U.S. Foreign Policy and China

For our parents

U.S. Foreign Policy and China

Security Challenges During the Bush, Obama, and Trump Administrations

Aiden Warren and Adam Bartley

EDINBURGH
University Press

Edinburgh University Press is one of the leading university presses in the UK.
We publish academic books and journals in our selected subject areas across the
humanities and social sciences, combining cutting-edge scholarship with high
editorial and production values to produce academic works of lasting importance.
For more information visit our website: edinburghuniversitypress.com

© Aiden Warren and Adam Bartley, 2021, 2022

Edinburgh University Press Ltd
The Tun – Holyrood Road
12(2f) Jackson's Entry
Edinburgh EH8 8PJ

First published in hardback by Edinburgh University Press 2021

Typeset in 11/13 Adobe Sabon by
IDSUK (Dataconnection) Ltd

A CIP record for this book is available from the British Library

ISBN 978 1 4744 5305 9 (hardback)
ISBN 978 1 4744 5306 6 (paperback)
ISBN 978 1 4744 5307 3 (webready PDF)
ISBN 978 1 4744 5308 0 (epub)

The right of Aiden Warren and Adam Bartley to be identified as the authors of this
work has been asserted in accordance with the Copyright, Designs and Patents Act
1988, and the Copyright and Related Rights Regulations 2003 (SI No. 2498).

Contents

Abbreviations and Acronyms

5G	Fifth generation
A2/AD	Anti-access and area denial
ABMT	Anti-ballistic Missile Treaty
ADIZ	Air defense identification zone
AI	Artificial intelligence
AIIB	Asian Infrastructure Investment Bank
APEC	Asia-Pacific Economic Cooperation
ARF	ASEAN Regional Forum
ASBM	Anti-ship ballistic missile
ASEAN	Association of Southeast Asian Nations
BRI	Belt and Road Initiative
BUILD	Better Utilization of Investments Leading to Development
CCP	Chinese Communist Party
CoC	Code of conduct
CSI	Container Security Initiative
CTBTO	Comprehensive Test Ban Treaty Organization
CUES	Code for Unplanned Encounters at Sea
DIUx	Defense Innovation Unit Experimental
DMZ	Demilitarized Zone (Korea)
DoD	Department of Defense
DPG	Defense Planning Guidance
DPRK	Democratic People's Republic of Korea
EAS	East Asia Summit
ECS	East China Sea
EEZ	Exclusive economic zone
ETIM	East Turkistan Islamic Movement
ETLO	East Turkistan Liberation Organization

EU	European Union
FBI	Federal Bureau of Investigation
FIRRMA	Foreign Investment Risk Review Modernization Act
FIU	Financial intelligence unit
FMF	Foreign military financing
FOIP	Free and Open Indo-Pacific
FoN	Freedom of navigation
FoNOPs	Freedom of the Seas Navigation Operations
FTA	Free trade agreement
G2	Group of Two
G20	Group of Twenty
IAEA	International Atomic Energy Agency
ICBM	Inter-continental ballistic missile
IDFC	International Development Finance Corporation
IMF	International Monetary Fund
INDOPACOM	Indo-Pacific Command
INF	Intermediate-range nuclear forces
IP	Intellectual property
IPR	Intellectual property rights
IPS	Indo-Pacific Strategy
IPSR	Indo-Pacific Strategy Report
IRBM	Intermediate-range ballistic missile
MDA	Maritime domain awareness
MIRV	Multiple independent reentry vehicle
MoFA	Ministry of Foreign Affairs
MSI	Maritime Security Initiative
NAFTA	North Atlantic Free Trade Agreement
NDS	National Defense Strategy
NMD	National Missile Defense
NPT	Nuclear Non-proliferation Treaty
NSC	National Security Council
NSS	National Security Strategy
OPIC	Overseas Private Investment Corporation
PBC	People's Bank of China
PLA	People's Liberation Army
PLAN	People's Liberation Army Navy

PNAC	Project for the New American Century
PRC	People's Republic of China
PSI	Proliferation Security Initiative
RIMPAC	Rim of the Pacific
ROKS	Republic of Korea Ship
S&ED	Strategic and Economic Dialogue
SCS	South China Sea
SLOC	Sea line of communication
SLBM	Submarine-launched ballistic missile
SME	Small and medium-sized enterprise
SOE	State-owned enterprise
THAAD	Terminal high-altitude area defense
TPP	Trans-Pacific Partnership
TRA	Taiwan Relations Act
UCESRC	U.S.-China Economic and Security Review Commission
UN	United Nations
UNCLOS	United Nations Convention on the Law of the Sea
UNSC	United Nations Security Council
UNSCR	United Nations Security Council Resolution
USNS	United States Naval Ship
USPACOM	United States Pacific Command
WMD	Weapon of mass destruction
WTO	World Trade Organization
XUAR	Xinjiang Uighur Autonomous Region

Introduction

From the purview of the world outlook in 2001 as George W. Bush stood at the podium to become the forty-third president of the United States, America seemed positioned to experience the extended benefits of the unipolar moment. Not simply was the U.S. the world's pre-eminent military power, the largest economic market, and a source for innovation and leadership, but it was so by a substantive margin. The rise at this time of China, touted by some as the emerging opponent to the liberal world order, was viewed in generally optimistic if not non-perturbed terms. While the challenges of China's military modernization, its broader territorial claims, and its human rights transgressions were noteworthy, they were also increasingly less worrisome; its military build-up had "been steady, but neither massive nor rapid, nor technologically very impressive."[1] By such measures, and with the manifold challenges of transitioning internal social-economic structures, China was considered to be too weak to confront the U.S. in Asia, and would remain so "well into the twenty-first century." Meanwhile, the project for "aligning" China with the world's institutions, entangling the Chinese Communist Party (CCP) within a web of multilateral associations and global economic relationships, seemed poised to offer at least a partial liberal political awakening.[2]

In looking back, these assumptions about the many benefits of engagement with China appear to have been over-sold, their key precepts seemingly anachronistic even by 2001 standards. Some twenty years into the twenty-first century, the United States and China have become locked within a contest of great-power competition. Partial decoupling in select critical technology industries

1

has begun to take place. The U.S.-China trade war, ignited in the anticipation of rectifying the large trade imbalance, has deepened across a spectrum of broadening charges. What began as the Trump administration's preoccupation with trade has become a generally bipartisan foreign policy to hold Beijing accountable for its disruptively protectionist policies and its theft of intellectual property. On these issues, observed Secretary of State Mike Pompeo at the February 2020 Munich Security Conference, "the United States has woken up."[3] In marking the conceptual and doctrinal shift in long-term views about the right policy for the People's Republic of China (PRC), the United States government under President Donald Trump has discarded the engagement policies attempted across the Bush and Obama years for the much less certain, and much more challenging, strategic competition of the Cold War years.

To say that the Trump administration deserves the full responsibility for this shift, however, is misleading. Engagement by one method or another has been the modus operandi of U.S. administrations since the time of Richard Nixon, deepening successively under presidents from Jimmy Carter to Barack Obama. While Trump has repudiated much of this engagement, more specifically at the diplomatic and military levels, the countries are still commercially, diplomatically, politically, and economically connected. What is observable here is that this process of engagement has been, in part, the means by which trial and error have defined Washington's strategic thinking over time. The continuities and changes in policy toward China in the context of North Korea, nuclear non-proliferation, the Asia-Pacific, military-to-military relations, emerging technologies, and climate change, among others, have resulted in appreciable and accumulative experiences that have driven policymakers to seek more accountability in policies with China.

Analysis of the available U.S. government documents, Congressional hearings, and security establishment reports reveals in this context an unmistakable and inexorable trend: the generation since 2001 of unmet engagement potential, miscarried diplomatic initiatives, and ultimately failed expectations has in no small way been consequential to the current progression toward confrontation. On this point, research illustrates that Bush and Obama engaged in an array of bilateral and multilateral initiatives to bridge the differences and manage the distrust with China, only to be, time and again, disappointed by half-measures, dispirited cooperation, and mistimed applications. By some accounts, these expectations for engagement by the end of the Obama years had long outrun their assumptions. "Across the ideological spectrum," observed Kurt M. Campbell and Ely Ratner in a noteworthy article, "we in the U.S. foreign policy community have remained deeply invested in expectations about China—about its approach to economics, domestic politics, security, and global order—even as evidence against them has accumulated." The strategic patience of these administrations, employed in the hope that China would adopt an enlightened leadership position in international affairs, required unwittingly ignoring the warning signs of Chinese belligerence, its assertiveness in diplomatic engagements, its bullying of allies, and its measured adoption of militarizing islands and the sea lines of communication in the South China Sea. The combination of past balancing, hedging, and engagement policies, the authors note, has been based on unrealistic assumptions about Washington's own level of engagement and the extent to which Beijing will cooperate.[4]

In attempting to add much-needed connective tissue to what can be defined as the most significant bilateral relationship in the world, this book seeks to unpack and illuminate the defining junctures across the three twenty-first-century American presidential administrations. How has each president's chief successes and failures been addressed by the next administration as they search for a workable formula with China? What legacies has each left when it comes to engagement in the security domains? To what extent have institutional and personal influences been consequential to both continuities and changes in each administration's China approach? Finally, has engagement as a mechanism for building trust and mitigating differences finally run its course, particularly as Trump attempts to drive a more transactionally driven, American-centered approach? This book addresses these questions. As such, while consideration is given to many mutual and overlapping areas in the bilateral relationship (including trade, economics, and culture), the core analysis of the book remains focused on the security relationship.

Setting the stage

It goes without saying that presidents George W. Bush, Barack Obama, and Donald Trump have all attempted to adapt and respond to the "rise" of China and the associated transformations of the bilateral relationship to the best of their understanding and capacity. In this equation, institutional and personal worldviews have, quite naturally, been influential to the setting of agendas, principles, and processes. At the same time, these presidential prerogatives have also been forced to compete with established and establishment perceptions and agendas, influencing the push and pull between policy and implementation. These influences have been especially visible in the twenty-first century as the challenge of China's rise and the implications of having to face another autocratic peer competitor have grown increasingly worrisome. It comes as no surprise, then, that at times each administration has fallen toward acrimony, particularly in relation to the extent to which engagement with China is necessary, the form of engagement that should be encouraged, and in some cases, the degree to which competition is preferable or more strategically sound. Here, the threat and engagement assessments among the different schools of thought have been demonstrably influential.

The engagement school has since 1972 largely prevailed in leading the policy debate toward China. Beginning more coherently under Carter with dual-use technology transfers, Bell helicopters and air-defense radar and communication equipment sales, presidents including Republicans Ronald Reagan and George H. W. Bush have supported, albeit not without disruptions, liberalizing restrictions on exports in dual-use and military application technologies—redefining the security relationship with the PRC.[5] Greater military-to-military relationships were pushed further by engagement proponents in the Clinton, Bush, and Obama administrations, despite subtle changes in security policies and attitudes toward Beijing. There are two main elements to this school. On the one hand, the "engagement-change" group assert that greater integration and diplomatic engagement in the international system will in the long term, via the help of liberal economic forces, alter the political orientation of the CCP from within. The other

4

side of this debate for the most part reinforces this argument, although it views China's internal political system as more stable and resilient to the influences of democratic institutions. This so-called "entanglement" group calls for "enmeshing China in a web of entangling relationships" to the point that any attempt to revise agreements or legal statutes will force major trade-offs in government and economic stability.[6] When China has been accused of by-standing on important issues of global governance, these proponents have reminded the U.S. government that China's unprecedented growth in governance institutions deserves credit, signifying further that the engagement policies have worked as they should. Indeed, if Beijing at times failed to meet expectations, it had in many ways deserved a pass.[7] The attempt to move this theme forward toward a more positive and inclusive involvement would converge with the "responsible stakeholder" engagement policy during the Bush years.

By the turn of the century, the discussion of China's rise and the achievements and failures of the engagement policies of the Clinton years had become an increasingly central topic, most noticeably of but not limited to the political right, garnering greater traction in security circles in Washington. Like the engagement school, the "China threat" school can be broken into two distinct classes. For one side, China's authoritarian government will be sure to seek to replace the United States in Asia and the world as it picks up the mantle of successorship from the former Soviet Union. In doing so, it will seek increasingly to export its illiberal institutions across the world, pushing the United States out of important markets and broader strategic domains.[8] The other side perceives a similar challenge, but it departs from the notion that the illiberalism of China's Communist leaders is significant.[9] Rather, it is the structure of the international system and the search for security maximization that will lead to greater conflict and eventually war. For both sides, greater and unwatched engagement with China will allow it to free-ride on the United States while it seeks to develop more comprehensively, to the point where it will challenge the U.S. While trends in this threat perception in the media reveal spikes in attention during presidential elections, spreading across military, economic, and governmental areas of concern, these trends have been more consistent in the Pentagon and among the security establishment.[10]

The Bush years, following 9/11, of course, witnessed a general dissipation of this literature with a new focus on the Middle East, but it did not altogether disappear. One of the themes of this book is to highlight the transition of these two schools in real time, from steady engagement to emerging disengagement in the policies of the Bush, Obama, and Trump administrations. There is no one point in time, despite the apparent hard-line policies of the Trump administration, when this transition began to occur. That said, there are notable markers across the years that suggest more of a transitioning phase. For some, this began as early as 2011 when the "pivot" to the Asia-Pacific, with a specific focus to countering China's influence, was codified into policy. For others, the major turning point was the emergence of the hardliner Xi Jinping in 2012. Notably, by 2015 even formerly optimistic "engagers" had begun voicing their increasingly critical observations of the divisive and epoch-changing rule of President Xi.[11] For a third group, Trump's divisive partial technology decoupling and the doctrinal shift in United States-China policy represent a more fundamental break. One of the reasons for this ambiguity in timing is that the established tenets of U.S.-China rivalry can be both materially defining and amorphous. In the areas of military modernization, Chinese island building in the South China Sea, proliferation of weapons of mass destruction, and Taiwanese defense, the challenge has been more pronounced and the revision of global norms more conspicuous. Meanwhile, the ambitions of Chinese leaders and the intentions of such projects as the Belt and Road Initiative (BRI), the "China Dream," and Made in China 2025, while depicted by some as pillars in a grand strategy to replace the United States in the Asia-Pacific, have been less clear. Additionally, China's engagement and growth in international institutions, including ratification of key agreements and legal bodies, suggests, at the very least, that its leadership is less rigid and uncompromising than many claim.

As this discussion suggests, while the acrimony in the security domain between the two states is hardly new, its complexion and position within the broader relationship has changed dramatically across the first twenty years of the twenty-first century. Several of these challenges, we note, have mushroomed over time to become more demanding: on the one hand, military and political developments in Taiwan policy in China have caused greater anxiety in the U.S. and as a result greater increases in arms sales to Taipei. On the other, the emboldening of U.S. alliances and security obligations has further heightened the perception of a U.S. containment policy in Beijing, influencing its development of strategic rocket forces in the province of Fujian, among others. Notwithstanding these differences, the United States and China have also been able to attain a means in which to handle their divergent security interests through a combination of adaptive policies, demands, and expectations, or in simple terms, working to live with such disparities with the chance that they would wane over time. Over the course of the 1990s and early 2000s, these broader management approaches often generated room for collaboration on both traditional and non-traditional security concerns, as Chapters 1 and 2 in this book illustrate.[12]

Looking to more recent times, it can be said that the U.S.-China security relationship is today a multifaceted and expanding mix of conflicting interests, combined with a deepening security dilemma. The current debate around China's Huawei and the development of future communications technology is emblematic of this point, observing the many political, military, and strategic implications, while at the same time noting this new and crucial service to the world. While this dichotomy can in part be attributed to the PRC's expanding capabilities and its increasing preparedness to use them, the United States has also been willing to respond to such provocations and developments with its own responses and pragmatic actions. It is not by coincidence, as such, that an intensification and diversification of security competition has taken place. In observing that China's military modernization since the mid- to late 1990s has dramatically narrowed the gap in capabilities with the United States, scholars note that these developments have been made primarily on the basis of impeding U.S. power projection capabilities in the Western Pacific and the wearing down of conventional U.S. military advantages in Asia. In an extreme scenario, some have argued that the cost for the U.S. military in undertaking a war with China has reached a threshold where the U.S. "could face defeat at the hands of the Chinese military in plausible scenarios."[13] The transition of these threats in more recent years in China's emerging defense and commercial technologies, including the domains of artificial intelligence, hypersonic weapons, and autonomous devices, has further underscored the quandary facing strategic planners in the United States.[14]

To be sure, since 2001, Bush, Obama, and Trump have all come to view Chinese military modernization in various ways as an attempt to render U.S. military forces in the Western Pacific inoperative. Whereas previously the PRC appeared to be willing to accept U.S. alliance movements, the upward trend reveals that, as its power and reach have grown, Beijing has become much more inclined to ratchet up tensions with those U.S. "friends and allies" who act, both symbolically and in reality, in a fashion that China perceives to be undercutting its national interests. Across the past twenty years, the PRC has regularly put pressure on the likes of Japan, South Korea, the Philippines, and Australia amid diplomatic disagreements, including the imposition of economic and diplomatic penalties, to coerce more reasonable responses. More recent observations have revealed that Beijing has, for some time, attempted to meddle in the domestic politics of some U.S. allies as a means to compel them to modify their policies.[15] That this marks a major shift in the long-held policies of Deng Xiaoping to not seek leadership, to concentrate on development and relationships, has been notably commented upon by analysts.

In this picture, China's maritime territorial disputes have taken on a new emphasis in U.S.-China security rivalry. Beijing's strengthening of its territorial and legal claims in the East and South China Seas has caused the United States to play a more prominent role in opposing such intimidation, bringing both states into more immediate contention. Specifically, China's formation of virtual-military bases through land reclamation in the South China Sea (SCS), and its continuing deployment of weapons and hardware on such structures, has propelled U.S. and regional apprehensions about an imminent armed conflict, noting also the limitations on freedom of navigation for both military and civilian vessels as the Chinese navy, Coast Guard, and maritime militia dominate the waterways.

Such assertions have presented the U.S. and its "friends and allies" with a mix of new and problematic challenges for which they have had little success in finding a definitive rejoinder. Combining these issues with other sources of tensions, including the BRI and Beijing's push for nuclear modernization, it has become evident that a form of balancing will continue to be a mainstay in both bilateral relations and U.S. presidential strategic thought.[16]

The role of the leadership

Despite Congress's growing role in the U.S. approach toward China, the president has been the central driver in defining the most appropriate responses in maintaining the stability of the U.S.-China relationship. Historically, the leaders of both states have operated as crucial sources of crisis supervision and circuit breakers amid times of spiraling frictions. In the lead-up to the twenty-first century, such examples included the 1979 transition to comprehensive normalization, the seminal exchange in the Taiwan arms sales communiqué in 1982, the aftermath of Tiananmen Square in 1989, Taiwan Strait crisis responses in the mid-1990s, the 1999 Belgrade embassy bombing, and in the late 1990s and early 2000s, the orchestrating of China's accession to the World Trade Organization (WTO). Across these historical events, the responses by the presidents and leadership teams on both sides of the Pacific were essential to sustaining the relationship and working out a way in which to reinvigorate ties.[17]

Of course, presidential leadership is difficult to measure. A starting point, at the most basic level, is: Can a president display effective leadership in the pursuit of realistically set goals? In foreign policy, the question might more resemble whether a president can guide or coerce disparate national and international identities, interests, and personalities to collectively adopt agreements or policies with far-reaching implications, including sanctions, war, or even the restraint of national power. According to some, by such measurements, leadership required political skills, bridging the natural relationships between coalition building and public, party, and legislative groups.[18] By implication, a lack of leadership is the inability to employ the vast powers of the White House, the people, and the legislative branch to implement the policies, doctrines, or visions of government. In times of uncertainty, leadership has required the further use of novel crisis management mechanisms, diplomacy, conciliation, and sometimes risks to national security—supported intimately with bureaucratic institutions whose role is to offset the flaws in the decision-making environment.[19]

As we note throughout the book, leaders can easily harm relations through a disregard of these processes. Trump's proclivity for tariffs, measures against Huawei, and extensive trade pressures against all parties, for instance, has together made attaining a strategy for dealing with China's provocations more difficult to achieve despite generally bipartisan support. For Obama, major challenges in the Middle East meant less spending on the "rebalance" and less focus on pushing back against Chinese assertions. As Chapters 4 and 5 illustrate, the freedom of navigation operations designed to protest Chinese assertions were conducted with little strategic outcome and with little aid from allies. For Bush, the notable transgressions between the Defense and State departments and the failure of strategy for stopping North Korean nuclear proliferation were in many ways attributable to his leadership and management flaws.

A second factor in this consideration is the role of advisers to foreign policy and doctrine. We note, for instance, the role of the China hardliners in the George W. Bush administration in forcing a more assertive policy toward China. In the Obama years, a clear leaning toward engagement, buttressed by more support for the State Department and alliance-building initiatives, was preferred. By contrast, the distinguishing feature of the Trump administration's China policy has been his preparedness to accentuate the domains of competition while reducing the chore of cooperation. As Trump has emboldened personal relationships with key China hawks, his proclivity to follow their advice above others and without critical input has damaged the reputation of the State Department and many in the security domains, who viewed engagement with Beijing as important.

As Trump and President Xi Jinping attempt to define and control the bilateral agenda, they have both allowed the central conduits of policymaking in the relationship to deteriorate. For context, the four cabinet-level dialogues established by Trump in April 2017 at Mar-a-Lago to address the expanding bilateral differences—encompassing economics, diplomacy and security, cyber affairs, and cultural ties—have all been discontinued. Meanwhile, military-to-military dialogues and lower-level diplomacy have mostly ceased. By the end of 2018, according to one observation, "phone calls, letters, and meetings between Trump and Xi" had become the "most important mechanism[s] for managing relations."[20] The implications, we note, are far-reaching, ranging across a spectrum from policy language and signaling misperception to personal animosity, divisive rhetoric, and antagonistic posturing, all of which can escalate relations to a point of crisis.

The latter stages of the book, in examining the Trump administration, illustrate these leadership flaws more acutely in both strategy and policy toward China. Put simply, Trump has established little in terms of a clearly defined set of priorities for China policy and, discernibly, only minimal internal desire and procedure to cultivate one. A case in point is the 2017 National Security Strategy, whereupon a major doctrinal shift was announced, labelling China a "strategic competitor" and a "revisionist state." By June 2019 Trump seemingly reversed this announcement by suggesting that Washington and Beijing were "going to be strategic partners."[21] Further, we note that while pressure and strong-arm tactics are oftentimes useful mechanisms for policy enforcement, their adoption in the absence of clearly defined goals, processes, and support can inhibit the intended outcome or miscarry, causing national or international backlash. As Trump has been clearly more preoccupied with applying pressure via public criticism, tariffs, military threats, export controls, and investment restrictions as the defining instrument to alter China's behavior, he has minimalized discussion of a mutual agenda or the value of incentives as ways to resolve difficulties in the relationship.[22]

Chapter synopsis

In examining the Bush, Obama, and Trump administrations and their responses to the security challenges presented by China in the twenty-first century, this book takes a departure from other representative presidential administration China policy books by including topics otherwise made vague by their limited attention in the literature.

In Chapter 1 (the first Bush administration) we examine the rise of the "China threat" and its relationship to policy in the Bush White House, particularly within the first year. Prior to the catastrophic events of 9/11, the U.S.-China relationship was heading toward increasing competition, as announced furtively by future national security adviser Condoleezza Rice in her 2000 *Foreign Affairs* article.[23] Original policy goals were spurred in no small way by the discussion of China's rise and its potential impact on American national security, observed to be deliberately challenging American leadership in the Asia-Pacific. Policy at this time was heavily influenced by China hawks in the Defense Department and notable advisers to the administration, part of a conservative network of China-threat proponents. While the discussions between the neoconservatives and the Cold War realists such as Colin Powell and Rice have been discussed more generally in the literature in terms of foreign policy, their consideration of China has been less clear. This chapter examines their influence and actions toward China more closely. It reveals that, while cooperation with the PRC after 9/11 was enthusiastically sought, it wasn't coherently given by the administration. On Taiwan, Bush remained in many ways ignorant of China's concerns, illustrating the worldview encompassed in the Bush doctrine and representing at this time China's still considerable distance from becoming a peer competitor.

The second Bush administration, Chapter 2 argues, marked a continuation of China-engagement strategies presaged by a closer relationship with the State Department in the White House and post-9/11 cooperation in counter-terrorism. To be sure, priorities in security-related domains, including the wars in Afghanistan and Iraq, North Korean nuclear proliferation, and the War on Terror, were major drivers of this ongoing positive relationship. At this time, too, Undersecretary of State Robert Zoellick's call for China to become a "responsible stakeholder," while pointing critically to areas of shortfall in China's global and regional duties, established the tone of the new bilateral relationship. This was to be one of engagement and cooperation with the aim of altering China's illiberal government from within institutional, diplomatic, and legal structures. Yet, notable frustrations on the security front proved more inhibiting than illustrated by the White House. Marked positives in cooperation such as in counter-terrorism, proliferation, and the Six-Party Talks were in many ways ephemeral and ultimately dissatisfying. The chapter observes further that Bush was inconsistent in his approach to questions on China's domestic counter-terrorism policies and even more so on U.S. cooperation in the Six-Party Talks. Despite what appeared in the media as a developing, friendly relationship, by the last years of the administration it had become discernible that Bush had inadvertently accepted progress in process in place of more tangible outcomes.

Though much more of an ideologue than his predecessor, the election of Barack Obama in 2008 saw a president determined to rebuild America's relationship with the Asia-Pacific after years of what some described as "benign neglect" during the Bush administration. As Chapter 3 will explain, however, notwithstanding these seemingly new efforts at cooperation, ongoing and emerging bilateral differences became a constant theme, as matters during the first term deriving from the "pivot" and Chinese assertions in the SCS came to the fore. In unpacking and defining the sources and drivers of the Obama administration's foreign policy toward China during its first term in office, the chapter sets out to: explicate the debates between the different groups in U.S foreign policy pertaining to China; articulate the U.S. national security concerns relating to China; provide insight into China's growing military power; discuss how the administration defined, rationalized, and expressed the "pivot"/"rebalance"; highlight the several continuities and departures of the "pivot"/"rebalance"; evaluate the various implications of and Chinese responses to the "pivot"/"rebalance"; and lastly, overall, present the consequences for U.S. foreign policy and security strategy in the region, and broader concerns for U.S.-China bilateral relations.

During its two terms in the White House, the Obama administration frequently endeavored to reassure Beijing that the United States was amenable to "a strong, prosperous and successful China that plays a greater role in world affairs," and that it did not seek to obstruct China's rise on the international stage. In response, China pledged to follow a "path of peaceful development." As Chapter 4 will illustrate, however, during its second term in office the Obama administration would continue to search for the "right" equilibrium pertaining to China, particularly on how to connect with the PRC on matters regarding stability and security in the Asia-Pacific region and beyond. Ongoing points of concern for Washington encompassed: trying to recognize the true basis of China's military modernization program; China's use of its military and paramilitary forces in disputes with states over territorial claims in the South and East China Seas; its noticeable progress in creating incendiary militarized structures in such contested waters; the strategic and security aspects of the BRI; and its continued threat to use force in unification tensions with Taiwan. While U.S.-China military-to-military ties improved during the Obama era, Washington overall continued to struggle in persuading Beijing that the policy of "rebalancing" toward the Asia-Pacific was not meant to contain China.

Like his predecessor, Obama attempted to cultivate a cooperative relationship with China while "guiding" discrepancies through discussion and through firmer approaches of "pressure, hedging, and balancing." In this regard, the administration began with the goal of pursuing mutually beneficial relations that could promote regional and global solutions while also balancing its strategy in response to China's more forthright assertions and claims in the region. Here, it unequivocally embedded the U.S.-China relationship within a comprehensive regional strategy. This "pivot" toward Asia (later redefined as a "rebalance") would also change in reaction to the changing strategic environment. Indeed, the notion of building a cooperative regional structure and cultivating productive relationships with rising powers (China most prominent among them) would increasingly move to a stance of strengthening security and economic cooperation with established U.S. partners and with new regional allies as a means to counteract the threat presented by China's maritime challenges. For the Obama administration, and over the course of the second term in office, while elements of cooperation and of competition oscillated back and forth, the latter became a more pronounced feature as China asserted its claims in the Western Pacific.

The fifth and final chapter examines the Trump administration's many changes to the United States-China bilateral relationship and the president's, by any measure, unconventional style of leadership and White House management. Remarkable differences in experience, behavior, priorities, and processes marked the administration from its two notable predecessors. Trump has ushered in a change of style and thinking about relations with China that has opened policy channels to new changes, and indeed policy reversals, deemed perhaps out of reach for his immediate predecessor. For many, including members of Congress, the accumulated complaints and frustrations of a sixteen-year bilateral relationship had finally produced a reaction in the White House that accorded action with accountability and rhetoric with policy. At least in the area of trade and later technology transference, the Trump administration's confrontational approach toward China has marked a notable departure in the level of confrontation Washington has been willing to risk with Beijing. The basis of the new approach has been a substantive shift in worldviews.

As the chapter demonstrates, serious inconsistency has marked the Trump administration's China policies and its approach to strategy in the Indo-Pacific concept. Long delays in implementation, coupled with diverging foreign policy priorities, have distracted the administration from what it defined, explicitly, as the greatest strategic threat of the new era. Meanwhile, Trump's unpredictable behavior, careless rhetoric, and rejection of liberal international norms have created a legitimacy problem as Asian regional partners decide whether to join in further American initiatives such as Trump's competitor to the BRI, the BUILD (Better Utilization of Investments Leading to Development) Act, and decide on how much they want to compete with China. As the administration enters its fourth year, Trump has yet to offer a vision for international security and relations with China going forward.

Last introductory thoughts

As the book will reveal overall, there is an exceptional yet perturbing convergence in the longer-term fundamental drivers and the short-term recurring ones at the core of U.S.-China relations. Together, they are pressing this relationship toward a more competitive domain, and the ensuing competition will likely draw in a wider array of issues and encompass more actors. Moreover, this is taking place while the traditional safeguards and stabilizers to competition that were in play are very much diminishing, if not completely breaking down. In examining the three U.S. presidents in the twenty-first century—Bush, Obama, and Trump—it is unclear as to whether a new U.S. president would or could fundamentally alter this intensifying dynamic or whether Xi Jinping would drastically shift course in the new decade and beyond. Many of these drivers are knotted to the personalities, material interests, and capabilities of both states, indicating, but not ensuring, their permanence. Consequently, it is evident that relations are perhaps moving toward a new period which, unlike previous ones, will be characterized by an amplified preponderance of competition and the enhanced probability of conflict and confrontation.[24]

Of course, in the months since the emergence of COVID-19, commentators and policymakers have differed over the kind of world the contagion will leave behind in its wake. That said, for the most part they have all argued that the world we are entering will be profoundly different from what existed before. Some envisage that the pandemic will create a new world order led by China; others believe it will prompt the demise of China's leadership. Some say it will put an end to globalization; others hope it will spur a new age of global collaboration. And still others have argued that it will amplify nationalism, destabilize free trade, and lead to regime change in various states—or all of the above. However, it is evident that the world following the pandemic will not necessarily be fundamentally different from the one that preceded it. In this regard, COVID-19 will not so much change the rudimentary direction of world history as accelerate it. The pandemic and the response to it have further uncovered the underlying characteristics of geopolitics today. As a consequence, the crisis promises to be less of a defining juncture than "a way station along the road that the world has been traveling for the past few decades."[25]

In this environment, deepening and intensifying bilateral competition, with its fundamental origins, will necessitate U.S. presidents to consider more imaginatively their positions on strategies to tackle the challenge, involving those options that seek to hinder and/or dull Chinese power as it expands and diversifies. Indeed, as the following chapters will reveal, obtaining an equilibrium in U.S.-China relations between cooperation and competition will be increasingly difficult to achieve as the latter becomes more pronounced, and the former contracts and is viewed to be of limited value.

1. The Bush Administration's First Term: Reconciling the China "Threat" with New Priorities

This chapter seeks to examine and unpack the Bush administration's approach toward the Chinese across two distinct phases during the first term in office: the events prior to September 11, 2001 and, following, the immediate post-9/11 years. While it is commonplace to say the terrorist attacks of 9/11 shifted the purview of the administration's foreign policy, we argue that until now the scale of this shift has not been properly accounted for in the literature in the China policy context. By all indications, the U.S.-China relationship under the Bush administration in 2001 was set to encounter the vicissitudes of a generational change in American strategic thinking. At the forefront of this shift lay the roots of a strategy for maintaining, in Charles Krauthammer's words, "a uniquely benign [American] imperium."[1] Unchallengeable power in the institution of the military, strategically waxed with the soft-power charms of democratic-liberal values, could be used, assertively and unilaterally if need be, to secure the liberal order of an American century. A general inclination of this theme in the literature has been to measure the characteristics by which a new imperial worldview was made possible by key neoconservatives in the administration.[2] At the same time, analysis of the early neoconservative movement within the Bush administration signified the emphasis of the rising China challenge in neoconservative and Republican thought. Nowhere was this more apparent, writes Maria Ryan, than in the *Weekly Standard*, where China outstripped Iraq and nearly all other foreign policy concerns.[3]

The China challenge undoubtedly marked the development of a Bush China policy during this first phase, but the extent to which it was formed on a strategy toward action continues to leave important questions unclear. As Andrew Scobell writes, while the hard-line stance on China in the early stages of 2001 may have been tactical, "designed to establish the Bush administration as a tough negotiator," its ideological dispositions tended also to confound relations, for instance, on Taiwan and missile defense.[4] This point of view clashes with Guy Roberts, who states that Bush operated a "clear-cut, comprehensible, and predictable policy toward China."[5] Accordingly, Bush navigated the diverse opinions of his advisers, driving a structured policy toward a managed engagement that sought to reduce the threat of China over time. Our examination finds little evidence to support this view. For instance, Bush's somewhat amateuristic approach to foreign policy stood in stark contrast to the experienced and powerful administrators of Donald Rumsfeld and Dick Cheney, who were given wide parameters to affect the U.S.-China relationship, a point not properly reconciled in Roberts's account. We argue also that conservative ideology played a critical role, reinforced by the image of an evolving China threat in publications and conservative thinking inside the Beltway. As this chapter illustrates, the China threat was a constant among administration officials. While the threat was rarely made explicit in public it was nevertheless a discussion of great importance behind closed doors.[6] Indicatively, even after 9/11, when a rebalancing of the U.S.-China relationship was pursued by Bush, not only do we find that it was done unevenly, but on the major issue of Taiwan, greater uncertainty became the norm.

The promises of a Bush China policy

For China policy, the first months of the Bush administration came to resemble an amalgamation of three themes, adopted and broadened throughout the 2000 presidential campaign: a reversal of Clinton's perceived soft China coddling, increases in military capabilities, including the sale of offensive weapons to

Taiwan, and the acceptance of the basic premise of the China threat—that China's rise would engage the United States in a life-or-death struggle for the free world. To the extent that a twenty-first-century China policy warranted such themes, Bush expressed the challenge as an emerging strategic threat. Deepening military cuts, combined with increasing deployment overseas during the Clinton years, had worked to soften, not strengthen, America's ability to meet the threat of a rising China, made evident by "its unresolved vital interests, particularly concerning Taiwan and the South China Sea."[7] For many, this wasn't necessarily unfair campaign posturing. Clinton had uncritically accepted the assumption that greater increases in trade, and the integration of China in the world economy, would result in an increasingly liberalized and perhaps democratized China. Significantly, he did this without making assurances in American military and strategic preponderance should the opposite prove true. This was considered a cardinal mistake.[8] But there was also an over-emphasis on U.S.-Chinese relations seemingly above and beyond relations with core allies in the region, namely, South Korea and Japan. For Bush, Clinton plied ignorance of China's strategic interests, of its desire to remake the balance of power in the Asia-Pacific in its image, forgetting also that these ambitions would include the "stealing of nuclear secrets or . . . trying to intimidate Taiwan," among other inimitable programs. How then could China be anything but a "strategic competitor"?

To be sure, this early posturing could not foretell the shape of a George W. Bush-Beijing relationship any more than Clinton's China bashing in the 1992 campaign could unmask his greater intentions toward a new trade relationship. From Carter to Clinton, all had extolled the virtues of a confrontational position against the "butchers of Beijing." All had turned from the hawkish rhetoric of the campaign trail to seek greater engagement with Chinese leaders. Yet, important distinctions in the composition of the new Bush team underscored a deeper, philosophical antagonism toward this potential successor to the Soviet Union than was evident in either the Clinton administration or the former Bush one. This came to identify itself first in the hawkish collection of former Cold War warriors who populated the senior roles as advisers to the president, a group even the conservative Ronald Reagan sought to avoid in his top advisory circle, viewing them as problematic.[9] We identify them here as belonging to two broadly defined groups, which we borrow from Scobell for reasons of simplicity. The "conservative hawks," the largest group in terms of numbers, advocated a hard-line policy on the question of potential peer competitors, favoring expansive military policies and assertive diplomacy. They included Vice President Richard (Dick) Cheney and Secretary of Defense Donald Rumsfeld, but the term covers also the many neoconservatives attached to the administration including Deputy Secretary of Defense Paul Wolfowitz.[10] "Conservative pragmatists" by differentiation were considered less hostile to peer competitors based upon their recognition of greater strategic uncertainties, and more selective about national security interests. These include National Security Adviser Condoleezza Rice, Secretary of State Colin Powell, and Deputy Secretary of State Richard Armitage. On the surface, many of these figures, veterans of the former Bush and Reagan administrations, appeared to differ significantly on substantive China points, including the level and sources of engagement.

On the broader debate, however, these differences defined the administration's initial stance toward China much less than their policy similarities did. Certainly, there was much consternation and disruption between Rumsfeld and Powell, for instance over policy toward Taiwan and U.S.-China military exchanges. But overall, their differences did not divert sharply on the big China issues. Rice's 2000 *Foreign Affairs* article is indicative in this respect: both "conservative pragmatists" and "conservative hawks" initially coveted the confrontational stance of the 2000 conservative opinion toward China. Yet, whatever their pretensions for moderating this assertiveness come 2001, there was little amelioration of the China "threat" in policies and speeches prior to 9/11. Bureaucratic wrangling over foreign policy was partly to blame. China policy, as much as foreign policy in general, was dominated early on by the influences of Cheney and Rumsfeld. But we also see in the leading documents, including the Pentagon's

21

draft *Defense Planning Guidance* (DPG) of 1992 and the Project for the New American Century's (PNAC) *Statement of Principles* and *Rebuilding America's Defenses*, the developing conscience of a Bush foreign policy where advisers, present and future in 2001, had been either leading consultants or signatories to their principles. At the top of the order, preparing the military to maintain a *Pax Americana* was shared among both groups. More significantly, these principles also included the mission to militarily expand the zones of democratic peace, and to deter the emergence of great powers and defend key regions, of which East Asia was the focus of these strategic considerations.[11] To contrast with Chinese opinion at the time, it was generally believed that such identifiers of the Bush administration—along with its willingness to use force, increased support for Taiwan, and greater emphasis on the U.S.-Asian alliance system—pronounced a view that Beijing was to be seen as an enemy and that containment would form any part of an engagement strategy with China.[12]

While this military and ideological exceptionalism—so broadly attributed to the neoconservatives—did not meet with widespread acceptance, nor was it wholly rejected. That Armitage supported, for instance, PNAC's January 1998 open letter to Clinton calling for regime change in Iraq or the August 2000 "Statement on the Defense of Taiwan," provocatively emboldening America's commitment to Taiwanese security, underscored this overlapping of priorities and views of the various advisers. As others have found, they were neither solely realists, idealists, or ideologues, but rather hybrids of all three. All embraced the idea, writes Melvyn P. Leffler, that only democracy preceded peace. All set about with "missionary zeal" to reinforce this conviction.[13] If we accept the guiding PNAC and DPG documents in their broadest terms, then we must also accept that for many the resulting agenda united advisers on the premise that only U.S. military power could obtain what John Higley describes as the "central means for unseating dictatorial regimes and promoting democracy and freedom worldwide."[14]

That said, there remains little agreement on how cohesive a neoconservative challenge to the conservative pragmatists—Powell, Rice, and Armitage—was in its thoughts or on how influential it was when it came to China policy. Not all challengers advanced the idea of a Cold War containment policy for China, and few were comfortable with the idea of nation building as a side-project for maintaining unipolarity;[15] there was no answer for what to do with China, for instance, should regime change actually take place. What the literature makes clear, however, is that their emergence as a counter-narrative to the Clinton administration's liberal trade agenda made popular headway among Republicans, culminating in the nomenclature of neo-Reaganism for a twenty-first-century foreign policy. This was a misnomer to be sure, but wide support among conservatives maintained an agreement with the broad brushstrokes of this neoconservative foreign policy agenda. After the 9/11 terrorist attacks, this agenda pronounced itself furtively in the Bush doctrine—where the search for security could be found in the threat of overwhelming force, a tendency toward unilateralism, "pre-emption" as official policy, American exceptionalism as the accepted ideology, and hostility toward multilateral institutions.[16] If we examine the lead-up to this eventful declaration, however, the challenge of China, which was considered, according to House Majority Whip Tom DeLay (Republican-Texas), to be the "leading national security issue of our time," loomed large as an originating threat instructive of these main points.[17] By September 30, 2001, the U.S. Quadrennial Defense Review had earmarked the China threat as requiring "a reorientation of the [U.S.] posture," taking into account "new challenges particularly anti-access and area-denial threats," indicative of China's new capabilities in missile technology positioned facing the Taiwan Strait.[18]

The China challenge, in truth, was less a neoconservative issue than it was a wider Republican one. The June 1998 House Select Committee on U.S. National Security and Military/Commercial Concerns with the People's Republic of China, established to examine the threat of Chinese nuclear espionage in the United States, united many in the Republican Party to countenance what was increasingly viewed as Chinese tenacity and arrogance in the face of a dominant American-led liberal order. As the report was to illustrate, the Chinese Communist Party (CCP) operated a deliberate and systematic program of espionage in America, with the intended aim of challenging U.S. power and leadership in Asia.[19] Mathew Rees of the *Weekly Standard*, afterwards a speech writer for President Bush and National Security Adviser Rice, wrote that there was no more sophisticated secret to have than American nuclear technology, now in the hands of the Chinese.[20] Indeed, the growing dialogue in the Republican Party about China's future had grown increasingly pessimistic. "China's military leaders are considering the possibility of conflict with the United States," wrote Zalmay Khalilzad of RAND, later to work with Rumsfeld at Defense. While the United States could ill afford to treat the Chinese as adversaries, their revisionist agenda nonetheless required constant checks on a coherent American China policy with sufficient and ready military capability. More focus should be given to enlarging defense agreements with not just Japan and South Korea but also among the member states of ASEAN (Association of South East Asian Nations) who have overlapping claims with China to islands in the South China Sea.[21] A chorus along this theme made its way around the conservative think tanks, following on from the sentiments articulated by the writers of the 1992 draft DPG and PNAC's *Rebuilding America's Defenses*.[22] In many ways the links between conservative republicans and the "neocons" on China failed to fully illustrate the major differences in policy approaches between the two groups, a point which confused the first months of Bush's China policy. For a lack of nuance, many attached themselves to the theme that the only way to secure peace in the Asia-Pacific, as remarked by John Bolton of the American Enterprise Institute, later Bush's ambassador to the United Nations (UN), was by reinforcing the old balance-of-power structure of the Cold War in East Asia.[23]

We will visit the China threat further below in detail, but it is worth noting the role of the president in this apparently negative slide toward an antagonistic China policy. Where did Bush's China views intersect and diverge with the emerging neoconservative establishment and the excited Republican China-threat bloc?

It has been fashionable to suggest that, on China at any rate, the neoconservative influence was tempered by the more moderating voices of Powell and Armitage at State.[24] Certainly this was the case during the April 2001 EP-3 reconnaissance plane incident, where restraint and diplomacy won above threats and posturing. But the claim fails to hold water when examined from the level of the system and the process of decision-making in the White House. While Bush may not have shared in certain neoconservative ideas about a containment strategy for China, it is important to note that he created an environment where these could be explored in greater detail and as plausible policy departures. The Bush doctrine and the invasion of Iraq after 9/11 make this point axiomatic. National security advice was dominated by the conservative hawks, which Bush failed to check by instituting the role of an honest broker in decision making. Rice, perhaps the one to adopt this role, could rarely manage to militate against their influence.[25] That this one-sidedness in policy advice should appear disconcerting is further illustrated by Bush's predilection to make decisions on gut intuition, often without deep introspection, and based on "strongly held convictions"; or to put it in the words of Jack Goldsmith, director of the Office of Legal Counsel, with "minimal deliberation, unilateral action, and legalistic defense."[26] On the score of decision-making efficacy, we might judge that Bush was not adequately equipped to moderate the dangers of a process too narrowed by its prejudices and dominating personalities, by a restricted information process, and by the lack of multiple advocacy, where alternatives to important decisions can be deliberated upon. He was in his own words not a foreign-policy guy. Where did this, then, position Bush on China policy?

If we place the China attitudes of the two periods before and after 9/11 in juxtaposition we in fact see two different Bushes. Of course, while this is to be expected given the emphasis of terrorism on U.S. policy after 9/11, it is also evidence of a disorderly decision-making process. At any rate, the United States could not afford to wage a war against global terrorism while waging a new Cold War against China. At this stage, the China challenge was perceived to be still in its infancy, while the People's Liberation Army (PLA) was considered a ponderous organization, its soldiers poorly trained and badly equipped, and its military capability estimated to be at least twenty years behind the United States.[27] The point is that a new attitude was quickly adopted toward China after

9/11, one in stark contrast to the administration's earlier confusion, which was reflected not just within the White House but also in greater public opinion. How to characterize the earlier attitude? In a speech delivered at the Ronald Reagan Presidential Library in November 1999, then Governor Bush hinged the shape of a future administration's China policy on the implicit charge that an ensuing China challenge was increasingly likely, albeit some engagement was also necessary. Accordingly, he held no misconceptions about the threat China posed; while the United States would "welcome a free and prosperous China," it would take assurances to manage its rise. At this point the presumption of a developing policy hung on the silence of whether the administration would find unwelcome an unfree yet prosperous People's Republic: it was, after all, an emerging peer competitor, to be dealt with "without illusion." These terms contained within them, to be sure, the origins of a neoconservative approach, beginning with a tougher and in some ways provocative Taiwan policy, to be reinforced by Rumsfeld at Defense, who refused to countenance an active engagement policy with formal military-to-military dialogues. There would be no point in giving the Chinese access to American intelligence sources, so went the thought, since the Chinese had never reciprocated to the same degree.[28] By January 2002, Bush expressed the U.S.-China relationship in striking new terms; a new opportunity, produced by a common danger, was erasing old rivalries, he announced. America would work with China "in ways we have never before, to achieve peace and prosperity."[29] There was to be no new Cold War containment policy in the offing; rather, all would share in the burden of waging the War on Terror.

The China "threat"

In its broadest sense, the China threat provoked a historical narrative that identified with the cataclysmic changes to the international system after World Wars I and II. As John J. Mearsheimer described in *The Tragedy of Great Power Politics*, "the cycle of violence" that the battlefields of Europe in the early twentieth century wrought will continue because the great powers, of which China is destined to become one, will cause a mutual fear to metastasize into a competition for power. Historically, this competition for power has led to cyclical conflict.[30] In the case of U.S.-China rivalry, the threat of pro-independence movements in Taiwan and Washington's continued, and ambiguous, support for its existence supplements this competition. Pundits seeking evidence had only to look to Chinese behavior in the years leading up to the inauguration of President George W. Bush to support this theory. Hyper-nationalistic reactions in China to the Chinese embassy bombing in Belgrade caused an uproar in anti-Americanism that contributed to suspending military-to-military ties (in truth a periodic affair); the conclusion of the Cox Report into Chinese military and nuclear espionage in Congress also featured as adding to Chinese military readiness; and Chinese tests of new long-range missiles continued to provide evidence for the assumption that new capabilities reflected new and emboldened intentions in China. Ideologically, economically, and militarily, China was set upon displacing the United States in Asia.

Top academic publications, reinforced by a series of anti-China volumes, offered a sense of analytical variety and therefore scientific legitimacy to the China threat, engendering further the sense of an impending conflict. Samuel Huntington's much-acclaimed *Clash of Civilizations* proved pivotal to this movement. More than a strategic affair, civilizational trends suggested not only that the United States was in a period of decline but that it was to be replaced in Asia with China's rise. Here was the very threat to the idea of a *Pax Americana* which had generated such passion in the neoconservatives, evidenced by a number of disconcerting trends in Asian affairs. In Japan, argued Christopher Layne in 1993, a strategic autonomy away from the United States and possibly toward China had already commenced.[31] Declining relations with Tokyo in 1995, which threatened to spill over to a trade war, seemed to add legitimacy to this charge. Clinton, forced to focus more on the region, found that more than Japan, China's neighbors had begun to reorient their economic growth to bandwagon on its growing economic output in the region. This was bolstered in addition by a cultural shift away from identifying with the way of the "West" toward an "Asia for Asians," adopted on the back of the economic successes of the Asian tigers—South Korea, Taiwan, Hong Kong, and Singapore—and China. This rejection, in part at least, of Western-style modernization in growing support of both local and Chinese successes was an affront to the notion of the American ideal. Moreover, it suggested an acceptance of China's governmental authoritarianism as opposed to Washington's emphasis on liberal transition, giving rise later to the concept of a "Beijing consensus." The United States, it seemed, was no longer the indispensable nation it appeared in 1996. As if to presage this altering of regional economies, Huntington wrote, Americans would be strongly inclined to reject China's, and Asia's, rise with military might, prompting in the process a negative spiraling in relations and possibly even conflict.[32]

By the beginning of the twenty-first century, and in the wake of the apparent end of what Francis Fukuyama called the ideological debate, many China watchers were discouraged to find that China had still failed to lay down its arms in deference to America's great victory over communism in the Cold War. Partisans attacked the Clinton administration as aiding this condition by increasing business and trade relations in lieu of more transitionally determinative policies such as demanding military transparency and greater respect for human rights. By this stage, and in accepting Fukuyama's thesis, many had come to perceive the disintegration of governmental reform in China as a characteristic of the greater limitation of communistic systems—leading to the corollary perception that China's collapse had become inevitable, if not imminent. China was bound to meet the "asymmetric transition from dictatorship to democracy," wrote the neoconservative China scholar and later Bush administration consultant Arthur Waldron—and it was America's duty to help engender this process.[33] It was a prospect that could begin as early as Bush's first term in office, he declared, a point later to be explored subtly in Rice's Foreign Affairs article.

More crucial to the debate at hand, a number of China-critical, if polemical, publications in the popular press brought greater emergency and attention to the evolving threat. The narrative was in part a reaction to the success of the publication in China of the widely popular China Can Say No, a manifesto arguing for a revolution against America's global hegemony.[34] Indelibly, its conclusions were not as charged as American reactions suggested them to be, denying that the publication was in fact a rearticulation of a wider image problem of American meddling explored first in Japan with the title *Japan Can Say No*. In China, the authors sourced their inspiration and motivation from the Taiwan Strait crisis of 1995, which had followed what was considered a provocative and insensitive visit by Taiwanese president Lee Tung-hui to the United States. Indeed, China's list of grievances by this stage was considered lengthy.[35] The authors wrote of the need for a clear divorce from American ideals, which they announced as imperialist pretentions cleverly masquerading as the principles of a benevolent superpower.

In a reverse pontificating of grievances, authors in America picked up on *China Can Say No* as a state endorsement of nationalistic aims which sought to displace the United States in East Asia. Because the book was published in the "controlled environment" of Beijing, Richard Bernstein and Ross Munro argued in the *Coming Conflict with China*, it demonstrated that the government gave its implicit consent to its anti-American conclusions.[36] Broadening Beijing's intentions beyond East Asia, Edward Timperlake and William Triplett argued in a similar theme in their book *Red Dragon Rising* that the appeasement of China, given its clear capabilities and authoritarian principles, would imperil the United States directly. "If the Communist Chinese," they wrote, "can gun down thousands of innocent civilians in order to ensure the regime's survival, it is only a matter of time before they turn their guns on the rest of the world to satisfy their territorial ambitions."[37] Nothing China could do, short of the complete and peaceful transition to liberal democracy these arguments proffered, would ever be enough to satisfy American demands.

It is worth extrapolating for a moment on the designation of this negative China imagery more broadly and how its origins as a manifestation of self-imagination in America inform part of the narrative. For whatever influence the authors above obtained over the China policy of the early Bush years, the fact that they nonetheless shared with many in the Bush White House a similar ideological predisposition, among many other themes, toward the threat of China suggests at the very least that a correlative relationship existed. Two points elaborate on their shared construction of China as an enemy-in-waiting. The first, as Chengxin Pan argues, is the proposition that fundamental observable truths exist and that these can with a level of sophistication describe and detail an objective and knowable world.[38] In this context, it could be plausibly stated that the Chinese will, in the Hobbesian understanding, seek greater measures in military preponderance in their search for global security and that this will create tension with the United States, and thereby, almost certainly lead to elongated conflict. The "obvious and disturbing analogy" of Wilhelmine Germany in the China image, Deputy Secretary of Defense Paul Wolfowitz was to argue, found its blueprint in this knowable and scientific tradition, to be built upon and mutually reinforced in publications as an analogy observable and scientific.[39] In the second point, identity reinforced the China threat as a product of sound logical necessity. If the United States was the exceptional nation, entitled subsequently to both "moral clarity and military hegemony," then not just China but any peer competitor would quite naturally take on the moniker of a "threat."[40] The conclusion to this designation was that any subsequent point counter to the threat image was considered immaterial, or a smokescreen, to larger Chinese ambitions perceived by policymakers.

If we accept these judgements then it becomes easier to understand where the China threat emanated from and subsequently why little was done about understanding China more thoroughly earlier. While the rise of the China-critical literature in the U.S. spurred a larger debate in Washington, it brought forth at the same time an unfortunate reality now augmented by divisions of the so-called China hawks and "panda huggers" (also known as the blue team/red team factions, named for China's offensive and defensive teams in military exercises) in and around the Bush administration. As Michael Pillsbury illustrated to the U.S.-China Economic and Security Review Commission (UCESRC) hearing in August 2001, there existed in government "very few people who can read Chinese who work on Chinese security matters, [and] close to none who can actually read a newspaper or an article published by the Chinese military or a Chinese government think tank." In fact, there was "no section of the United States Government whose job it is to gather and translate and to learn what the Chinese are saying."[41] The first two recommendations to be made by the commission in July 2002 were to rectify this apparent and glaring deficiency.[42] But the problem was as much a fundamental lack of interest as it was a budgeting one.

For one school of thought, the answer for America was clearly to rearm irrespective of any new comprehension of the Chinese language; the United States government did "not need any more translations to be made."[43] This was the doctrine of the so-called blue team of China hawks, representative of the many neoconservatives, although only a few were counted among its members. Accordingly, to know that "China views the U.S. as its present and future enemy," argued Richard Fisher, a senior fellow at the time at the Jamestown Foundation and adviser to the UCESRC, required a belief not only in the certainty of such claims, but that they could be discovered without interacting with either Chinese sources or materials. With this, judgment was made that Beijing was preparing for war over Taiwan, and that until the regime collapses "the PRC leadership will resort to increasing appeals to nationalism or even launch into nationalist military crusades, for which the United States would likely be a target."[44]

No blue team members took on positions in the Bush administration, yet it is enough to say they played a role in narrowing the opinion for those that did. On this point, they were like-minded thinkers among conservative Bush advisers who circled Washington's security establishment and at times provided consulting services to the White House. But they were also the links to the public for information deemed too controversial to be echoed by officials, driven by leaks sometimes in an attempt to push advisers toward policies more in line with their views. Bill Gertz is perhaps the leading figure in this charge, considered to break more stories about "China's misdeeds" per year than any other, often "based on top-secret intelligence reports" handed down through partisan intelligence officers and Congressional aids.[45] His method of delivery at the same time was as much the promulgation of the China threat as it was often a personal attack on those members of the China knowledge community at variance with his hawkish views.

These China intellectuals, nominally grouped as an association of "panda huggers," were charged with being soft on China. In fact, they often accepted similar views in terms of China perceptions, differing, however, on the costs the United States could be prepared to incur and on those the Chinese were prepared to accept. In short, it was believed the blue team could be counted upon to assert combative China policies, and that they were confident in the power of the United States and "unconcerned about Chinese retaliation against U.S. interests."[46]

It is difficult to gauge the influence of the blue team on China policy in the White House. They were, in the words of Mark Lagon, a member of the Senate Foreign Relations Committee, "a network which works actively together to shift our policy on China."[47] For some at least, their persuasive powers accorded a sense of authority, influencing, it was believed, Rumsfeld's animosity toward military-to-military dialogues.[48] But such views were also undertaken by advisers closer to the president, the most prominent of these being John Bolton, whose partisan championship for a new and stronger U.S.-Taiwan relationship was well acknowledged. In keeping with the blue team assumption of unbeatable U.S. strength in military arms, he advocated consistently for independence for Taiwan on the basis that any Chinese threat to respond with force was pure "fantasy."[49] When reviewing U.S. policy toward Taiwan in the first months of the Bush administration, it is possible to see the assumptions and advice arising from such blue team recommendations at work.

China policy in the first nine months

The first months of the Bush administration reveal the contours of a broadening U.S.-China schism in everyday relations. The two larger incidents in this shift occurred over a hardening of Taiwan policy and the April 1 EP-3 reconnaissance plane collision with a Chinese F-8 fighter jet. These events were at the same time punctuated by smaller, insensitive obstacles seen by Beijing as evidence of a new arrogance in Washington. The decision to officially meet the Dalai Lama in the White House on May 23, the president's early criticism of Chinese assistance to help build a fiber-optic network in Iraq, and an unprecedented decision to allow Taiwan's President Chen Shui-bian liberal terms for a U.S. visit set an unambiguous tone about the nature of the new relationship. For Chinese observers, this was evidence that the new Bush administration had begun office convinced that China had become America's "biggest rival and [that] it was imperative to take preventative measures before it was too late."[50]

Undoubtedly, the relationship between the United States and Taiwan represented the fundamental flashpoint between Beijing and Washington. The architecture of the Taiwan Relations Act and the three U.S.-China joint communiqués provided the legal framework for a U.S.-Taiwanese relationship consistent with the one-China policy. But it was not considered to be consistently adhered to. By the first months of the Bush administration, policymakers were considering proposals for the largest sale of American weapons to Taiwan, dramatic not just for its monetary value but also for its technological sophistication and offensive capability. This wasn't such a departure in Taiwan policy from previous administrations; each president retained the right to judge arms sales on the basis of the threat from mainland China, although the Chinese argued this abrogated the "reduction" clause of the third U.S.-China Joint Communiqué. Indicatively, however, a decided and strategic leaning toward Taiwan had occurred. To emphasize the point, Bush rejected the "three no's"—no change to the one-China policy, no support for independence in Taiwan, and no support for Taiwanese membership in international organizations—and ignited instead controversy over his pledge to do "whatever it took to help Taiwan" should a conflict occur.[51] He would send no high-level dignitary to China to reciprocate Vice Premier Qian Qichen's March 2001 visit, and he appeared on a public radio program to suggest that his administration would drop "strategic ambiguity," a policy established to deter both Beijing and Taipei from aggravating relations, for outright support for Taiwan.

These points caused much consternation. Indeed, Bush seemed to be sending mixed signals. The administration sought no changes to the status quo on China policy, Condoleezza Rice asserted during the campaign, which included no deviation from the one-China policy. In fact, the new administration saw trade with China and the opening of its markets as potential game-changers for a twenty-first-century U.S.-China relationship. Why then the erratic behavior? There are two main contending points to this discussion. Basing judgments for policy on the creation of an effective deterrence against the apparent threat of China, Bush's hawkishness enabled the administration to avoid policies detrimental to U.S.-China cooperation, circumventing at the same time a crisis in the Taiwan Strait, or so this argument proffers.[52] An adjoining rationale for this position for some was that Bush's language to the Chinese was more conciliatory than what was promulgated in the media. His comments to Qian Qichen in March suggest he believed his developing China policies were hardly a cause for concern: "Nothing we do is a threat to [the Chinese] and I want you to tell that to your leadership."[53]

The second example is Colin Powell's remarks on the administration's decision to allow President Chen to layover in the United States for three days on his way to Latin America. The White House will "reassure the authorities in Beijing," commented Powell to the media, "that there is nothing in the president's transit that they should find disturbing or in any way modifying or changing or casting any doubt on the policy that exists between us and the People's Republic of China."[54] This was all well and good provided the Chinese read these remarks as intended. But as the second point illustrates, there was little reason for them to do so. Contending forces within the administration and in Congress on China, pulling between hostility and cooperation, were thought to be behind the considerable disharmony on the China question. By this measure, Bush in fact lacked a coherent and cohesive China policy or at the very least, one he could follow without disruption. It may have been that Bush genuinely meant to establish greater working relations with Beijing and that his Taiwan policy was less charged than his Chinese counterparts assumed. But this belief would have been a naïve one. The point is that it gave no agency to Chinese leaders and their beliefs or thoughts about the Taiwan issue, acknowledging still less that the last Taiwanese president to visit the United States caused a crisis to erupt in the Taiwan Strait, or that Chinese authorities were hyper-sensitive to any perceived changes in the status quo of the U.S.-Taiwan relationship directly bearing upon their plans for military modernization.[55]

Bush's National Missile Defense (NMD) program proved an additional cause for consternation in the relationship, again directly bearing upon the Taiwan question. Missile defense had been a rallying call for neoconservatives and Republicans, emboldened by the 1998 Rumsfeld Commission to adopt a system countering perceived new threats in proliferation of missiles and weapons of mass destruction. Rejecting the Central Intelligence Agency's emphasis on fact-based analysis, the Rumsfeld Commission turned the methodology on its head to accept a hypothesis-based one, stressing the measurement of capabilities over intentions. This was an attempt to account for the "unknown unknowns," to cover even for information policymakers were unaware they were unaware of. Importantly, it took as its starting point certain preconceived ideas about the intentions of states in question—zero-sum engagement, selfish aims, revisionist agenda, and maximization of power—proceeding afterwards to measure the available information against them.[56] By this equation, Bush's May 2001 announcement of the administration's decision to deploy ballistic missile defenses unnerved many, but the implications for the Chinese and the Taiwan issue were particularly felt in Beijing.

China's rise in the United States and its association with the China threat literature suggested an implicit relationship between the NMD and China. The 1998 Defense Authorization Act had already begun mandating the study of ballistic missile defense for Taiwan. By the beginning of the new century, arms sales to Taipei contained within them military equipment, including advanced air-to-air and anti-ship missiles, "that could be eventually linked to a theater missile defense system."[57] Beijing's seemingly tepid response to the May announcement led some to believe that the Chinese were willing to move on from the NMD issue for greater assurances on World Trade Organization (WTO) admission and for China's application to host the 2008 Olympic Games. This position dismissed, however, the significance of the NMD issue for Beijing. Further, it disregarded the fact that between 1998 and 2001, with the announcement that the U.S. would leave the Antiballistic Missile Treaty (ABMT), Chinese leaders had launched a "multi-pronged campaign opposing U.S. missile defenses," and that a cottage industry of anti-NMD-issue articles in think tanks, the media, journals, and the popular press had transformed the issue in China, as Jing-dong Yuan observed, "into a household topic."[58] By this stage, it was evident that Chinese concerns were driven as much by their limited capabilities to deter Taiwanese independence as they were by increasing uncertainty over Washington's intentions toward China. These considerations for Beijing forced leaders to upscale their missile program across the Taiwan Strait and fast-track military modernization.[59]

On April 1, a U.S. EP-3 Orion reconnaissance aircraft collided with a Chinese F-8-II "Finback" over waters 65 miles from Hainan Island, China, temporarily putting the issue of the NMD on hold. The Chinese fighter and its pilot, Wang Wei, were lost and the EP-3 was forced to make an emergency landing on Chinese soil. Following the landing, its twenty-four U.S. crewmen were detained and the Chinese demanded an apology with reparations for an accident they accused the American crew of perpetrating. By many accounts, the first crisis of the new Bush administration showed a potential for uncontrollable escalation. Bush demanded the immediate release of the crew and plane while the Chinese reciprocated with demands for the U.S. to cease its reconnaissance missions. By April 12 the affair had fizzled out through no small feat of diplomatic engagement on the side of the Bush administration.

On the surface, the resolution of the EP-3 incident appeared to reflect the diligence of the State Department machinery, the abrogation of decision-making input by China hardliners Rumsfeld and Cheney, and the steady hand of the president. In many ways this was the case. But a fundamental incoherence within the Bush administration's China message was also present, a point illustrated by a desperate unease between the State and Defense departments. At the time when aerial surveillance near China had been increasing, Chinese fighter pilots had also raised their risk taking to a point where an accident was increasingly possible. It would be an understatement to say that the Chinese were unhappy with the increasing abuse of what they considered their airspace within their 200-mile exclusive economic zone. At any rate, it was not considered in the State Department or the White House in these early days that a clear mechanism for crisis relief between China and the U.S. should be established. In this, an easy consensus was reached among all parties in the administration that Washington had a right to fly such missions, irrespective of Beijing's feelings and of the consequences. Bush instructed the State Department that the U.S. was in no way to apologize for the accident, especially since it was clear the Chinese pilot had been in the wrong.[60]

In Beijing, by contrast, the incident produced images analogous to ones witnessed during the 1999 Belgrade bombing of the Chinese embassy by NATO forces. Once again, Chinese people were made to feel humiliated by the American "bully," whose dry, legalistic responses, and inability to apologize, were perceived as insensitive to say the least.[61] The nationalist outcry alarmed Chinese authorities in no small way, hardening their initial response to the incident. At the same time, the laborious communication between the PLA and the political leadership made their demands more critical, their responses slow, and the crisis appear drawn out. With Jiang Zemin out of the country and the 2002 successorship dilemma not yet abated, the PLA stood firm on message. In this, their accusation of American fault was accepted as the official story and adhered to, the reaction to which required substantial U.S. conciliation.[62]

The first twelve hours following the accident went by without a word from the Chinese about the American servicemen, alarming the Bush administration. Indeed, they could not know at the time that poor crisis architecture in Beijing had compounded the challenge of authority in the chain of command. Immediate assumptions in the Bush administration appeared to draw the opposite conclusion; alarmed about the lack of communication, Bush announced in the Rose Garden on April 2 that the time had come to release the crew. "Every day that goes by," he asserted, "increases the potential that our relations with China could be damaged."[63] Whether or not Bush was apprised of the potential for this communication to be misconstrued, the magnification of the spectacle in the media by the president worked to tighten the inflexibility of the Chinese response, still confused by bureaucratic channels. Among observant China watchers in the U.S., it was believed that conciliating Beijing's desire for an apology over the EP-3 incident was a prospect worth considering, since the issue was as much about giving face as it was about the shock of the discovery in China that U.S. spy planes were regularly flying so close to the mainland. With the Rose Garden address, however, the public in China demanded swift reprisals, as Susan Shirk notes, escalating a dilemma that Beijing would like to have kept quiet.[64] In the meantime, Chinese messaging revealed an attempt to talk tough while acting in a way that suggested leaders were more pragmatic about a solution. On April 4, Powell publicly responded for the first time with "regret" for the accident and the loss of the Chinese pilot, seen as an attempt to lower the temperature, then sitting at alarming levels. By this stage, Bush too was looking for a "way out," abandoning efforts to lower the tensions between the two nations to Powell. Bush resisted also the recommendation to move an aircraft carrier closer to Hainan while instructing staff to resist in public any anti-China sentiment.[65] On April 6, Bush followed Powell's lead in articulating the administration's "regret" for the loss of the Chinese pilot, intimating that the United States was seeking a de-escalation of the crisis.

By April 12 the crisis had ended with a semblance of an apology; however, neither side achieved its aims considered for a successful resolution. Ambassador Joseph Prueher presented a formal letter to China's foreign minister, Tang Jiaxuan, on April 11, perceived as acquiescing to Chinese demand. Insofar as the United States was "very sorry" for the loss of the Chinese pilot and for landing an American aircraft on Chinese soil without clearance, it did not accept responsibility for the accident or for the pretext of the flight.[66] This was acceptable to Beijing, who read the letter to the Chinese population as an apology of sorts. Left unaddressed was the Chinese demands for the ceasing of U.S. reconnaissance flights close to China's borders and the question of the EP-3 aircraft, which Beijing forbade to leave Chinese soil under its own power. This annoyed Rumsfeld's Defense Department, which perceived the administration's response as too conciliatory, contributing later in the month to a greater inflexibility on weapons sales to Taiwan. In the conservative press, William Kristol and Robert Kagan attacked the Bush administration as perpetrating a national humiliation brought about by the direct consequences of a "deliberate Chinese policy" to make America appease Chinese leaders. Bush had shown that Washington feared "the political, strategic, and economic consequences of meeting a Chinese challenge."[67]

As to whether the debacle revealed either consistency or nuance in the administration's China policy, there exists little substantiating evidence.[68] Certainly, Bush did well to deflate the crisis, leaning on his capable diplomats to "find a way out" of the dilemma. But as John Garver articulates, the change in attitude toward China, from arrogant antagonist to conciliatory diplomat, emerged more from a realization of changed power realities in Beijing.[69] The point is made in Bush's decision to escalate the crisis by appearing on television on April 2, forcing the Chinese to harden their own response in the face of an excited domestic populace. Indeed, other considerations internal to the Chinese leadership were likely to play a role in its response.[70] But the decision to hold the American servicemen hostage to an apology and the ceasing of U.S. reconnaissance missions gave the Bush administration little room to maneuver. Any de-escalation would require a voluntary response from Beijing.

To be sure, the administration had cards to play in the form of objecting to China's application for the 2008 Olympic Games, rejecting China's WTO admission, and selling advanced weaponry to Taipei. At the same time, Bush needed the Chinese to support a new sanctions regime in the UN against Iraq. A postcrisis analysis in the 2002 UCSRC illustrates these points. Bush may have misperceived the initial Chinese response as something more sinister and calculating, a perception trumpeted by Kristol and Kagan in the popular press. It was perceived that in a crisis the Chinese may "not escalate at the same pace or by the same means as the West, causing the West to miss the level of commitment the Chinese are applying." In other words, unless the Chinese were correctly understood, which it wasn't entirely sure they were, the United States ran the risk of implementing policies inadequate to their design and intention. As such, and in simpler terms, greater attention was needed to understand Chinese leaders, their structure of government, and their style of dealing with foreign affairs.

For some, the relative stability in relations in the aftermath of the incident suggested that a newfound respect, if not commonality, had emerged between the Bush administration and Chinese leaders. Accordingly, momentum toward a greater rapprochement was achieved. Bush's comments calling for more a "constructive and productive relationship" and Powell's visit to Beijing in late July were seen as emblematic of this new relationship.[71] Yet, we find caution for this reasoning. To dismiss other seemingly more intractable issues over Taiwan, missile defense and the Dalai Lama for a less tangible diplomatic victory tends to put the cart before the horse. Indeed, the trigger had not been dismantled; Washington continued its disturbing flights close to the Chinese mainland and Beijing delayed the return of the plane to the United States. Moreover, by mid-April 2002, the topic of arms sales to Taiwan again dominated the bilateral relationship. Although Bush in the end would not include the sophisticated Aegis radar system in the arms package, he did approve a provocatively large weapons cache, including four Kidd-class destroyers and 12 P-3C anti-submarine aircraft, with the promise to help Taipei obtain eight diesel submarines. Three days later, on the 26th, Bush announced the United States was prepared to do whatever necessary to defend Taiwan, an announcement which encouraged and legitimized Taipei's search for independence.[72] From this purview, the vitality of this new momentum appears suspect, its characteristics unmeasured. While Bush may have sought to compartmentalize the Taiwan issue, as some suggest, he risked the perception that the successful resolution of the EP-3 incident could deprioritize the core interest of Taiwan in U.S.-China relations.[73] At the same time, the Defense Department was unwilling to play by a similar understanding, ceasing all military-to-military exchanges following the EP-3 incident, with any continuance of dialogue to be decided by Rumsfeld on a case-by-case basis.

The post-9/11 honeymoon

The immediate post-9/11 relationship between the Bush administration and Beijing provides one of the more contrasting episodes in behaviors in American foreign policy. Indeed, it might be said that the negative spiraling of U.S.-China relations could only have been righted with the disruption of an event so dramatic in its revulsions as the 9/11 attack on American soil. Whatever the administration's evolving policy for China, the succession of events in the wake of the attacks—the War on Terror, sanctions on Iraq, the war in Afghanistan—reoriented the relationship to the status of a strategic partnership in the fight against global terrorism. In speeches and policy announcements thereafter, discussions of human rights, missile technology transfer, and trade infringements were watered down if not entirely jettisoned; perceived anti-China bills in Congress dissipated; and the general inclination was that with the new focus on terrorism the United States had much to lose in competition with Beijing.[74]

In the immediate aftermath, President Jiang Zemin, too, was quick to offer his country's condolences and to help track down the perpetrators. By all accounts, Beijing took the opportunity to restart the relationship with the Bush administration, backing UN Resolution 1373 to use force in Afghanistan, a major departure in China's non-intervention policy; sending a counter-terrorism team to Washington as a sign of willingness to share intelligence; agreeing to allow the Federal Bureau of Investigation to operate in Beijing on a limited basis; and agreeing to frameworks on sharing intelligence, law enforcement, and terrorist financial tracking data. More importantly, Beijing aided Washington in bringing its all-weather ally Pakistan over to the war effort, a point considered paramount for basing U.S. forces and aircraft close to the war zone. Perceptively, a great rebalancing of the relationship had taken place as well on the American side.[75] By October 2002, Bush had met with leaders twice in the U.S.—with Vice President Hu Jintao, later Jiang's successor, in April in Washington, and again with Jiang at Bush's ranch in Crawford, Texas—representing what appeared to be an unprecedented level of diplomatic engagement. This was to be followed by further rhetorical gestures toward China as a "great power" and the relationship as a "constructive strategic partnership," stoking the Chinese government's reputation as a legitimate and high-standing member of the community of nations. Human rights were dropped as a major concern in the White House and tacit support was given for China's Strike Hard campaign against separatists in Xinjiang and Tibet. In Washington, the China-threat elements of the administration and Congress were silenced, adding further credence to the belief that a reset had begun. Such was the basis of this new engagement and charm offensive.

Perhaps the most remarkable point, however, was that this rebalance occurred at the same time as a greater emboldening of the U.S.-Taiwan relationship took place, brought about by new weapons packages and the signaling of increased support for Taiwanese democracy. This led some to consider that Bush had achieved, in the face of the preceding four decades, the most comprehensive and successful U.S.-China relationship on American terms since the Nixon administration. Key departures in Chinese foreign policy—its marginalization of anti-American propaganda, its support for UN intervention in Afghanistan and global anti-terror activities, and importantly its decision to join the WTO—were emblematic of a positive shift that could be largely credited to an effective Bush China policy.[76] These early prognostications were justified still by the strong position of the United States, at the time the world's sole superpower, and by the major sources of leverage still open to the government, including decisive international support for the War on Terror and the U.S.-led international order; decision-making power over important issues such as terrorism (and the naming of the Xinjiang separatists as a terrorist organization), the Olympic Games committee, and the WTO and the question of China's smooth entry; and, importantly, Taiwan. Moreover, owing to glaring deficiencies, Chinese military modernization efforts were to be viewed as inadequate, even if rapidly advancing, at the time for Beijing to respond appropriately to the Taiwan threat. By the early years of the Obama administration this apparent leverage had been exhausted.

To be sure, this agreeable new diplomatic partnership could not hide for long the major challenges lurking below the surface. Upon closer examination, the new rebalance appeared little more than a recess in an increasingly troubled relationship, what Chinese scholar Jia Qingguo identified as a period of "reduced differences, rising tensions."[77] Core differences not only remained but in fact continued to worsen despite the new ostensible cooperation in the War on Terror. The administration's decision to pull out of the ABMT in June 2002, and its perceived implications for a theater missile defense system, drew troubling associations for Beijing with the Taiwan question, heightening the threat of a greater U.S.-Taiwanese defense relationship. This unilateralism in Washington concerned Beijing deeply, but it was also viewed as a major setback for multilateralism, and particularly a failure for Beijing's multilateral regional security forum, the Shanghai Cooperation Organization.

Discernibly, as time moved on there appeared for Beijing to be little strategic benefit in its support for the Bush administration's War on Terror. As Aaron Friedberg argued in early 2002, Beijing may have agreed, albeit reluctantly, with intervention in Afghanistan on the basis of international cooperation, but it was bound to see any further American action in Iraq, or even Iran or North Korea, as counter to its strategic interests.[78] Unresolved core interests, temporarily set aside in a moment of crisis, were not solved, nor even discussed with reference to a settlement amenable to a more long-term cooperative partnership. Rather, while the administration sought a new working agreement on relations, commissioners on the U.S.-China Economic and Security Review Commission plotted on the terms of a regime change in China. The honeymoon in U.S.-China relations, ostensibly, would be an ephemeral one. By 2003, Friedberg's thesis had proven disconcertingly prescient for the Bush administration: White House officials could not deny that while cooperation on anti-terrorism had been forthcoming, maintaining the cordial atmosphere between both states had become, in Adam Ward's words, "an increasingly effortful and gravity-defying affair."[79]

Within this context, the relationship between Bush and Taiwan continued to represent the fundamental difference in the U.S.-China relationship. In August 2002, Bush signed the U.S. 2002 Supplemental Appropriations Act, requiring legislation to treat Taiwan as comparable to a NATO ally. The Act was specific to legislation aimed at recovery in the United States from terrorist attacks, but it included detailed provisions on Taiwan, referring, for instance, to Taiwan military leaders and elected officials as "covered allied persons" in an attempt to provide immunity from the International Criminal Court. For Beijing, this was seen as further incremental change to the one-China policy in Washington. Beijing summoned the U.S. ambassador to protest these new provisions. Other points of friction were also articulated around this time to Colin Powell on the side of the ASEAN Regional Forum in Brunei by the Chinese foreign minister, Tang Jiaxuan, in an attempt to drive home the magnitude of the issue. The Chinese were "seriously concerned about the upgrading of the U.S.-Taiwan relationship and strengthening of the military links between the United States and Taiwan," Tang pressed to newspapers. Not surprisingly, Powell gave short shrift to these representations, responding once again that on the question of arms sales and the Supplementary Appropriations Act, they were for the "purpose of making sure that the Taiwanese are able to defend themselves and are in no way an attempt to move away from our 'one China' policy." If Powell was heard to complain that the Chinese were "constantly seeking reassurance from the U.S. about its policy toward Taiwan," his actions nonetheless appeared to obfuscate the implications of U.S. policy on the Chinese side or recognize that they were forcing the Chinese to continually re-evaluate their commitment to cooperation with Washington.[80]

In December 2003, the new U.S.-China relationship threatened to fall apart as elections in Taiwan once again brought the question of independence to the fore. Bush's pro-Taiwan posturing of the first years had come home to haunt the administration and its new emphasis on U.S.-China cooperation. Increasingly vocal opposition to Beijing and threats toward formal independence in Taipei caused the administration to reassess the relationship. President Chen Shui-bian, with leaders of the Democratic Progressive Party (DPP), pushed for greater constitutional reforms that Bush administration officials believed would catalyze an unwanted confrontation with Beijing, prepared in the event to respond with force. This caused Bush to take "extraordinary steps," writes Robert Sutter, to deflate the tension, publicly rebuking, with Chinese premier Wen Jiabao, the Taiwanese president in front of reporters in Washington, D.C. on December 9.[81] But the immediate problem was not to be deterred easily. By late October 2004, further public calls by the State Department for the de-escalation of Chen's pro-independence stance were met with few results. Indeed, by this time administration officials including Bush himself had come to think of Chen as a walking "landmine" for U.S. policy, a point not lost on opposition forces in Taiwan who used the epithet to publicly berate Chen and the DPP. This deterred Chen to some degree. But part of the problem lay in the fact that, short of a direct constitutional amendment toward permanent separation, Chen felt confident enough in U.S. support to pursue incremental steps toward independence.[82]

In further exacerbating bilateral complexities, Rumsfeld's Defense Department at varying intervals appeared to aid escalation more than deflation. In looking briefly back to a leak of the 2002 Nuclear Posture Review, it is evident that plans by the Defense Department considered the use of nuclear weapons in "a military confrontation over the status of Taiwan." This apparent broadening of U.S. nuclear doctrine, which had been focused on North Korea, Iraq, Iran, Libya, and Syria, was in stark contrast to states that were considered to be the more immediate threat.[83] In the wake of further departures in the ABMT in December 2001, the arms sales to Taiwan in April, and the perceived change in the policy of strategic ambiguity, the potential targeting of China for nuclear weapons use was to be seen as yet another step in an increasingly challenging U.S. policy toward China. To stoke the anger of Beijing further, in March 2002, Rumsfeld sent Deputy Secretary of Defense Paul Wolfowitz to Florida to meet with the Taiwanese defense minister, Tang Yiau-Ming, visiting unofficially to attend a meeting of the U.S.-Taiwan Business Council, along with the assistant secretary of state for East Asian and Pacific affairs, James Kelly. This was the highest-level meeting to occur since the change in diplomatic recognition in 1979.[84] Rightly, this appeared as justification for the belief that U.S.-Taiwan military cooperation was more than what Bush had assured Chinese leaders. Although their discussion was not made public, another leak, this time to Reuters, revealed that while Bush had assured no changes to U.S. Taiwan policy in personal meetings, his administration continued to view Taiwan as a nation under American protection.[85] Seemingly, the new focus on global terrorism had failed to significantly alter the administration's view of China as a strategic competitor.

Conclusion

The U.S.-China security relationship in the first Bush term reveals an administration always in two minds on engagement with China. To be sure, Bush displayed a noteworthy predilection for pragmatism, witnessed first with the successful diplomatic conclusion of the EP-3 incident and followed by the dramatic shift in priorities and attitudes, from competition to partnership, after 9/11. But there were also hard-headed elements of the Bush administration disposed to view this partnership as ephemeral and self-serving. The logic of engagement, according to these views, reflected the arithmetic of great-power equations more than the theories of comparative gain and liberal-economic awakening. While perhaps centered in the Pentagon, these views were shared more broadly across the key policymakers and advisers within the administration who viewed China's rise with foreboding unease. In terms of policy, these dichotomous views precipitated at times incoherence and miscalculation, even as cooperation was pushed in the wake of military operations in the Middle East and counter-terrorism collaboration in the War on Terror. Chapter 2 examines this miscalculation more clearly in the second Bush administration, but it is noteworthy that its genesis takes place in the first term. In summary, while Bush sought to reorient the relationship toward a more cooperative and constructive partnership, he did so while also buttressing U.S. support for, and selling increasingly sophisticated weapons to, Taiwan, dismantling the ABMT, and adopting militarily challenging policies—with little thought to Chinese counter-policies and reactions.

These perceptions and their resulting actions originated in the China-threat image, which came to emerge at the beginning of the administration. Many appointees accepted the basis of this threat—that China's rise would hasten the inevitable clash between Washington and Beijing as China's autocratic leaders sought to assert more authority in global affairs. Indeed, this view, we note in subsequent chapters, became increasingly prevalent as the Obama and Trump administrations sought to deal with a progressively revisionist China under President Xi Jinping. Until 2008, at least, this was not accepted by Bush and many China observers as a fait accompli. That said, Bush harbored observable misgivings about Chinese intentions. Notably, he would not seek to dispel the notion that China would seek to challenge the U.S.-led liberal international order or that the Pentagon should be forced into pliant engagement with the PLA. These attitudes were to have knock-on effects, the most notable of these was, as of 2004, Rumsfeld's continued hold on military exchanges, causing "major headaches for Defense-affiliated organizations attempting to conduct cooperative programming with Chinese counterparts."[86] If the administration believed this contradiction to reflect a timely and calculated policy, the Chinese found it disconcerting.

While it is clear that discernible patterns of cooperation and policy had begun to emerge by the end of the first administration in the security sphere, little of a clear-cut, predictable strategy existed. Noteworthy changes in style and policy—such as the "Anything but Clinton" mantra, the adoption of theater missile defense, the pivot from strategic partner to strategic competitor, and subtle changes to the military posture, to name a few—marked its departures from the former administration. In a number of cases, these changes appeared to represent more a capitulation to rhetoric than substance. But there appeared at the same time only casual, and often mistaken, reference to China's perception of these changes. These perceptual differences took place most prominently on Taiwan policy, the results of which emerged more coherently in the second administration with China's Anti-Secession Law.[87] In the short term, these tensions were masked by the new cooperation in counter-terrorism and the war in Afghanistan, new economic agreements, and the expansion of diplomatic engagements. With 9/11, long-term differences were compartmentalized and put aside; administration China hawks were silenced; and focus was redirected toward Afghanistan and Iraq.

Notwithstanding the more overt changes to policy toward Taiwan and military exchanges, by the end of the first term Bush appeared nonetheless to be continuing much of Clinton's focus on engagement. By mid-2002, in fact, unprecedented top-level interaction between President Bush and President Jiang, and between the Department of State and the Ministry of Foreign Affairs, led to historic new agreements on information sharing, nuclear non-proliferation, counter-terrorism cooperation, United Nations sanctions regimes, and state intervention. In China, noted national security adviser Condoleezza Rice, authorities remarked that Bush had "gone the extra mile,"[88] that human rights protests had notably quietened, that the WTO admission process was smoother, that support for China's 2008 Olympic bid was forthcoming, and that Chen Shui-bien's attempts at independence were censured. For the White House, Bush, too, found new support in Beijing for UN intervention in Afghanistan, help in procuring Pakistani support for military basing, and new transparency in military policy and development. By 2005, this engagement had come to represent the administration's ongoing China policy.

2. The Bush Administration's Second Term: Searching for the Responsible Stakeholder

The second Bush administration, this chapter reveals, continued its notable shift in attitudes and style in its approach to dealing with China. Noteworthy changes in personnel—with Colin Powell, Richard Armitage, and Paul Wolfowitz out—presaged greater support for more engagement with Beijing as Condoleezza Rice became secretary of state. Strategic priorities in the ongoing War on Terror, the wars in Afghanistan and Iraq, and the threat of nuclear proliferation in North Korea made for significant anchors in this paradigm shift. At the same time, there was also reason to believe that important changes in China's behavior and makeup could develop significantly along the lines of the theory that more engagement, and not less, would work to soften authoritarian rule on the mainland as economic integration reinforced the liberal status quo. The defining moment for this shift emerged in September 2005 with Undersecretary of State Robert Zoellick's call for China to become a "responsible stakeholder." Looking beyond narrow national self-interest, Zoellick proselytized, China had done well to seek out constructive partnerships in dealing with global problems in a mature and collaborative manner. Notwithstanding this apparent "peaceful rise," however, inaction on issues pertaining to proliferation, military transparency, the Six-Party Talks, and unhelpful policies toward Taiwan would continue to be sources of frustration. But this was also a call for many in the United States to move beyond the tendency to view China "solely through the lens of fear." In this regard, the United States would need to "intensify" its engagement with China so as to meet the "challenges of the new century" and protect the foundations of the liberal world order.[1] Here was a statement that the Cold War analogies and zero-sum perspectives of the first Bush administration, as epitomized in the neoconservatives, no longer applied. It was under this framework that the China engagement-change theory found its most ardent application taking place during the second Bush administration.

"Conditional acceptance" of China's rise, and not "strategic competitor," forecast the new policy approach. Certainly, this proved a continuation from the final years of the first Bush administration. But it wasn't until 2005 that the failure of Bush's hawkish and non-cooperative approach to issues such as North Korean nuclear proliferation was formally recognized, or that it was realized that meaningful results there could not take place without significant Chinese support. To Bush's credit, the administration turned diplomatic engagement with Beijing into a robust new exercise, comprising even new exchanges with Secretary of Defense Donald Rumsfeld's department. Symbolized in the senior dialogue talks between Zoellick and the Chinese vice foreign minister Dai Bingguo, this engagement was undertaken as a project of Secretary of State Rice's "transformational diplomacy," supplemented by a 13 percent increase in budget for foreign affairs, the largest in the budget proposals for the fiscal year 2005.[2] Recognizing the new threats to international and regional security, new challenges required America's diplomatic corps to focus on areas in Asia and Africa previously considered peripheral to U.S. interests.[3] Discernibly, the bilateral relationship entered a level of significance usually held only for strategic partners.

Over the course of the next four years, however, observable inconsistencies in this new diplomatic engagement came to illustrate the notable and poorly hidden differences in rhetoric and practice. Distraction and unilateralism, as this chapter will illustrate, constituted the mounting problems in the policies toward Asia. To be sure, not all have accepted this adumbration of affairs. Bush had done more than any other to strengthen America's position in Asia, noted Rice, and contrary to the naysayers, writes Michael Green, former senior director for Asian affairs at the National Security

Council (NSC), "most major players in Asia have used the war on terrorism and the conflict in Iraq to align more closely with the United States."[4] On the account of military and formal relations with "allies and friends," these points have tended to ring true. At the same time, however, they masked the downsides of the economic, political, and diplomatic relationships, which had come to demonstrate that Bush's views and priorities were largely at variance with Asia's problems.[5] Military relationships were bolstered; U.S.-Japan ties were strengthened, and with Prime Minister Junichiro Koizumi, Japan set upon a path to military normalization with greater support for Taiwan sovereignty under the U.S.-Japan Joint Security Consultative Committee. But this was undertaken at the same time as relations with South Korea soured demonstrably, first under President Kim Dae-jung and then under Roh Moo-hyun, as Bush rejected the Sunshine policy. Additionally, Rice participated haphazardly in Southeast Asian regional diplomatic engagements, "snubbing" in July 2005 the ASEAN (Association of Southeast Asian Nations) post-ministerial conference (PMC) and later the ASEAN Regional Forum, only to join engagements the following year in an attempt to counteract sentiments that the region had become "unimportant to the administration."[6]

By the end of the second Bush term, devastating results from Pew polls revealed that support for the administration in the Asia-Pacific had dropped dramatically from the early years, even among staunch allies in Japan and Australia.[7] The overall trend in U.S. behavior toward Asia, it appeared, remained unchanged from the first years. As Mel Gurtov further observes, while the administration sought to bolster Cold War-era alliances in Asia with an emphasis on balance-of-power politics, it was being upstaged by Beijing as it sought to intensify regional integration in free trade agreements, increase and pursue consistent participation in dialogue groups such as ASEAN + 3 and the East Asia Summit, and undertake new commitments to regional initiatives such as the ASEAN Treaty of Amity and Cooperation (which Bush refused to sign) and the Joint Declaration on Strategic Partnership for Peace and Prosperity.[8]

Critique of the Bush administration's policies with China reveals a similar uneven trend. Unprecedented cooperation on counter-terrorism, weapons non-proliferation, and North Korean denuclearization occurred. Chinese participation in new regulatory frameworks, non-proliferation protocols, and dialogue groups was sought after and in many respects obtained, reinforcing the prospect that "habits of cooperation" could strengthen other initiatives toward cooperation and liberalization.[9] This process was considered a principal accomplishment for U.S.-China relations in the administration. According to Victor Cha, former director of Asian affairs at the NSC, the United States under Bush "achieved a pragmatic, results oriented, cooperative relationship with China . . . that greatly enhances regional stability."[10] Indeed, these points are difficult to disprove. In terms of qualitative significance, however, their denotations are methodologically deceptive. T. J. Pempel makes the point: many of the positive evaluations of Bush's Asia policies have been creatively unfalsifiable, made on the basis of the lowest possible standard.[11] If engagement with Beijing had worked to stabilize relations and foster regional optimism, for instance, it had done so only after engagement had deteriorated to new lows following the troubles created by Bush. Further, if "real progress" on North Korea had taken place, it had done so only after five years of hawkish unilateralism had failed to produce results. By the end of 2008, Bush's engagement with China had come full circle to reflect the "comprehensive partnership" of the Clinton years. The addendum to this trial-and-error cycle, for many, has been the opprobrium that the method resulted in too much error.

What comes to the fore in the analysis of these security relationships is the misconception in the White House that the "constructive" partnership was interpreted analogously on each side and in terms of American priorities and challenges. This was a concern raised, in fact, as early as 2005 as the trends of engagement in counter-terrorism and non-proliferation initiatives became more definitively contrary to American intentions. But the trends of the partnership at this time were not considered correlative. By the end of the Bush years, however, it was too late to correct the error that in the lingering anticipation of cooperative outcomes, the administration had accepted progress in process as the measurement of positive results.[12] The shortfall in expectations would come to bear directly on the Obama administration's expectations and policies for China.

Accommodating for process: U.S.-China counter-terrorism cooperation

The extraordinary circumstances of September 11, 2001 gave authority to the view that a radical revision of U.S.-China engagement was warranted in the face of an older and more sinister enemy in terrorism. In a volte-face from former antagonistic sentiments, U.S.-China cooperation was redressed under the banner of the War on Terror. More than a threat to world peace, here was a common interest the United States and China could use to smoothen the first tumultuous months of Bush's initial year in office. The new strategic relationship, subsequently, became known as the three C's of a "candid, cooperative and constructive" partnership.[13] To broadcast the turn-around of affairs by the end of 2001, the State Department's coordinator for counter-terrorism, Francis X. Taylor, moved to announce that "U.S. and Chinese leaders had fostered a robust, multi-faceted and evolving partnership designed to confront . . . global terrorism."[14] This included the introduction by April 2002 of regular expert-level consultations on counter-terrorism and financial monitoring, including information sharing across law enforcement agencies and the Treasury Department's Operation Green Quest. These initiatives would expand in time to include the establishment of a Federal Bureau of Investigation (FBI) liaison office in Beijing in October, the signing of the Container Security Initiative (CSI) in July 2003, an increase in participation in international conventions against terrorism, and the announcement of reconstruction aid for Afghanistan, including the removal of debt obligations. Along with Beijing's diplomatic support for the invasion of Afghanistan, and its aid in convincing Pakistan to "accept" U.S. basing rights, these were publicized as being major contributions to the War on Terror and broader U.S.-China relations.

This optimistic picture of cooperation, to be sure, worked at first to distract many conservative pundits from the China-threat narrative. Inside the White House, the first years of this enhanced cooperation produced many new China-engagement supporters, eager to build rapport with their Chinese counterparts. On the nuances of new joint programs, administration officials found keen participation, noting that, outside of official biannual meetings, American and Chinese counter-terrorism officials and experts were constantly in touch and actively working together on a broad range of issues. On examining the progress of this engagement on the big questions, however, the aggregate trend marked a departure from this more cooperative relationship. While the White House was responsive to critics of this new engagement, underscoring the unprecedented changes to China's behavior, it could not hide the fact, or its dissatisfaction, that progress was irregular and fundamentally disappointing. The hearings of the U.S.-China Economic and Security Review Commission here are revealing. The lack of Chinese cooperation in the areas of nonproliferation and counter-terrorism, commissioners of the panel acknowledged, had brought to question the basis of their interests. If the Chinese government didn't act to stop "weapons proliferation to terrorist-sponsoring states," despite their proclamations to do so, the logical analysis was to conclude that it had become government policy to use cooperation to thwart such programs. With the exception of one or two notable studies, the underbelly of this cooperation has escaped greater scrutiny in the U.S.-China relationship during the Bush years.[15]

In practice, the Bush administration sought to differentiate counter-terrorism cooperation between military aid and financial, political, and diplomatic help. It should not be surprising, at this stage, that attention to hard military attributes was given priority, particularly when considering the military campaigns in Afghanistan and later Iraq. That said, political and diplomatic backing was still considered necessary for long-term success. Sixty-nine nations within this category of aid were reported in the Department of Defense's Fact Sheet released in June 2002 as being most helpful in the War on Terror. What is notable, as Bonnie Glaser observes, is that not only did China fail to make the cut, but it was seemingly upstaged by countries such as Eritrea and the United Arab Emirates whose contribution was considered minimal and less important, publicly, than China's.[16] This may have been a case of inter-departmental politics; many were still skeptical of Chinese intentions and suspicious of cooperation, especially Rumsfeld's Defense Department. Whatever the justification, the omission presaged an early apprehension and disingenuousness about the new relationship, a point made increasingly explicit in Congressional hearings and government documents in later years.

What is perhaps more notable, however, is that this exclusion also took place on the questions of political, diplomatic, and intelligence cooperation, considered the "backbone" of U.S.-China counter-terrorism cooperation. In close examination, two trends emerged in the early years that would ultimately bode ill for any effectual changes under the engagement-change approach. The first pertains to the questionable concessions in Bush's cooperation with China, seen to be made in the purview of a strictly contractual agreement, and thereby making the basis of the new engagement a questionably shallow enterprise. In return for agreeing to open an FBI liaison office in Beijing, for instance, Attorney General John Ashcroft declared the East Turkistan Islamic Movement (ETIM) in northwestern China a terrorist movement, thus legitimizing Beijing's Hard Strike campaigns against domestic "splittists." This appeared to contradict the administration's policy of broadening terrorism to include "legitimate economic and social issues" brought about by Chinese policies in Xinjiang (discussed further below).[17] It was not by coincidence that in December Assistant Secretary of State James Kelly was forced to defend the ETIM designation as a step based on evidence and "not as a concession to the PRC."[18] As such, outside of this contractual arrangement the rhetoric on Chinese counter-terrorism aid was dialed down considerably.

The second consideration relates to public documents and press releases countering the positive relationship fostered in the White House. While all agreed that Chinese cooperation would be beneficial to combatting the War on Terror, few could point to certain specifics on how this new and "unprecedented" relationship would or should unfold, even in a purely diplomatic and information-sharing context. On counter-terrorism cooperation, for instance, observers found it difficult to articulate the extent to which China had actually been helpful in "routing out al Qaeda both in Afghanistan and around the world" or the specific role al Qaeda played in China's counter-terrorism strategy. For at least one observer, the administration had made it unclear

"what exactly there was to talk about" on "intelligence sharing or law enforcement work."[19] This skepticism, we find, was
never adequately addressed by the administration, whose spokesman continued to praise Chinese cooperation even as gaps in the
partnership began to surface. While China was not expected to
provide military cooperation in the War on Terror, noted General
Tommy Franks and Admiral Dennis Blair in an April 2003 briefing, neither the Central nor the Pacific commands could explicitly convey in detail how the Chinese had been helpful in other
areas. On the question of shared intelligence, Beijing had not been
"specific enough, particularly as compared to cooperation from
the Philippines, Singapore, and Malaysia."[20]

Similarly, by December 2003, the director of the Office of
Terrorism Finance and Sanctions Policy at State, George A. Glass,
could only prevaricate on the ambiguity of U.S.-China counter-
terrorism finance cooperation. While bilateral dialogues occurred,
they revealed little, for instance, about how the Chinese froze the
assets of terrorist organizations, "how they implement freeze orders
domestically," or whose assets they were actually freezing. In terms
of information sharing, the Chinese "tell us they do [it]," but the
implication was the department received no other information.[21]
Meanwhile, extensive hearings on counter-terror initiatives in the
Terror Finance Program before Congress mentioned China's participation only twice, and only to say that their restraint in joining the
Financial Action Task Force had been unhelpful.[22] When Treasury
Assistant Secretary Kenneth Lawson, of the Office of Enforcement,
discussed the nature of America's inter-agency and overseas cooperation on counter-terrorism in May 2002 with Congress, China
was again notably missing from any mention.[23]

Other observations reveal similar inconsistencies. We observe
that selective participation in key counter-terrorism financial bodies by China has been the norm, demonstrating consistency with
Chinese interests. But a carry-on from this has also been further
selectivity within these institutions in terms of information and
intelligence sharing.[24] Part of this objection occurred on the basis
of Taiwanese participation in international counter-terrorism initiatives, which had, according to State Department documents,
"impeded broader cooperation on APEC [Asia-Pacific Economic

Cooperation] counterterrorism and non-proliferation activities," and caused the Chinese to further reject participation in the Egmont Group, an information-sharing collective of over 100 financial intelligence units (FIUs) across the world.[25] Moreover, while the 2004 establishment of the People's Bank of China (PBC) FIU was touted by the State Department as further broadening U.S.-China cooperation in the areas of capacity building and expertise exchange, reports a year later illustrated that information sharing had stalled. The PBC, the State Department noted, had been "hesitant" to work with counterpart organizations in the United States despite their proclamation to do so.[26]

The pattern emanating from this engagement illustrates that while the administration sought to bolster the cooperation narrative, it did so even as evidence demonstrated a sense of reluctance, and even duplicity, in Beijing. That this was an issue considered meaningful to both countries, an area where the United States shared a common interest with China, "which has also been a victim of terrorism," seemed to underscore the triviality of the new relationship.[27] Indeed, consecutive State Department *Country Reports on Terrorism* in the final Bush term revealed the growing dichotomy as statements became shorter, less descriptive, and increasingly apathetic. By 2010, these descriptions had become quite negative, noting that the People's Republic of China did "not always distinguish between legitimate political dissent and the advocacy of violence to overthrow the government and has used counter-terrorism as a pretext to suppress Uighurs."[28]

The Container Security Initiative: a microcosm

The CSI offers another case with which to assess the excessive publicity in U.S.-China counter-terrorism cooperation. The CSI was designed to screen containers in the busiest ports across the world before shipping to the United States. There was significant momentum in the security establishment to begin a framework for cooperation on this front, the most obvious case for which, and one of the many lessons of 9/11, was how easy it had become for terrorist organizations to majorly disrupt airlines around the world. In post-9/11 assessments of American security, shipping containers emerged as one of the greatest threats, likened to a "modern-day Trojan horse" tied to a "slow-moving cruise missile."[29] In economic terms, the damage from closing one port per day in the United States due to a terrorist event would cost an extraordinary $4.8 billion.[30] Discernibly, the CSI required significant diplomatic resources to establish a "declaration of principles," later extended to international partners incorporating the world's top twenty ports. Within a series of bilateral and multilateral platforms, the Bush administration sought to meet a working criterion that largely eliminated the many concerns among states, encompassing: the costs of burden sharing, thought to be significant; disruption to port efficiency and authority; concerns over sovereignty; and inconsistencies in operation platforms, notwithstanding other perceptual, technical, and political differences.[31] To this end, CSI was a notable success.

The fact that by 2002 China accounted for 40 percent of world container volume and 42 percent of U.S.-bound cargo made it an important partner in this initiative. To be sure, any terrorist attack on an American port would have knock-on effects on world seaborne trade affecting China, but the further risk to Chinese ports from terrorism was considered enough to make cooperation mutually beneficial. It was no surprise therefore that President Jiang Zemin was quick to offer Beijing's support to the administration, with China joining officially on July 29, 2003. Barring access to internal government documents, it is difficult to assess the value of this initiative from the outside. However, some tentative conclusions can be made from the basis of the data that is available. What comes to the fore, and as other terror initiatives also illustrate, is that cooperation became in many ways one-sided and comparatively marginal compared to other U.S. CSI partnerships.[32] In public, U.S.-China cooperation was touted as being exceptionally close: the two countries stood "shoulder-to-shoulder," announced the commissioner of customs and border protection, Robert Bonner, "in the world on terrorism and in our mission to protect the global trading system."[33] Behind closed doors, the attempt to speed up the slow-moving project in China produced an agreement so watered down that any realistic ends became threatened with over-burdened and unrealistic means. In seeking to "respect the sovereignty of China," U.S. technicians would receive no direct access to Chinese ports, including no access to customs computer systems or data outside of the strict boundaries of the agreement, and could only request reinspection of containers (by Chinese agents) upon the condition that substantial new evidence warranted it.[34] Coupled with the lingering problems of container shipping in general—the archaic and paper-heavy logistical system, often incomplete and falsified bills of lading, and even the theoretical impossibility of pre-screening a large percentage of containers—the CSI deal with China proved to offer little more than an expensive public relations initiative.[35] That said, both the administration and Beijing would continue to argue that cooperation had taken place.

Such challenges emanating from Chinese CSI cooperation were illustrative of the major differences in the relationship, sidelined in 2001 in the interest of counter-terrorism cooperation. While moderates on both sides sought to demonstrate the intimacy of the relationship in the public domain, they could not hide the counter-narratives that, in China, some state media outlets had glorified the terrorist attacks on the Twin Towers, or in the U.S., some administration officials had advocated for active regime change on the mainland.[36] Unmet potential in CSI cooperation, indicatively, was more than a simple divergence of legal and political systems. Clashes in ideological values played a notable and disrupting factor, no doubt exacerbating the already wide and mutually reinforcing trust deficit. Researchers examining longer-term strategic trends were quick to note that Beijing's engagement with the CSI and other terrorism initiatives had been mostly opportunistic and used to buttress the regime by emboldening cooperation with Washington. "Superficially," Denny Roy observed, Beijing had "checked all the right boxes," gaining international approbation as a partner in the War on Terror. Ingeniously, however, it had at the same time successfully yielded the banner as America's top potential adversary to al Qaeda, all the while encouraging opposition to U.S. hegemony.[37] For others, China's concerns about U.S. intentions, its access to Chinese port data, and intelligence were amplified by Bush's foreign policy unilateralism and the administration's hawkishness toward the regime. The result was that while the Chinese were verbally willing to participate, their aims were to practically limit the access of the Americans whose jobs were to assess the containers. As Andrew Erickson observes, aside from the standard arguments around American interventionism in Chinese affairs, the idea of stationing American intelligence units on Chinese soil fostered the belief that they would seek to "hunt rabbits while cutting grass," or, in other words, gather intelligence while operating under the agreement of the CSI.[38]

By 2006, hearings in Congress revealed that there was "very little track record" in China's support for the CSI.[39] Compared to other partners, Chinese authorities had been exceptionally slow-moving. While signing on to the initiative in 2003, it was noted, Beijing had extended discussions a further two years before any meaningful agreement was met. Further, negotiations revealed that Chinese demands had been extremely particular, to the extent that "China consistently refrained from committing itself too easily, leaving room for future in-depth consultations."[40] Meanwhile, 70 percent of all cargo containers from the world's major exporters destined for the U.S. were already meeting processing expectations under the initiative.[41] Shanghai and Shenzhen became operational as pilot ports under the new watered-down agreement in mid- and late 2005, respectively. By 2008, however, they remained the only two ports under the CSI, with Ningbo, Guangzhou, Qingdao, and Tianjin, four of the six Chinese ports within the world's top fifteen, continuing to remain outside the agreement.

By this time, and even as early as 2005, many within the China expert community had become increasingly critical of China's counter-terrorism cooperation, even as more engagement became the norm. While the opinion of the State Department was that China had "actually been a supportive actor" on the question of terrorism, many noted that this support had been at times vague and for the most part unmeasured. The administration had made it unclear what success in U.S.-China cooperation might look like, noted members of the Review Commission, what the "benchmarks" or "measures" for success were, or how the responsible-stakeholder definition should apply. Rather, as China continued to "stand on the margins" on the important issues, the administration risked accepting the process as the standard without any plausible expectation of an outcome.[42]

In truth, as far as counter-terrorism with China was concerned, the focus by 2006 had been redistributed to managing the wars in Afghanistan and Iraq. While there were a few notable programs to come in 2006 and 2007, counter-terrorism cooperation had by this time largely run its course as a vehicle for engagement in the administration and Congress. Certainly, the CSI continued to operate in Shenzhen and Shanghai; China became a member of the Megaports initiative, and, in 2006, the United States began training Chinese customs officers on ship interdiction practices and at-sea handling of weapons of mass destruction (WMD)-related, dual-use technologies. At this time too, Chinese authorities granted the Bush administration rights to put a Coast Guard liaison office in Beijing.[43] Yet, it is difficult to qualify these initiatives and programs without further access to internal documents. Very little information exists to suggest they added substantially to, or even took away from, U.S.-China ties in terms of their relationship-building goals. A general assessment reveals that while this cooperation had not transformed U.S.-China relations in any significant way, its service in stabilizing the troublesome relationship following 9/11 had been remarkable. To be added to this conclusion is the point also that no terrorism incident occurred in the maritime domain between U.S. and Chinese ports. In terms of long-term trends, however, there is little to suggest that substantial progress had been made in bridging the trust deficit.

By the final two years of the Bush administration, counter-terrorism cooperation had narrowed to Congressional concerns focusing almost exclusively on China's treatment of its Uighur people and its continued armed sales to the Middle East. At this time, too, a shift in perceptions in Congress, ranging from encouraging cooperation to something between apathetic and more assertive policies, was advocated. This corresponded with concerns about the increase of Chinese weapons in the Middle East broadly and Afghanistan and Iraq more specifically. In 2007, for instance, U.S. military personnel found Taliban forces in Afghanistan using

Chinese-made HN-5 surface-to-air missiles. Meanwhile, Iranian-made anti-aircraft missiles, operating close to the Persian Gulf, were found to be uniquely similar to designs by the China Precision Machinery Import and Export Corporation, a state-owned enterprise (SOE), questioning to what extent Beijing had been complicit in such arms proliferation.[44] While there were notable inconsistencies in pointing to this Chinese small-arms proliferation in the Middle East, the more specific being that authorities could not tell when the weapons had been transferred or if they were explicitly Chinese-made, since they were missing serial numbers, the trend in proliferation nonetheless pointed challengingly upward. In 2008, the director of national intelligence, Michael J. McConnell, sounded a further alarm by mentioning China's continued violation of UN sanctions on non-proliferation norms, noting pointedly that PRC arms sales to the Middle East had become "destabilizing" and "a threat" to American forces.[45]

Turning a blind eye: the Uighur issue

By many accounts, unrest in northwest China had been motivated by Beijing's policies of planned Han migration into the Xinjiang Uighur Autonomous Region (XUAR). Such overtures included further the unequal distribution of economic benefits and resources, and central government energy needs—expropriated by an "almost entirely Han workforce." This had fostered the perception that government policies had turned Uighurs into second-class citizens, breeding dissent against the Party.[46] China's Strike Hard campaigns in 1996 and again in 2001 were aimed at terminating this dissent under the banner of defeating the "three evils" of "extremism," "terrorism," and "separatism." Until 9/11, however, many examples of what were retrospectively labelled as terrorist activities in the region had not been acknowledged by Chinese authorities as "fitting the terrorist label." These included incidents formerly acknowledged as "riots" and led by "a small number of ruffians."[47] This is not to ignore the fact that terrorist attacks had taken place in the XUAR or that minority groups and organizations such as ETIM may have been complicit in their involvement. China's fear had been based on the notion that Xinjiang separatists might have become emboldened via transnational Islamic extremist groups so as to perpetrate attacks against the government in support of independence.[48] The concern in the United States, by contrast, was that the comprehensive labeling of Uighur peoples and XUAR minority groups with legitimate grievances could be used, with a compliant international environment, to justify the wholesale repression of a people.

The notable absence of information substantiating these claims against minority organizations such as ETIM and others led many observers to dismiss the terrorist designation as opportunistic. Two of these groups, the World Uighur Congress and the East Turkistan Information Center, were non-governmental organizations based in Germany and were "engaged in the publication of news and information in support of the Uighur independence movement."[49] The East Turkistan Liberation Organization (ETLO), according to China's Ministry of Public Security, had received funding from al Qaeda and training from the Taliban in Afghanistan.[50] Meanwhile, Chinese officials claimed ETIM was supported by al Qaeda and responsible for a broad range of terrorist activities carried out in China. Yet, like the ETLO, much about ETIM was unknown or unsubstantiated. According to U.S. government sources, most were unaware of the existence of ETIM prior to 9/11, and only learned about it after China's Foreign Ministry named and labeled it a terrorist organization shortly after the New York and Washington attacks. Even then, Shirley Kan observes, Beijing did not blame it for any alleged incidents and no group calling itself ETIM claimed responsibility for any prior alleged attacks.[51] In the early post-9/11 years Chinese authorities appeared willing to go as far as suggesting that all Uighur separatists in the XUAR had links to al Qaeda, although this generalization was later reduced to a thousand or so extremists.[52]

Bush's policy on the Uighur terrorist front marked a pragmatic if at times maladroit approach to these claims. For China's "good behavior" in the War on Terror, writes Joshua Kurlantzick, Bush sought to reward them by compromising on the ETIM decision, placing it on the list of terrorist organizations at the State Department.[53] According to Assistant Secretary of State James

Kelly, the president did this while simultaneously stating his administration's opposition to any efforts that would use the cloth of counter-terrorism to silence political or religious views. Further concessions, however, seemed to illustrate an apparent disagreement in the administration over the role of China policy and human rights as the State Department refused to put the group on its Terrorist Exclusion List, which would prevent any member from entering the country. Meanwhile, State's annual human rights report continued to note that China had "chosen to label all of those who advocate greater freedom in [Xinjiang] . . . as terrorists" and that the department's view was contrary to this belief.[54] Subsequently, in 2003, the administration dropped its habitual sponsorship of criticizing China's human rights record at the UN Commission on Human Rights, suggesting an explicit break with the State Department. In the following year ETIM was finally placed on the exclusion list.

These concessions returned to haunt the administration as the pretense of Chinese claims came to be factored into the administration's decisions about what to do with Uighur detainees held at Guantánamo Bay, Cuba. By 2004, twenty-two Chinese Uighurs were being held at the detention camp on the island, fifteen of whom the Defense Department were ready to release on the basis that they were considered low risk. Five were thought to be in the wrong place at the wrong time when they were initially detained. Meanwhile, few, if any, had ties to regional terrorism, let alone al Qaeda, although most were uncompromising critics of the Beijing government. Under the terms of the "cooperative" and "constructive" relationship the Chinese might have expected these dissidents to be returned, where it was believed they would be executed as enemies of the state.[55] For the Chinese, at least, it seemed that this demand would be met, especially since human rights had been played down inside the White House.

To Bush's credit, he was unwilling to allow this to happen. But he was unwilling at the same time to set the detainees free in the United States, agreeing instead to keep them in Cuba in limbo. What is significant here is that Bush used the Uighurs' association with ETIM to suggest they were unsafe for release, using the arguments provided by Beijing to justify their continued imprisonment.

If the Chinese needed evidence to support the claim that the administration's rationale for constructive engagement masked ulterior motives, this seemed to be a defining juncture. Bush appeared to deny Chinese demands to return the Uighurs, while accepting Beijing's terrorist charges so as to keep them in Guantánamo in breach of their human rights. By 2008, this pretense for Bush came undone in the U.S. Court of Appeals in Washington as it sought to overturn the terrorist distinction. Noting that all "intelligence documents" associated with the charges appeared to come from a single source, which was the Chinese government, the judges ruled that there was no supporting evidence to keep them locked up on terrorist charges.[56]

Bush, in fact, had become more critical of China's counter-terrorism campaign against the Uighurs in these later years. He appeared with Nobel Peace Prize nominee Rebiyah Kadeer, a formerly detained Uighur businesswoman, in June 2007, objecting to the arbitrary imprisonment of Uighurs in China. In 2008, Bush further denounced Beijing's actions in the XUAR while addressing human rights and honoring Uighur Muslims in a speech on religious freedoms. But these were also pushed along by an increasingly vocal Congress, which sought to tighten the counter-terrorism relationship in the White House. Heightened Congressional concerns over the designation of ETIM as a terrorist organization in October 2006 had led to a considerable backlash against the administration's ostensibly aimless policies. This was followed by House resolutions in September 2007, charging the PRC with manipulating the campaign against terrorism to "increase cultural and religious oppression of the Muslim Uighur people." In 2008, Senate Resolution 574 condemned China's pre-Olympic clampdown on Uighurs following worrying and violent trends in Xinjiang.[57]

Greater scrutiny of U.S.-China anti-terrorism cooperation had begun to reveal the superficiality of the relationship by the middle of this second term. This scrutiny was headed by the U.S.-China Economic and Security Review Commission, but aspects of the relationship had also begun to emerge from other Congressional committees. By the final years of the Bush administration, many of the commissioners had yet to be convinced that there was solid evidence for the claims that the Chinese had been a supportive influence in the fight against terrorism, or that their aid had substantially buttressed administration initiatives.[58] For some, the lack of Chinese exchange between the military, intelligence, and security communities seemed to suggest at least that this cooperation was dubious. That the Chinese should "repeatedly" refuse to cease new arms sales to Iran, after substantial reports that PRC weapons were finding their way to the Taliban, did not seem to reflect the actions of a "cooperative" partner in the War on Terror.[59] For others, it had become convincingly apparent that Chinese cooperation was designed to address exclusively Chinese interests and their problems with separatism in Xinjiang, leaving the United States to deal with the Middle East and Southeast Asia where terrorism was the defining problem.[60]

Proliferation and North Korea

Aside from the realm of counter-terrorism, another major point of U.S.-China cooperation emerged by the second administration under similar circumstances of suspicion in Congress. Non-proliferation in the post-9/11 security environment was to be considered "one of the foremost priority concerns of the United States government," a point requiring Bush to seek multilateral support.[61] Indeed, this formed part of Robert Zoellick's mandate to create a new diplomatic engagement with Beijing, one that would draw Chinese authorities more into a leadership role in the Six-Party Talks with North Korea. By 2005, U.S.-China cooperation on non-proliferation revealed, like the case of counter-terrorism, two increasingly diverging narratives in Washington. On the one hand, administration officials sought to bring the dialogue to focus primarily and positively on China's development in international institutions and non-proliferation regimes. This participation was considered to be behavior-changing, illustrated by the dramatic change in China from international pariah in the early 1990s to global multilateral partner by 2005. Moreover, it was considered unrealistic to judge China's participation in a vacuum of solely non-proliferation activities. The relationship was multifaceted, demonstrated by the intensification of cooperation and engagement on counter-terrorism and maritime security and the growth in military dialogue in the second term, notwithstanding the robust expansion and inter-dependence in trade and finance.

On the other hand, cooperation had failed to produce the results sought, and expected, by the administration and Congress following 9/11. As in the experience with counter-terrorism, the administration found the Chinese to be unreliable partners. Before long, White House officials were being probed by an irritated Congress as to why efforts to thwart the proliferation activities, contrary to Chinese promises, of violating Chinese entities had proven extremely marginal; why any opportunity to treat violations of the Nuclear Non-proliferation Treaty (NPT) with sanctions was opposed; and why such opposition had worked to sabotage the efficacy of non-proliferation regimes on North Korea and Iran.

On the surface, the new level of engagement in the post 9/11 climate worked to deepen commitment to existing non-proliferation frameworks in Beijing. Important agreements undertaken during the first years of the Bush administration in China—including the 2002 agreement to publish and enact new export control regulations, the joining in May 2004 of the Nuclear Suppliers Group, and subsequent support for UN Security Council resolutions (UNSCRs) on North Korean and Iranian nuclear proliferation—proved that engagement had worked to loosen the Party's grip on its former objections to liberal institutional agreements. In 2004 and again in 2005, Beijing produced white papers more specifically outlining its counter-proliferation objectives in the form of "China's National Defense" and "China's Endeavors for Arms Control, Disarmament, and Non-proliferation," respectively. These activities, Assistant Secretary of State Paula A. Desutter observed, demonstrated an "impressive array of commitments."[62] The Chinese had shown a disposition to meet the White House halfway and had displayed an interest in joining the Australia Group and the Missile Technology Control Regime.

Notwithstanding the above undertakings, there were notable and wide differences in terms of implementation. For many, China had not lived up to its promises in non-proliferation, a point made evident by the consistent transference of dual-use nuclear technologies by Chinese companies to Iran. For some, Beijing displayed a frustrating refusal to meet the expectations of not only American sanctions regimes, but even unanimously backed UNSC agreements. While it had signed on to UNSCRs in 2006, 2007, and 2008 calling for Iran to suspend its nuclear enrichment, it sought at the same time to water down any imposition for the UN to enforce sanctions against Tehran. Meanwhile, China's ambassador to the UN, Wang Guangyu, was caught assuring Iranian leaders that "as a matter of principle," authorities in China would "never" support sanctions in the Security Council.[63] By some accounts, this was an active attempt to subvert the UNSC, demonstrated further in July 2007 when a PRC entity was caught attempting to ship "a large amount of chemicals used to make solid fuel for ballistic missiles" to Iran in violation of Resolutions 1737 and 1747.[64] These were issues, according to the State Department's Bureau of Verification, Compliance and Implementation, that increasingly defined the divergence between policy and action in Beijing. Accordingly, here was evidence that China's rise, despite its many new memberships in regional and international agreements and bodies, was not translating into the responsible stakeholder many had hoped.

Patterns of Chinese weapons proliferation seemed to lead to one of two conclusions: either authorities in Beijing were unaware that China's corporations, including its SOEs, were participating in weapons proliferation, or they were complicit in such activities. All indications seemed to suggest it was the latter. PRC entities, Defense Intelligence Agency director Vice Admiral Lowell Jacoby testified, appeared to remain illegally involved "with nuclear and missile programs in Pakistan and Iran," in some cases without the government's knowledge, but for the most part with the implied consent of authorities.[65] The point was driven home by the fact that serial proliferators appeared to operate in China absent of any intervention. By 2004, Bush had imposed sanctions against Chinese entities on over sixty occasions, amounting to an impressive increase of 650 percent from the preceding eight years of the Clinton administration. From the White House, the narrative put forth following these sanctions was that "the Chinese have heard us loud and clear," and had agreed as a result to take domestic proliferation seriously.[66] This was at least the working narrative at State and Defense, whose interlocutors, it was noted, "had every reason to believe that they [their Chinese counterparts] shared the philosophy underlying non-proliferation."[67] This wasn't necessarily untrue. Yet, the point seemed to highlight a gap between further action and policy in the administration as engagement and process continued to be prioritized.

Consecutive hearings on China's proliferation practices from 2005 to 2008 in Congress revealed that no change had actually taken place despite a robust growth in U.S.-China bilateral relations and increasing Chinese participation in non-proliferation regimes. Non-transparency on all Chinese actions regarding proliferation remained the norm, while rejection of any meaningful sanctions regime threatened to significantly undermine the NPT. Meanwhile, serial proliferators continued to be sanctioned, often multiple times, by the American government without any corresponding action in China to shut down at the least the major players. By 2008, State and Defense officials had come to view personnel from the Chinese Ministry of Foreign Affairs (MoFA), who they dealt with "almost without exception," as largely powerless operators on proliferation issues. Put another way, while dialogue took place and agreement on the major issues of North Korean proliferation was consensual, the authority to make decisions was ostensibly located elsewhere in the party hierarchy. The Chinese, it transpired, had not at the same time made it clear where authority resided within the government to address these questions.[68]

In truth, while Washington and Beijing agreed on the seriousness of the threat of proliferation, the heart of the problem was based on a fundamental difference of perception on what the correct solution should be. In short, authorities in Beijing viewed support for sanctions as not only counterproductive to non-proliferation, but also destabilizing to regional security. This was based on a long and personal history with sanctions during the Cold War, but it included also a healthy mistrust of American intentions in Northeast Asia, judged on the basis of the highly destabilizing Iraq War in the Middle East. When the moderate reformist president of Iran, Mohammed Khatami, reached out to the Bush administration in 2003 for comprehensive negotiations on terrorism, nuclear weapons, support for groups like Hezbollah, and the Israel issue, for instance, Dick Cheney and Donald Rumsfeld killed the proposal.[69] Afterwards, when Iran was charged with violating the NPT, sanctions were proffered as the catchall solution. For Chinese authorities, it was this attitude that underscored the "complicated root causes . . . and symptoms" of proliferation more than any Iranian defense policy.[70] As the 2005 white paper "China's Endeavors for Arms Control, Disarmament, and Non-proliferation" was to further illustrate, the greater national interest lay in the need to guard against regional and international instability, a point made in consideration of the hawks in the Bush administration. While the topic of North Korean and Iranian nuclear proliferation remained the highest significance for Bush, routinely engaged upon, according to Don Mahley, deputy assistant secretary of state for international security affairs, at the highest levels of the relationship, these countries were notably missing from any mention in the document.[71] The greater challenges to the international non-proliferation regime, according to the document, were considered instead to be the Bush administration's apparent secession on key items: its break from the Anti-ballistic Missile Treaty and its refusal to join the Comprehensive Nuclear Test Ban Treaty, the Prevention of an Arms Race in Outer Space resolution, and the Amended Protocol on Landmines, as case points.

Meanwhile, Iran's contravention of the NPT was to be viewed less as a violation of the treaty than a failure to honor its obligations. This was a play on words to be sure, undermining the administration's efforts to arrest Iranian nuclear ambitions. But even as Beijing sought to engage with UNSCRs, punishing Iran for its violation, it continued to declare that no evidence of nuclear proliferation existed. If this was proof of double dealing on Beijing's behalf, it was not picked up in the White House with any apparent fanfare. Whatever the UNSC Resolutions 1737 in December 2006, 1747 in March 2007, and 1803 and 1835 in 2008 sought to achieve, Beijing continued to consider them unhelpful while adhering only loosely to them. Meanwhile, Tehran, Shen Dingli has argued, continued to push its uranium enrichment forward despite the resolutions, threatening in the process to sue the Western countries involved.[72]

The more significant and long-term result of this behavior in Beijing was that it worked to delegitimize the "responsible stakeholder" narrative pursued by Bush and Secretary Rice, which came under increasing criticism in the United States. Certainly, there was much to praise in China's evolving policies on non-proliferation, including the substantial increase in U.S.-China cooperation and its participation in non-proliferation bodies. However, John Garver makes the point that to maintain the theme that sanctions were ineffective while seeking to consistently weaken them in the UN, to make them voluntary, and to ensure that they did not interfere with Chinese investment in Iran's energy sector, smacked of shameless opportunism.[73] That Beijing sought further to fill the vacuum left by retreating Western and East Asian firms in the face of sanctions reinforced this sense of duplicity. It had become clear that the Chinese did not in fact care very deeply about proliferation despite their pretensions.

Subsequently, there was a discussion to be had in the administration about Beijing's propensity to ignore the spirit of the UNSC sanctions and its consistent objection to the Proliferation Security Initiative (PSI) in the UNSC. The PSI was introduced by Bush in May 2003 to cover what had been hitherto a substantial gap in interdiction law. It had been proposed in the aftermath of the failure to legally seize Scud missiles captured on the North Korean vessel *So San* headed for Yemen in 2002, and based on the 1992 UNSC presidential statement that "members of the Council commit themselves to working to prevent the spread of technology related to research for or production of such weapons [as WMDs] and to take appropriate action to that end." The PSI was widely accepted and adopted as representing the spirit of non-proliferation.[74] On the surface, authorities in Beijing applauded the cooperation among PSI members while they agreed to examine their position toward the initiative. In practice, however, and as time progressed, Chinese objections to forced interdiction clauses weakened the UNSC response so that any action undertaken in the name of the PSI was to be committed on the basis of consent and "in accordance with the Charter."[75] Upon this reading, Beijing threatened to veto any resolution that sought to endorse the original PSI emphasis on forceful interdiction, which had underscored the gap missing in interdiction law and non-proliferation.

These reservations, it was announced in September 2005 by China's director general of the Department of Arms Control at

the MoFA, Zhang Yan, were based on the fact that forceful interdiction was considered to be illegal, "beyond the permission of
current international law."[76] In fact, endorsement in the UNSC
would have created further justification and precedence for legal
measures, vitiating these concerns. But it was considered that
Beijing was concerned lest its own ships become targets of the
PSI, as witnessed by the 1993 interdiction of the Chinese vessel
Yinhe, suspected of shipping chemicals to Tehran. This was to say
nothing of the increase in sanctions against Chinese entities trading with Iran and North Korea in violation of UNSC injunctions.
It came as no surprise therefore that China's objections to the
PSI continued to baffle many observers and Congressional Commission members who were assured by the administration that
the Chinese were sympathetic to America's concerns, recognized
the value of the PSI, and were working unprecedentedly with the
administration to counter proliferation. For some, China's actions
were nothing but "willful government-supported proliferation," a
point which ensured the administration and the European Union
(EU) would continue to embargo arms sales to the PRC.[77]

The real test of the so-called U.S.-China strategic relationship would take place over the question of North Korea's nuclear
proliferation.[78] Pyongyang's decision to leave the NPT and pursue nuclear weapons capabilities in January 2003 caused the
Bush administration to deepen its engagement with the PRC in
the hope of staving off the emerging threat of a rogue nuclear
strike. This decision was made on the basis that China maintained
considerable influence over the regime, delivering 80 percent of
North Korea's economic needs.[79] The emphasis on North Korea
soon came to form the basis of the U.S.-China relationship for the
duration of the Bush years. Like cooperation on non-proliferation
and counter-terrorism, the administration found a generally receptive Beijing, which worked to help pressure North Korea into the
first trilateral talks in April 2003, followed by the first round of
the Six-Party Talks in August, and the second round in February
2004. By the end of the first Bush administration, the State Department was praising China's efforts as hugely rewarding and crucial
to the establishment of regular negotiations, despite further non-
compliance by North Korea with demands.

As with non-proliferation, troubling behaviors in Beijing and within the Bush administration drew perceptions and actions on either side counter to the cooperation each sought. Bush moved quickly in 2001 to establish a major policy review of U.S. relations with North Korea, laying emphasis on two themes, as Charles L. Pritchard, U.S. special envoy for negotiations with North Korea, writes: "Anything but Clinton (ABC)," which included the sidelining of the 1994 Agreed Framework, and the principle that "bad behavior was not to be rewarded."[80] All prior agreements on dialogue with the North Koreans were to be judged on the basis of this new and ostensibly arbitrary standard. Bush's justification here rested on the analysis that while the United States had been abiding to the 1994 agreement, Pyongyang had not only consistently threatened to break it, but had in fact pursued a uranium enrichment program in violation of it. Meanwhile, there was little caution in the administration given to statements about North Korea or its leader Kim Jong-il with regard to the process of denuclearization. Over time, the regime was to be labelled as a partner to Iraq in the "axis of evil," an "outpost of tyranny," and a dictatorship led by a "tyrant" who "starves his people."[81] If there was a plan to this remarkably arrogant behavior in the White House, Pritchard makes the point, the only logical explanation was that Bush had over-stated Pyongyang's interest in "joining the international community," believing as a result that it could be "forced to alter its behavior without serious direct engagement by the United States."[82]

For some, this approach to a sophisticated problem was evidence of a dangerous dualism in North Korea policy, driven by a fractious pull between disparate groups in the Department of State and hawks in the NSC and at Defense. Many noted, too, the influence of Vice President Cheney, who had, in many ways, overtaken the narrative and direction of policy.[83] The first notable account of this was Colin Powell's cause to retract comments that the administration would largely continue the former administration's focus on diplomacy and negotiation. Certainly, this was preferred by Pyongyang, which likely misunderstood the political and policy process in Washington as the changeover in administrations occurred.[84] Prior to 2006, this stance was perceived as too conciliatory for a member of the "axis of evil" by many hawks in the administration. While the military option was removed from the table, a strategy of "isolate and confront" came to dominate the diplomatic doctrine for neoconservatives. Meanwhile, regime change was loosely discussed by senior members of the administration, illustrated by John Bolton in April 2003 in response to North Korea's objections to multilateral dialogue. Pyongyang, he challenged, would be encouraged to "draw the appropriate lesson from Iraq that the pursuit of weapons of mass destruction is not in their national interest."[85] By February 2006, influential Democrats on the Armed Services Committee, the Foreign Relations Committee, and the vice chair of the Intelligence Committee in Congress were prodding for a change in policy, noting that the results of the administration's policies had not led to the "elimination, freeze, or even a slowing of North Korea's nuclear and ballistic missile activities."[86]

By 2006, it had become apparent that U.S. and Chinese views of North Korean nuclear ambitions and ideas about the right policy approach to denuclearization were working at cross-purposes. While both agreed on the need for denuclearization, they departed sharply on the question of regime change in Pyongyang. For Beijing, regime change would be considered tantamount to a regional crisis, exacerbating not just the regional security makeup but also domestic stability, as the refugee crisis extended into neighboring provinces. Indeed, while the United States continued to envelop its eastern seaboard with a Cold War alliance system, Beijing was unwilling to harden its approach to North Korea for fear of pushing it toward collapse. Its response to Bush's attitude and policy approach therefore was to side with Pyongyang on the charge that the administration had not done enough to assuage apprehensions of an aggressive and unilateral intent in Washington.

In an interesting point, Victor Cha makes the claim that regime change in North Korea had been early on rejected by the Bush administration in terms of a military solution and that while some may have harbored such sentiments, it was never the subject of internal meetings. Accordingly, all the public criticism of the administration on the issue had missed the strategy laid out by Bush that diplomacy was first and foremost. The point missing in Cha's account, however, was the significance of optics in these policies, if indeed Bush followed such a program. Neither the Chinese nor the North Koreans could have known about the internal thoughts of the administration, and even if such sentiments were verbally communicated by the White House, there was no reason to take these statements at face value. Secretary Rice notably illustrates in her account that while Bush was informed that regime change might be taken off the table if greater diplomatic overtures were used, he was convinced nonetheless that regime change "by other means" would take place. [87] Given these dichotomous views, it should be unsurprising that this emphasis on stability for China had gone largely unappreciated in the White House. Bush was quick to reject this interpretation of Chinese views, but he did so even as Cheney made it a point to publicly denounce any negotiations with evil "tyrannies" as a lost cause. Indicatively, the point failed to mitigate China's concerns. It was not by mischance, Shirley Kan makes the point, that while Bush was calling for "firm resolve" in late 2005, China's Hu Jintao was calling at the same time for "greater flexibility."[88]

This misinterpretation of Chinese concerns came to sully the understanding and point of engagement in the White House. When North Korea exploded its first nuclear device on October 3, 2006, administration officials noticed the Chinese were visibly shocked. They had assured Bush that Kim Jong-il did not have the capability that the U.S. intelligence services said he had. Pyongyang had not only kept Beijing in the dark, but it had made the Chinese look credulous by lying about its progress and intentions. "There was no country more outraged by the nuclear test," observed Victor Cha, "than China."[89] When sanctions were put forth in the UNSC, Chinese authorities moved quickly to approve them. Certainly, these behaviors in China—its activities in getting North Korea to the table and applying sanctions against proliferation violations—were considered highly unusual, and outside the norms of Chinese diplomacy.[90] This seemed to suggest that they viewed the nuclear tests as a sign of great embarrassment, if not a threat to the national interest, forcing them to take a more hardline approach in dealing with Kim. The mistake was, however, in trusting in Beijing to go beyond a point where the danger of regime collapse became increasingly likely. It was here that Bush misjudged Beijing's participation in the Six-Party Talks, believing that their interests were mutually shared, that a nuclear North Korea was a threat to regional security, and that Beijing could use its considerable leverage to force Pyongyang into compliance. It was under these assumptions that Rice sought, on October 18, to reassure Japan and other regional allies that Pyongyang could not possibly maintain its aggressive nuclear posture, noting that any "further action by the North Koreans will only deepen its isolation, which is pretty deep right now."[91] When Beijing refused to fulfil these expectations, these assumptions began to fall apart.

It had become clearer by the end of the year that China could not be relied upon to lead the Six-Party Talks in a way consistent with U.S. policy aims. While it had voted to enact UNSC Resolution 1718—preventing, among other things, nuclear weapons technology or materials, including other major weapons, being traded with or supplied to North Korea—there were also notable objections to China's cooperation. Namely, it would not contribute to CSI interdictions of North Korean ships, nor go beyond the measures of UNSC sanctions to limit oil and other energy supplies to North Korea. Moreover, administration officials were alarmed to discover that not only were luxury goods to Pyongyang not curtailed in Beijing, but that they had in fact increased year on end.[92] When the next set of meetings between the U.S., China, and North Korea resumed in December 2007, Assistant Secretary Christopher Hill discovered that no change in behavior had occurred despite the sanctions. Economic interaction between Beijing and Pyongyang, meanwhile, continued uninterrupted.

Interaction with the Chinese on the North Korea issue had come to underscore two disillusioning and impenetrable truths. The first was that whatever the provocation, Beijing was unwilling to give up on its only ally, preferring instead to muddle through the disappointments. The second was that Bush administration policy could not continue on its usual course of relying on the Chinese to leverage Pyongyang into giving up nuclear weapons. This mood was even more visible in Congress, who charged the president with failing to use "maximum carrots, maximum sticks, and maximum focus" in the denuclearization of the peninsula.

The administration, Gary L. Ackerman (Democrat-New York) argued, had to stop "outsourcing our foreign policy to China and to negotiate directly with the North Koreans to get them to abandon and dismantle their nuclear program."[93] This charge, and subsequent North Korean actions, seemed to presage a consequential change in negotiations as Assistant Secretary Hill was given authority to negotiate one-on-one with Pyongyang, offering flexibility rather than isolation in return for denuclearization. Immediate results followed the February 13, 2007 Six-Party Talks with North Korea's agreement to shut down its Yongbyon nuclear facility and allow verification. By 2008, dismantlement of the Yongbyon facilities was ongoing, with only minimal interruption on the basis of slow fuel transfers.

Conclusion

In the broadest terms, the U.S.-China relationship by the end of the second Bush administration appeared to make new and remarkable strides toward a more long-term and stable partnership. Many could point to greater and unprecedented cooperation in areas traditionally characterized by frustration and indifference. Indeed, despite Bush's predilection for unilateralism and hawkishness on strategic matters, the administration appeared outwardly at least to reject the theory that confrontation between rising and status-quo powers was a fait accompli. Part of this perception lay in Beijing's, albeit selective, embrace of regional and international institutions, and its public engagement in non-proliferation at the UN. More significantly, the new emphasis on turning China into a "responsible stakeholder" through engagement and inclusion within international institutions offered a policy both tough and appropriately conciliatory. Nowhere was this more evident than in China's hosting of the Six-Party Talks and, in the final year, its help in urging North Korea's apparent turn toward denuclearization.

With hindsight, the learning curve—from unilateral antagonist to multilateral partner on North Korea and U.S.-China relations—served to illustrate Bush's flexibility and pragmatism in his approach to dealing with China. The most notable change in this regard was Bush's about-face on North Korea policy from isolation and confrontation to interaction and conciliation. Observably, the "Anything but Clinton" doctrine was dropped, and the good-behavior policy was discarded as a prelude for negotiations. Progress toward denuclearization, it appeared, seem to finally flow forth. It is worth noting, too, that this flexibility occurred alongside notable departures in the administration, among them Colin Powell, Richard Armitage, and Paul Wolfowitz in 2004, and Donald Rumsfeld in 2006. Additionally, Bush's trust in and support of Secretary of State Condoleezza Rice was consequential to this flexibility, her diplomatic program prioritizing enhanced dialogue and engagement with Beijing. By 2008, Bush had become an emphatic supporter of engagement, noting that the U.S. and China could coexist in a "cooperative and constructive, yet candid" manner, and that it should be the mandate of future administrations to adopt this policy.[94]

Of course, the point also serves to demonstrate inconsistency and uncertainty in broader policy approaches. At points, Bush appeared neither consistently flexible nor observably methodological. This was demonstrated clearly in the administration's policy toward China's internal anti-terror policies and Uighur nationals held by the American military. More strikingly, there appeared no mechanism for evaluating these policies in light of administration objectives. For members of the Economic and Security Review Commission, the Bush administration had shown an alarming predilection for appearing too happy with the process of cooperation and not upset enough about the lack of verifiable results.[95] Indeed, on these questions, the second administration displayed a deft obfuscation. This had become apparent also to notable conservatives who were to remark that Bush had given Beijing little incentive to seek punitive measures against North Korea, noting that little was expected until the administration ceased its "endless praising of Beijing for its thus far fruitless efforts."[96] The point was made more explicit on China's policies toward non-proliferation. Viewed in aggregate, China's formal actions on non-proliferation commitments in 1991, 1994, 1998, 2000, and 2002 had occurred only "after the application of pressure from the United States, including in the form of the imminent or actual imposition of sanctions."[97] Yet, outside of sanctions against proliferating Chinese entities, Bush avoided applying such pressure. By mid-2008, the deteriorating agreement with North Korea on denuclearization, for many, demonstrated the point that Bush had been too preoccupied with means and not ends.

At a closer look, Bush's focus on engagement proved in many ways unfulfilling and at times even deceiving. Many were to note that this connective tissue on major administration concerns such as terrorism, non-proliferation, and North Korea was both marginal and elusive. While it was argued that numerous and substantive high-level meetings between Bush and Chinese president Hu Jintao made for a notable break with the former administration, for instance, it was also acknowledged that these meetings had proven largely symbolic gatherings.[98] Meanwhile, lower-level engagement had proven equally frustrating for interlocutors at State and Defense, who complained that their counterparts held little authority to action agreements. The correlation between administration policy and this dislocation between dialogue and authority still awaits further analysis. In light of mistaken assumptions concerning Chinese policy and nuclear non-proliferation, however, a tentative hypothesis is that this dialogue was misplaced, and the internal Chinese politics of these issues misunderstood.

Lastly, whereas the counter-terrorism relationship was instrumental in improving ties following 9/11, its management over time, and specifically after 2005, ultimately precluded the necessary trust-building cooperation needed. This is not to say the administration was largely to blame or that it was negligent. Indeed, the chapter reveals that, more than in any other domain, the Bush administration was at times both innovative and resourceful in its counter-terrorism relationships. China too was an active partner, cooperating for instance on international policy toward Afghanistan, some information sharing, and on issues such as the CSI. But these were also low-risk domains for cooperation, touching upon security-related issues of mutual interest. When it came to weapons proliferation, human rights, and North Korea, by contrast, engagement became much more strained and cooperation more ambiguous. Meanwhile, the issue of China's persecution of the Uighur people, and its handling of its own domestic terrorist challenges, struck as obvious and opportunistic policies to aggressively control domestic reaction to other hugely unpopular policies in the XUAR. By the end of the Bush administration, these policies in Beijing were increasingly reflected in Bush's more stubborn position on human rights and specifically religious freedoms.

3. The Obama Administration's First Term: The Promises of the "Pivot"

The chapter will outline and assess Obama's first four years in the White House in relation to an increasingly intensifying relationship between the United States and China. Though much more of an ideologue than his predecessor, Obama addressed the American public with firm truths about what he saw as China's new military and political assertiveness. While the president thought he could build a more constructive engagement and connectedness with the People's Republic of China (PRC), his "pivot"—later "rebalance"—to the Asia-Pacific signified a more assertive approach, which would proceed to engender tensions during the administration's second year in office. Specifically, Obama sought to rebuild America's relationship with the Asia-Pacific after what some described as "benign neglect" during the Bush years, while also reinforcing the system of alliances in the region with a new level of participation in regional dialogues and new security partnerships.

Notwithstanding the "pivot," emphasis by the administration was also placed on both states to collaborate more on shared interests, as conveyed by Secretary of State Hillary Clinton during her first official trip to China in February 2009.[1] Clinton argued that it was crucial for the global community that China and the United States work together on areas pertaining to security, peace, and prosperity. In discussing the global economic crisis, she said that "we have to look inward for solutions, but we must also look to each other to take a leadership role in designing and implementing a coordinated global response to stabilize the world's economy, and begin recovery." With more emphasis on anthropogenic climate change, Clinton noted that both states were bound to "develop and deploy clean energy technologies designed to speed our transformation to low-carbon eeconomies," incorporating "renewable energy, the capture and storage of CO_2 from coal plants, and energy efficiency in our buildings." Additionally, she affirmed that the Six-Party Talks, participation in international peacekeeping efforts, and mid-level military-to-military dialogues would be undertaken.[2]

As this chapter will illustrate, however, despite these seemingly new attempts at cooperation, ongoing and emerging bilateral differences became a persistent theme, as issues during the first term emanating from the "pivot" and Chinese assertions in the South China Sea (SCS) came to the fore. In unpacking the sources and drivers of the Obama administration's foreign policy toward China during its first term in office, the chapter sets out to: elucidate the debates between the divergent camps in U.S foreign policy pertaining to China; articulate the U.S. national security concerns relating to China; provide insight into China's growing military power; discuss how the administration defined, rationalized, and articulated the "pivot"/"rebalance"; highlight the various continuities and departures of the "pivot"/"rebalance"; assess the various ramifications and Chinese responses to the "pivot"/"rebalance"; and lastly, overall, present the implications for U.S. foreign policy and security strategy in the region, and broader concerns for the U.S.-China bilateral relationship.[3]

Divergent camps in the discourse

In echoing the optimistic sentiments expressed by Clinton during the very early months in office, the Obama National Security Strategy (NSS) of May 2010 emphasized the administration's pursuit of a "positive, constructive, and comprehensive relationship with China." However, by the time of the document's release in mid-2010, tensions and at times dichotomous elements in national interests had begun to surface in the relationship. By this stage Obama was more prepared to call out certain provocative behaviors of the PRC as well as express what he thought was the need for

China to "lift its game" in taking on a "responsible leadership role" commensurate with its great-power status. In this regard, the NSS document, like Robert Zoellick's "responsible stakeholder" speech in 2005, emphasized the need to "work with the United States and the international community to advance priorities like economic recovery, confronting climate change, and non-proliferation." That said, a firmer tone was clearly on display. The document conveyed that the U.S. would also monitor China's military modernization program and "prepare accordingly to ensure that U.S. interests and allies, regionally and globally, are not negatively affected."[4]

On a broader level, the administration again called on China to "make choices" that reflected its position and "rise" through contributing to "peace, security, and prosperity." To undertake this approach, the NSS advocated a range of fora, including the newly established Strategic and Economic Dialogue, to "address a broader range of issues, and improve communication between our militaries in order to reduce mistrust." While acknowledging that both states could not be expected to agree on every issue, the administration would remain "candid on our human rights concerns and areas." With this in mind, the divergences should not "prevent cooperation on issues of mutual interest, because a pragmatic and effective relationship between the United States and China is essential to address the major challenges of the 21st century."[5]

In elucidating the broader sentiments of the NSS, it is evident that Obama was attempting to seek a balance in terms of moving forward across multiple domains. While this approach would attempt to foster a "pragmatic and effective relationship," and keep Chinese military advances and assertions in check, it would also press China to step up from its, at times, laggard status in the global commons. Notable Chinese objections to, and non-participation in, Bush-era institutions such as the Proliferation Security Initiative were behind such concerns. As the next section will illustrate, the Obama NSS was clearly reflective of a divergent set of U.S. viewpoints encompassing well-established, yet in some instances, emerging perspectives on how to adjust and adapt to China's global trajectory. Much more than Bush, Obama was willing to accept many of the policies established in the administration preceding his own, adjusting them when necessary according to his purview and relationship with Beijing.

During the earlier stages of the Obama administration, many U.S. commentators and policymakers became progressively worried about China's expanding economic and political reach in the world—described often ominously as "China's rise"—and what it would mean for global U.S. economic and political interests. This was a return undoubtedly to the China-threat narrative of the early Bush years, in some ways still very much alive in Congress and among Republican establishment foreign policy analysts. For several analysts and policymakers, China's growing global power and influence was a "malign threat" that needed to be impeded, while conversely, others believed that it was an unavoidable occurrence that needed to be "steered and managed." By the end of the first Obama administration, a growing chorus, sharply critical of China's aggressive expansion of its island-building programs in the SCS, its continued theft of intellectual property, and its bewildering denial of Pyongyang's sinking of the *Cheonan*, a South Korean naval ship, killing forty-six, had nonetheless undermined the feeling that a positive and constructive relationship with China could at all be a realistic policy.[6]

Those who viewed China's trajectory as being "malign" argued that while Beijing's leaders may have described their growth as a "peaceful rise" with no ambitions for challenging U.S. regional leadership or liberal international norms, what they were actually doing was biding their time, conserving their strength, and waiting for the opportune moment to emerge. In other words, China was perceived to be adhering to many international norms as a strategy, but in reality, was seeking to undercut and ultimately supplant U.S. international power and influence.[7] U.S. policymakers and analysts in this camp also argued that Chinese leaders sought to trigger divisions in U.S. alliances, generate economic inter-dependence with U.S. friends, and even go as far as arming U.S. adversaries.[8] Regardless of its pointed declarations of assistance in the U.S. anti-terrorism campaign, according to this view, the PRC's frequent breaches of its non-proliferation obligations in reality contributed to strengthening illiberal states, some of which had provided sanctuary to global terrorists. Additionally, policymakers in this domain asserted that Beijing, with its deeply illiberal and assertive leadership, was essentially a threat to U.S. interests, and that the political system needed to change significantly if the United States would ever be able to attain a productive bilateral connection. From this viewpoint, U.S. policy needed to concentrate on methods to redefine the PRC from *within* while "attempting to contain PRC foreign policy actions and economic relationships around the world where these threaten U.S. interests."[9]

Others, embodying concerns touching on the major power challenge of China's ascent, argued that Beijing officials viewed the world as a state-centered, competitive environment where power was used as a means to increase the nation's wealth, influence, and ultimately, its ability to revise international norms. Only by this method could the Chinese Communist Party assure its perpetual survival. In this regard, a militarily powerful China with significant international economic linkages would be able to wield substantial political influence so as to induce U.S. friends and allies to make different choices, and thereby, potentially impinge upon the United States' broader capacity to translate its impact around the world. At the beginning of Obama's time in office, these commentators, analysts, and policymakers argued that China was already exploiting the global financial crisis to improve its access to international energy sources, building lasting and influential relationships with regional American partners, buttressing support for illiberal governments, and pushing the United States out of the Asia-Pacific. In response, the United States needed to develop a wide-ranging strategy in order to stymie China's expanding power through bolstering its existing regional alliances and creating new connections, increasing overseas investments, improving American global competitiveness, and maintaining a strong military presence in Asia and elsewhere as a counterbalance to growing PRC power and influence.[10] As John Bolton, the former ambassador to the United Nations, observed, if China was "doing what comes naturally," then the administration's policy needed to better reflect these concerns.[11]

A third and influential view at the time pertained to those who advocated the "accommodation and management" of China's economic and political rise. It was thought that as China became more economically inter-dependent with the international community, it would therefore have a greater interest in pursuing balanced international economic interactions and relationships.[12] In this light, China would have a vested concern in collaborating on ways and means to tackle the global economic crisis and the flailing international financial system. It was also viewed that prosperity in the PRC could potentially inspire Chinese society to move in a direction that would advance a materially better-off, more educated, and cosmopolitan population. According to this viewpoint, this "type" of emerging Chinese demographic would yield a more globally conformist set of views that would seek to avoid conflict with the United States. Moreover, it was also argued that such developments could ultimately engender a desire to press the state for greater political pluralism, openness, and inclusiveness, and that this trend would likely continue as China's trajectory moved in an upward fashion.[13]

In the "accommodation and management" perspective, U.S. policy would work more intimately with the PRC so as to foster these positive developments, but also to seek ways to reciprocally benefit both states by collaborating on critical global issues such as the international financial system, alternative energy sources, climate change, and medical research. Perceiving China as a "threat" or attempting to restrain it, the proponents in this domain argued, could create adverse policy consequences that could quickly veer into the military domain.[14] Along this line, David Shambaugh argues, the "logic and strategy of integrating China remains" the only realistic policy.[15] Other ramifications could entail an emboldening of Chinese nationalism with a strong anti-American bias, a deterioration in PRC governance, the augmenting of Party power and ensuing cutback of reforms, and/or a progressively more detached United States that the international community might see seceding away from the global order.[16] Intensifying such debates was of course the persistent and ongoing effect of globalization, which had inextricably tied together U.S. and PRC interests much more tightly than in the 1990s and even early 2000s. These extensive inter-linkages made it progressively more difficult for either state to take independent actions without spurring far-reaching, inadvertent consequences that could negatively impact other policy interests.

U.S. national security concerns and China

Notwithstanding the above debates, the first term of the Obama administration would see an increased expression of concern from officials in the executive branch and in Congress regarding China's expanding military expenditure, its frustrating passivity toward North Korean aggression, its assertiveness on maritime issues, and its continual crackdown on free expression domestically. Some of these concerns related to the overall drive of China's military build-up, the absence of and apparent lack of respect for military transparency, persistent examples of attempts to attain U.S. military secrets, and military and technological support to autocratic states and other internationally dubious actors. While the United States and China maintained some degree of high-level dialogue on military matters during this period in time—and as alluded to above, they had resumed deputy-ministerial defense consultations in June 2009 after an eighteen-month hiatus—the lack of communication and distrust of each other's true motives remained a source of consternation.[17]

Of course, it was the incidents and actions of the PRC in the South China Sea that would alter the perceptions over time of those U.S. policymakers who sat in the "accommodation and management" camp. On March 9, 2009, for instance, the Pentagon reported that PRC ships and aircraft operating in the SCS were acting in an increasingly assertive fashion toward two U.S. Navy ocean surveillance vessels operating in the area (USNS *Impeccable* and USNS *Victorious*). The American ships were operating approximately 75 miles south of Hainan Island, the location of the PRC's Yulin Naval Base and where China had been operating new ballistic missile and nuclear attack submarines.[18] According to a Pentagon report, the episode involved five Chinese vessels that "shadowed and aggressively maneuvered in dangerously close proximity to USNS *Impeccable*, in an apparent coordinated effort to harass the U.S. ocean surveillance ship while it was conducting routine operations in international waters." The crew members aboard the opposing ships, two of which were within 50 feet of each other, waved Chinese flags and told the U.S. ship to leave the area. After the *Impeccable* notified the Chinese ships "in a friendly manner" that it was pursuing a safe route to leave the area, two of the Chinese ships halted "directly ahead of *Impeccable*, forcing the ship to conduct an emergency 'all stop' in order to avoid collision." In a provocative move, "they dropped pieces of wood in the water directly in front of *Impeccable*'s path."[19] According to Major Stewart Upton, a Pentagon spokesman, "The unprofessional maneuvers by Chinese vessels violated the requirement under international law to operate with due regard for the rights and safety of other lawful users of the ocean."[20]

One of the most concerning aspects of the altercation was that it occured a week after positive military discussions had taken place with the PRC on February 27–28, 2009. After meeting with the deputy chief of the general staff, Ma Xiaotian, the U.S. undersecretary of defense for East Asia, David Sedney, described the meeting as "the best set of talks" he had experienced.[21] Following the incident, the United States formally protested to the Chinese government, arguing that the *Impeccable* had been operating in international waters. The Pentagon reported that it had sent a guided-missile destroyer, USS *Chung-Hoon*, to the SCS to assist the *Impeccable* as it continued its reconnaissance. Under the 1982 UN Convention on the Law of the Sea (UNCLOS), a state's territorial waters extend 12 nautical miles and its "exclusive economic zone" (EEZ) 200 nautical miles from its shoreline. Additionally, ships from other states are permitted free navigation in a state's EEZ, including freedom to fish, lay pipelines and cables, and conduct scientific research. It was within this EEZ that the *Impeccable* was operating. In response to the March 2009 incident, Chinese officials asserted that as a military ship, the *Impeccable*'s movements contravened the UN convention's EEZ obligations.[22] According to Foreign Ministry spokesperson Ma Zhaoxu, "the Chinese Government has always handled such activities in strict accordance with the above regulations. Engaging in activities in China's exclusive economic zone in the SCS without China's permission, U.S. navy surveillance ship *Impeccable* broke relevant international law as well as Chinese laws and regulations."[23] While there was a clear dichotomy between the two views on who violated international law, the March 2009 maritime incidents can be viewed as a defining point in the expanding military operations by the PRC in areas that U.S. military forces had routinely operated in unimpeded.

For security officials in the administration, these activities and indeed the reinterpretation of UNCLOS and customary international law by Beijing in the SCS were hardly a surprise. In fact they were considered to be more of a response commensurate with the rate and scale of China's military modernization, including the "acquisition of advanced foreign weapons, continued high rates of investment in its domestic defense and science and technology industries, and far-reaching organizational and doctrinal reforms."[24] Indeed, the modernization of China's national defense has been considered by some Chinese commentators to be a key component of the four modernizations, encompassing the modernization of industry, agriculture, and science and technology. In briefly looking back to Deng Xiaoping's original design, defense was considered a lower priority than modernization in other fields. As China's economic growth since the mid-1990s had enabled it to increase its overall state revenue, the pace of China's defense modernization naturally intensified.[25]

In other areas, the People's Liberation Army (PLA) was pursuing a comprehensive transformation from a mass army designed for protracted wars of attrition to one capable of fighting and winning short-duration, high-intensity conflicts along the periphery against high-tech adversaries.[26] It was these sentiments that in part explained U.S. concerns when in March 2009, the PRC proclaimed that it would expand its military budget during the year by 14.9 percent (to 480.69 billion yuan, or approximately $70.2 billion), making it the twenty-first year of double-digit increases in PRC military expenditure.[27] U.S. military planners and other American military authorities argued that PRC enhancements appeared principally geared toward a Taiwan "emergency" and strategies to thwart the military forces of an external entity—most probably the United States—in the event of a dispute over the Republic of China. The report maintained that this build-up posed a long-term threat to Taiwan and ultimately to the U.S. military presence in Asia.[28]

Of course, outside the specific military domain, other related areas also came to the fore during the Obama administration's first term in office. Economic and trade issues gradually became more complicated and remained a significant source of acrimony and tension. By 2008, the total volume of U.S.-China trade reached approximately $409 billion, with the PRC becoming America's second-largest trading partner. In addition to the substantial and expanding U.S. trade deficit with China (which climbed to $266 billion in 2008), bilateral issues emerged based on China's inability or disinclination to protect U.S. IPR and the PRC's trade and currency policies.[29]

The lead-up to the "pivot"

Tensions deriving from economic and trade issues are in many ways reflective of how the relationship has moved from one of building optimism in the 2000s to one today that is periodically antagonistic. From the U.S. perspective, China's trajectory and transition toward a Westernized free-market state had failed to materialize, disappointing many who at the time were optimistic about what the partnership could yield. As the notions of Chinese moves toward a "user-friendly" liberal market economy faded and as crackdowns on dissent to restrict the access of Western businesses increased, the positive Bush-era views of U.S. policymakers further diminished. This of course only became further exacerbated with accusations that China was engaging in levels of cyber espionage and stealing American industrial secrets. Obama was the first U.S. president to go into the public domain with his list of frustrations, describing China as a "free rider."[30] In an August 2014 interview with the *New York Times*, the president noted that China's reluctance to take on global obligations had enabled it "to secure the benefits of the global trading system with none of the responsibilities." As further observed, "they are free riders. And they have been free riders for the last 30 years and it's worked really well for them . . . And I've joked sometimes, when my inbox starts stacking up. I said can't we be a little bit more like China? Nobody ever seems to expect them to do anything when this stuff comes up."[31] In more specific terms, China's leadership simply felt reluctant to pay economic and political costs toward stabilizing the global economy, mitigating climate change, castigating rogue regimes and aggressive states, and pressuring nuclear proliferators.[32]

To be sure, Obama continued to push China toward broader global obligations in areas such as maintaining sanctions on Iran, which ultimately led to the marked deal in mitigating Iran's breakout capability in creating nuclear weapons. Additionally, he also reached an understanding with President Xi Jinping, Hu Jintao's successor, to regulate greenhouse gases—laying the foundation for the Paris Agreement on climate change. Indeed, the Obama administration announced its intent to attain an economy-wide target for reducing its emissions by 26–28 percent below its 2005 level by 2025 and to strive to decrease its emissions by 28 percent. In a reciprocal agreement, China declared its objective to achieve the peaking of CO_2 emissions around 2030, or even earlier, while also seeking to increase the portion of non-fossil fuels in primary energy consumption to around 20 percent by 2030.[33] Notwithstanding these positive interactions, Obama, since 2010, was already in the throes of placing greater emphasis on emboldening U.S. alliances in Asia, drawing closer to Japan and South Korea and providing explicit support to members of the Association of Southeast Asian Nations (ASEAN), concerned about China's claims to the SCS.[34]

Before the terms "pivot" and "rebalance" came to prominence in the administration's rhetoric, a final attempt was made to ease the relationship and seek more mutually accommodating positions on what the administration perceived as emerging security challenges in the East and South China Seas. In September 2009, the administration agreed to a Chinese invitation for a joint statement during Obama's visit to China in November, whereupon the U.S. president presented the Chinese with an innocuous list of mutual interests and goals. The speech, more than demonstrating the administration's attempt to justify further engagement, however, was misinterpreted, or deliberately misrepresented, by Chinese authorities to suggest that Washington now associated the "acceptance" of China's territorial sovereignty as acceptance of Chinese territorial claims. As stated:

> The two countries reiterated that the fundamental principle of respect for each other's sovereignty and territorial integrity is at the

core of the three U.S.-China joint communiqués which guide U.S.-China relations. Neither side supports any attempts by any force to undermine this principle. The two sides agreed that respecting each other's core interests is extremely important to ensure steady progress in U.S.-China relations.[35]

It is no surprise that Chinese authorities regard territorial integrity and the maintenance of sovereignty as being central pillars to the national interest. The United States had consistently adhered to such principles in joint statements before, but new and heightened elements of Beijing's sovereignty claims over Taiwan, the Diaoyu Islands (known in Japan as the Senkaku Islands), and the islands, rocks, shoals, and waters of the SCS, increasingly clashed with the long-standing U.S. policy to reject such unilateral territorial expansion. The perhaps inadvertent endorsement of such "core interests" was not the most apt choice of words and senior U.S. officials in subsequent statements thereafter would struggle with definitional nuance and application. At the same time, Beijing's turn to referring to these terms when it viewed Washington as backing away from its statement, also displayed a new assertiveness in China's foreign policy.[36]

To some extent, the Obama administration's early efforts at seeking a more measured approach to China's evolving foreign policy created anticipation in Beijing that the new administration was going to be, overall, much more accommodating than its predecessors. Such optimism was scotched when, in early 2010, the Obama administration behaved in customary fashion by selling arms to Taiwan, condemning Beijing for breaching Internet freedoms, and orchestrating a meeting between the president and the Dalai Lama. Due to the earlier encouraging language, this continuance of "standard policy" came as a genuine disappointment in China, spurring some sentiments of duplicity and generating domestic calls for a sterner foreign policy approach. In 2010, for example, when North Korea attacked South Korea twice, killing South Korean sailors, soldiers, and citizens, Beijing attempted to shift the blame to Washington and Seoul and to protect Pyongyang from any international consequences. Initially, the Obama administration in nuanced fashion asked China to liaise with

North Korea in addressing its behavior. When Beijing objected, however, Washington turned to Japan and South Korea to organize a response to Pyongyang's hostility, which ultimately led to increased intelligence collaboration between the three states and coordinated U.S.-South Korean exercises in the Yellow Sea. As Chinese authorities quickly came to realize in December that North Korean belligerence was generating moves by other states in the region toward strengthening their respective alliances, they intensified their efforts to discourage Pyongyang from undertaking further provocations.[37] For some, such as retired admiral Michael McDevitt, to resolve this dilemma the alliance needed to persuade Beijing that its security concerns were understood, and "the allies should attempt to assuage Beijing's strategic concerns regarding U.S. presence north of the DMZ." That said, he noted, Washington and Seoul should also implement—but should not state—a more negative assurance to China. Indeed, "in response to the shelling of Yeonpyeong Island," for instance, "the allies conducted drills in the West Sea (or Yellow Sea), which China had warned it considered a sensitive area. These drills were a tangible reminder of the 'costs' Beijing assumes because of its tolerant approach to North Korean behavior."[38]

The United States also took other measures to address tensions emanating from sovereignty differences in the region. At the ASEAN Regional Forum (ARF) in July 2010, Hillary Clinton stipulated that while the United States took no stance on the sovereignty disagreements in the SCS, it would see nonetheless that they be handled peacefully. In this context, she suggested that a way forward would be the creation of a set of multilateral confidence-building measures and codes of conduct, remarking further that disputants should explain their demands in adherence to international law. As stated:

> The United States supports a collaborative diplomatic process by all claimants for resolving the various territorial disputes without coercion. We oppose the use or threat of force by any claimant. While the United States does not take sides on the competing territorial disputes over land features in the South China Sea, we believe claimants should pursue their territorial claims and accompanying rights

to maritime space in accordance with the UN convention on the law of the sea. Consistent with customary international law, legitimate claims to maritime space in the South China Sea should be derived solely from legitimate claims to land features. The U.S. supports the 2002 ASEAN-China declaration on the conduct of parties in the South China Sea. We encourage the parties to reach agreement on a full code of conduct. The U.S. is prepared to facilitate initiatives and confidence building measures consistent with the declaration.[39]

While this suggestion was extensively endorsed in Southeast Asia, there was also a stern diplomatic response from the Chinese foreign minister. This consequently led U.S. southern counterparts to lean in the direction of being "more willing to cooperate with the United States and with one another in ways that might have long-term payoffs for U.S. interests in the region."[40]

At this time, an additional eruption of regional tensions occurred to put Chinese assertiveness on display, prompting U.S. regional partners to further assess their postures toward China. In September, Japanese authorities detained the captain of a Chinese fishing boat near the Diaoyu/Senkaku Islands for reckless behavior and illegal fishing. In response, the United States reiterated its long-standing policy toward the islands, in which it again took no stance on their fundamental sovereignty, but acknowledged Japan's administrative control, and as such, Article V of the U.S.-Japanese Security Treaty was very much applicable. Around this period Beijing escalated its movements in the sea and air around the islands and eventually declared an air defense identification zone (ADIZ) in the East China Sea (ECS) that incorporated the contested area. The inflammatory creation of the zone was condemned by the United States and other states in the region as an unnecessary escalation, and saw Washington send out B-52 bombers to the area to emphasize its continuous freedom of navigation (FoN).[41]

Defining and articulating the "pivot"

Having been lost in the wilderness in Afghanistan and Iraq, the Obama administration sought to readjust and embolden its position in the Asia-Pacific region. With a clear eye on China's movement and trajectory in the region during the 2009–2010 period, Obama's first term would see a strategic shift in response to the coordinated issues of SCS island reclamation, military modernization, the expansion of maritime naval, Coast Guard, and militia units, and the threat of a further ADIZ in the SCS. Given the definitional debates, including the delineation and interchangeable uses of the terms "pivot" and "rebalance," it is worth providing some much-needed clarity, to which this section now turns. According to Jonathan G. Odom, the Obama approach during his first two to three years in office saw a strategic shift toward security in the Asia-Pacific region, encompassing three defining pillars: (a) a "pivot" toward U.S. relationships with states and organizations in the Asia-Pacific region, (b) a "rebalance" of the U.S. military presence in the region, and (c) an emphasis on maintaining and advocating a rules-based international order.[42]

In providing clearer chronological separation to the terms "pivot" and "rebalance," Richard Weitz argues that while in the initial stages "Asian pivot" and "back to Asia" were the terms of choice, they "were no longer in fashion" since U.S. policymakers wanted to emphasize that the U.S. "had never left Asia." As such, policymakers preferred to underline the elements of continuity in the administration's strategy with those of its predecessor, noting in actuality, that even before the announcement of the Pentagon's Asian orientation, the United States had been quietly strengthening its forces in the region. As such, the terms of choice, Weitz continued, shifted to a "rebalance," encompassing two separate processes: a military rebalancing of its global resources from other regions to Asia, as well as a rebalancing within the Asia-Pacific region, reducing the concentration of forces from northeast Asia to a more broadly distributed emphasis throughout the entire region.[43]

This definitional articulation of the "rebalance" was promulgated on October 11, 2011 with Secretary of State Hillary Clinton's article entitled "America's Pacific Century" in *Foreign Policy*. She argued that over the course of the preceding decade the U.S. had been preoccupied with conflicts in the Middle East, specifically the ongoing wars in Iraq and Afghanistan. Clinton contended that the magnitude of U.S. resources and capital expended on these wars had been a miscalculation, and that it was crucial for the U.S. to redeploy its energy in regions where it could attain the maximum impact on its contributions, such as the Asia-Pacific. In the twenty-first century, she further articulated, Asia would represent the predominant market for growth, with many Asia-Pacific states becoming central players in the global geopolitical arena of the future. As stated:

> The Asia-Pacific has become a key driver of global politics. Stretching from the Indian subcontinent to the western shores of the Americas, the region spans two oceans—the Pacific and the Indian—that are increasingly linked by shipping and strategy. It boasts almost half the world's population. It includes many of the key engines of the global economy, as well as the largest emitters of greenhouse gases. It is home to several of our key allies and important emerging powers like China, India, and Indonesia.[44]

Here, Clinton described economics as a significant motivation for the "pivot" or "rebalance," writing that "open markets in Asia provide the United States with unprecedented opportunities for investment, trade, and access to cutting edge technology," and that "our economic recovery will depend on exports and the ability of American firms to tap into the vast and growing consumer base in Asia."[45] Additionally, the region was home to nearly half the world's population and therefore it was in the interest of the U.S. to dedicate an increased level of engagement to this region. While Clinton identified the Asia-Pacific as having various challenges—noting severe pollution, North Korea's capricious and unstable nuclear weapons proliferation, and cyber security breaches—it was the trajectory of China and the increasingly troublesome territorial disputes in the SCS that appeared to be the most significant driver of what would be defined as the "pivot." That is, as a means to safeguard the free flow of commerce, the U.S. "must" maintain its historic role of security guarantor and protector of international shipping lanes. This entailed maintaining that FoN was implemented in accordance with international law, particularly in disputed maritime domains such as the ECS and SCS. "Strategically, maintaining peace and security across the Asia-Pacific," the article extrapolated, "is increasingly crucial to global progress, whether through defending freedom of navigation in the South China Sea . . . or ensuring transparency in the military activities of the region's key players."[46]

Of course, the strengthening of alliances with states in Asia, solidifying and developing regional economic structures, advocating multilateral institutions, and emboldening traditional "friends and allies" in the region were foremost in this policy shift. Specifically, this would entail a methodical rebalancing of U.S. resources and attention to the Asia-Pacific region while maintaining a continuous diplomatic dialogue with historical allies Japan, South Korea, the Philippines, Australia, and Thailand. Greater focus would also be placed on relationships with India, Indonesia, Singapore, New Zealand, Malaysia, Mongolia, Vietnam, and Brunei as emerging regional players of significance. In this regard, the U.S. would seek to play a more energized and consistent role in the multinational institutions of the region, including Asia-Pacific Economic Cooperation (APEC) and ASEAN, while seeking new trade agreements with the Trans-Pacific Partnership (TPP).[47] As Clinton states:

> I have called [the "pivot"] "forward-deployed" diplomacy. That means continuing to dispatch the full range of our diplomatic assets— including our highest-ranking officials, our development experts, our interagency teams, and our permanent assets—to every country and corner of the Asia-Pacific region. Our strategy will have to keep accounting for and adapting to the rapid and dramatic shifts playing out across Asia. With this in mind, our work will proceed along six key lines of action: strengthening bilateral security alliances; deepening our working relationships with emerging powers; engaging with regional multilateral institutions; expanding trade and investment; forging a broad-based military presence; and advancing democracy and human rights.[48]

In many respects, these words from Clinton were a rearticulation of Condoleezza Rice's transformation diplomacy, albeit with a greater and more strategic focus on Asia and the Pacific. In cultivating the definitional basis and rationale for the "pivot," President Obama during late 2011 and early 2012 also specified the intensifying role the U.S. would come to play in the Asia-Pacific region.

In an address to the Australian parliament on November 17, 2011, Obama first formally outlined his Asia-Pacific foreign policy strategy.[49] He stated that his objective was to guarantee that "the United States will play a larger and long-term role in shaping this region and its future, by upholding core principles and in close partnership with our allies and friends."[50] This would entail the pursuit and maintenance of security, "which is the foundation of peace and prosperity." Further, he articulated, "we stand for an international order in which the rights and responsibilities of all nations and all people are upheld. Where international law and norms are enforced. Where commerce and freedom of navigation are not impeded. Where emerging powers contribute to regional security, and where disagreements are resolved peacefully."[51] In echoing these sentiments, National Security Adviser Tom Donilon observed that the main focus was to define and reiterate the norms and rules of the Asia-Pacific region, so as to ensure that commerce and navigation remain fluid, and "that emerging powers build trust with their neighbors, and that disagreements are resolved peacefully without threats or coercion."[52]

As for the logistics and details of the "pivot," proclaimed steps included troop deployments to Australia, new naval deployments to Singapore, and new areas for military cooperation with the Philippines. While overall reductions in U.S. defense spending were still envisaged, the military presence in East Asia would be nonetheless expanded, "more broadly distributed, more flexible, and more politically sustainable." Other strands in the plan pertained to a new defense planning document that would elaborate on the justification for the rebalancing to Asia while retaining an emphasis on the Middle East, joining the East Asia Summit (EAS), one of the region's leading multinational organizations, and building momentum in negotiations to create a nine-state free trade agreement known as the Trans-Pacific Partnership (TPP) (including Australia, Brunei, Chile, Malaysia, New Zealand, Peru, Singapore, the United States, and Vietnam, with the possibility at the time of Canada, Mexico, and Japan joining the TPP discussions).[53] As discussed above and reiterated by the president, the four developments spurring the "pivot" clearly pertained to: Beijing's expanding military capacity and its escalating assertions regarding contested maritime space, with consequences for FoN and the United States' ability to maintain power in the region; the increasing economic significance of the Asia-Pacific region to the United States' economic well-being; the conclusion of U.S. military operations in Iraq and Afghanistan;

and efforts to reassure "friends and allies" in the region that the United States was still committed to the region amid concerns emanating from the U.S. federal government's imminent cuts to defense spending.[54]

The military element of the administration's Asia-Pacific strategy was further articulated in the January 2012 Defense Strategic Guidance. The report described plans to embolden U.S. treaty alliances in the region with Japan, South Korea, Australia, the Philippines, and Thailand—and to expand cooperation with "emerging partners" in order to "ensure collective capability and capacity for securing common interests."[55] Additionally, in regard to the growth of China's military power, it stated that the U.S. must respond with "greater clarity of its strategic intentions in order to avoid causing friction in the region . . . [and] make the necessary investments to ensure that we maintain regional access and the ability to operate freely in keeping with our treaty obligations and with international law." In articulating the "primary mission of the U.S. Armed Forces"—including the protection of U.S. national interests and meeting the objectives of the 2010 National Security Strategy—the Joint Force needed to recalibrate its proficiencies and make discerning additional investments to succeed in applicable missions, one of which included China. As a means to conceivably dissuade prospective challengers such as China, and to preclude them from realizing their more ambitious and revisionist goals, the United States must sustain its capacity to project power in applicable regions where access and freedom to operate are challenged. In these domains, high-tech opponents would "use asymmetric capabilities, to include electronic and cyber warfare, ballistic and cruise missiles, advanced air defenses, mining, and other methods, to complicate our operational calculus." As such, the seminal report argued that the Pentagon would "invest as required to ensure its ability to operate effectively in anti-access and area denial (A2/AD) environments." This would encompass the implementation of the Joint Operational Access Concept, maintaining undersea capabilities, constructing a new stealth bomber, upgrading missile defenses, and "continuing efforts to enhance the resiliency and effectiveness of critical space-based capabilities."[56]

Continuities and departures

Despite much of the discourse at time, several commentators argued that there were some facets of the Obama administration's "pivot" that represented merely an extension rather than the marked transformation of U.S. policy as many have indicated. In this line of thinking, the administration followed an extensive procession of U.S. governments who had, since the end of World War II, pursued a security strategy in the Asia-Pacific that was gauged toward sustaining a substantive military presence in East Asia, and including the United States in core diplomatic movements in the region.[57] As articulated by Evan A. Feigenbaum:

> I think that notion of a "shift" is overstated . . . There's no question that the United States is paying a lot of attention to what's happening in Asia, but this notion of some gigantic pivot obscures the degree to which there are some really central pillars of American policy in the Pacific that have roots that go back decades. It isn't as if the United States suddenly woke up in the last year or two and discovered that it ought to play an important role in security in Asia. The notion of some gigantic pivot isn't helpful because it suggests that the United States is kind of a herky-jerky superpower that swings wildly from focusing on one thing to focusing on another thing.[58]

According to this observation, the administration hastened and broadened policies that were already underway under the Bush administration, encompassing an emphasis on the southern and western parts of the region involving operations via revolving deployments (rather than through creation of permanent bases). Additionally, Obama extended Bush proposals such as improving relations with existing allies in Asia, negotiating the TPP, and cultivating new partnerships with Vietnam, India, and Indonesia. As conveyed by Robert Sutter, Bush's program, while engaged in turning countries in Southeast Asia into a "second front" for the War on Terror, expanded Washington's bilateral and institutional influence in a series of agreements that further sought to tighten the bond between U.S. and regional partners.[59]

Discernibly, the counterpoint for many observers, despite this apparent continuity between administrations, was that Obama's "upgrade in U.S. diplomatic visibility and presence in the Asia-Pacific" was more than just an extension. Under the Bush administration, many "Southeast Asian leaders in the region felt they had been neglected by the United States."[60] This was conveyed by ASEAN secretary general Surin Pitsuwan, when he described Secretary Clinton's visit to the ASEAN Secretariat in February 2009 as being a sign that America was ending "its diplomatic absenteeism in the region." As further stated:

> You have said the U.S. is ready to listen. We are also ready to listen, Madame Secretary. Your willingness to listen will go a long way to winning friends and partners, and reassuring allies in the region. Your visit also emphasizes the importance of ASEAN in the regional architecture. ASEAN, with its 41 years of history, has been an anchor of stability, peace, and harmony for the region. As a region, ASEAN and East Asia is ready, able, and willing to work with the United States in the search for solutions to global impasses, including bridging the cultural divide.[61]

In a symbolic move that illustrates the perceived emphasis of the shift, the trip by Clinton to Asia was not only her first overseas trip after formally becoming secretary of state, it was also the first time someone holding the said position had actually visited the ASEAN Secretariat. For many, the administration's enhanced emphasis in its approach to the Asia-Pacific region was defined as a change of means, in terms of resources and leadership, as well as a shift in policy goals. Notwithstanding the prevalent (continuum/departure) debates at the time, it is clearly evident that the policy was a marked response to the tensions in Sino-U.S. relations and featured at least three broad new elements of U.S. policy, encompassing: "new military priorities and deployments; an arguably more integrated and region-wide approach to the Asia-Pacific; and a vision of the region's geography to include the Indian Ocean." Ultimately, such elements would see the "Indo-Pacific" term come to the fore in the mainstream foreign policy vernacular and broader security discourse.[62]

U.S. security policy, the "pivot" and its ramifications

As indicated, the most transformative moves of the "pivot" were to be found in the security domain. While the envisaged deployments of troops and military hardware to Australia and Singapore signified an expanded U.S. presence, they also demonstrated that Obama's "pivot" embodied the elements of a strategic choice on "selective primacy," which, due to Washington's concerning fiscal situation, would see a push toward a more specialized force structure in the future.[63] In assuring that reductions in defense spending would not compromise the U.S. presence in the Asia-Pacific, the Department of Defense's January 2012 Strategic Guidance document sought to minimize cuts in the size of the navy, concentrating reductions instead on army and marine ground forces.[64]

The "selective primacy" approach began in April 2012 when a company-size rotation of 200 to 250 marines were initially planned to be deployed through an existing Australian military facility at Darwin for approximately six months at a time. The size of the rotation was to increase progressively across several years toward a force of 2,500 Marine Corps personnel, or a full marine air-ground task force. The United States and Australia also revealed strategies that would entail U.S. military aircraft having greater access to Royal Australian Air Force facilities. Additionally, the two militaries purportedly reassessed the degree to which the U.S. Navy could have more access to Australia's naval bases, with HMAS *Stirling* in Perth specifically identified as an ideal location that could provide the "U.S. Navy a sorely needed place to refuel, re-equip and repair on the Indian Ocean."[65] Aside from the broadening of U.S.-Australia military ties, discussions also included drone flights from a coral atoll in the Indian Ocean. Australian and U.S. officials at the time argued that the Cocos Islands could be an "ideal site for U.S. surveillance aircraft, including unmanned, high-altitude Global Hawk drones that could conduct spy flights over the South China Sea."[66]

In an attempt to emphasize the point that the new military collaboration was not directed at China, Australia's foreign minister, Stephen Smith, exclaimed that "Australia maintains positive and separate relationships with both the U.S. and China and strengthening our relations with one of these countries does not detract from our relationship with the other."[67] Prime Minister Kevin Rudd echoed these sentiments, indicating that there was a trust-building mechanism between the U.S. and China. In this regard, he argued that the Australian government did not believe it had to "choose between its longstanding alliance with the United States and its expanding relationship with China"; nor did the United States and China believe that they must make such a choice. In fact, he emphasized, Australia did not approach China as an adversary, but rather, favored a policy "aimed at encouraging China's peaceful rise and ensuring that strategic competition in the region does not lead to conflict."[68]

In Singapore, the U.S. planned to post four littoral combat ships at the city-state's naval facility.[69] The Philippines and the United States also discussed military cooperation possibilities, including the rotation of surveillance aircraft, a greater transferal of U.S. troops on assignment, and more joint military simulations.[70] Broadly speaking, the U.S. Navy's focus on the strategic "maritime crossroads" of the Asia-Pacific region, according to chief of naval operations Admiral Jonathan Greenert, would "station several of our newest littoral combat ships at Singapore's naval facility," start rotational deployments of marines to Darwin, and "help the navy sustain its global forward posture with what may be a smaller number of ships and aircraft than today." Further, Greenert elaborated, Singapore would undertake cooperative counter-piracy or counter-trafficking operations around the SCS, which could entail "Poseidon aircraft or unmanned broad area maritime surveillance aerial vehicles periodically deployed to the Philippines or Thailand to help those nations with maritime domain awareness." Of course, the rationale conveyed pointed to the disputed sovereign concerns of the oil-rich reefs and islands in the SCS, and the fact that the region is the shortest route between the Pacific and Indian Oceans, including the world's busiest shipping lanes containing half the globe's oil tanker traffic.[71]

While Obama administration officials regularly argued that their emboldened approach to the Asia-Pacific was not exclusively gauged toward any specific state, most commentators believed it was clearly, at least in part, responding to China's expanding influence and trajectory. To be sure, the Chinese were to read this increasingly as the strengthening of Washington's long-term containment strategy. For Obama, Beijing's preparedness to engage in assertive claims to contested maritime territory in the South and East China Seas, as well as via large and unprecedented live-fire military exercises, maritime patrols, provocation of Vietnamese oil exploration vessels, and confinement of Vietnamese and Philippine fishing boats, was a principally concerning rationale for an enhanced American presence. It should be noted that China was not in isolation in undertaking such assertive measures to safeguard claimed territory in the SCS. Patrol ships from Indonesia, Malaysia, the Philippines, and Vietnam also apprehended and impounded fishing vessels of other states found operating unlawfully in claimed areas (albeit not to China's level). According to some analysts, the administration appeared to achieve a reasonable level of success when periodically leaning toward the more confrontational side of its approach. For instance, when the U.S., Vietnam, and other East Asian states diplomatically pushed back in 2010 against what they saw as Chinese infringements in the SCS, China was forced "to join multilateral negotiations with Southeast Asian countries over a Code of Conduct (CoC) in the South China Sea." Further, when Vietnam made overtures to bolster U.S.-Vietnamese ties (as well as deepen its ties to India and Japan) this spurred Beijing toward improving its relationship with Hanoi, thereby contributing to a reduction of frictions.[72]

Given this expanded diplomatic profile in the Asia-Pacific, it should be unsurprising that some in China fixated purely on the perception that the "pivot" sought to separate China from its neighbors while thwarting its military advancement. This was the view carried by many in the PLA, which had long been distrustful of U.S. objectives in the region. Accordingly, one response was to improve China's anti-access capabilities and to seek more assertive measures in defending China's territorial claims (rather than less). The "rebalancing" therefore engendered sentiments from some analysts who argued that containing China could actually make it more difficult (immediately and down the track) for the United States to secure China's collaboration on such ongoing matters associated with Iran and North Korea.[73]

There were also concerns that the "rebalance" could have consequences for U.S. economic interests, particularly given China was the United States' second-largest trading partner, its third-largest export market, and the largest foreign holder of U.S. debt. Here, the possibility of worsening, already distressed, U.S.-China strategic confidence was perceived by many as potentially making China *less* receptive to U.S. concerns about its economic policies and about access for U.S. firms in the Chinese marketplace. In simple terms, "pressing China" in the realm of security could make Beijing less inclined to compromise on significant decisions in the broader global economic system. This could also mean that states in the region could react negatively against an expanded U.S. involvement in regional issues if it was viewed to be increasing tensions, or attempting to compel such states to "choose" between two critical partners.[74]

A shared criticism of the Obama approach, therefore, was that it could be unnecessarily provoking China while inadvertently steering U.S. allies and partners—among them the Philippines, Japan, and Vietnam—to believe that they had more U.S. support for their differences with China than Washington was essentially willing to offer. Analysts who contributed to this disapproving view argued that the "rebalancing" was over-engrossed in military rudiments and was undermining already impaired U.S.-China strategic trust and fueling regional instability instead of abating it. According to Robert S. Ross, the Obama policy unnecessarily compounded Beijing's insecurities and would only spur "China's aggressiveness, undermine regional stability, and decrease the possibility of cooperation between Beijing and Washington."[75] As an alternative to inflating "estimates of Chinese power and abandoning its long-standing policy of diplomatic engagement," he continued, "the United States should recognize China's underlying weaknesses and its own enduring strengths. The right China policy would assuage, not exploit, Beijing's anxieties, while protecting U.S. interests in the region."[76]

In contrast, other critics suggested that the military side of the "rebalancing" was inadequately vigorous, resulting in a U.S. policy that was at times comparable to "speaking loudly" but "carrying a shrinking stick."[77] For Dean Cheng and Bruce Klingner of the Heritage Foundation, the "pivot" was weakened by the reality that the U.S. military was limited in the requisite resources necessary to execute such a strategy. Even as the quantity of threats to regional order in Asia continued to expand, there was not "a commensurate increase of U.S. capabilities." While Obama claimed at the time that there would be no forces cut from Asia, reductions in the overall U.S. force structure would nonetheless stymie America's global power projection and "force sustainability capabilities."[78] As such, Cheng and Klingner contend, "it is unrealistic to think that the United States can sustain a half a trillion dollar cut in defense spending, let alone the trillion dollar cut currently pending Congressional action, and still maintain its current level of commitment, much less augment it, as implied by the administration's avowed pivot."[79]

China's reaction to the "pivot"/"rebalance"

Cautious of Washington's objectives, China responded by building up its own military and pressing its sovereignty demands in the region. Coinciding with a marked leadership change in 2012, the hawks in the Chinese military had come to attract the full attention of the new Xi Jinping leadership, attaining as a result a substantive funding boost.[80] As further conveyed by Xiang Lanxin, there was "even a demand from the military to re-enter the Communist Party's Politburo Standing Committee in the coming 18th Party Congress, from which it has been absent since the 15th Congress in 1997, when the party decided to push for the professionalization of the military to reduce its political power."[81] In looking back to Xi's time as China's vice president, he had also articulated cautious trepidation during a visit to the United States in February 2012, shortly after the Obama "rebalancing" strategy was officially launched. As stated, "China welcomes a constructive role by the United States in promoting peace, stability and prosperity in the Asia-Pacific. At the same time, we hope the United States will respect the interests and concerns of China and other countries in this region."[82] Despite such restrained sentiments, Chinese officials frequently posed questions on the extent to which the U.S. "rebalance" was, in actuality, conducive to peace, stability, and prosperity, and whether, notwithstanding U.S. assurances to the contrary, it was in fact intended to "contain" or "encircle" China.

In providing more forthright speculation pertaining to U.S. shifts, China's deputy foreign minister with responsibility for the United States, Cui Tiankai (who is at the time of writing China's ambassador to the United States), coauthored an article with a fellow diplomat, Pang Hanzhao, raising questions about the United States' "true motive" in "rebalancing" to the Asia-Pacific. It was unclear what "signals" the administration "wanted to send to China and the region," they remarked. Moreover, to avoid escalation the U.S. needed to "convince China" and others "that there is no gap between its policy statements on China and its true intentions." In highlighting the areas of concern in the administration's determination to strengthen its alliance system in Asia, they laid particular emphasis on U.S. plans to develop a ballistic missile defense system in the region, efforts to expand the joint operating effectiveness of U.S. naval and air units, and the potential for the U.S. to interfere in regional areas of difference.[83] As further articulated:

> Instead of trying to resolve specific problems between the United States and China simply as they stand, they tend to magnify the problems out of proportion by seeing them through the lens of competition for domination between major powers and by speculating and analyzing China's intentions in the worst possible light . . . In the course of returning to the Asia-Pacific, the United States has been vigorously strengthening its alliance system, advancing the anti-ballistic missile system in the Asia-Pacific, pursuing "sea-air battle" and intervening in the disputes between China and its neighbors.[84]

These concerns were clearly evident at a security summit in Singapore in June 2013, when Major General Yao Yunzhu, director of the Center for China-America Defense Relations at the PLA's Academy of Military Sciences, informed Secretary of Defense Chuck Hagel that the "rebalance" was perceived in China as an "attempt to contain China's rising influence and to offset the increasing military capabilities of the Chinese PLA." By this stage, U.S. government officials had "on several occasions clarified that the rebalance is not against China," though these assurances fell on deaf ears.[85] The most common assertion from Chinese critics was that the United States' drive to maintain a higher profile in Asia—including its commitment to multilateral groups such as ASEAN and intensification of its military partnerships—was undermining the region by encouraging states to press their territorial demands vigorously. Additionally, Chinese proponents were also at the time critical of the core economic strategy relating to the Trans-Pacific Partnership (TPP), described by many as being an initiative that intentionally omitted China, impeded regional economic assimilation, and complicated ASEAN's leadership role in advocating trade and investment liberalization in the region. At the Obama-Xi summit in June 2013, Obama consented to a request from Xi for consultations on U.S. progress toward a TPP agreement, viewed as moving dialogue further in this area.[86] Additionally, at the S&ED meeting in July, China agreed to progress toward a more "substantive" stage in discussions over a joint investment treaty that would, if the U.S. had its way, emulate the investment obligations of the TPP.[87]

Regardless of the economic and trade arguments pertaining to the TPP, many contended that it was the geopolitical-security aspects that were the decisive driver of the initiative. Indeed, some at the time considered the TPP to be a threshold in assessing U.S. mettle and credibility in the Asia-Pacific region. Here, proponents argued that the TPP would demonstrate the pre-eminence of the United States' incorporation into Asia's economic and diplomatic edifices, signifying that Congressional indecision or rejection of the TPP could make the administration's "rebalancing" strategy look relatively feeble and divisive. As stated by Jeffrey A. Bader and David Dollar, "If they succeed, there will be substantial benefits for their nations and a big diplomatic win for the Obama administration. If they fail, the accord risks getting bogged down in U.S. presidential politics and puts into question the rebalance to Asia."[88]

Likewise, many Asian policymakers would construe a failure of the TPP in the United States as a representation of diminishing U.S. attention in the region and its incapacity to sustain its strategic and material presence. By contrast, certain critics of the TPP argued that such opinions were inflated, and that the strength or weakness of wider bilateral political and security relationships depended more on states' evaluation of their political and security interests than on terms associated with a U.S. trade agreement.[89]

According to Daniel Slane and Michael Wessel, those who argued that the TPP was crucial to thwarting China's aspirations were disregarding the fact that those states were not "rushing into China's embrace." In fact, it was evident, the authors continued, that "several of the TPP participants are more interested in stronger alliances with the United States which aren't dependent on preferential trade relations and new trade agreements."[90] Put differently, such states needed the United States as a broader counter to China, with many noting that the TPP was not "a factor in assessing the risks that China poses . . . our 'pivot to Asia' does not need to be anchored by a new preferential trade agreement."[91] Despite these sentiments, however, while China was not necessarily on the radar for TPP membership, its growing trajectory as a regional economic power with active overseas trade and investment initiatives was an important factor to any TPP assessment.[92]

Indeed, those supporting the TPP, including President Obama, often defined it as a platform for upholding U.S. leadership in Asia in the face of China's rise, arguing that through the agreement the United States would "write the rules" for regional trade and investment and help redefine a stronger, rules-focused regional order. Further, some analysts optimistically reasoned that in many ways U.S. and Chinese goals for trade liberalization and regional norms could be reciprocally strengthening—rather than mutually exclusive—in advocating the goal of free trade in the Asia-Pacific region.[93] Of course, these dichotomies in viewpoints would persist across Obama's second term in office and through to the 2016 U.S. presidential election. As the next chapter illustrates, the emerging complexities and transition of global politics throughout Obama's tenure in office, as well as the intensifying partisanship that was permeating the strategic thinking of U.S. policymakers, came to complicate the administration's message and strategy in dealing with China's upward trajectory.

Conclusion

When assessing Obama's first-term approach to China, it is evident that in dealing with difficult challenges the administration's record is varied. To some extent, it was remarkably successful in strengthening the U.S. diplomatic apparatus in the Asia-Pacific and was somewhat controlled in handling tensions when they arose. That said, the Obama administration also made some noteworthy missteps, particularly in the areas of rhetoric and public diplomacy. After the first two years in office, it became noticeable that such assertions rendered China even more challenging and further undermined the possibilities for cooperation with the United States. Specifically, Obama employed frank and robust language about "pivoting" back to Asia as the United States retreated from the wars in Afghanistan and Iraq. At the most rudimentary point, this approach, according to some policymakers, was imprecise— in that they felt the United States had never abandoned Asia and consequently did not need to "pivot" *back*.

In fact, as discussed during this chapter, many contended that the plans later accompanying the so-called "pivot" were in the strategic mix well before Obama began his presidency. These plans included sending littoral combat ships to Singapore and negotiating the TPP, as mentioned, as well as dispatching more submarines to Guam, rotating F-22 aircraft through Japan, and entering a free-trade pact with South Korea. Regardless of the "continuities vs. departures" debates pertaining to the Obama "pivot," it *was* the Obama administration that would actually oversee the implementation, emboldening, and refinement of such plans, as well as new significant elements added to the equation. In this regard, the Obama administration sent upper-level representatives to Asia more regularly and strategically than its predecessor; enhanced relations with Burma (also called Myanmar); joined the EAS; signed the Treaty of Amity and Cooperation in Southeast Asia, the founding document of ASEAN; and saw to it that the EAS and the ARF, often criticized as symbolic "meet and greets," essentially tackled crucial security matters.[94]

Notwithstanding these commendable diplomatic advances, the assertive language about a "pivot," while at times justified, did feed into Chinese conspiracy assumptions about purported U.S. containment and encirclement policies. Paradoxically, the language also generated some difficulties with U.S. allies in Asia. While the emphasis of the U.S. presence in the region was intended to be comforting, it also led the United States into areas where it maladroitly intimated that it might not necessarily be able to cope with multiple global challenges at once, and thus, unsurprisingly, some of the said allies became concerned that the United States might pivot *away* again should difficulties evolve in other regions. In acknowledging the perhaps slight miscalculation, the administration let go of the term "pivot" and substituted it with the more benevolent "rebalance." But by this stage, many of the fractious interactions that are so prevalent today were already in play. As indicated, upon securing office, the Obama administration's initial efforts in fashioning optimistic sentiments that it was going to be much more engaged than its predecessors ultimately encountered difficulties as it searched for the right medium in its China approach. Because of the earlier optimistic language of the administration, the perpetuation of a "traditional" policy would come to the fore as a genuine frustration in China, spurring sentiments of duplicity and generating internal calls for a sterner foreign policy. These of course were exacerbated when the Obama administration sold arms to Taiwan, condemned Beijing for violating Internet freedom, and coordinated a visit for the president to meet with the Dalai Lama.

Tensions in East Asia became significantly greater over the course of the first two years in office. Subsequently, the Obama administration found itself using military assets on a relatively frequent level so as to send signals to Beijing that it would counter assertive PRC actions in the East and South China Seas. In the context of other actors in the region, such as in its relations with the Philippines surrounding the Scarborough Shoal, Beijing took advantage of the "incitement" by others in attempting to legitimize Chinese endeavors to establish jurisdiction over territory that China had long claimed as its own but not administered. At other intervals, such as its 2012 announcement of a new administrative unit encompassing the mostly unoccupied Paracel and Spratly Islands and the Macclesfield Bank, the PRC behaved aggressively, even without any apparent provocation. As will be discussed in the next chapter, China generated much concern throughout the region by undertaking substantively sized land reclamation and infrastructure projects on contested reefs, leading U.S. secretary of defense Ashton Carter to chastise Beijing at the

May 2015 Shangri-La Dialogue. The Obama administration was, in the main, right to critique provocative Chinese behavior and regularly proclaimed the international community's FoN in the East and South China Seas. The administration was also appropriate in the way it reacted to contentious Chinese actions, via revitalizing its regional alliances, consolidating partnerships with non-allies, and assisting its regional partners to expand their abilities to monitor and counteract Chinese assertiveness. While such actions did not immediately address the region's problems, they were clearly an attempt by Obama to have Beijing understand that there were advantages—to itself and everybody—in behaving in a less assertive, more encouraging fashion, not unlike what it had pursued for most of the first decade of the new millennium.

In terms of collaboration, the areas relating to non-proliferation, intervention in regional and civil conflicts, and climate change saw a varied record from Obama. On nuclear proliferation, while there were extensive obstacles—and at times reluctance—in moving China toward addressing North Korea's persistent advancement of nuclear weapons and delivery systems, much more progress was made in steering Iran toward an agreed cessation of its nuclear program. China signed up to relevant UN resolutions against both states, albeit only after working to dilute them. More significantly, it persisted in its efforts to hinder progress by regularly offering fiscal reprieve to Pyongyang and Tehran. While Beijing and Washington worked closely together on North Korean denuclearization in the Six-Party Talks, particularly from 2006 to 2008, they ultimately broke down in the last year of the Bush administration, not to be revitalized since. After a three-year stand-off with minimal communication, the Obama team determined that such an approach was also not working, and pushed the "Leap Day" arms control agreement of February 2012, where the administration made a substantial offer to resume discussions. While this was promptly scuppered by North Korea's use of ballistic missile technology in a satellite launch, the administration did attain some recognition for undertaking this diplomatic response, and in the process, made it clear to all rational spectators where the actual obstruction was based.[95]

But as far as areas where both states worked well together during the first term are concerned, it was the issue of climate change where positives were made. This would culminate in the 2014 APEC summit, where Obama and Xi achieved what appeared to be a marked step toward addressing issues emanating from greenhouse gas emissions. Here, China pledged that it would reach peak carbon emissions by approximately 2030 and agreed to produce 20 percent of its future electrical energy from non-carbon sources. Additionally, there was headway on several other issues in the U.S. relationship with China, from enhanced military-to-military ties, to consequential dialogues on how to prevent confrontations at sea, to the foundations for a bilateral investment treaty, to more easily secured visas for business travel and tourism. Overall, it was the broader challenges posed by China's rise—and the Obama administration's "pivot"-based response in addressing such challenges—that provide insight into how the relationship would undergo further transformation, and intensification, during Obama's second term in office, particularly with Xi Jinping's decisive leadership coming to the fore in 2012. As discussed in the next chapter, as a means to further strengthen regional security and discourage China from resolving its territorial disputes through intimidation, the United States would again seek to balance and maintain a vigorous presence in Asia, given Xi's approach, while attempting to energize military, diplomatic, and economic ties with allies and other regional partners.[96]

4. The Obama Administration's Second Term: Balancing Continuities and New Realities

In the twenty-first century U.S. foreign policymakers have had to address significant questions pertaining to the type of relationship the United States should pursue with the People's Republic of China (PRC) and how to adapt to China's "rise." After more than thirty years of double-digit economic growth, China's economy has become the second largest in the world and according to some estimates—notwithstanding the fallout from the COVID-19 global pandemic—will overtake the United States by 2027. Of course, accompanying its economic trajectory, China has also developed and cultivated its global strategic reach and extended range of power projection capabilities. During Obama's two terms in office, the administration repeatedly attempted to assure Beijing that the United States was receptive to "a strong, prosperous and successful China that plays a greater role in world affairs," and that it did not seek to impede China's trajectory on the world stage. China, in response, promised to adhere to "the path of peaceful development."[1] As this chapter will illustrate, the Obama administration during its second term in office continued to search for the "right" equilibrium pertaining to China, particularly on how to engage with it on issues concerning stability and security in the Asia-Pacific region and beyond. Ongoing points of concern for Washington included: understanding the true rationale behind China's military modernization program; China's use of its military and paramilitary forces in altercations with states over territorial claims in the South China Sea (SCS) and East

China Sea (ECS); its marked progress in establishing provocative militarized structures in such disputed waters; the strategic and security aspects of the Belt and Road Initiative (BRI); and its persistent threat to use force in pressing toward unification with Taiwan. While U.S.-China military-to-military ties improved during the Obama era, Washington continued to struggle in persuading Beijing that the U.S. policy of "rebalancing" toward the Asia-Pacific was not meant to contain China.[2]

Many of these ongoing and even new concerns for Obama were exacerbated by China's change in leadership in November 2012, at first considered by many as a positive sign for the growing relationship. China's new president, Xi Jinping, was a noted princeling and suspected reformer. He was considered to be pro-business, hardworking, low-key, and a modernizer with plans to bring China more rigorously into the twenty-first century as a great power.[3] Moreover, Xi's established links with the United States, including frank discussions with Obama and Vice President Joe Biden, were thought to offer a chance at emboldening and improving engagement, particularly on issues such as Taiwan, cyber security, China's human rights record, North Korea, and Iran's proliferation, among notable others.[4] As this chapter brings to bear, however, Xi's bold and all-encompassing leadership developed quickly to significantly impact the Obama administration's strategic calculi.

Here, two defining planks of the Xi era would come to the fore as sources of consternation among Obama officials. The first was when China began constructing military bases out of barely existent atolls in the SCS in 2013, and the second was when Xi launched the ambitiously economic, but very strategic BRI (formerly "One Belt, One Road"). It soon became evident that China's trajectory and intent under Xi was perhaps moving *away* from the previous statements that seemingly embraced, or at least acknowledged, notions of global leadership, a shared community, and common interests.[5] Additionally, the Chinese nationalist drive would further intensify under the Xi leadership, evident when in 2015 China launched its "Made in China 2025" plan. As one thread of the broader "China Dream," Beijing authorities sought to reduce China's dependence on foreign technology, while steering the substantial resources of the state toward supporting the advancement of "national champion" companies across ten strategic industries.[6]

Like preceding presidents, Obama endeavored to develop cooperation with China but also to control differences through dialogue and through sterner methods of "pressure, hedging, and balancing." This was, indelibly, a position adopted on the back of Bush's difficulties with Chinese cooperation in the War on Terror and the domain of nuclear non-proliferation, despite the administration's strong engagement-focused policies. Observably, some hedging was needed since Chinese leaders would not always keep to the spirit of agreements. The weight given to each element of this engagement policy shifted over the course of Obama's two terms in office, while remaining a predominating force. The administration began with the goal of pursuing a cooperative relationship that could foster regional and global solutions while also balancing and toughening its strategy in response to China's more forthright objectives and claims for the region. Additionally, it unequivocally embedded the U.S.-China relationship within a comprehensive regional strategy. This "rebalance" toward Asia (initially described as a "pivot") also changed in response to the altering strategic environment. Indeed, the notion of building a cooperative regional structure and cultivating productive relationships with rising powers (China most prominent among them) would progressively move to a position of bolstering security and economic cooperation with established U.S. partners and with new regional allies as a means to counteract the threat presented by China's maritime challenges. For the Obama administration, and over the course of its second term in office, while elements of cooperation and of competition oscillated back and forth, the latter became a more prominent feature as China asserted its claims in the Indo-Pacific.[7]

The emergence of Xi Jinping and the "China Dream"

One of the most significant developments to impact the Obama administration's China policy during its second term was the coming to power of Xi Jinping. Preceding his attainment of the top position, it looked as though Xi was going to be a more willing participant in extending a "collaborative hand" to Obama. During a visit to the United States in February 2012, Xi said he had reached an agreement with President Obama and Vice President Biden where the two states would launch a "new path of cooperative partnership between major countries featuring harmonious coexistence, sound interactions and win-win cooperation."[8] While both agreed that certain elements for this "new model" in U.S.-China relations were already underway, the Obama administration reassured Beijing that it welcomed "a strong, prosperous and successful China that plays a greater role in world affairs." In response, Chinese authorities stated that they welcomed "the United States as an Asia-Pacific nation that contributes to peace, stability, and prosperity in the region."[9] With this in mind, both parties also acknowledged that the relationship needed to keep working on ways to mitigate the potential for tensions to escalate into conflict, with many observers in both Washington and Beijing pointing to a somewhat veiled yet prevalent distrust on both sides of the U.S.-China relationship. As conveyed, notwithstanding the United States' "new model of cooperation" rhetoric, it concurrently remained committed to executing a strategic "rebalancing" to the Asia-Pacific, conceived, in part, to assure Asian allies anxious about the strategic assertions of China's expanding aims in the region.[10]

Xi and his Chinese leadership formalized their positions at the Chinese Communist Party's 18th Congress in November 2012, as well as Xi's realization of the seminal role of state presidency, which would take place at the opening session of the 12th National People's Congress in March 2013. Here, Xi would be expected to serve as president for two five-year terms, until 2023.[11] In their early stages in office, Xi and his colleagues advanced a firm desire to strengthen and improve the U.S.-China relationship. Xi quickly accepted Obama's request to attend the June 2013 presidential summit, which presented an opportunity for continued dialogue minus the ceremonial formalities that previous Chinese leaders had stipulated during their respective visits to the United States. Under Xi, China's new leaders demonstrated a greater readiness to put pressure on North Korea over its nuclear program, while also agreeing to participate in a new phase of "substantive" negotiations with the United States over a bilateral investment treaty, abandoning some provisions that had hindered discussions in the past. With the White House alleging that cyber infringements into U.S. government and private networks were attributable to official Chinese actors, they agreed to create a high-level working group on cyber security. Additionally, they also committed China's military to an ambitious program of high-level exchanges and moderate operational collaboration with the United States' military. Xi signified he would keep working with the U.S. in addressing global climate change by lowering the intake and manufacturing of hydrofluorocarbons (HFCs),[12] and subsequently would sign a significant joint statement.[13]

Despite these more cooperative sentiments, however, it was also evident that several areas of mistrust would remain pronounced in the new Xi-Obama era. Unsurprisingly, skepticism remained especially evident on matters pertaining to national security and more broadly Washington's interests in the Asia-Pacific. For one, the U.S. government continued to view China's intensifying military modernization as being designed, in part, to inhibit the U.S. military's autonomy of movement in Asia and prevent a U.S. intervention in the occurrence of Chinese use of force against Taiwan. The immediate concern was that China's emboldened use of intimidation in disputes with its neighbors over territory in the East and South China Seas could undercut the stability on which the wealth of the region depended.[14] While such points in the bilateral continuum were in many ways expected, there were other more significant changes taking place within China that would come to the fore across the second term of Obama's time in office, namely, Xi's "China Dream."

The "China Dream" emerged in reference and strategy in November 2012, coinciding with Xi's appointment to the top post within the Chinese Communist Party (CCP). Extrapolating on its meaning and significance in his first address to the nation as head of state on March 17, Xi called upon China to "make persistent efforts, [to] press ahead with indomitable will, [to] continue to push forward the great cause of socialism with Chinese characteristics, and [to] strive to achieve the Chinese dream of great rejuvenation of the

Chinese nation." While not going into explicit detail on the logistics associated with the "dream," he did argue that "to realize the Chinese road, we must spread the Chinese spirit, which combines the spirit of the nation with patriotism as the core and the spirit of the time with reform and innovation as the core."[15] If this was evidence of a new policy to export its ideology or even its large labor force to new areas, this was not yet on the administration's radar. While ambitious, calm, and symbolic, the seminal speech nonetheless coincided with an intense 200 days in office in which Xi would press for a remarkable array of policy changes and adjustments at an astonishing pace. At this time, the "China Dream" brand was embedded into Party doctrine, establishing stringent new rules governing the behavior of officials, guiding parameters on what ideas could be openly "accepted" and discussed, and even going as far as firmly (and specifically) muzzling a liberal newspaper in southern China over its endorsement of "constitutionalism."[16] An emerging theme of China's new foreign policy, looking back, was the extent to which these first movements would herald the departure from Deng Xiaoping's long-standing policy of "*taoguang yanghui, yousuo zuowei*" (keeping a low profile while contributing in selective areas) toward an approach that was more assertive and conflict-driven.

Discernibly, the "China Dream" sought to expand upon China's strengths in business and development construction while turning the country into a defining global leader with an avant-garde technological base. As a first plank in this dream, in September of 2013, Xi revealed the Belt and Road Initiative. Initially, this was undertaken in response to Secretary of State Hillary Clinton's call in October 2011 to create what she described as a "New Silk Road" initiative so as to boost trade and therefore stability in West Asian states.[17] Of course, in adopting this initiative for the Chinese state and positioning it under their "One Belt, One Road" banner, Xi and the Beijing authorities moved briskly in establishing an ambitious infrastructure investment program that would seek to internationalize the renminbi and build greater investment opportunities for the country's state-owned enterprises (SOEs) across land and sea routes connecting Eurasia and the Indian Ocean. Other developments also took place at a rapid pace including the

119

establishment of the Asian Infrastructure Investment Bank (AIIB), while stipulating objectives to eliminate poverty in China by the end of 2020, the 100th anniversary of the establishment of the CCP. Xi further ratcheted up the pressure on Taiwan, describing it as a "political issue that can't be passed on for generations," and proceeded to execute a long-held strategy to construct substantive military bases in the SCS.[18] For a nation that had long eschewed large and dramatic changes to foreign policy, China's leaders seemed to be making a bold new statement about the capabilities of its new and ostensible great-power status.

It is worth extrapolating here further on the visionary goals centered around the "China Dream" and the "great rejuvenation of the Chinese nation." Noticeably, these new sentiments and policies "tapped into a deep reservoir of national pride and further solidified his [Xi's] popularity." By 2015, this rejuvenated pride allowed Xi to launch a marked restructuring of the People's Liberation Army (PLA), transforming it from a "bloated, corrupt, untested and inward-looking military" to one far more proficient in driving China's power abroad. Moreover, he coordinated the addition of "Xi Jinping Thought" into the Party's constitution to steer the state into a "new era" of national revitalization, including the elimination of term restrictions on his presidency, effectively permitting him to remain in control for life.[19] These actions would over time prove disconcerting markers for the Obama and Trump administrations, presaging a new era of enhanced state control in China and an emboldened foreign policy mandate.

As was anticipated, it was on the international stage where Xi's bolder pillars of the "China Dream" would become a source of alarm, debate, and tension for U.S. policymakers and analysts. As signified, his ambitious foreign policy agenda pertaining to the launching of the AIIB, the amplification of Chinese claims in the SCS via substantial land reclamation projects, developing military trajectory, and—perhaps most ambitious of them all—the BRI, posed many security and strategic questions to the Obama administration's second term in office. Of course, such aspirations and provocative strategic footholds that these policies evoked, were also accompanied by Xi's intensification of the Party's extensive system of ideology, propaganda, surveillance, and control, deemed an imperative ingredient to achieving the "China Dream." In this regard, during Obama's second term, there was an ongoing and persistent expansion of the Party's control over national power, which will likely extend deep into the late 2020s or beyond.[20]

China's military modernization during Obama's second term

In seeking to find some form of equilibrium or balance, it was the issue of China's masked and by all measures offensively orientated military modernization that would prove to be one of the most significant challenges for the administration. It was evident earlier on during the second term that the new Chinese leadership would seek the development and even expansion of a vigorous military in ensuring the "Dream's" realization. Specifically, Xi underscored the PLA's warfighting capabilities as the primary goal of China's military modernization endeavors,[21] encompassing the enhancement of its "real combat awareness" with the capacity to "fight and win wars."[22] As part of this equation, and solidifying his support, Xi undertook a concentrated anti-corruption operation throughout the armed forces, investigating and punishing high-level officers across the military's leadership.[23] Aside from reaffirming loyalty to and compliance with Xi, the reforms increased the speed at which modernization would take place, including the creation of a more efficient joint command system, the advancement of training to replicate the circumstances of real warfare, the augmentation of skilled and qualified personnel, and the improvement of supervision through the Central Military Commission.[24]

Unsurprisingly, China's military modernization was buttressed by a steady rise in military expenditure carefully watched by the Obama administration. According to Department of Defense (DoD) estimates, China's military budget expanded at an inflation-adjusted average of 9.7 percent annually over the period from 2003 to 2012. In continuing this trend into Obama's second term, China's officially announced budget for 2013 emerged at $114 billion, representing an increase of 10.7 percent over 2012. While these figures were considered to be substantive, China's actual military expenditure as assessed by the Pentagon was thought to reach at least $215 billion. Of course, these observations and indeed prognostications about the extent of China's opaque military modernization had begun more concertedly with the Bush administration. By the final years of Obama's first term, the Defense Strategic Guidance report, led by the DoD, had come to reflect the administration's evolving concerns, arguing that "the growth of China's military power must be accompanied by greater clarity of its strategic intentions in order to avoid causing friction in the region."[25] As a means to maintain a contingency, the report continued, the United States must "continue to make the necessary investments to ensure that we maintain regional access and the ability to operate freely in keeping with our treaty obligations and with international law."[26] Whether or not the "rebalance" to the Asia-Pacific had set out to be a primarily political and economic program, by 2013 increasing concern over China's military modernization had begun to alter the focus to include more military features.

Observing this debate within Washington, and through Obama's interlocutors, Chinese authorities repeatedly reassured administration officials that the PRC was committed to peace and to working within the international system, and emphatically not trying to undermine it. Chinese leaders also indicated that they did not have the aspirational goal nor the capacity to confront the United States' posture in Asia. In statements following his summit meeting with Obama in June 2013, Xi once again promised that China was "firmly committed" to a pathway that would attempt to engender "peaceful development."[27] Despite such assurances, however, Obama officials continued to press China to adopt a more transparent position and "clarify" some of its modernization activities.[28] By May 2013, further alarming aspects of China's military developments had required Obama to seek greater explanation in terms of Chinese intentions. As one DoD report noted, China's military modernization looked increasingly offensive, "designed to improve the capacity of [China's] armed forces to fight and win short-duration, high-intensity regional military conflict" with the United States in mind.[29] While the "principal focus and primary driver of China's military investment" was represented by Taiwan, it was also observed that China's military modernization was focused on developing a broader suite of capabilities for "protracted-scope projection" and missions in evolving spheres such as cyber, space, and electronic warfare, as well as other operations, comprising anti-piracy exercises, peacekeeping, humanitarian support and disaster relief, and regional military actions.[30] As such, greater dialogue on these developments was required to mitigate against misunderstandings, potential accidents, and escalations.

More than the simple development of existing capabilities, the Chinese military trajectory appeared to be orchestrating a build-up that was aimed toward deterring an American intervention by U.S. forces in a conflict in the Western Pacific. The United States defined such proficiencies as "anti-access/area-denial" operations while the PRC described such missions as "counter-intervention operations." Whatever the designation, Pentagon officials perceived a cause for concern in the PLA Navy's "carrier killer" anti-ship ballistic missile DF-21D, which provided China with "the capability to attack large ships, including aircraft carriers, in the western Pacific Ocean." Additionally, China had test-flown an autochthonously produced fifth-generation stealth fighter prototype, the J-20, and looked to be building a second advanced stealth aircraft, tentatively recognized as the J-31. The Defense Department perceived such planes as possible game-changers in China's "ability to strike regional airbases and facilities," which would ostensibly include U.S. military bases in Asia. Finally, China's purchase of an aircraft carrier in 2012, while described by some commentators as being more symbolic than a truly defining military projection of tangible power, was viewed as indicative of new and strategic blue-water navy ambitions. Obtained from Ukraine in 1998 and renamed *Liaoning*, the ship, defense officials observed, would attain operational efficiency "in three to four years" and likely herald the building of "several aircraft carriers over the next 15 years."[31]

The Chinese leadership's perception of its national security was clearly centered on its interpretation of predominant global movements blended with its internal situation. As indicated in the 2015 defense white paper's evaluation of the national security position, Beijing anticipated that an overall favorable external environment would remain in place for at least several more years.[32] Specifically, what was meant by "favorable" was what Chinese leaders perceived to be a period which, while acrimonious at varying intervals, would be stable enough to provide a "strategic window of opportunity" where China could enhance its broader national potency, global competitiveness, and overall "sway" with minimal serious threats. Some Chinese analysts at the time, however, also noted that from 2020 and beyond, China might be required to adapt to emerging realities and challenges, including heightened U.S. strategic attention, perceived threats from a militarily stronger Japan, a precarious global economy, and the necessity to refine and maintain its own economic development paradigm.[33] Aside from these realities, the white paper also identified another positive trend: the continual shift toward a multipolar world, which China believed would coincide with the apparent weakening of the United States' superpower position. Here, China's "comprehensive national strength, core competitiveness and risk-resistance capacity" would be able to take advantage of this trend while continuing to "increase" China's ever "growing international standing and influence."[34]

Given Beijing's threat perception—and following the lines of such documents as "China's Endeavors for Arms Control, Disarmament, and Non-proliferation" from 2005—the U.S. "rebalance" to the Asia-Pacific, with an augmented military presence and alliance network, appeared as the central source of regional volatility. Accordingly, Obama's "interference" in China's SCS affairs and reconnaissance operations targeted at China were the essential motivations for authorities to protect maritime interests. As the defense white paper was to state, "some external countries are also busy meddling in South China Sea affairs; a tiny few maintain constant close-in air and sea surveillance and reconnaissance against China. It is thus a long-standing task for China to safeguard its maritime rights and interests."[35] Other apparent threats mentioned included Japan's alleged remilitarization; "offshore neighbors" that antagonize Beijing in maritime zones; purportedly secessionist forces in Taiwan, Tibet, and Xinjiang; and ostensibly "anti-China" forces practicing a democratic revolution in China. Conspicuously, Chinese authorities were to note, these mounting challenges to the national interest intensified as the government's search for greater control over energy resources, the sea lines of communication, and assets overseas increased.[36] Rather than seek to reassure neighbors and global powers like the United States that these concerns were more benign and defensive, however, Chinese analysts sought instead to emphasize the security challenges and the need for a stronger navy.[37] Additionally, China would require more progressively advanced, long-range, precision, smart, unmanned, and stealthy weapons to aid the country in its search for a greater controlling stake in the region. In pointing to the emergence of new technological frontiers of tension, the 2015 defense white paper also argued that outer space and cyberspace would become pivotal conflict domains, including the assimilation and intensification of information technology into warfighting (so-called "informationization").[38]

Of course, a significant attribute in China's military modernization drive during the Obama administration was in the nuclear domain. Since the beginning of the Bush years, the number of Chinese nuclear warheads had more than doubled, and by the end of Obama's tenure in office China had built up its stockpile to an estimate of approximately 280 nuclear warheads.[39] Around 234 warheads were assigned to China's land- and sea-based ballistic missiles, while the remainder were assigned to non-operational forces, such as new systems in development, operational systems that could increase in number in the future, and reserves.[40] More specifically, China increased its deployment of new nuclear delivery systems for every part of its nuclear triad, including new mobile intercontinental ballistic missiles (ICBMs), new submarine-launched ballistic missiles (SLBMs), and a new bomber that could carry nuclear cruise missiles. The types of nuclear weapon it developed over this period included the MIRVed Dongfeng-41 ICBM and a potentially MIRVed SLBM, the Julang-3.[41]

For many within the Obama administration, China's persistent drive to modernize its nuclear arsenal was a central part of a long-term program to develop more survivable and robust forces consistent with its nuclear strategy of assured retaliation. In this regard, the Chinese government had adhered to its goal of strengthening its capabilities for strategic deterrence and nuclear counter-attack by refining the strategic early warning, command

and control, rapid reaction, and survivability and protection capabilities of its nuclear forces. In agreement with its self-declared minimum-deterrence posture, Xi maintained that China was focused on making qualitative improvements to its nuclear arsenal rather than significantly increasing its size. As indicated, these included the development of new capabilities in response to the ballistic missile defenses and precision-guided conventional strike systems being deployed by the U.S. and other states.[42]

However, during Obama's second term in office, and as China continued to expand, refine, and modernize its nuclear capabilities, it became progressively more difficult for the administration to rationalize the extent to which these developments had become essential to merely ensuring China's second-strike capability. Indeed, there was much speculation from administration officials that China's nuclear program was potentially transitioning its capacity from a strategy of *minimum* deterrence to one of *limited* deterrence. Under a "limited deterrence" doctrine, China would need to bolster the targeting of its nuclear forces with the capacity to hit cities, which would encompass expanded deployments and greater refinement.[43] In simpler terms, China's expanded nuclear objectives, conditions of use, and targets signified that these weapons were being developed to actually increase its warfighting capability. More specifically, China wanted to have the option to use its nuclear missiles prior to a nuclear strike, conceivably in tandem with its conventional missiles to deter further adversarial aggression or interference.[44] This suggested that Beijing was prepared to transition to the more assertive strategy of limited nuclear deterrence. In fact, according to one analyst, Susan Turner Haynes, there are some within China who have allegedly advocated for such strategic change.[45] Indeed, while China's defense white paper of 2015 maintained that "China has always pursued the policy of no first use of nuclear weapons and adhered to a self-defensive nuclear strategy"[46]—so as to provide minimum deterrence in the form of a credible second-strike capability—the country's rapidly modernizing nuclear forces at the time pointed to possible future shifts in its nuclear strategy and "trends that are today pushing the two powers toward heightened strategic competition."[47]

Territorial concerns and the South and East China Seas in the second term

While China's military modernization was in itself a source of concern for U.S. policymakers during the Obama administration, when assessed in the context of China's assertions in its maritime disputes, the potential for escalation became seemingly more apparent. As Obama officials were to note, China had for an extensive period of time placed a firm emphasis on addressing its sovereignty and territorial integrity, a priority manifested in its decades-long attempt to bring Taiwan under its jurisdiction. A similar importance had driven China into a succession of quarrels with its neighbors over maritime territory in the South and East China Seas. Beijing's ever-increasing preparedness to wield its maritime power and developing economic influence in such disputes, both directly and indirectly, continued to engender concerns in Asia and in the United States that China's "peaceful rise" might turn into something more troublesome upon further power aggrandizement.

In the context of the ECS, China is in an ongoing territorial dispute with Japan over the autonomy of a group of uninhabited islets, known in Japan as the Senkaku Islands and in China as the Diaoyu Islands. The islets were also claimed by Taiwan, which referred to them as the Diaoyutai Islands. While the United States did not take a position in the debate, it maintained a firm interest on the matter as it was applicable to the obligations of the U.S.-Japan Treaty of Mutual Cooperation and Security, which encompasses areas under Japanese administration. Japan-China acrimony over the islets had been fairly high at varying intervals since September 11, 2012, when Japan's government acquired three of the islands from their private Japanese proprietors, a transfer that China proclaimed at the time was comparable to "nationalizing" the islands. From this point onward, China would sustain an almost uninterrupted presence within relatively close proximity to the islets and frequently deploy vessels within the 12-nautical-mile territorial sea waters surrounding them. Specifically, it principally sent in ships from the two civilian agencies, China Maritime Surveillance and the Bureau of Fisheries, but it also dispatched navy vessels and military

127

aircraft into close contiguity with the islands. In response, Japan intensified its coast guard patrols and the operations undertaken by its Japanese Self Defense Force combatant planes. Chinese representatives signified that among their important objectives was to compel Japan to recognize that the status of the islets was actually "in dispute," an admission that Japan refrained from observing. Several commentators at the time argued that China may have been attempting to destabilize the case for potential U.S. interference in a dispute over the islets by contending that the Chinese positioning nearby demonstrated that they were no longer administered exclusively by Japan, and therefore, did not sit within the range of the U.S.-Japan Security Treaty.[48]

The Obama administration sought to clarify this delineation in Section 1286 of the National Defense Authorization Act for Fiscal Year 2013. Here, the view of Congress was that "the unilateral action of a third party"—a reference to China—"will not affect the United States' acknowledgement" of Japanese administration over the islands, thereby reasserting the United States' pledge to Japan under Article V of the Security Treaty. Both Secretary of State Hillary Clinton and Secretary of Defense Chuck Hagel sought to reaffirm this viewpoint.[49] As Clinton stated, "although the United States does not take a position on the ultimate sovereignty of the islands, we acknowledge they are under the administration of Japan and we oppose any unilateral actions that would seek to undermine Japanese administration."[50] Likewise, Hagel affirmed that "the United States opposes any unilateral or coercive action that seeks to undermine Japan's administrative control . . . we do recognize they are under the administration of Japan and fall under our security treaty obligations."[51] Characteristically, the Chinese Foreign Ministry condemned these statements as "ignorant of facts and indiscriminate of rights and wrongs."[52] After the Obama-Xi summit in June 2013, National Security Adviser Tom Donilon summarized President Obama as informing his Chinese equivalent that while the United States did not take a stance on the sovereignty of the contested islets, "the parties should seek to de-escalate, not escalate; and the parties should seek to have conversations about this through diplomatic channels and not through actions out on the East China Sea."[53]

As is well documented, it was the second term of the Obama administration that would see the SCS become a major U.S. security concern as tensions between competing claimants intensified. China had continued to maintain widespread, though inexact, assertions to substantial portions of the SCS, abundant in oil and gas deposits as well as fisheries, and a vital pathway through which a substantial portion of global trade passes. China physically commanded the Paracel Islands and seven reefs among the Spratly Islands.[54] Territory claimed by Beijing was also claimed in part by Brunei, Malaysia, the Philippines, and Vietnam, and in totality by Taiwan, with the most acrimonious of territorial differences being those between China and Vietnam and China and the Philippines. The SCS bordered a U.S. treaty ally, the Philippines, and has remained a key strategic channel for the U.S. Navy.[55] The Obama administration endorsed attempts by China's competing claimants to posit their concerns of perceived contraventions in the SCS on the dialogue agenda for regional consultations. In response, China, which contended that the disagreements were best managed between the opposing claimants bilaterally and in isolation, opposed what it perceived to be U.S. attempts to "internationalize" the disagreements. Obama also openly implored the Association of Southeast Asian Nations (ASEAN) and China to proceed with long-delayed discussions over the wording of a mandatory code of oversight that would regulate behavior in the SCS and encompass specific dispute resolution procedures. ASEAN and China announced on June 30, 2013 that they would undertake official consultations on a code of conduct at a meeting in China in September 2013.[56]

U.S. strategy, options, and responses to the East and South China Seas

The second term would certainly test the mettle of the Obama administration, particularly regarding the extent to which its strategy for deterring China's land reclamation actions would be sufficient and effective in addressing the issue. The main action in question was the plausibility of undertaking an approach to counter China's so-called "salami-slicing" method—a strategy that sought to incrementally secure a greater level of control over applicable land, waterways, and airspace in the East and South China Seas—and whether the predominant U.S. approach could be effective without spurring escalation. Various critics argued that the Obama administration did not have a coherent, all-encompassing strategy for addressing these "salami-slicing" maneuvers, and that the U.S. strategy was simply inadequate.[57] Others within the administration at the time conveyed their concerns with much emphasis relating to China's land-building activities on the basis that they were undermining stability, while additionally being inconsistent with assurances China had made under the (non-binding) 2002 Declaration on the Conduct of Parties in the South China Sea.[58] Further, China's provocative establishment of an air defense identification zone (ADIZ) in the ECS in 2013—an airspace over land or water in which the identification, location, and control of aircraft is cooperatively undertaken by civilian air traffic control and military authorities to the benefit of a state's national security—warranted an assertive, if proportional response from the United States. This was perceived by policymakers as an effort by Beijing to augment its claims over contested territories, such as the uninhabited Senkaku/Diaoyu Islands. More drastically, China's actions and claims by this stage seemed to proffer the question of whether such actions might herald a further emboldening of claims in the question of a South China Sea ADIZ.

On this specific matter, current and former Obama administration members were to respond in a unified and defiant voice. The administration would "oppose China's establishment of an ADIZ in other areas, including the South China Sea," observed Evan Medeiros, a former director of Asia affairs on the National Security Council, noting further that "we have been very clear with the Chinese that we would see that [setting another ADIZ] as a provocative and destabilizing development that would result in changes in our presence and military posture in the region."[59] In the Senate in May 2015, David Shears, assistant secretary of defense for Asian and Pacific security affairs, responded to law makers by stating that the administration was "actively assessing the military implications of land reclamation and are committed to taking effective and appropriate action."[60] The United States would consider sending ships and aircraft to within 12 nautical miles of constructed reefs near the Philippines and other islands to show its dedication to freedom of navigation (FoN) in one of the world's most active shipping lanes.[61] In this regard, the United States under Obama would proceed to fly and publicize reconnaissance flights that ran in close proximity to several of the claimed land structures, provoking Chinese admonitions to depart from the area.[62] Through publicizing the magnitude and pervasiveness of the reclamation and construction, the administration attempted to reaffirm a further message that it was unequivocal in its support for FoN.[63]

The Obama administration further ratcheted up public diplomacy to draw more attention to China's unilateral actions in the region. In a speech at the Shangri-La Dialogue in May, Defense Secretary Ash Carter remarked emphatically that there would be no mistaking America's commitment to open and free waters, emphasizing that "the United States will fly, sail, and operate wherever international law allows, as U.S. forces do all around the world."[64] These comments were made in effect to reassure partners in Southeast Asia of America's commitment as much as they were a signal to put Chinese leaders on notice about possible American responses should further provocations occur. Carter additionally appealed for a halt on island reclamation by all claimants, including China, and indicated that the administration would discuss the matter with Vietnam directly. More shrewdly, in restating the United States' extensive interest in the SCS, Carter drew attention to international legal doctrine, signed and ratified by Beijing, to convey the point that "after all, turning an underwater rock into an airfield simply does not afford the rights of sovereignty or permit restrictions on international air or maritime transit."[65] Chinese spokesmen, unsurprisingly, vigorously denied this interpretation of the law.

By mid-2015, the White House was operating on multiple fronts to restrain or contain China's assertive, and by all measures belligerent, policies in the SCS. Obama expanded Washington's security cooperation further with Japan, Malaysia, Indonesia, and, notably, the Philippines and Vietnam, seeking additionally to enhance the more strategic elements of Manila's and Hanoi's maritime resources. This comprised delivering equipment and infrastructure support to the Vietnamese coast guard, helping the Philippines create a National Coast Watch System to improve its maritime domain recognition, and performing sea reconnaissance maneuvers with Indonesia, including flights over the SCS for the first time.[66] While such actions (other than statements directly referencing the land reclamation activities) were aimed toward counteracting China's increasingly assertive maritime endeavors, Obama was at times limited with what he could do to directly prevent China's island-building activities. Namely, options for responding to those activities appeared to offer one of two conclusions: either the administration could choose a course which would elicit a strong and perhaps critical response, causing the Chinese to react more challengingly; or else otherwise, it could adopt a position that might be seen as inadequate if China did not change direction.[67]

Indeed, there was no easy solution to this issue. Obama sought to cultivate more workable options for imposing costs against further Chinese actions, but he was forced ultimately to rely on existing activities and intensifying them until such other options were presented. These included: sterner statements to China underscoring the ramifications of its ongoing island-building activities, and more generally, shifting the U.S. tone of dialogue to add greater pressure; improved publicizing, to the community and governments in the region and globally, of China's land reclamation movements and other applicable activities in the region, as well as their probable repercussions for international law and the impact on the global commons; opposing land reclamation endeavors in contested waters by both China and other claimants; improving the capability of allied and affiliate states in the region to maintain maritime domain awareness (MDA), coast guard patrols, and fishing fleet ventures in the area; the additional bolstering of U.S. security cooperation with allied and partner states in the region, particularly with India, to the extent of establishing an alliance for balancing China's assertiveness; increasing arms sales to Taiwan; and expanding U.S. Navy operations in the region, including FoN operations.[68]

Despite these Obama endeavors across 2014–2015, however, the Chinese appeared to repeatedly spurn efforts to cease and desist their island building. Critics were to note that a number of non-offensive military protests, such as a three-week deployment to the Philippines of a P-8 squadron to conduct flights over the Spratlys, did not deter China from its ongoing land reclamation ventures. What's more, nor did its impromptu nature indicate a clearly defined purpose.[69] Meanwhile, in September 2015, alarming questions emerged following the construction of what appeared to be military facilities on the islands, large enough to host offensive, combat aircraft.

By this stage, many critics argued that the Obama administration needed to go much further in considering the Pentagon's list of policy options for addressing provocations in the SCS. For some, a greater and more coherent presence involving intensified and constant surveillance by the surface fleet and air assets was needed, including further expansion of operations by U.S. warships within the Spratly archipelago, and live-fire exercises, intended to signify how the navy might approach these militarized islets—all as a means to convey American concern for Chinese actions and demonstrate that the United States was viewing China intently. Such responses, they argued, would also make it clear that the United States did not fear a conflict at sea with China. For others, Obama's approach during this defining period on the SCS issue appeared to reveal one of two things: either the Pentagon's Asia "toolkit" did not, in fact, exist or, more likely, Obama was reluctant to adopt the requisite provocative policy options that would compel China to truly re-evaluate its *own* actions. "In either case," Mark Mazza of the American Enterprise Institute remarked, "U.S. conventional deterrence is weakened and the United States has shown itself unwilling or incapable of responding to what is, in the case of island building, admittedly an extremely tough policy problem."[70]

This is not to say that there were not activities undertaken to add logistical rigor to Obama's suite of policies. In late March 2015, the Senate agreed to a budget resolution that would enable the Senate Budget Committee to support a "comprehensive, multi-year partner capacity building and security cooperation plan in the Indo-Pacific region, including for a regional maritime domain awareness architecture and for bilateral and multilateral exercises, port calls, and training activities of the United States

Armed Forces and Coast Guard."[71] The joint security operations envisaged in this adjustment—in particular collaborative MDA operations—were one such Congressional effort to embolden U.S. security strategy in Southeast Asia. The National Defense Authorization Act, presented by the Senate Armed Services Committee for the fiscal year 2016, approved $50 million to deliver equipment, materials, and training to Southeast Asian nations so that they could construct maritime domain awareness facilities to tackle mounting sovereignty challenges in the SCS. This was introduced formally at the Shangri-La Dialogue by Defense Secretary Carter, who called for a new security initiative to assist regional states enhance their maritime capabilities.[72] As stated:

> I am pleased to announce that DoD will be launching a new Southeast Asia Maritime Security Initiative. And thanks to the leadership of the Senators here today . . . and others, Congress has taken steps to authorize up to $425 million dollars for these maritime capacity-building efforts . . . by taking steps now to ensure the regional architecture that has reinforced norms, stronger institutions and alliances, more capabilities, and deeper connectivity, we can ensure our successors at the Shangri-La Dialogue in twenty years will be talking about the challenges and opportunities presented by the rise of yet other Asia-Pacific nations.[73]

As a defining point of consternation and acrimony between the U.S. and China, the SCS and accompanying activities would remain an issue across Obama's second term in office and continue deep into Trump's tenure. Indeed, since 2013, the PRC has constructed and fortified artificial islands on seven locations in the Spratly Island chain, and sought to stymie other states in their pursuit of economic or other activities within the exclusive economic zones they are permitted under the UN Convention on the Law of the Sea. Ultimately, many analysts have contended that Obama was unsuccessful in credibly pushing back against China's island grabbing in the SCS, which has since only intensified despite the decision by the Permanent Court of Arbitration in The Hague repudiating its territorial claims there. Instead, the administration continued to rely on rhetoric or symbolic actions that taken together were limited.

For some analysts, the "salami-slicing" activities of China's reclamation efforts had cumulatively altered the strategic appearance of the SCS during Obama's years in office, to the extent that China has now consolidated its influence over the strategic corridor between the Indian and Pacific Oceans—through which one third of global maritime trade passes. Additionally, it has also secured a substantive stake in the region's natural resources, "coercing other claimants seeking to explore for oil and gas in territories that they themselves control under the United Nations Convention on the Law of the Sea. Vietnam, for example, has been forced to scrap a project on its very own continental shelf."[74]

China's Belt and Road Initiative and strategic footholds

It is clear that the Chinese government views a growing economy as vital to maintaining social stability. By 2013, President Xi was well aware that China faced a plethora of significant economic challenges that could impede future development, including distortive economic policies that had caused an over-dependence on fixed investment and exports for economic growth (rather than on consumer demand), state support for state-owned entities, a weak banking system, disparities in income, increasing pollution, and the comparative deficiency in the rule of law in China. Xi promised to address these issues by applying policies to embolden the position of the market in the economy so as to foster innovation, make consumer expenditure the major power of the economy, increase social safety net coverage, boost the expansion of less-polluting businesses (such as services), and crack down on official state corruption. The capacity for the Chinese government to apply such modifications, it was viewed, would likely play a significant role in determining whether the state could continue to sustain comparative economic growth rates. Clearly, China's rising economic power had enabled it to become progressively engaged in global economic policies and projects, particularly infrastructure expansion. In this regard, the BRI signified a grand strategy by China to finance infrastructure throughout Asia, Europe, Africa, and beyond. If efficacious, China's economic ingenuities could, it was viewed by Beijing, markedly expand its export and investment markets and increase its "soft power" globally.[75]

As a means to revitalize China's economy and boost its "soft power," while also attaining strategic footholds in key locations around the world, President Xi launched two projects intended to spur connection and integration across continents: by land, an endeavor known as the "Silk Road Economic Belt" and, by sea, an endeavor known as the "21st Century Maritime Silk Road." Taken together, these inextricably linked projects would become the BRI. A central pillar of the initiative encompassed the support of PRC institutions facilitating transportation and energy infrastructure schemes in a variety of states, with particular focus on identifying and removing those impediments that could undermine investment, trade, and people-to-people links. Additionally, the BRI was intended to assuage congestion in the Chinese economy and stir new economic activity to China's western region.[76] As China does not issue its own authoritative figures, the size and scope of PRC financing, investments, and loans dispensed under the BRI are contested.[77] From the perspective of the Obama administration, the BRI was much more than just an infrastructural/economic program. While the economic motivations were certainly comprehended, the BRI was also perceived by many in the administration to be an avenue by which Beijing could cultivate diplomatic and security interests so as to: attain key energy supply links, and, perhaps more concerningly, enable future Chinese military or intelligence usage of Chinese-constructed ports and other infrastructure for strategic purposes.[78]

While the aforementioned perceptions certainly garnered traction, Chinese authorities made concerted efforts to assure the international community that the BRI was primarily about infrastructure, trade, investment integration, and connectivity. In fast-forwarding to a 2017 statement by President Xi:

> The Belt and Road Initiative calls for joint contribution and it has a clear focus, which is to promote infrastructure construction and connectivity, strengthen coordination on economic policies, enhance complementarity of development strategies and boost interconnected

136

development to achieve common prosperity. This initiative is from China, but it belongs to the world. It is rooted in history, but it is oriented toward the future. It focuses on the Asian, European and African continents, but it is open to all partners. I am confident that the launch of the Belt and Road Initiative will create a broader and more dynamic platform for Asia-Pacific cooperation.[79]

With its inception coinciding with the Obama administration's second term in office, the BRI was viewed with caution from the outset, and perceived much differently to how Chinese leaders articulated it. According to Jacob Stokes, while the United States' involvement in Central Asia was diminishing as its role in Afghanistan was winding down, the advent of Chinese involvement across Eurasia, the Indian Ocean, and the Middle East would clearly test Beijing's capacity to balance economic competition and cooperation with strategic desires—and overall, its capacity to "work with, rather than against, neighbors and global political powers."[80] That is, "if Chinese actions go beyond the basic protection of its investments into broader geopolitical actions, international perception of China's future foreign interventions could give credence to suspicions of Beijing's imperialistic desires. Such a dynamic has characterized China's relations in the East and South China Seas in recent years; a westward corollary is not hard to imagine."[81] Likewise, in Europe, China has engendered economic influence through expanding trade relationships and BRI-related infrastructure investments not conditional on standards for democratic governance and human rights, particularly in Eastern Europe, Greece, and Italy. According to Andrea Kendall-Taylor and David Shullman, this form of engagement will ultimately translate into political and strategic leverage and coercion, as it already has in many countries in Asia.[82]

Indeed, across both the Obama and Trump administrations it is evident that the BRI has provided China with the opportunity to expand its military objectives and overall strategic presence. By the start of 2019, Chinese state-owned operations were being run in approximately 75-plus ports and terminals out of 34 states, and in Greece, Pakistan, and Sri Lanka, PRC investment in ports has been followed by high-level visits from Chinese naval vessels. Beijing also revealed that it would implement separate adjudication courts for BRI projects, thereby using the scheme to foster an alternative legal system—compared to international legal norms—girded by Chinese rules. Indicatively, such advances have also transferred to the political domain. For instance, in Ethiopia and Sudan, the CCP has trained officials on ways and means to adjust and "cultivate" public perceptions in the media, extending guidance on what legislation to pass, and which monitoring and surveillance technologies to utilize. Possibly the most notable endeavor has been China's campaign to foster its vision of a "closed Internet." Under the umbrella of "cyber-sovereignty," Beijing has propagated the notion that states should be permitted to, as one official document stated, "choose their own path of cyber development, model of cyber regulation and Internet public policies." In this regard, it has pressed for discussions about Internet authority that would benefit states and prohibit delegates from civil society and the private sector from playing an active role in spurring accountability, and broader questions relating to privacy.[83]

It is evident that during Obama's second term in office, the BRI transferred from a policy of purported investment, infrastructure, and connectivity, to one that clearly presented security-related questions and points of consternation for the administration. In encouraging SOEs to capitalize in high-risk markets in favor of the BRI, the PRC in effect was able to gain controlling stakes in assets such as strategic ports and stipulate technical/logistical standards such as railroad track indicators or types of satellite navigation systems for the next phase of its global economic advancement. While such decisions may have appeared as initially questionable from the context of a liberal political system and a market economy, they now appear as a more strategically coherent grand strategy in the PRC to overtake the United States as the lender and leader of choice.[84] At a regional level, prominent Chinese commentators and analysts also contended in frank terms that the BRI was purely and simply rolled out as a strategic instrument to respond to and thereby counteract the Obama administration's "pivot" to Asia.

In 2015 Justin Yifu Lin, a leading policy adviser and a former chief economist at the World Bank, specifically claimed that President Xi initiated the BRI to offset U.S. policies such as the "pivot"/"rebalance" and the Trans-Pacific Partnership (TPP). He also argued that China should use its economic assets including its large foreign reserves and knowledge in constructing infrastructure to bolster its position in the region. Similarly, Tang Min, councilor in the Chinese State Council, observed that China and many developing economies had been excluded from the U.S.-led TPP and that these states required a "third pole," namely the BRI. Many China observers in the United States initially downplayed the initiative's significance, implying that it was a public relations ploy meant to depict China as a benign power, a project intended to embolden Xi's legacy, or an impractical scheme that China, which had struggled with some development initiatives in the past, would fail to implement.[85]

Several analysts at the time argued that this apparent underappreciation was somewhat evident within the administration itself. Congress did not hold a single hearing dedicated to the BRI; nor did the U.S.-China Economic and Security Review Commission, a body that Congress created in 2000 to monitor bilateral trade and security issues. Additionally, at both the 2015 and the 2016 summits of the U.S.-China Strategic and Economic Dialogue (S&ED), the highest-level yearly meeting conducted between the two states, U.S. and Chinese officials specified approximately 100 points of prospective teamwork without commenting on the BRI once. Further, in their public statements, U.S. officials had a propensity to mention the initiative only in passing and in ambiguous terms.

According to Gal Luft, the United States' incapacity to appropriately respond to the BRI was particularly concerning given that Washington inadvertently helped hasten Beijing's interest in the project. As he specifies, the "pivot," or "rebalance" to Asia that Barack Obama commenced in 2011 "may have been somewhat limited, but it had nonetheless intensified China's perceptions of encirclement by the United States and its allies"—real or embellished—as well as the Obama administration's de facto exclusion of China from the TPP. Such actions essentially stymied many of China's aspirations in the Pacific, "leading Beijing to seek strategic opportunities to its west."[86] Other commentators argued, however, that it was a delicate form of competition, but one that many in the Obama administration saw as the most important geopolitical power struggle in the world. As stated by Michael Green, "It's not a black-and-white contest between us and China, even though the president has presented it that way to sell it to Democrats . . . The Pacific Partnership puts pressure on the Chinese to up their game. We are somewhere between direct competition over who will make the rules and a competitive liberalization that will eventually create some common rules around the world."[87]

Former Australian prime minister Kevin Rudd, who was based at Harvard University at the time, concluded that in both China and the United States there was a rush "to believe that the two countries are now locked into some sort of irreversible and increasingly fractious zero-sum game." While China was seeking to develop its political and diplomatic influence across Asia, principally through its formidable economic presence, there was little evidence "that Beijing had any intentions of fully revising, let alone replacing, institutions like the United Nations, which have served China's interests well." Instead, China would most likely pursue a stronger voice in the several enduring reform processes of the system, and within each of the institutions would maintain the overall Chinese rubric of "greater multipolarity" and a "more democratic order." That said, Xi had also "ended former paramount leader Deng Xiaoping's foreign policy orthodoxy over the past 35 years of 'hide your strength, bide your time, never take the lead,'" and in its place, was more inclined to incorporate a "more vigorous, activist and assertive international policy to advance Chinese interests both in the region and beyond." For Rudd, notwithstanding certain tensions that permeated bilateral relations, "the political machinery of the China-U.S. relationship—anchored in regular, working-level summitry between the two presidents and supported by the framework of the high-level meetings of the Strategic and Economic Dialogue and its subsidiary policy working groups—is functioning reasonably effectively."[88] But despite these rather optimistic sentiments of Rudd, it was evident that the BRI—whether in response to Obama's "pivot"/"rebalance" or the TPP, or whether as a part of Xi's strategic global posture—would remain a source of U.S. foreign policy conjecture and debate deep into the Trump administration's tenure in office.

The North Korea nuclear issue

One of the most significant security challenges for the United States in its relationship with China has been the North Korea nuclear program. For years, the United States and the international community have sought to negotiate a conclusion to North Korea's nuclear and missile advancement and its trade of ballistic missile technology. Such endeavors have been replete with phases of crisis, impasse, and cautious progress toward denuclearization. Overall, North Korea has remained a significant challenge for the global nuclear non-proliferation regime and a specific source of friction for the Sino-U.S. relationship. The United States has pursued a range of policy responses to the proliferation challenges presented by North Korea, involving military collaboration with U.S. allies in the region, extensive sanctions, and non-proliferation mechanisms such as export controls.[89]

By the end of Obama's second term, the administration's "strategic patience" approach was under significant pressure, and deemed by many critics to be an unbridled failure in its appeasement disposition. Indeed, during Obama's tenure in office, North Korea had conducted four nuclear weapons tests: in 2006, 2009, 2013, and two notably advanced tests in 2016. Although highly disputed by analysts at the time, Kim Jong-un claimed that the marked January 2016 test was thermonuclear in nature.[90] This apparent technological breakthrough was also declared by the regime back in December 2015 when Kim, on a visit to the Pyongchon Revolutionary Site, indicated that the North Korean state had developed such thermonuclear capabilities.[91] Of course, many in the international community queried such advancements, while others had the audacity to scoff and even laugh at these pronouncements. Notwithstanding the bold January 6, 2016 declaration, many analysts still argued that while *this* test could have been of a boosted fission device, it was not possible to necessarily ascertain the test's specific nature without obtaining the requisite particles in the atmosphere, and taking such particles to a radionuclide monitoring station for analysis.[92] With that said, it was clear that the January test was different and illustrative of the progress the hermit regime was making in its technological quest to unify a long-range missile with a powerful nuclear device. As such the test garnered extensive international condemnation, and saw China, a traditional ally of the regime, adjust its approach and increase its support for a UN resolution to apply further sanctions against the North Korean state.[93]

For the Obama administration, the 2016 test continued the long line of obfuscation by the North Korean regime, where it had historically veered from a periodical willingness to negotiate, on the one hand, through to recalcitrant and provocative actions, on the other. For instance, after extensive diplomatic meetings during the first Obama term—a visit from former president Jimmy Carter to North Korea in April 2011; a July 2011 meeting between the U.S. special representative for North Korea policy, Stephen Bosworth, and the North Korean first vice foreign minister, Kim Kye-gwan; and a February 2012 bilateral meeting in Beijing—an agreement to halt uranium enrichment in exchange for U.S. food aid was reached in early 2012.[94] In an apparent conciliatory shift, North Korea subsequently announced its suspension of uranium enrichment at the Yongbyon Nuclear Scientific Research Center and said that it would not conduct any further tests of nuclear weapons while such productive negotiations involving the United States were taking place. The agreement required the cessation of long-range missile tests and also included permission for International Atomic Energy Agency (IAEA) inspectors to monitor operations at Yongbyon. In affirming this move, the United States said that it had no aggressive intentions toward North Korea and was prepared to improve the bilateral relationship.[95] However, in what can be viewed as a representation of both North Korean actions and bilateral relations between the two states, Pyongyang launched a provocative long-range missile test in April 2012, two months after the agreement. While not necessarily surprising, the agreement and backflip again reflected the limitations of the Obama administration's "strategic patience" approach to Pyongyang.[96]

Clearly, the United States and China share a mutual concern in peace and stability on the Korean Peninsula, and ultimately, attaining verifiable denuclearization of the peninsula. With China operating as North Korea's leading provider of fuel and food resources and its most formidable political ally, the Obama administration, much like its predecessor, regularly called on Beijing to provide greater leverage in its relationship with Pyongyang—by encouraging North Korea to move away from its provocative behavior and toward denuclearization. During Obama's second term Washington specifically pressed Beijing to bolster its application of UN sanctions against North Korea. As observed by then-national security adviser Tom Donilon in a speech on Asia policy in March 2013, any "prospects for a peaceful resolution" necessitated "close U.S. coordination with China's new government." In this regard, "no country, including China, should conduct 'business as usual' with a North Korea that threatens its neighbors." To facilitate "a clear path to ending North Korea's nuclear program," China's overall "support at the UN Security Council and its continued insistence that North Korea completely, verifiably, and irreversibly abandon its WMD and ballistic missile programs" was imperative.[97]

Since the death of former North Korean leader Kim Jong-il in December 2011 and the succession of his son Kim Jong-un as North Korea's supreme leader, Chinese-North Korean relations have gone through intermittent periods of strain and tension. North Korea repeatedly disregarded China's admonitions not to carry out rocket launches and nuclear tests, and in May 2012 provoked anger in China when its navy boarded a Chinese fishing boat and incarcerated the crew for more than two weeks.[98] These episodes were subsequently followed up with a sequence of firm Chinese actions against North Korea. In January 2013, for instance, shortly after China's new leaders began their new roles, China endorsed United Nations Security Council (UNSC) Resolution 2087 denouncing North Korea's December 2012 rocket launch. In March, China supported Resolution 2094, which reinforced existing sanctions against North Korea in response to the state's February 2013 nuclear test. In April 2013, Xi Jinping warned Pyongyang during a speech at the Boao forum in Hainan that "no one should be allowed to throw a region or even the whole world into chaos for selfish gain."[99] The statement was widely construed to be pointed at the young and precocious new leader. In May 2013, China's state bank, the Bank of China, called for the account of North Korea's primary foreign-exchange bank, the Foreign Trade Bank, to be shut down.[100] Meanwhile, in late June, Chinese leaders insulted North Korea by accommodating a high-profile visit by the South Korean president, Park Geun-hye, when they had yet to host Kim Jong-un. During the meeting with President Park, Xi delivered what was understood to be another stern notice to North Korea, stating that "China's stance in working to achieve peninsula denuclearization is firm, and its attitude is serious and sincere . . . [China] opposes the action of any party in wrecking peace and stability," a statement clearly referring to the North Korean state.[101]

North Korea was a significant topic of dialogue both at the conference between President Obama and President Xi in June 2013 and at the fifth round of the S&ED in July 2013. After the S&ED, the State Department remarked that both states "agreed on the fundamental importance of the denuclearization of the Korean Peninsula in a peaceful manner," and on "the importance of working together to ensure full implementation of UNSC Resolution 2094 and other relevant resolutions by all UN Member States."[102] China has an extensive history of being committed to delivering material sustenance to the Pyongyang regime based primarily on concerns about the destabilizing ramifications should the regime collapse—which China considers could entail military conflict, floods of North Korean refugees entering China's northeast provinces, and potentially, a reintegrated Korean Peninsula that would no doubt involve the United States in the equation right on China's doorstep. Such potential scenarios have been a source of concern for China and have clearly contributed to its participation, albeit at times lackluster, in pressurizing North Korea and endorsing and implementing sanctions against the regime.

Indeed, the administration's perception of China's somewhat passive approach to the North Korea issue led Obama to formally call for a heightened and more tangible involvement in the equation. In February 2013, for instance, the United States House of Representatives passed a resolution denouncing North Korea for its "flagrant and repeated violations" of UNSC resolutions and for other provocations. The resolution, however, also called on the PRC to pressure North Korean leaders to curb their provocative behavior, relinquish and dismantle their nuclear and missile programs through curtailing crucial economic support and trade to North Korea, and adhere to all relevant international agreements and UNSC and IAEA resolutions. Additionally, the House called on China to take specific and "immediate actions to prevent the trans-shipment of illicit technology, military equipment, and dual-use items through its territory, waters, and airspace that could be used in North Korea's nuclear weapons and ballistic missile programs."[103]

In assessing the last year of the Obama administration, it is evident that despite varied Chinese support for UN resolutions—particularly in the context of improving implementation and execution—the North Korean nuclear issue would escalate to unprecedented levels as the regime proceeded to undertake its fifth nuclear test. On September 9, 2016, the anniversary of the founding of North Korea, the U.S. Geological Survey detected a 5.3 magnitude earthquake at the regime's nuclear testing site. North Korea swiftly acknowledged it had completed a nuclear test in a provocative announcement, stating that it had successfully constructed a warhead small enough to place onto the end of a missile and had the capacity to counter or impede any attacks from its adversaries. Analysts believed the explosion's yield to be between 10 and 20 kilotons, an explosion significantly larger than all previous tests carried out by the regime.[104]

The test drew immediate international condemnation. President Obama called it "a grave threat" to international security and stated that the regime's actions had only destabilized the region. In the previous two years, the prevailing consensus on the North's nuclear program had been that it was predominantly a political symbol, and the only power asset Pyongyang had to feasibly garner tangible economic and diplomatic responses. However, with the pace of both nuclear and missile testing intensifying, the prospect of North Korea actually unifying a nuclear warhead and missile technology onto one device could no longer be considered farfetched. As stated by Kelsey Davenport, the director for nonproliferation policy at the Arms Control Association, "It is likely now that North Korea could at this point put a nuclear warhead on a short- or medium-range missile which could reach South Korea, Japan and U.S. military installations in the region."[105]

145

As the last decisive setback for Obama's "strategic patience" policy, the two 2016 North Korean nuclear tests coincided with a sequence of missile advancements in the same year: the first being the launch of a two-stage, solid-fueled and submarine-launched missile in August; and the second, in September, being the test of three new aluminum-bodied versions of Scud missiles with a 1,000-kilometer (620-mile) range. As Davenport again states, "All this activity is aimed at expanding the size of North Korea's nuclear arsenal and expanding its delivery options . . . It is taking steps to quality-improve its missiles, using solid fuel so they can be deployed more quickly, and extending their range. The trajectory points to a growing North Korean nuclear threat and the next U.S. administration will have to prioritize that threat."[106]

Aside from condemning North Korea, the Obama administration again warned China that it would blacklist Chinese businesses and banks that continued to do illicit business with North Korea through failure to sufficiently execute UN sanctions against Pyongyang. The sterner U.S. approach reflected the administration's frustrations with China and the perception that it was not rigorously enforcing existing sanctions to help curtail Pyongyang's nuclear and missile program, which U.S. policy in terms of both sanctions and diplomacy had failed to dent. In October 2016, just after North Korea conducted its fifth and largest nuclear test, U.S. deputy secretary of state Antony Blinken emphasized to Chinese officials the necessity for China to be much firmer in its enforcement of sanctions, while U.S. national security adviser Susan Rice and secretary of state John Kerry, stressed the importance of comprehensively blocking financial flows to Pyongyang during a meeting with Chinese state councilor Yang Jiechi in New York on November 1, 2016. In response to the U.S. caution, Beijing officials said they believed pressure alone on North Korea would not work and that they opposed any U.S. actions that would impact Chinese commercial entities. With President Barack Obama's administration in its final weeks, U.S. officials said that any major steps would likely be left to the incoming Trump administration in January 2017.[107]

Many analysts have argued that the Obama administration's repeated calls to China regarding the firmer implementation of

UN sanctions on North Korea saw an overall improvement in the PRC's actions. But while Chinese officials may have been somewhat swayed by Obama's pleas during 2016, it was during the defining year of 2017 that the Chinese leadership—in response to the security implications emanating from potential U.S. strike options of the said year—had no choice but to intensify and step up its sanctions application. In this regard, China adhered more closely to the range of caps stipulated by UNSC sanctions relating to the import of North Korean coal, Pyongyang's largest export item. In February 2017 it indicated that it was suspending all imports of coal from North Korea for the rest of the year. A former UNSC panel member, however, did make the comment that it was too early to declare if Beijing's conformity was "merely cosmetic" or if it "signal[ed] a shift" in sanctions enforcement. It must be noted at this point that while coal imports from North Korea were indeed cut, China continued to import certain metals even though Security Council Resolution 2321, passed in September 2016, banned countries from importing copper, nickel, silver, and zinc from North Korea. In assessing China's performance, the former panel member again observed, the "real test is time."

In under a year, not long after Obama's departure from the White House, North Korea would test a long-range missile that potentially could reach not only the west coast of the United States but also the east coast, including New York City and Washington, D.C. With the high likelihood that this long-range missile could also adequately possess a nuclear warhead that could survive the vast distance and violent re-entry into the earth's atmosphere, and be accurate enough to strike in close proximity to the above targets, a new threshold of horror was passed. Of course, aside from U.S. responses, the role of Chinese participation would be a crucial requirement, to the extent that 2017 would see an increase in the Chinese enforcement of UNSC sanctions. While Chinese trade and aid to North Korea was already at a reputedly smaller level than previous contributions, clearly Beijing was very much concerned with the bellicose rhetoric of Trump and the administration's seeming preparedness to undertake preventive strike options against North Korea—not to mention the catastrophic ramifications that this would present to the

Chinese state. Although still a point of consternation and debate for U.S. commentators and policymakers alike, by 2017–18 it was evident China had agreed to progressively more stringent UNSC sanctions resolutions and, to an unprecedented degree, appeared to be implementing these measures.[108] Of course, as a reflection of the U.S.-China bilateral relations in the context of North Korea, this semblance of progress and participation would not necessarily remain static.

Conclusion

During September 2016, President Barack Obama undertook his last trip to Asia, marking what some viewed as the final lap in his acclaimed "rebalance." The narrative of this policy as proclaimed by current and former administration officials was unsurprisingly optimistic—explicating the audacious but cautious implementation of a strategy from its first day in office. However, behind the facade and as indicated during this chapter, what actually transpired was a much more challenging terrain. In seeking to carry out a fresh cooperative strategy that presented strategic security assurances to Beijing, while urging it to join with the United States in solving common global challenges, the Obama administration was often caught in a perpetual struggle to find the optimal balance.

In briefly looking back to the first term as a point of reference, the conciliatory rhetoric rooted in Obama's November 2009 speech (that he did not seek to contain China and that Beijing was pivotal to Washington's global agenda) led commentators to articulate a new "G2" strategy. As an indication, they highlighted the fact that the administration did not authorize arms sales to Taiwan in its first year in office, and that the president declined a meeting with the Dalai Lama. However, during the first year and a half, varying developments undercut the earlier period of optimism. In the case of China, Beijing disappointed America's G2 strategy by not providing ample political capital on climate change at the 2009 Copenhagen summit (although it would rectify this during the second term in Paris in 2015); and moreover, it emboldened its territorial claims in the East and South China Seas. In response,

Obama bolstered relations with its allies such as South Korea and Australia, both of whom were prepared to participate in signature Obama ventures like climate change, nuclear security, and global health. In terms of trade, beginning with the National Export Initiative in the 2010 State of the Union speech, Obama fostered a marked improvement on trade that connected the nation's economic revival and job creation to export promotion, ultimately contributing to the enactment of the U.S.-Korea Free Trade Agreement and the advocating of the TPP. More significantly, Obama provided more "face time" to Asia. He went against the practice of one annual trip to Asia after the United States joined the East Asia Summit in 2011, and traveled outside the predictable Northeast Asia course to Indonesia, India, and Australia as part of a broader G20 strategy that included Asia. The 2016 trip mentioned above was the eleventh of Obama's presidency, and was both a culmination and contribution to the "pivot" as declared in a seminal speech to the Australian parliament in 2011.

In the context of Obama's second term, the administration attempted to execute a nuanced strategy with Beijing, balancing compartments of competition and cooperation that resulted in substantial (albeit varied) agreements on climate change in Paris, counter-proliferation (Iran and North Korea), and cyber security. Of course, these relative achievements were countered by persistent Chinese land reclamations and military infrastructure construction efforts on atolls in the SCS, and antagonistic patrolling in the ECS in spite of international criticism and U.S. FoNOPs reprisals. Additionally, the Obama administration at times struggled to come to terms with President Xi's lofty ambitions associated with the BRI and overall strategic assertions. Clearly, the "pivot's" legacy was markedly impacted by the demise of the TPP. The twelve-member free-trade pact, the first to include the world's second- and third-largest economies, was not just an agreement limited to trade and commerce. From an Obama perspective, the agreement had the capacity to impact much more than just tariffs, with the potential to play a decisive role in engendering marked reforms on labor, the environment, food safety, intellectual property, cyber security, the digital economy, development, and other applicable standards—not to mention the potential for the U.S. to redefine the rules of law governing trade in the region.[109]

Overall, the second term of the Obama administration exhibited a complex configuration, with the tracks of expanding cooperation and managing friction that were evidently defining the bilateral relationship. Both states sought to manage the antagonistic side of the bilateral relations by collaborating on issues where their concerns converged as they simultaneously confronted each other over their marked disparities, especially when China continued to advance its claims to sovereignty in the East and South China Seas. In tit-for-tat fashion, China also saw a U.S. presence in the region as indication to sustain its assertive strategies that the United States saw as incendiary. While such scenarios could have seriously escalated, cautious and rational dialogue on both sides continued to predominate.[110] Like the administrations that came before, Obama strived to expand collaboration with China but also to manage varying dichotomies through discourse and through the approach of "pressure, hedging, and balancing." The emphasis accorded to each component of this engagement policy altered over the course of Obama's two terms in office, while remaining a prevailing force often in search of an equilibrium.

5. The Trump Administration: Conflicting Narratives and Aberrant Departures

This final chapter examines the Trump administration's many changes to the United States-China bilateral relationship and the president's, by all measures, unconventional style of leadership and White House management. Remarkable differences in experience, behavior, priorities, and processes clearly distinguished the administration from its two notable predecessors. Notwithstanding Trump's bombastic approach to politics, his derision of American democratic and indeed diplomatic processes further cast the president himself as an outlier through attacking not only adversaries and peer-challengers, but also long-standing allies and regional partners. These "principles" epitomized in the Trump worldview were indeed the embedded promises of the "Make America Great Again" campaign to put "America first" and foremost in diplomatic engagements and trade agreements around the world. Insofar as the strategic challenge to United States' interests in the Asia-Pacific has underscored the administration's key foreign policy agenda, the approach to managing such affairs, we find, have occurred largely outside of the White House domain. When it has come to China, Trump, despite the more consistent and considered approaches of his State and Defense departments, has shown a disposition for destabilizing and impromptu flip-flops, provocative and discursive hyperbole, and tunnel vision on trade differences.

At the same time, Trump has ushered in a change of style and thinking about relations with China that has opened policy channels to new adjustments—and indeed policy reversals—deemed perhaps out of reach for his immediate predecessor. For many, including members of Congress, the accumulated complaints and frustrations of a sixteen-year bilateral relationship had finally produced a reaction in the White House that accorded action with accountability and rhetoric with policy. At least in the area of trade and later technology transference, the Trump administration's combative approach toward China has marked a notable departure in the level of confrontation Washington has been willing to risk with Beijing. The basis of the new approach has been a substantive shift in worldviews. The "strategic patience" of the previous administrations, mixed with engagement and varied levels of coercion, had failed to bring China more in line with the liberal world order and broader American interests. In fact, under Chinese president Xi Jinping, these policies appeared to have led to an almost complete reversal of Washington's intentions. The previous assumptions of the former administrations, that "the current international order benefits China, and capitalism brings with it democracy," observed one Congressional co-chair, "have been shattered and abandoned, even by those who fervently advocated them."[1]

As the chapter illustrates, while there have been notable changes to America's National Security Strategy (NSS), presaging a turning point for dealing strategically with an emboldened China in security matters, there has also been continuity in terms of the structures and principles laid down by presidents Bush and Obama. Long-standing alliances have been bolstered, despite at times complaints about their shortcomings. Further, Trump has approached the Association of Southeast Asian Nations (ASEAN) and other regional groupings in a conciliatory and open manner, again despite his antipathy for multilateralism. In the Asia-Pacific, the administration has adopted the Indo-Pacific Strategy (IPS) to deal increasingly with the strategic challenge of China. By some accounts, with the exception of a region-wide economic-strategic partnership, Trump has actually been "more active in fulfilling the material factors of the pivot" than Obama, increasing the number of troops and weapons systems in East Asia.[2] Of course, there have also been considerable departures. It goes without saying that Trump's management of the administration's China approach has been problematic. While he has pursued dramatic policy reversals in the search for a new trade deal, the relationship with China and the strategy for the Indo-Pacific have in many ways been rudderless. Diplomatic summitry, followed by symbolic high-level meetings, have replaced regular and valuable lower-level engagements, denying bilateral connections that in the past have been crucial to addressing differences and locating opportunities. This has left important gaps in understanding the terms of conduct in the emerging competitive environment. The implications, including the rising potential for crises and the exploitation of new strategic domains such as, for instance, cyberspace, are considerable.[3] Meanwhile, budget allocations for Indo-Pacific programs and Southeast Asia regional security cooperation initiatives have been repurposed for other areas.

As the chapter also demonstrates, serious inconsistency has marked the Trump administration's China policies and its approach to strategy in the Indo-Pacific concept. Long delays in implementation, coupled with diverging foreign policy priorities, have distracted the administration from what it defined, explicitly, as the greatest strategic threat of the new era. Meanwhile, Trump's unpredictable behavior, careless rhetoric, and rejection of liberal international norms have created a legitimacy problem as Asian regional partners decide whether or not to join in further American initiatives such as Trump's competitor to the Belt and Road Initiative (BRI), the BUILD (Better Utilization of Investments Leading to Development) Act. As the administration concludes its fourth year amid major disruptions emanating from COVID-19, U.S. race protests and subsequent riots, and the further deterioration of trade talks, Trump will remain increasingly limited in offering a vision for international security and relations with China going forward. "If the 'responsible stakeholder' notion has been overtaken by reality, what replaces it?" asked David Stilwell, assistant secretary of state for East Asian and Pacific affairs, in December 2019, three years into the Trump administration. More significantly, what was Washington for, if not a liberal world order?[4] These questions have not been adequately addressed by the Trump administration.

Trump's presidential style, implications, and broader security challenges

By the time of the 2016 presidential elections, marked changes in China's behavior toward the United States, its direct and unabashed challenge to the liberal international world order, and its flagrant theft of intellectual property (IP) had become consistent themes among the candidates. For Donald Trump, the origins of these challenges could be directly linked to the policy choices of previous administrations, namely, their attachment to globalism, nation-building, trade, and immigration. While these were typically denoted as benchmarks of American exceptionalism, Trump painted this worldview as being fundamentally flawed, squandering the unprecedented gains achieved with the end of the Cold War while handicapping Americans via unfair trade regimes, endless wars, and thankless nation-building exercises. In this respect, the legacies of the Bush and Obama administrations were, rather than principled and realist-oriented crafted policies, a blend of hedging, transitional, and at times, incrementalistic approaches that shifted across both administrations to unsatisfactory ends.[5] In a blustering exercise of campaign politics, popular policy promises, and unbridled arrogance, the Trump campaign offered a remolding of American grand strategy centered on quantitative and material zero-sum gains.

The policy roots of these dramatic changes warrant particular notice since they mark significant departures in long-standing norms. In contrast to his two predecessors, Trump's management of the presidential transition and the divisive changes he wrought to the staff system created a noteworthy vacuum in foreign policy nuance. Part of this had been a consequence of Trump's campaign promise to "drain the swamp" of the establishment political class; to deconstruct the administrative state by centralizing power in the Oval Office and among the key advisers employed by Trump to carry out the "America First" agenda.[6] Over time, this promise has turned into something more unsettling than many had originally conceived. Initially, Trump's foreign policy team, marked by their many connections to the military and big business, promised a sense of continuity. Discernibly, if Trump suffered from a notable paucity in political experience, an absence of familiarity with foreign and economic policy, and a tendency to improvise in speeches in aggrandizement of unrealistic policy proposals, it was considered that these responsible and knowledgeable advisers would step in to correct the excesses. In this context, assessments of the administration's first year are quick to note Trump's restrained foreign policy despite his vociferous rhetoric.[7] Secretary of Defense James Mattis, National Security Adviser Herbert R. McMaster, Secretary of State Rex Tillerson, Ambassador to the United Nations Nikki Haley, National Economic Council director Gary Cohn, and White House chiefs of staff Reince Priebus and later John F. Kelly, were all to perform this function at times during the first year.

However, these advisers and cabinet secretaries were not to last long. Priebus was dismissed in late July 2017, while Cohn, McMaster, and Tillerson exited by mid-2018. In the White House alone, the turn-over-rate for assistants to the president in the first twenty months amounted to an unprecedented two thirds of those appointed in the first year.[8] Meanwhile, hundreds of mid-level national security positions by the end of 2017 had yet to be filled—with many noting also the increasingly limited pool of qualified professionals Trump could draw upon as Republican "never-Trumpers" boycotted the administration.[9] There were several consequential outcomes to these disruptive changes in the administration. The first was that the significant amount of unfilled positions forced the White House to lean on staff to wear multiple hats in different and complicated roles. The defining example in this context was the president's son-in-law Jared Kushner, who was placed in charge of the Office of American Innovation, managing a Middle East peace plan between Israelis and Palestinians, renegotiating the North Atlantic Free Trade Agreement, and negotiating a U.S.-China trade deal, among other roles. To be sure, Kushner is an outlier in this respect. But the point reinforces the claim that Trump's ad hoc and changeable management of staff led to more dysfunction than stability, at least in terms of national security. Observers were to note that Kushner did not get along with Tillerson, whose State Department was relegated to the role of a back-up foreign policy outfit, denuded of funds and staff, and often left out of the loop. Meanwhile, Priebus tried, unsuccessfully, to curb the authority of Kushner, who neither worked within the White House chief of staff's management arrangement, nor for many months had the security clearance to undertake the many delicate roles he was given.[10]

A second outcome has been the notable disruption to the policy process. With competing staff arrangements, poorly defined roles, and the absence of a clear structures, roadblocks emerged in the management of decision-making systems and policy implementation. This was exacerbated, further, by changes to the cabinet and senior policy positions such as the director of national intelligence, which tended to correspond with further shakeups to sub-cabinet positions responsible for overseeing key bureaucratic roles. While it is not unusual for presidents to hire and fire staff based on their suitability and efficacy, constant changes can work to frustrate presidential decisions, impede policy processes, disrupt information flows, and adversely affect communications. As illustrated further below, while Trump's IPS has received much fanfare, it has remained significantly under-resourced and depressed in policy significance due in many ways to an incoherent policy process and misplaced roles.

In the context of China, these troubling developments in Trump's foreign policy apparatus stressed greater focus and nuance in the Oval Office, as weakened national security and foreign policy processes became the norm. Emphasis here goes to Trump's decision-making structure, his aptitude in directing foreign policy, and notably the relationship between these two domains and his worldview. In assessing these characteristics, Trump's policy choices in the first term have revealed less a careful and calculated decision-making process than a muddled vision to "Make America Great Again." The observable outcome in the administration's first initiatives in Asia, in this context, was the tendency to create greater levels of anxiety. Here reassurances toward regional multilateral commitments, such as the Trans-Pacific Partnership (TPP), were replaced by undiplomatic demands for greater financial contributions to long-standing security relationships. Trump was to calm this apprehension with pragmatic visits to the region in 2017, but mixed messaging and the failure to define a cohesive approach left regional partners unsatisfied. In contrast to Bush and Obama, Trump has illustrated an unapologetic contempt for process, resistance to a coherent strategy—so as to "keep 'em confused"—a reflexive contrarianism in diplomatic and political behavior, and a consistent eschewing of expert opinion.[11] On foreign affairs more specifically, Trump is considered "intellectually lazy," a president who doesn't read, yet contradicts and disparages the intelligence community.[12] These points, we note, have coalesced to meet unsatisfactorily with Trump's worldview, wherein international relations are considered zero-sum and power is divisible in primarily quantifiable terms. Money, jobs, trade volume, military assets, financial deals, and economic markers are counted as the beacons for successful policy while ideational factors are marginalized.

The point is exemplified in Trump's decision to reject the TPP. For the president, this was a deal where the benefits for Americans were traded for the false promises of liberal globalism, not just in business, but also in terms of labor, workers, and trade. Aside from greater market access and trade volume, the more "compelling strategic rationale for the TPP," as many former national security officials and think tank experts noted, including in July 2015 Trump's future secretary of defense, James Mattis, was its potential to balance against a regional reliance on the Chinese market, therefore denying China the leverage to shape the region in its own image.[13] Moreover, it would allow the United States and like-minded partners to control the liberal norms of global trade and force China to work *within* rather than outside of them. Part of Trump's decision at this point reflected his party's "Anything but Obama" creed. To be fair, once the more strategic and calculating aspects of the TPP became clearer to Trump, he did seek to review his position. By this time, however, the window for American initiative in negotiations had dissipated, likely forcing Trump to drop the review.[14]

A further converging point here is the re-emergence of the China "threat" theme in the Trump administration. This appeared in greater nuance and momentum in fact by the end of the Obama administration, according to David Lampton, as a "tipping point" loomed under the crumbling support for positive U.S.-China ties. By 2015, "important components of the American policy elite" were increasingly "coming to see China as a threat."[15] Noticeably, many were beginning to call for a reassessment of the policy of engagement that included some parts balancing and some parts open containment.[16] These sentiments manifested and collided with the Trump administration, reinforcing the authority of the perceived "threat" in two significant ways. In the first, Trump brought into the administration China-threat alarmist Peter Navarro, whose inflammatory books on Chinese trade practices stoked Trump's further pursuit of upending the U.S.-China trade relationship. A second hawk in this picture has been Michael Pillsbury, who has argued more eloquently that China has pursued a "secret strategy to replace America as the global superpower," and that it has relied upon gullible administrations to execute its plan.[17] While both belong to the fringe of a wider security dialogue concerning China, they have guided Trump toward an increasingly hostile relationship with Beijing, followed in tow by an uncommonly compliant Congress. In the second reinforcement, these advisers, along with other Trump policy loyalists, have combined the near two decades of complaints against China's trade practices in the World Trade Organization, its theft of IP, and its currency manipulation, to make an ardent case for retaliatory trade practices.

The result of this culmination of worldviews, policy priorities, and perceptions of threat has been a disjointed and at times confused shift in U.S. doctrine from strategic engagement to strategic competition with China. This shift has taken place more coherently in the State and Defense departments. For Trump, however, the referent object has been, almost absentmindedly, the trade relationship and more specifically the trade imbalance. Indeed, as a campaign promise, Trump made bold proclamations to reduce the trade deficit and bring America back into positive trade relationships with all international actors. While it was never considered by some that such trade demands would actually result in a tangible policy to reduce the deficits, many were by 2017 willing to voice their deep dissatisfaction with China's unceasing theft of IP, forced IP transfers for companies operating on the mainland, cyber intrusions into high-tech American firms, and the clandestine and commercial means by which Chinese agents sought to obtain sensitive military and commercial assets. By this stage, too, Xi Jinping's increasingly mercantilist trade practices had become more visibly evident in the BRI's development plan, which had led to strategic acquisitions of maritime ports in the Indian Ocean, and substantial leverage over participating economies.[18] Finally, part of this equation must necessarily also encompass Congress, which has viewed Chinese economic policies as progressively zero-sum, and aimed at disrupting America's military advantages in new-generation technology areas.

It was these converging views in Congress and the administration that allowed Trump, more than Obama or any other predecessor, to merge the many commercial and strategic issues with the trade deficit in July 2018 to begin the U.S.-China trade war. Long-standing tensions, reaching back as far as the first years of George W. Bush, had accumulated to meet at this point. At first, Trump's escalation of punitive tariffs on Chinese items, and subsequent iterations, were viewed by Congress as inflammatory and possibly destabilizing, harming U.S. farmers and consumers and American businesses in China. But there were also, Navarro observed, voices that could find justification to use the trade war as finally seeing an end to the "domination of the industries of the future" and the "discriminatory, unreasonable practices" of the Chinese government.[19]

While many would disagree with Trump's methods, others were also happy to see Washington finally holding Beijing accountable for its many perceived abuses of the relationship. For Defense officials and security establishment insiders, this turning point in perception occurred in mid-2017 with a report by the Defense Innovation Unit Experimental (DIUx) outreach group. In noting that China's 13th Five-Year Plan called for investment in the trillions of yuan in priority technologies, it outlined how increased Chinese purchases of U.S. artificial intelligence (AI), robotics, and virtual reality entities, among other critical technology areas, had strained America's competitive edge in areas of emerging technologies key to U.S. national security. Considering that many of the dual-use products produced by these commercial entities had substantial military applications, mastering them ahead of competitors, it was argued, would "ensure that we will be able to win the wars of the future."[20] By 2017, the report concluded, Chinese entities had already invested $1.3 billion in American firms. According to some analysts, the report presaged a "qualitative shift in U.S. thinking" on China since it represented the first time America had failed to keep pace with China in key emerging industries.[21]

While Chinese purchases of critical technology firms had already raised considerable attention in Congress, the DIUx report and the trade war offered opportunities to broaden control over the sale of sensitive technology companies. In 2018, the escalation of the trade war turned into a partial decoupling in critical emerging technology industries when Trump, led by Congress, enacted the Foreign Investment Risk Review Modernization Act (FIRRMA), to curb the acquisition of commercial firms considered valuable to U.S. national security. By 2019, these actions, more than an extension of the trade war, had become an escalation in the strategic tug-of-war between the U.S. and China. Combined with the decrease in government-to-government dialogues, and Trump's ambivalence toward any form of engagement outside of leadership summitry, the new dialogue fostered in China was a resigned progression toward a "cold war in selective areas" of trade, the economy, and technology. According to one general in the People's Liberation Army (PLA), whereas before many believed the U.S. containment strategy to be "formerly selective," concentrated in the military domain, the trade war and FIRRMA had broadened it to include new economic areas. For another, the potential to "avoid conflict or competition" had become increasingly difficult since "now there is no incentive for relations."[22]

The Indo-Pacific strategy and China's military "threat"

In 2017, the Trump administration moved to shift America's National Security Strategy (NSS) from its core focus on counter-terrorism and nuclear proliferation in the Obama years, to one that sought to portray the "re-emergence of long term strategic competition" by revisionist powers. Accordingly, U.S. national security had been deeply impacted by the challenge of states such as China and Russia, who were "determined to make economies less free and less fair, to grow their militaries, and to control information and data to repress their societies and expand their influence."[23] Notwithstanding the change to a more competitive posture, there were notable overlaps with the previous administration, including an emphasis on alliances, democracy building, military development, and homeland security. This was unsurprising, since these facets formed the basic architecture of all national security strategies across at least the last four presidents. For some, however, the 2017 NSS marked the turning point in U.S. doctrine from strategic engagement to strategic competition with China.[24] Observers seeking to confirm this shift were to look no further than the more unambiguous 2018 National Defense Strategy (NDS), which called for a "fundamental shift in the armed forces toward preparing for war against China or Russia."[25] Followed by the launching of the trade war in June, and Vice President Mike Pence's provocative speech to the Hudson Institute in October, the new era of great-power competition in the Trump administration's vision placed China square in front as the emerging security threat to the United States.[26]

Peculiarly, the White House has at varying intervals portrayed this narrative in paradoxical and ambiguous terms. While Trump has taken credit for the NDS, for instance, the president's comments have largely avoided the key point of the new era of competition with China. In remarks at the release of the document, Trump, rather than explaining the core assumptions of meeting the military and strategic challenge of China and Russia, excoriated allies for not paying enough for collective defense.[27] Discernibly, while the NDS had pursued a critical tone, noting the impact of China's "military modernization program" and its aims for "regional hegemony," Trump has consistently avoided this characterization of competition with China.[28] Nor has he sought to explain what the new emphasis on strategic competition will mean for U.S. foreign policy over the long term. Here his State of the Union addresses are revealing. Despite the apparent "massive shift" in doctrine, China was mentioned only once in 2017 with respect to trade, once briefly in 2018 to say that China and Russia had presented the U.S. with a new era of competition, and twice briefly in 2019 in the context of trade and the Intermediate-Range Nuclear Forces Treaty (INF Treaty). In October 2018, Pence marked China's aims "as nothing less than to push the United States of America from the Western Pacific and attempt to prevent us from coming to the aid of our allies" with its increasingly sophisticated military.[29] Yet, by 2020, Trump announced that this military challenge had been largely abrogated. America's military under his watch, he announced, had been "completely rebuilt, with its power being unmatched anywhere in the world," noting further that relations with China had "changed" for the better, and that "we have perhaps the best relationship we've ever had with China, including with President Xi."[30]

Discussion pertaining to China's military modernization among Pentagon and Defense officials diverged significantly from this narrative. Indeed, much of the focus and strategic direction for the NSS and NDS can be seen to have originated, except in the areas of immigration and trade, almost exclusively from Defense and National Security Council (NSC) personnel. The most notable facet of this divergence from Trump's focus has been the need for a coordinated "whole-of-government approach." For many commentators, the need for a more holistically encompassing focus was plain, and considered urgent, since China's own whole-of-government strategy—consisting in part of political warfare, lawfare, economic leverage through programs such as the BRI, and military modernization to obtain such aims as control over the South China Sea (SCS)—had already majorly disrupted America's strategic edge.[31]

At the same time, many in the new administration regretted Trump's rejection of the TPP and the "rebalance" of the Obama years, perceived as strategically well placed to meet Washington's aims in the Asia-Pacific. While Obama was criticized for not spending enough on military development and on such initiatives as the Southeast Asia Maritime Security Initiative (MSI), the "rebalance" was nonetheless a useful and strategic recalibration of American assets to meet the China challenge. By contrast, Trump's posture upon entering office seemed to offer "confrontation without competition,"[32] critics noted, lacking a "coherent, integrated national strategy for the Asia-Pacific region," and one in particular that dealt "with an increasingly powerful and assertive China."[33] Movement in Congress by Senator John McCain (Republican-Arizona) sought to boost this focus for Trump in the Asia-Pacific to the sum of $7.5 billion under the scheme of an Asia-Pacific Stability Initiative. While the Defense Department was to pick this up in May of 2017, its focus remained attached to militarily energizing allied and partner bases, thus falling short on regional consensus building and economic engagement mechanisms.[34] Still, this was a start to having Trump redefine his focus to shift toward a whole-of-government approach instead of the more siloed concentration on trade.

By the end of 2018, however, Trump was yet to meet in strategic terms what his administration had promised in policy speeches and documents including the NSS and the NDS. On the IPS, pushed first by Secretary of State Rex Tillerson in October 2017, Trump repackaged Obama's emphasis on the "rebalance" to announce a vision for a "free and open Indo-Pacific"[35] (FOIP). Here, priority was given to promoting regional stability and prosperity, with many noting the use of the terms "governance" and "cooperation," considered out of place in Trump's "America First" foreign policy. This was to be followed in May of 2018 by further policy branding with Secretary of Defense James Mattis's rebadging the U.S. Pacific Command (USPACOM) as the Indo-Pacific Command (INDOPACOM), broadening the emphasis of America's strategic reach.[36] In some ways, these moves were seen largely as responses to China's regional military and economic expansionism, and out of touch with the Asia-Pacific's many problems, the most exigent of which has been under-development. By the beginning of 2019, Trump had failed to offer the region a substantial counterbalance to the BRI above criticisms of China's predatory economic practices and its militarization of the SCS. The BUILD Act, led by Congress and announced by Secretary of State Mike Pompeo in June, was to be the first "down payment on a new era in U.S. economic commitment to peace and prosperity in the Indo-Pacific region," but offered only marginal funds and was perceived by some to be an inferior replacement for the TPP.[37]

The administration's budget proposals for the IPS cast further suspicion on the shift toward competing with China observed in the NSS and NDS. On the first point, the administration's first two budgets actually diverted funds from the Asia-Pacific to drive assistance toward "strategic allies in the Middle East." In 2018, the State Department's budget request for the Indo-Pacific region in its Foreign Military Financing (FMF) scheme, an assistance mechanism to drive development of military capabilities in partner states, amounted to just 1 percent of the FMF budget. This equated to roughly the budget allocation for Tunisia of $40 million, while countries such as Jordan and Egypt received $350 million and $1.3 billion respectively.[38] A second, similar story captures the ostensibly low priority of the Indo-Pacific at the Department of Defense (DoD). When INDOPACOM called for an Asia-Pacific security initiative, modeled on the former European Reassurance

Initiative in 2015, it was dismissed. Meanwhile, the Obama-era MSI budget request for the financial year 2018 shrank to $84 million from $98 million the previous year for the entire region. These programs were restored somewhat by the end of 2018 in Congress—who provided much-needed leadership in these budget allocations—with the Asia Reassurance Initiative Act, but they nonetheless remained considerably under-funded given the apparent strategic threat of China in the Indo-Pacific.

By June 2019 the administration appeared to be more fully prepared to follow through with the NSS and NDS, though significant roadblocks were still visible. Pompeo added more weight to the Indo-Pacific region, making notable trips to the Philippines in February, India in June, and Japan for the G20 summit on the 27th of that month, followed by a stop in South Korea on the 29th. In August, the secretary travelled to Thailand to participate in the annual ASEAN ministerial meetings, where he was to follow on to Australia on the 3rd, and to Micronesia on the 5th. By this stage, the June 2019 Indo-Pacific Strategy Report (IPSR) had emerged so as to further buttress the original salience of the China challenges noted in the NSS and NDS.[39] However, the whole-of-government approach continued to lag behind the administration's emphasis on the military domain. The BUILD Act, the economic arm of the IPS, was passed in Congress in October of 2018, and with it survived the Overseas Private Investment Corporation (OPIC), which was originally slated for elimination in the 2017 budget.[40]

At the end of 2018, OPIC, the key financial vehicle for balancing against the economic power of the BRI, had not changed its focus from middle-high-income countries or its emphasis on financial services and renewable energies. Critics were quick to point out that the initiative had failed to adequately counter the BRI, which had mandated a focus on low-income countries and on infrastructure projects, and, what's more, had taken far too long to address the threat.[41] It was only by January 2020 that the U.S. International Development Finance Corporation (IDFC), the successor to OPIC, had become operational. By this stage, the Trump administration appeared to be at least two years behind in addressing the threat of China recognized in the NSS, the NDS, and the IPSR.[42]

While there has no doubt been an expanded understanding of what the Indo-Pacific means to America's most demanding long-term challenge, there remains a glaring disparity between how the administration and Congress continue to plan for Indo-Pacific security concerns compared to other international issues. For some, the accumulative impact of ongoing wars in the Middle East, a focus on Russia/Ukraine, budget cutbacks, under-investment in sophisticated military resources, and the magnitude of America's liberal-order-building strategy in past administrations had left the U.S. armed forces ill equipped for great-power competition in the Indo-Pacific.[43] Certainly, the NSS aimed to address this predicament of "strategic insolvency" by resetting the Defense Department's focus toward preparing for great-power war, as opposed to multiple smaller conflicts, while "urging the military to prioritize requirements for deterrence vis-à-vis China." That said, Chinese counter-intervention systems were likely to continue destabilizing America's capacity to project power into the Indo-Pacific, elevating the danger that China may use limited force to accomplish a fait accompli triumph before America could react. Overall, Washington's chance of "denying this kind of aggression" placed a "premium on advanced military assets, enhanced posture arrangements, new operational concepts and other costly changes."[44]

In the Pentagon, despite the Trump administration's expansion of the budget for the military, and its promising reversal of the apparent erosion of America's military competitive advantage "over any potential enemy," China's military modernization continued to cause notable unease.[45] Certainly, this anxiety could be traced back to almost every Pentagon budget analysis in the Bush and Obama administrations looking at China's growing military prowess. But by the beginning of 2017, observers assessing this modernization had begun to discuss Beijing as possessing "near-peer competitor" status capabilities. To be sure, many were to note that Beijing could not deploy large numbers of conventional forces across the globe. Nor had its modernization aims been outside of the capabilities already attained by the United States military.[46] At the same time, however, China's investment in AI, hypersonic missiles, anti-access/area denial (A2/AD) capabilities, and 5G networks proved disruptive shifts in the balance of

America's military deterrent. By 2019, this dialogue had become increasingly alarming among Defense officials. In discussing military priorities, Elbridge Colby, former deputy secretary of defense for strategy and force development, remarked that the military threat from China and Russia had become so demanding that the Pentagon was required to do either "less of everything else," including the wars in the Middle East, or do "it more efficiently." Everything, he observed, "not directly connected to readying our forces to fight China or Russia should be considered under a harsh and skeptical light."[47]

These comments presaged a conceptual shift in the perception of China's capabilities more broadly across Washington and among members of Congress, the Pentagon, and Defense. Although Chinese military capabilities were considered to be closing the gap—as a "near-peer competitor"—on America's military, in other areas, the PLA had already reached parity or indeed had surpassed American capabilities. In AI in particular, China's robust government support for research institutes and intelligence-related start-ups, and greater linkages between commercial and academic actors had actually put it on a par with Washington. Meanwhile, its advantage in high-performance computing, through multi-level government support and with the world's only two supercomputers, was projected to surpass U.S. capabilities in 2020.[48] In the maritime zone, too, China's force projection in the East and South China Seas had increased to the point where superiority in numbers of PLA Navy (PLAN) vessels, including the world's largest (paramilitary) coast guard forces, and its only maritime militia force, could possibly overwhelm and render null the superiority of America's more advanced surface vessels. This was not to say that outside of the first island chain—reaching from the Kuril Islands in Japan down to the Malaysian peninsula—China could project this force. Beijing's blue-water navy was considered yet to be threatening in this area. But part of China's modernization activities, including its advanced weapons programs, had been designed explicitly to target U.S. weaknesses and exploit American vulnerabilities.[49]

In examining the SCS and Beijing's A2/AD capabilities, these vulnerabilities cloud the question of whether the United States could win a potential war with China in the littoral waters off the

Taiwan coast. China's notable build-up of highly accurate anti-ship ballistic missiles (ASBMs), multi-role intermediate-range ballistic missiles (IRBMs), and anti-ship cruise missiles are considered by some to be game-changing weapons, capable of hitting moving ships at sea. A second disturbing feature was that the U.S. Navy had not "previously faced" such a threat by ASBMs, nor was it sure how it would respond to such a broad spectrum of missile systems in a high-end conflict scenario.[50] By April 2018, the new commander of INDOPACOM, Admiral Philip Davidson, was willing to go as far as to suggest that the Chinese could feasibly "control" the SCS in all circumstances short of a war with the United States.[51] By January 2020, others were to posit that the United States had lost its advantage "throughout the spectrum of operations" in the SCS, allowing China to obtain "escalation dominance" since it had the "power to deter any U.S. turn towards escalation."[52]

The question of whether the United States could defend Taiwan from a concerted Chinese attack was considered equally ambiguous. The U.S.-China Economic and Security Commission's 2019 annual report to Congress noted explicitly that the "cross-Strait military balance has decidedly shifted in China's favor in recent years" and that this "change presents a major challenge both to Taiwan's ability to defend itself and to the United States' ability to intervene effectively in a cross-Strait conflict."[53] While the PRC was not yet believed to have the military capability to successfully invade and capture Taiwan, it could nonetheless keep the United States from coming to its aid under its formidable A2/AD blockade. Part of this equation also involved the question of resolve. While the United States and China might have a balance of capabilities, and therefore no deterrent, in a match-up for Taiwan, the Chinese on the other hand embraced a determination that accepted higher costs than the United States "in most contingencies." Given the trends in China's military modernization and this calculation of resolve, Chinese capabilities were forecast not merely to just overcome U.S. forces, but rather to "outmatch" the United States on the Taiwan question.[54]

For policymakers, at this stage, the perception of China's military modernization needed to extend beyond the realm of the PLA to include facets of foreign policy, trade, and the economy, considered to add subtle force multipliers to Beijing's military strategy. If the United States habitually separated the government and private sectors, China and Russia were seen to integrate their own applicable sectors to compete unevenly for a more authoritarian international order. Here, the question of whether China represented a "near-peer competitor" became further obscured. Strategic investments in 5G and cultivating overseas relationships of dependency under the guise of the BRI were believed to provide an "impetus for the PLA's development of strategic delivery capabilities and overseas bases."[55]

In other areas, the new China-Russia axis, identified by Defense as working to undo the liberal world order piecemeal, added further stress to the American military in the Western Pacific. Meanwhile, the U.S. had never faced an adversary of comparable size and economic sophistication to the one China now presented. While the United States spent more on its military than any other nation, it was also a global military. China by contrast, spent increasing amounts on military development in select areas of A2/AD, to keep the United States out of the first island chain. In material terms, by 2017, China had 317 warships and submarines, compared to 283 in the U.S. Navy, operating mostly in its claimed littoral waters. Only 60 percent of the U.S. Navy, by contrast, was situated in the Pacific. Further projections by the Pentagon indicated that by 2025, the PLA would have approximately 30 percent more fighter aircraft and four aircraft carriers in the Pacific and further "guided-missile destroyers, advanced undersea warfare systems and hypersonic missiles."[56] Under these terms, China had at least partially become a peer competitor.

Trump and maritime territorial disputes in the South and East China Seas

Free and open Indo-Pacific region and the National Security Strategy

It has been evident thus far during Trump's tenure in office that U.S.-China strategic competition in the SCS and ECS has formed a key component of the administration's more assertive approach toward

China, and broadly speaking, its endeavors for advocating its concept for the Indo-Pacific region.[57] Indeed, across the sequence of declarations and reports, the Trump administration has articulated a goal to promote a "free and open Indo-Pacific" (FOIP), incorporating an approach that seeks to combine U.S. strategies toward East and South Asia, two regions that have often been addressed in relative separation. In this direction, Trump has displayed a willingness to go further than Obama, broadening the NSS to define the Indo-Pacific as stretching from "the west coast of India to the western shores of the United States."[58] Others have described the geographical expression more generally as including the western reaches of the Indian Ocean littoral. Perhaps more significantly, regional partners, initially wary of Trump's antipathy toward regional groupings, have extended support for the expanded concept, and thereby, strengthened the administration's agenda. Indian prime minister Narendra Modi defined the region as extending from "the shores of Africa to that of the Americas,"[59] while Japanese prime minister Shinzo Abe described it as a "broader Asia" that has broken down traditional geographical boundaries, and "is now beginning to take on a distinct form . . . the Pacific and the Indian Oceans are now bringing about a dynamic coupling."[60]

While the Trump administration's rollout of the Indo-Pacific strategy was initially somewhat ambiguous and slow to develop, officials have since made more detailed policy pronouncements in articulating the strategic concept. In many ways, the strategy is an amalgamation of former and current policy themes, but it goes further in identifying the emerging challenges emanating from China's growing global influence across economic and military modernization domains. As the Trump NSS illustrates, "a geopolitical competition between free and repressive visions of world order is taking place in the Indo-Pacific region." Additionally,

> although the United States seeks to continue to cooperate with China, China is using economic inducements and penalties, influence operations, and implied military threats to persuade other states to heed its political and security agenda . . . China presents its ambitions as mutually beneficial, but Chinese dominance risks diminishing the sovereignty of many states in the Indo-Pacific.[61]

Further, while the Trump administration's NSS goes into greater detail in articulating what it perceives to be a wide range of threats presented by China, it has diverted sharply from Obama's emphasis on engagement and cooperation. In fact, despite Trump's promises to push back against Beijing, specifying a growing list of malicious Chinese practices on "every conceivable playing field," there has been no noticeable attempt to hedge or provide a mechanism for dialogue.[62] In more specific terms, it has been the Chinese advancement in the Indo-Pacific region that has appeared to cause the most consternation, thus the perception advertised has been that any further dialogue would only embolden this advancement.

In the economic domain, China's infrastructure investments and trade strategies have enabled it to reaffirm and buttress its geopolitical ambitions. Its attempts to construct and militarize atolls in the SCS have "endangered the free flow of trade, threaten the sovereignty of other nations, and undermine regional stability." Coinciding with this, the NSS illustrates, China has undertaken a rapid military modernization campaign intended to restrict U.S. access to the region while enabling itself to attain a freer rein there. The document calls for states in the region to endorse a "sustained U.S. leadership" that fosters "a collective response in upholding a regional order respectful of sovereignty and independence." Of course, aside from political and economic responses, the NSS emphasizes the need to "maintain a forward military presence capable of deterring and, if necessary, defeating any adversary," strengthening its longstanding military relationships and encouraging the development of a strong defense network with its allies and partners.[63]

A further and intrinsic strategic motivation for the IPS, here, has been the emergence and convergence of India and South Asia as a significant hub for maritime traffic and control of important sea lines of communication. With the administration embracing a new era of strategic competition, these aspects formed necessary national security objectives for a U.S. Pacific strategy, thus comprising a more comprehensive approach to the Indian Ocean region and the Pacific. The Trump administration has sought therefore to align India more tightly into regional fora and organizational constructs, including restarting a concept initially founded during the Bush administration: the "Quad," a four-member group encompassing the United States, Japan, Australia, and India. In April 2018, Alex Wong, a deputy assistant secretary in the U.S. State Department, added further legitimacy to the concept by recognizing the historical and contemporary context of South Asia, with emphasis on India, and the extent to which it could play a defining role in the Pacific more broadly. This point stressed India's role as a democratic state that subscribed to "a free and open order," and therefore one "that can bookend and anchor the free and open order in the Indo-Pacific region." Perceptively, while Trump was noted to downplay the American tradition of democracy promotion in his speeches, his national security chiefs sought nonetheless to secure its application in the broader strategy for the Indo-Pacific. As such, administration policy has come, Wong remarked, "to ensure that India does play that role" of democratic defender and "does become over time a more influential player in the region."[64]

The Trump administration's overarching strategy in the SCS and ECS

For the Indo-Pacific strategy to be fully realized, the administration has sought to maintain the approach of criticizing China's assertive actions in the SCS, and reiterating the U.S. stance on issues relating to the SCS and ECS on a more persistent level. In continuation of the Obama legacy, it has also sought to maintain and expand the U.S. naval presence and Freedom of Navigation (FoN) activities in the SCS with "gray-hull" military assets and in recent times, U.S. Coast Guard "white-hull" vessels. On top of this, INDOPACOM has maintained overflight operations in the SCS and ECS with U.S. Air Force bombers, noted as visibly minimal yet objectively substantial. If the Trump administration has been criticized for not doing enough in terms of deterring Chinese assertions to ownership of the SCS under its nine-dash line claim, commander of Pacific Air Forces General Charles Q. Brown observed, then such views were blind to a more active regional deterrence. While U.S. Air Force FoN operations don't "get as much press as what you hear about with the freedom of navigation and the maritime environment," the strategy was nonetheless working "because we do get calls from [Beijing]."[65]

In an attempt to add more rigor to the strategy, Trump has also sought to reinforce the U.S. military presence and operations in the Indo-Pacific region on a broader scale, developing new U.S. military models of strategies for thwarting Chinese military forces. This has even gone as far as including other punitive measures, where possible, including for example in May 2018, the DoD's decision to "disinvite" China from that year's RIMPAC (Rim of the Pacific) exercise, as its behavior was described as being "inconsistent with the principles and purposes" of the exercise.[66] Further, part of the strategy has called for upholding and improving diplomatic ties and security cooperation with allied and partner states. Trump had been working "intensively" in trying to "counter China's military assertiveness," Mattis remarked in 2018, adding that the White House had been diligently "cozying up to smaller nations in the region that share American wariness about Chinese intentions."[67] That said, Trump also called upon regional partners to deliver maritime-related security support to the strategy, urging allied and partner states to do more independently and in coordination with one another to protect their interests in the SCS.[68]

By some measures, the administration's proactive diplomatic engagement, at least at the elite level, among Indo-Pacific countries has strengthened the U.S. presence in the region. Maritime-related security assistance under the Indo-Pacific MSI has been revamped, extending on the Obama administration's Southeast Asian MSI of 2015 to deliver, at the outset, $425 million in maritime security backing to designated states over a five-year period.[69] What's more, the administration increased U.S. defense and intelligence cooperation with Vietnam and Indonesia.[70] In November 2018, former national security adviser John Bolton came out more forcefully on the side of regional actors by stating that the U.S. would dispute any bilateral deals between China and other claimants to the SCS, noting that the open corridor for international shipping was not for the sole use of any one state. While Bolton welcomed negotiations in principle, "the outcome has to be mutually acceptable, and also has to be acceptable to all the countries that have legitimate maritime and naval rights to transit and other associate rights that we don't want to see infringed."[71] This developing support for regional partners was reinforced again in March 2019, in more forthright terms, when Secretary of State Pompeo declared that "any armed attack on Philippine forces, aircraft, or public vessels in the South China Sea will trigger mutual defense obligations under Article 4 of our Mutual Defense Treaty [with the Philippines]."[72]

Finally, the long association between China's actions in the SCS and its use of "gray zone" paramilitary vessels to intimidate and control movement around strategic islands has been put on notice. Chinese Coast Guard vessels and large militia fishing trawler units have been at the forefront of Xi Jinping's strategy to control the waters surrounding claimed assets in the SCS. Classified as "gray-hull vessels painted white" due to their large size and military features, and as "little blue men" in the militia units, their part in China's strategy, noted Abraham Denmark, a former deputy assistant secretary of defense for East Asia under Obama, was to harass as much as possible its rival claimants and demonstrate and assert claims from a threshold just below conflict. While forming collectively the largest maritime force in the Indo-Pacific, these vessels were also "state-organized, -developed, and -controlled forces operating under a direct military chain of command," clearly denoting their military, rather than civilian, purpose. By 2018, the Defense Department was ready to challenge these navy features in the SCS, noting in subsequent reports that China's use of them had come to play "a major role in coercive activities to achieve China's political goals without fighting."[73] In January 2019, the Pentagon alerted its counterpart organization in China to the fact that it would no longer view China's Coast Guard cutters and maritime militia vessels as civilian units. The administration would now address "incitements" by them in the same fashion as it would react to provocations by Chinese navy vessels.[74] That this was a major shift in Washington's approach to challenging Beijing's strategy and authority in the SCS has gone relatively unnoticed.

Freedom of navigation program

Aside from military and rhetorical reassurance programs, a major plank in the Trump administration's broader IPS has been its freedom of navigation (FoN) program. It has been long-standing U.S. Navy policy to contest what the United States deems to be disproportionate or otherwise illegal maritime claims made by other states, and thus, undertake actions of operational rights under international law to deny legitimacy. Extending as far back as 1979, the FoN program has required a multi-pronged approach, including diplomatic endeavors, operational assertions by U.S. Navy ships, and a global approach that is gauged toward not just China, but other states where applicable. Of course, this notably changed with the Obama administration and, consequentially, President Xi Jinping's island-building project. While Obama sought to ratchet up America's response to China's glaring territorial grab in the SCS, these initiatives proved largely ineffective during this time. Obama coordinated the military aspects of the FoNs with a strategized diplomatic protest for each mission. But these protests were too few—the U.S. Navy conducted just two FoN operations (FoNOPs) in 2015 followed by three more in 2016 with no noteworthy change to China's behavior.

Under the Trump administration, the DoD has emboldened the original FoN program, intensifying operations to the tune of six FoNOPs in 2017 and five in 2018. These have coincided with further assertions, deploying warships more frequently to waters in close proximity to artificial islands China has militarized with aircraft shelters, runways, deepwater harbors and, most recently, short-range missiles. Moreover, it has pressed its allies to contribute their ships to future missions.[75] Certainly, these have been considered improvements in America's counter-legitimacy protests. By September 2018, Defense was willing to state that the administration had monitored and physically protested against China's "excessive maritime claims" and, "through operational assertions and activities" designed "to preserve the rights, freedoms, and uses of the sea and airspace guaranteed to all nations by international law," had successfully weakened China's claims.[76] By November 2019, Secretary of Defense Mark Esper pronounced that the United States had conducted "more freedom of navigation operations in the past year or so than we have in the past 20-plus years."[77] As with other features of Trump's evolving China policies, however, it is not clear to what extent such maneuvers have been managed successfully or strategically between Defense, State, and the White House. For instance, when Trump called Xi in March, 2017, to ask China to do more in restraining North Korea's nuclear program, it was, surprisingly, just hours after INDOPACOM had sent the USS *Stethem* on a FoN exercise past Triton Island in the Paracel archipelago. Predictably, Xi didn't respond well to the request, noting "negative factors" in the relationship. Moreover, there has been the question of whether the FoNOPs have contributed to weakening China's claims rather than destabilizing regional security through "gunboat diplomacy," especially since Trump has lessened the emphasis of diplomacy more generally.[78]

While the Trump administration has argued that these operations have contributed to the broader FOIP concept, and have even forced China to "reassess" its strategic posturing at various intervals, they have also come precariously close to causing escalation. A point of significance, here, is that while the administration has sought to increase FoNOPs, it has done so while shrinking military-to-military relations and diplomatic talks designed to de-escalate tensions and minimize misunderstandings. Concurrently, as the Trump team has escalated its FoN program, Chinese authorities have also sought to display resolve to counter the operations with Chinese navy vessels and PLA Air Force units. The result has been a steady increase in "unsafe and unprofessional" encounters. In one notable instance, the U.S. Navy destroyer *Decatur* was harassed by and barely escaped from a collision with a Chinese destroyer. According to navy reports, the Chinese vessel passed the U.S. destroyer in dangerously close proximity, within approximately 45 yards, on the port side, causing the U.S. destroyer to veer sharply to starboard. Chinese officers, meanwhile, were heard to demand *Decatur* to change course or "suffer consequences." According to one commentator, "this is the first time we've had a direct threat to an American warship with that kind of language."[79]

Such incidents have been indicative of a broader trend in U.S-China encounters in the SCS. Since 2016, the U.S. Navy has recorded eighteen dangerous or "unprofessional" altercations with Chinese military forces in the Pacific. For the Trump administration, most of these provocative maneuvers against American military assets took place during the first year. Three of them, in February, May, and July of 2017, involved Chinese fighter jets executing what Washington perceived to be "dangerous" intercepts of U.S. Navy reconnaissance aircrafts.[80] Indicatively, the potential for an accident at sea, not unlike the 2001 EP-3 incident, had progressively worsened, motivated by the greater risks the PLA Navy and Air Force seemed prepared to take. Meanwhile, risk management agreements have lapsed. In 2015, China signed onto the multilateral CUES (Code for Unplanned Encounters at Sea) framework, joining the United States to manage the risk of accidents at sea. While it is worth praising CUES as a step toward building greater risk reduction platforms between Washington and Beijing, it has not stopped provocative military maneuvers from taking place. Indeed, notable flaws continue to inhibit the full applicability of CUES, the principal one being that it does not cover China's Coast Guard and maritime militia vessels, which predominate in the SCS and operate under the People's Armed Police and the Central Military Commission. Further, since April 2018, China has begun landing aircraft and transferring electronic jamming hardware, surface-to-air missiles, and anti-ship missile systems to its freshly constructed facilities in the SCS, heightening the chances of escalation rather than diminishing them.[81]

China's militarization of islands in the SCS is worth further examining here. In July 2018, reports indicated that China was covertly testing electronic warfare assets recently fitted at fortified island-bases. Designed to confuse and/or disable communications systems, the placements were set to aid the PLA in housing, storing, and replenishing navy vessels in the area, providing further relief and support for China's claims and its "active defense" program.[82] Again in July 2018, Chinese state media revealed that a PLAN search and rescue ship had been based at Subi Reef, the first time that this type of ship had been permanently stationed at one of China's occupied sites in the Spratly Islands.[83] In assessing the extent to which China has enhanced its position in the SCS, some have gone as far to say that China has attained a marked foothold and commanding presence there. From its various stations now operating on disputed islands, as Admiral Philip Davidson commented for the Senate Armed Services Committee on April 17, 2018, once occupied, China will be able to extend its influence thousands of miles to the south and project power deep into Oceania. The PLA will be able to use these bases to challenge U.S. presence in the region, and any forces deployed to the islands would easily overwhelm the military forces of any other South China Sea-claimants. In short, China is now capable of controlling the South China Sea in all scenarios short of war with the United States.[84]

Of course, other developments have also been a point of consternation for the Trump administration. The DoD has observed that while China has challenged foreign military activities in its maritime zones in a fashion that is incompatible with the rules of customary international law (as specified in the United Nations Convention on the Law of the Sea (UNCLOS)), the PLA has in recent times begun performing the equivalent kinds of military actions inside and outside the first island chain in the maritime zones of other states. For U.S. policymakers, this is illustrative of a double standard when it comes to international law and is a further sign that Beijing seeks to ignore or change norms wherever it can. Despite China being a state party to the UNCLOS, for instance, its domestic law restricts military activities of other parties in its exclusive economic zone (EEZ), including intelligence gathering and military evaluations. At the same time, the PLA has progressively undertaken military actions and maneuvers in other states' EEZs: in 2017, for instance, it performed air and naval operations in Japan's EEZ; sent AGIs (intelligence-gathering ships) to the Aleutian Islands, probably to examine testing of a U.S. terminal high-altitude area defense (THAAD) system; and sent a further AGI to observe a multinational naval simulation in Australia's EEZ. PLA operations in external EEZs have also taken place in Northeast and Southeast Asia, and an expanding number of operations are also transpiring well beyond the Chinese domains.[85]

For Chinese analysts, these actions are, rather than illustrations of China's new revisionism, responses to the Obama administration's "pivot" and the Trump administration's accelerated positioning of military assets in the area to counter China's claims. As Wu Shicun, president of the National Institute for

South China Sea Studies in Haikou, observes, "China will take the necessary measures to increase the cost of such provocative actions by the U.S. and other relevant countries . . . Otherwise the actions of the provocative parties will only be more frequent and unscrupulous."[86] In challenging the legal aspect of the issue, Zhang Junshe, a senior research fellow at the PLA Naval Military Studies Research Institute, argued further that Trump's "excuse" of using freedom of navigation did "not stand because international law never allowed U.S. warships to freely enter another country's territorial waters."[87] According to this claim, the U.S./Western definition of freedom of navigation was considerably wider, comprising in its assessment operations of different types undertaken by both commercial and military vessels and aircraft in international waters and airspace. An alternative term for discussing the U.S./Western definition of freedom of navigation is "freedom of the seas," indicating "all of the rights, freedoms, and lawful uses of the sea and airspace, including for military ships and aircraft, guaranteed to all nations under international law."[88] By contrast, when Chinese officials argue that China is a proponent of freedom of navigation, they are pointing to its *own* narrow interpretation of the term, and thus, not conveying agreement with, nor an endorsement for, the U.S./Western definition of the term.[89]

Reconciling resources and strategic imperatives in the Indo-Pacific

Certainly, the absence of agreement in definitions between China and the United States on the rules of the road in the SCS only elevates the risk of a catastrophic misunderstanding or mishap. But aside from this, and as briefly touched on above, the expanding perception of conflict has been exacerbated by some U.S. concerns that its vessels and crews are in decline after seventy years of undisputed preponderance across the Pacific Ocean. Indeed, budgetary debates pertaining to the United States' capacity to execute its broader security strategy, and not just in the Indo-Pacific region, have been extensive and varied. With U.S. naval commanders concerned that their ships and crews are on the defensive, a reassessment of the navy's strategic and expenditure priorities has come to the fore in policy and security discourse. As the Trump administration presses the navy to be more assertive in the SCS and broader Indo-Pacific, it is doing so, according to some analysts, with a limited number of resources, while in juxtaposition, the Chinese are expanding and modernizing their suite of options.[90]

As such, many analysts have come to question the extent to which the Trump administration can sufficiently resource and sustain its strategy for competing with China in the SCS and ECS, especially insofar as financing and sustaining the maritime-related security assistance as presented in the above sections is concerned. Funding levels for security support to states in the SCS, they contend, represent only a minor proportion of funding levels for U.S. security assistance beneficiaries in other regions, such as the Middle East.[91] As argued by Eric Sayers, there is a sizeable and constant chasm between the level of significance the U.S. government has affixed to the Indo-Pacific and "what annual appropriations continue to prioritize at the State Department and Pentagon." While there has no doubt been an expanded understanding of what the Indo-Pacific and U.S.-Chinese competition exemplify to America's most demanding long-term challenge, there remains a glaring disparity between how the administration and Congress continue to plan for Indo-Pacific security concerns compared to other international issues. As Sayers again states, "This is not to argue that other priorities, such as European Command and countering Russian [sic] in Ukraine, are not important. They are and deserve budgetary support. But some will argue that this budgetary emphasis demonstrates a bias towards those theaters at the expense of Asia."[92]

While Trump clearly wants to amplify the U.S. presence in the SCS and the broader FOIP program, the push and pull of economic factors, where an understanding of America's long-term stance in the Indo-Pacific by senior leaders and Congress is reconciled with budgetary limitations, need to be addressed. As indicated, in recent years Congress has undertaken critical measures in the region, including the creation and backing of the MSI in 2015, funding of the Palau Compact in 2017, resourcing some of the Indo-Pacific Command's unfunded requirements in 2018, offering funds for dioxin remediation in Vietnam, and restructuring and increasing the lending threshold for OPIC as part of the BUILD Act. Notwithstanding these activities, and as noted above, there is a gap between the level of resource dedication to the region when compared with the substantial objectives the Trump administration has set for itself. As the administration's "mental map of the Indo-Pacific matures," the next stage in executing this approach on China will "fall to elected officials, and senior congressional staff to prioritize resource levels for the region commensurate with the great power competition we find ourselves in."[93] Despite the rhetoric of Trump et al., "an outdated superpower mindset in the foreign policy establishment," one critique offers, "is likely to limit Washington's ability to scale back other global commitments or make the strategic trade-offs required to succeed in the Indo-Pacific," leaving initiatives like FOIP precariously balanced.[94]

A post-INF world: implications for the U.S., Indo-Pacific allies and partners, and China

In assessing further departures in Trump's foreign policy, the United States' decision to withdraw from the 1987 Intermediate-Range Nuclear Forces (INF) Treaty is likely to have deep implications for U.S. alliance relationships in the Indo-Pacific and elsewhere, and will likely (re)shape allied deterrence postures. The Trump administration publicly argued that Russia's violation of the INF Treaty was the primary cause for its decision to withdraw from the pact in August 2019. However, it is evident, as many administration officials have made clear, that China's growing force of INF missiles has also been an important factor in their decision. While the treaty prevented the United States and the Soviet Union (and now several Soviet successor states, primarily Russia) from possessing ground-based weapons with a range of 500–5,500 kilometers (300–3,000 miles), China conversely has faced no such impediments or restrictions. Most concerning is the sheer fact that a substantial proportion of China's (primarily conventional) missiles fall within this range, notably threatening U.S. naval forces in the Indo-Pacific region. As stated by U.S. Defense Secretary Esper, a forthright U.S. "adjustment" should not come as a shock to China: "We have been talking about that for some time now . . . And I want to say that 80 percent of their inventory is INF range systems. So that should not surprise that we would want to have a like capability."[95]

Not surprisingly, much of the INF Treaty discourse has largely focused on the dynamics surrounding U.S./NATO-Russian relations. Far less attention has been paid to the regional dynamics in the Indo-Pacific. The discussion that has taken place has primarily involved debates among Washington-based experts on whether or not the United States should continue, de facto, to uphold the treaty's restrictions even after its expiration—as a means of preserving the international arms control regime while attaining the potential strategic benefits from deploying previously restricted missiles. Of course, this Washington-centered debate has ignored the fact that any potential deployment and diplomatic decisions will not reflect U.S. preferences alone, but will also need to take into account the perceptions, concerns, and preferences of U.S. allies and partners, and of course, China.

Illustrative of those advocating that the U.S. move quickly in the Indo-Pacific to take advantage of its new post-INF flexibility are Toshi Yoshihara and Jacob Cohn from the Center for Strategic and Budgetary Assessments. In a *National Interest* article, they argue that U.S. policymakers "should reclaim" strategic options that have the capacity to reinstate "U.S. power and prestige in the post-INF era."[96] In reaffirming such views, Timothy A. Walton and colleagues argue that theater-range missiles would "yield strategic dividends," particularly if fielded in numbers and in a fashion sufficient to introduce ambiguity in the adversary's strategic calculus. Further, an "appropriate" deployment would contribute to a credible U.S. warfighting posture and would play an important role in denying the adversary's operational aims should deterrence fail. These advantages, they argue, "would in turn augment U.S. conventional deterrence, an essential ingredient to the stability of key regions around the world."[97]

In building upon these arguments, Mark Montgomery and Eric Sayers, and similarly Max Boot and Nathan Levine, argue that INF-range missile deployments will shift the current dynamic in the Asia-Pacific to benefit the United States. Levine points to the strategic advantages of the weapons being "stationed in unsinkable, out-of-the-way locales like northern Japan, Guam, the southern Philippines, or even northern Australia,"[98] while Montgomery and Sayers contend that deployments will "reassure allies and partners and deter Chinese behavior in Southeast Asia."[99] Neither, however, provide any evidence that they have researched the views of policymakers or opinion shapers in these states to see if they share these conclusions. Even in Sugio Takahashi and Eric Sayers' "America and Japan in a Post-INF World," where the authors aptly acknowledge that "deployment of ground-based strike systems will hold some controversy in Japan," they ambiguously state that "the answer to this controversial issue must be found by the Japanese government and public."[100] While Clive Williams also acknowledges that such U.S. deployments would undoubtedly have implications for U.S. allies in Asia, like Takahashi and Sayers, he offers very little in terms of detail and domestic considerations of the said countries.[101]

On the other hand, Tom Countryman and Kingston Reif represent a group of thinkers who argue against deployments primarily because they lament the demise of the INF Treaty and want to preserve its limits. They point to the rhetoric of Fu Cong, director general of the arms control department at China's foreign ministry, who warns that Indo-Pacific states should "exercise prudence and not allow the U.S. deployment of intermediate-range missiles on their territory," intimating that it would be an unwise decision that could get them caught in a crossfire between the United States and China. On this point, Countryman and Reif argue, securing basing agreements "would require a major investment of political capital from Washington at a time when the Trump administration has done significant damage to several of these alliance relationships."[102] They and Zack Brown argue that the deployments would be militarily ineffective and that U.S. deployments could spur China to accelerate its own deployments over its vast land area, and as such, "U.S. security and the security of its allies would suffer."[103] Mark Cameron correctly asserts that with the question of potential deployment sites, "the answer is not obvious. Guam is a potential candidate, but it is one island that could be counter-targeted by China. Deployment to South Korea, Japan, and Australia would likely be controversial in those countries."[104] In what can be deemed as one of the few analyses that takes serious account of the views of U.S. "friends and allies," Pranay Vaddi cites the need for consulting with Indo-Asian allies, because absent serious discussions, missile deployments could engender a rift between allies, and could even undermine U.S. relationships and "play into China's hands."[105]

That said, U.S. concerns about China's growing IRBM arsenal are shared by Washington's Asian allies and partners, particularly Japan and Taiwan. While these countries would like to see a revised INF treaty that incorporates China, Beijing has rebuffed U.S.-Russian efforts to globalize the accord. As stated by Chinese state councilor Yang Jiechi: "China develops its capabilities strictly according to its defensive needs and doesn't pose a threat to anybody else. So we are opposed to the multilateralization of the INF."[106] Clearly, as China continues its economic and military trajectory, asserting power through a whole-of-government long-term strategy, it will continue to pursue a military modernization approach that seeks Indo-Pacific regional authority in the short term, and displacement of the United States to achieve global pre-eminence in the future. The United States and its Asian and Pacific allies and partners now face several important strategic decisions related to arms control diplomacy and the potential deployment of INF-range systems. These changes necessitate a clear-eyed appraisal of the threats faced, an understanding of the shifting character of warfare, and a transformation of how the Defense Department conducts its strategy. With the Trump administration's seeming preparedness to keep all options alive, a "post-INF world" in the context of the Indo-Pacific region no doubt adds further complications to the equation.

The Belt and Road Initiative (BRI) and the Trump response

While the trade war, critical-area technological decoupling, China's military modernization, and assertions in the South and East China Seas have been the major areas to attract attention in assessing U.S.-China challenges during the Trump tenure, China's Belt and

Road Initiative has also warranted increasing government examination. The BRI was officially launched in 2013 by Xi Jinping to bring together Beijing's strengths in infrastructure development capabilities, its excess capacity in labor and infrastructure resource pools, and its large wealth surplus to link regional networks and, ultimately, pathways to Europe in partnerships for development. Formerly "One Belt, One Road," the BRI consists of the Maritime Silk Road through the Indian Ocean and the Silk Road Economic Belt through central Asia, but it has also developed to include more pathways and linkages to regional and global actors not historically associated with the ancient Silk Road.[107]

With its elevation to Party constitutional significance, the national prerogative for the political and economic development of the BRI has caused many to look at the more strategic implications of the projects. Some analysts have gone as far as to describe Beijing's BRI drive as having ulterior geopolitical motives akin to the Marshall Plan—a method for China to generate strategic advantage in its geographical domain, just as the United States used economic statecraft to strengthen its position in Western Europe in the wake of World War II—and as a modern manifestation of Halford Mackinder's early-twentieth-century theory that controlling Eurasia was a precondition for global hegemony.[108] Others have described the BRI as part of China's "grand strategy," using all aspects of national power to "assert [China's] influence and reshape at least its own neighborhood."[109]

By the beginning of the Trump administration, these narratives had yet to coalesce into a unified response. In fact, the first months offered a complete reversal of the negative anti-China sentiments brought about during the campaign. As critics were to note, Trump seemed to improve U.S.-China relations almost from the beginning by abandoning the TPP on day one in office. Further "upbeat" meetings and discussions with Foreign Minister Wang Yi and state councilor Yang Jiechi in February and March brought to focus the State Department's interest in solving the North Korea issue. Notable first discussions, analysts observed, played toward soliciting China's influence to moderate Pyongyang's destabilizing behavior, downplaying other critical areas of Trump's China agenda. Notwithstanding the periodical and clumsy statements from the Trump administration, by March 8, Chinese authorities had begun characterizing U.S.-China relations as "transitioning steadily and developing in a positive direction."[110] On the BRI more specifically, Trump appeared to turn sharply from Obama's inward hostility by agreeing to send a delegation to the One Belt, One Road Forum in May. It was only in December that a marked shift on this discussion occurred, when the NSS stated, without specifying the BRI, that the administration was concerned by what it saw as China's attempt to "displace the United States in the Indo-Pacific region, expand the reaches of its state-driven economic model, and reorder the region in its favor."[111] The document further noted that the reconstruction and modernization of development investment should be a priority for the United States so as to "not be left behind as other states use investment and project finance to extend their influence."[112] In terms of a clear-cut policy, however, the White House had yet to specifically state how it would deal with China's increasingly influential, and by all accounts nefarious, BRI practices.

An interesting point here is that while Trump was repositioning American foreign policy to focus on trade, initiatives in Japan continued to build upon projects complementary to the Obama administration's "rebalance." These included the Expanded Partnership for Quality Infrastructure, an alternative, transparent initiative to the BRI, and the FOIP concept, initiated by Prime Minister Shinzo Abe in 2007. In November 2017, leaders from the U.S., Australia, India, and Japan met in Manila for a quadrilateral dialogue—led by Abe—to agree on a vision for seemingly upholding the liberal international order in the face of the advance of China's growing economic and military might. However, little consensus was achieved.[113] Trump specified areas for cooperation in alternative trade, transit, and financing frameworks with several Indo-Pacific partners, as well as a rebooted version of the Quad. But by this stage it was a somewhat ignorant position, akin to operating, as one analyst called it, a foreign policy strategically adrift and on autopilot.[114] Japan and Australia were in the midst of completing the successor to the TPP, the Comprehensive and Progressive Agreement for Trans-Pacific Partnership, and while they did not participate in the BRI, they did not want to isolate China completely.

Trump's rejection of the TPP and the administration's lack of strategy for meeting China's challenge to the liberal international order in Asia upset the other members of the Quad, who sought a more nuanced policy agenda vis-à-vis China that dovetailed engagement with economic tools of containment. Despite Trump's lack of vision for policy in Asia, Abe vowed to "press forward with the [FOIP concept] in order to maintain and strengthen a free and open maritime order based on the rule of law in the Indo-Pacific and make the Indo-Pacific a global commons that brings security and prosperity to all nations without distinction," noting that it "can cooperate with any country, including China, as long as it agrees with this kind of approach."[115]

By the end of 2017, Trump's disconnect with Asia on the issue had emboldened Washington's allies to seek cooperation elsewhere. As one analyst remarked, the Trump administration's lack of leadership in meeting the security challenges of the Indo-Pacific led allies like Japan to break the "shackles of the long-time bilateralism approach with the United States."[116] In May 2015, Japan had revealed its five-year, $110 billion proposal to support private financing of "quality infrastructure" projects, using benchmarks that focused on a project's elongated expenditure viability, local job innovation, and environmental sustainability.[117] By 2017, Tokyo and New Delhi conveyed their vision for an "Asia-Africa Growth Corridor," described as being a "people-centric sustainable growth strategy" that would yield and foster economic connectivity between the two continents via infrastructure enhancement, vocational education, and collaborative projects in areas such as agro-processing and pharmaceuticals.[118] In the economic and trade area, Japan and India emerged as the replacement leaders for the otherwise unengaged Washington.

By late 2018, and following on from tensions in U.S.-China relations deriving from the trade war, a semblance of a unified policy began to establish itself in the administration. In fact, by this stage, U.S. opposition to the BRI had become increasingly unwelcoming. At the Asia-Pacific Economic Cooperation summit, Vice President Pence spearheaded the administration's new opposition to the BRI by informing state leaders (including President Xi) that Washington viewed Beijing's BRI negotiations as engaging in "so-called 'debt diplomacy'" and that it would begin addressing these issues in policy terms as a threat to regional stability. In describing PRC loans, Pence noted further that these negotiations were "opaque at best, and the benefits flow overwhelmingly to Beijing."[119] Accordingly, the economic model Beijing had offered in BRI negotiations, in lieu of the traditional Bretton Woods institutions like the International Monetary Fund and World Bank, had been a smokescreen for obtaining economic leverage over host states. While the IMF may have made it difficult for states to obtain funds for development, it hadn't cornered them into one-sided debt-for-equity swaps once development projects had turned sour through a lack of economic means to sustain them. The Paris Club agreements were put in place to see that this could not happen.

In more frank terms, in March 2019, Secretary Pompeo proclaimed the BRI to be "a non-economic offer," and the administration was "working diligently to make sure everyone in the world understands that threat." As stated:

> Their moving into the South China Sea is not because they want freedom of navigation. Their efforts to build ports around the world aren't because they want to be good shipbuilders and stewards of waterways, but rather they have a state national security element to each and every one of them . . . but when you're showing up with a non-economic offer, whether that's through state-facilitated, below-market pricing or handing someone something knowing that you can foreclose on their nation shortly, so predatory lending practices, that's not straight and we are working diligently to make sure everyone in the world understands that threat . . .[120]

While PRC funding certainly had the potential to improve the significant infrastructure deficit in beneficiary states, China's early implementation of the BRI was viewed to be inconsistent, and, at times, one sided in its execution. Moreover, it enabled principally Chinese developers "to benefit by cutting corners and evading responsibility for legal, social, labor, environmental, and other issues."[121] With agreements often concluded in haste, many projects suffered from an inability or refusal to undertake feasibility studies and environmental and social impact evaluations, as well as financing terms that would have generated manageable debt obligations for recipient states. As such, there have been instances where such issues "have begun to alienate local communities and taint the BRI brand," while other countries have sought to renegotiate the terms of their BRI agreements.[122]

Having come to terms with the vacuum that the rash TPP departure had created, and attempting to respond to the BRI, the Trump administration constructed its own strategic mechanism. This began in 2018 in Congress, who pushed the Trump administration to implement the BUILD Act and establish the new IDFC by combining current U.S. government development finance functions.[123] Having eliminated some sixty-two agencies when coming to office in 2017, the administration's apparent shift was a stark contrast to earlier policy pronouncements. Of course, in slowly recognizing that China's development push contained significant strategic elements, the BUILD Act and the IDFC were critically designed, according to Pompeo, to "provide opportunities for American companies to compete overseas and create jobs here at home, a critical component of the President's national economic strategy," while strengthening "the U.S. government's development finance capacity, offering a better alternative to state-directed investments and advancing our foreign policy goals."[124] Further, they were proffered to fill the space produced by a lack of resources from other bilateral and multilateral investors, and as such, to offer quick "no questions asked" capital for infrastructure projects in these places. In praiseworthy terms, one observer offered, the IDFC presented something distinct from China's version of large state-to-state lending by offering "a private sector, market-based solution." According to this narrative, the BUILD Act sought to fill a gap in the BRI unfulfilled by Chinese financing. "China does not support lending to small and medium-sized enterprises (SMEs), and it rarely helps local companies in places like Africa or Afghanistan grow."[125]

Notwithstanding the good intentions of the BUILD Act, the sheer reality has been that it and the IDFC have both been created and restructured to serve as a bulwark against the strategic dimensions associated with China's BRI infrastructure investment. In an era of emerging technologies and the intersections these present to global security, the BUILD Act has been Trump's attempt to apply strategic muscle to balancing China's growing influence across a plethora of domains. One such example has been cyber security. China's state-backed private-sector investments have provided telecommunications infrastructure to a large portion of the global South. And while there are immense infrastructural benefits attained by some recipient states, there have also been marked opportunities for China to embolden their political and strategic reach in the region, driving Internet platforms that uniquely enhance China's strategic leverage in cyberspace. As this theoretically means that the Chinese government can control the infrastructure, it in effect has access to information when needed, including significant amounts of data that could provide China with an advantage over the U.S. in intelligence collection.[126]

Given the concerns emanating from the transition from 4G to 5G and the expansion of telecommunications giants Huawei and ZTE to Western and non-Western states, the associated infrastructural foothold in developing states has clearly presented concerns for the Trump administration as it attempts to constrain Chinese companies and execute its broader security strategy. In such non-Western states, according to some analysts, the U.S. has lost significant strategic and political ground in this area. While the U.S. was asleep at the wheel, this line of thinking asserts, China made a concerted effort, and extensive progress, to secure ownership of the physical infrastructure using the manifold platforms associated with the Asian Infrastructure Investment Bank, the Silk Road Fund, the Industrial Commercial Bank of China, the Export-Import Bank of China, and the China Development Bank, which are all mandated to support projects through the BRI. Currently, while the IDFC could bring some balance back to this disequilibrium, "American and most other western companies do not have similar support from their governments."[127]

In finally understanding the strategic imperative, the Trump administration has responded by placing restrictions on the ability of U.S. firms to do business with Huawei, as well as pressuring allied states to ban Huawei from their respective 5G networks.[128] While this links to the trade war and economic tension between the two states, Trump security officials have maintained that the expansionary and competitive nature of Huawei presents a national security risk to telecommunications equipment that could be applied to reconnaissance and/or cyber-related activities by the Chinese state. Huawei has denied these assertions, but the United States has proceeded to advise and coax if necessary other states to steer their business dealings away from Huawei and from cooperation with China on infrastructure projects under the framework of the BRI.[129] For Trump, there are notable reasons for doing so, not the least being that China forbids an equal tender process for its own telecommunications infrastructure. More significant, however, is that Chinese commercial law under Xi has mandated the subordination of all commercial interests in support of the state, requiring private corporations to abide by all state requests. With Huawei's capability to navigate the Internet and telecommunications infrastructure in associated states, and given China and Huawei's conspicuous secrecy around government-corporation links, Trump administration security officials have sought to push hard against its adoption, at least in allied states.

To this end, the Trump administration has not been completely successful. While Australia and Japan have effectively blocked Huawei from their 5G networks, some states, such as Germany, remain undecided. With the British prime minister, Boris Johnson, throwing down "the gauntlet to U.S. President Donald Trump" with his 2020 "decision [at the time] to defy his warnings and allow Huawei to be part of the United Kingdom's next-generation 5G telecom infrastructure," Berlin's decision on which 5G network it will choose has been watched closely in the White House given its ability to influence how other European states may follow.[130] While the controversy surrounding the choice of Huawei as a 5G network supplier in Germany may surprise some observers, for China's state-controlled media, the issue is reflective of the high-stakes game associated with the Trump-led campaign of pressure and intimidation against its allies.[131] From Beijing's perspective, the subsequent distrust the U.S. has spurred between it and Berlin has only contributed to the broader narrative that the Trump administration seeks to "decouple" the American and Chinese economies. As illustrated on August 23, 2019, in true Trump fashion on Twitter, "Our great American companies are hereby ordered to immediately start looking for an alternative to China, including bringing your companies HOME and making your products in the USA." While the president cited the International Emergency Economic Powers Act in legitimizing his authority for such an order, he later said on August 25, 2019, that he had "no plan right now" to activate the law, leaving many commentators to once again question his seemingly on-the-run policy decisions on crucial matters pertaining to national security.[132] The ad hoc policy gestures and threats have confused not only the Chinese, but also U.S. law makers, unclear about America's leadership and intentions vis-à-vis the Chinese.

Trump's relations with diverging states

Aside from the above bilateral complexities, other broader strategic considerations pertaining to Trump's policies toward the states of North Korea and Taiwan need elaborating, to which the next section now turns.

North Korea

There are few examples that provide a better microcosm of Trump's security strategy than the administration's approach to North Korea. From the early stages of his tenure in office, it was clear that Trump wanted to move away from the very limited "strategic patience" approach of the Obama administration. Whereas Kim Jong-un had very clearly defined goals and redlines, and overall "knew what he was going to get" with Obama, Trump's erratic style, with its revolving door of high-level representatives, bold statements, pseudo-machismo tweets, and inability to fully articulate or define denuclearization, clearly challenged the certainty that Kim had enjoyed with Obama in charge. Indeed, when Trump addressed the UN General Assembly in September 2017, he said that if the U.S. was compelled to defend itself or its allies, it would have "no choice but to totally destroy North Korea." Describing Kim as "Rocket Man," Trump said the North Korean leader was "on a suicide mission for himself and for his regime." In response, Kim called the U.S. president "mentally deranged" and warned that he would "pay dearly" for threatening to destroy North Korea. Further, he added, Trump's comments "have convinced me, rather than frightening or stopping me, that the path I chose is correct and that it is the one I have to follow to the last."[133]

Despite Kim's preparedness to respond to Trump's bellicose words, in simple terms, Trump was able to rattle Kim's cage. However, coinciding with this was an intensification and fast-tracking of North Korea's capacity to unify its missile technology with a nuclear device that could potentially hit the United States mainland. On September 3, 2017, North Korea demonstrated that it had achieved this feat and was now in a position where it could feasibly reach the east coast of the United States with a nuclear device. In conducting its sixth nuclear test, the hermit regime claimed the device tested was a hydrogen bomb and the test was a "perfect success." Seismic activity signified it was its largest nuclear test to date at 3:30 UTC. The initial estimate from the Comprehensive Nuclear Test-Ban Treaty Organization (CTBTO) was that the seismic event's magnitude was approximately 5.8, took place at a very shallow depth, and was in the immediate vicinity of North Korea's Punggye-ri test site. Based on the seismic data, several analysts assessed the device to possess an explosive yield in excess of 100 kilotons TNT equivalent, which was significantly higher than North Korea's previous nuclear tests. While Pyongyang's pronouncement that the device was a hydrogen bomb could not be objectively substantiated, the greater yield was indicative of a boosted fission or thermonuclear device. The CTBTO's seismic estimate was later revised to 6.1 on September 7, 2017.[134]

As the above events unfolded, it was clear to China's leadership that Trump's threat, and perhaps even preparedness to use pre-emptive/preventive force, as well as the mobilization of U.S. forces and the THAAD missile system in close proximity to its shores, was too much for Beijing to sit idly by and "wait and see." And despite the ground-breaking, albeit questionable, meeting in Singapore in 2018 between Donald Trump and Kim Jong-un, it was clear that North Korea would remain a source of ongoing consternation between the United States and China. Indeed, while the U.S. and China have both committed to the goal of denuclearization in North Korea, there have been many instances where they have disagreed on the optimal means for moving forward in attaining that goal. One of the main criticisms has been China's often compromised and/or softer approach toward North Korea, reflected particularly in its inclination to seek less ardent UN sanctions than the U.S. and its complete repudiation of international assessments that North Korea had purposefully sunk the ROKS *Cheonan* in 2010. In response, the Trump administration has frequently ratcheted up its rhetoric toward China's sanctions implementation (or lack of), describing their response as being "at times inconsistent, but critical."[135] Specifically, in the domain of "significant commodities," the PRC has been chastised by the administration for selectively permitting certain items while limiting others. In tweeting his own White House statement on the issue, the president stated that "President Donald J. Trump feels strongly that North Korea is under tremendous pressure from China because of our major trade disputes with the Chinese government. At the same time, we also know that China is providing North Korea with considerable aid, including money, fuel, fertilizer and various other commodities. This is not helpful!"[136]

As a source of bilateral tension, the Treasury Department responded by identifying those mainland-based commercial entities, Hong Kong-based shipping companies, and PRC nationals who had purportedly contravened U.S.-North Korea sanctions.[137] In 2018 and again in 2019, the United States led efforts requesting that a UN sanctions committee declare that North Korea had acquired refined petroleum commodities at quantities substantively greater than UN sanctions allowed, and that all new transfers should cease. North Korea was alleged to have obtained the above-quota petroleum products through illegal ship-to-ship transfers at sea. In both instances, in what was viewed as a seemingly bold strategic political maneuver, Russia and China blocked the UN committee from proclaiming that Pyongyang had contravened the yearly limit for importing refined petroleum products, which are key for its economy.[138] In articulating the administration's frustration, Nikki Haley, U.S. ambassador to the United Nations, stated:

Now for China and Russia to block it, what are they telling us? Are they telling us that they want to continue supplying this oil? The sanctions committee has what it needs. We all know it's going forward. We put pressure today on China and Russia to abide and be good helpers through this situation and to help us continue with denuclearization. This undermines that approach.[139]

That said, notable Chinese gestures across the 2018–2019 period included, at times, an improved capacity to execute UN sanctions regimes. In this regard, many analysts have even gone as far as to acknowledge the sanctions as playing a dramatic role in cutting North Korea's exports and imports, and thereby, fostering the thaw in relations between North Korea and South Korea, and ultimately, opening the pathway for the two summits between Donald Trump and Kim Jong-un, held in Singapore and Hanoi respectively.[140] Additionally, the announcement of Trump's June 2018 summit with Kim contributed to a thaw in the heretofore frosty China-North Korea ties. Subsequently, since March 2018, Kim has visited China four times and Xi has visited North Korea once, in June 2019. Not surprisingly, China was clearly taken aback by the, at times, recalcitrant and unpredictable behavior of both Trump and Kim, particularly during the acrimonious and escalatory period of 2017 and early 2018. Further, the prospect of U.S. strike options, the potential escalation to war on the peninsula, a U.S.-led occupation, the elongated presence of the U.S. military in very close proximity to China, and/ or the flood of North Korean refugees across its border—all these were regarded as totally unacceptable scenarios to the Chinese state. As such, aside from its endorsement and execution of firmer UN sanctions, the PRC has also consistently urged all parties to embark on "phased and synchronized steps" in a "dual-track approach" to a political resolution of issues on the Korean Peninsula, with one track concentrating on denuclearization and the other on instituting a peace process.[141] Of course, in the period after the Trump-Kim summit in Hanoi in February 2019, progress between the U.S. and North Korea became moribund at the negotiating table, where discussions ended in stalemate over what the United States described as unreasonable and disproportionate North Korean requests for sanctions relief, in exchange for only a limited submission of its nuclear capabilities.[142]

Despite a subsequent brief and symbolic meeting between Trump and Kim at the demarcation line between North and South

Korea in the demilitarized zone on June 30, 2019, the failure of the Hanoi summit to produce tangible steps to advance denuclearization and peace building clearly impacted whatever progress had taken place between the two states. On January 21, 2020, a counselor to Pyongyang's mission at the United Nations in Geneva announced that North Korea would no longer adhere to its self-imposed moratorium on nuclear and long-range missile testing.[143] The representative, Ju Yong-chol, stated that the April 2018 moratorium was conceived to "build confidence with the United States," but given that the Trump administration "remains unchanged in its ambition to block the development" of North Korea, Pyongyang has "no reason to be unilaterally bound" by its earlier pledge.[144] The Geneva comments reaffirmed those of Kim Jong-un at the 7th Central Committee of the Worker's Party of Korea, where he revealed the incendiary but expected swing in North Korean policy toward negotiations with the United States. Kim indicated in April 2019 that North Korea's attitude to negotiations with Washington would alter if the United States did not embrace a more accommodating negotiating position by the end of the year. The extent to which relations shifted across 2019 is evident when looking at the statements of Kim. The leader of North Korea began 2019 by restating his commitment to "neither make and test nuclear weapons any longer nor to use and proliferate them," noting his "firm will to . . . advance towards complete denuclearization."[145] By the end of the year, Kim instead cautioned that North Korea would "steadily develop indispensable and prerequisite strategic weapons for national security,"[146] while its nuclear deterrent will "be properly coordinated depending on the U.S. future attitude" toward Pyongyang.[147]

To add further dissatisfaction to the Trump administration in its dealings with China, Kim held summits with Russian and Chinese leaders throughout 2018 and 2019 in addition to his two with Trump.[148] The more troubling outcome of these, despite the pretensions to deal bilaterally with the United States, was that on December 16, 2019 Russia and China both recommended the partial repeal of UN Security Council sanctions on North Korea, as a means to re-establish a diplomatic course of action. Preceding the draft resolution's publication, the Russian ambassador to the

United Nations, Vasily Nebenzya, announced on December 11 that "sanctions will not substitute for diplomacy. It is impossible to reach an agreement without offering something in return."[149] Of course, these announcements repudiated all previous attempts of the United States to meet in a conciliatory manner with North Korea in search of an agreement. While it is unsurprising that the trilateral discussions held between China, North Korea, and Russia have received significantly less international interest than the optics associated with U.S.-North Korean diplomatic summits, their outcomes have been noticeably more effectual in their disruption of U.S. strategy to deal with North Korea.[150] The trilateral fora have clearly concentrated on converging the three states' positions so as to embolden Pyongyang's posture in ongoing negotiations with Washington. While Russian foreign minister Sergey Lavrov observed on November 8, 2019 that the autonomous trilateral grouping should not be perceived as a substitute for the U.S.-North Korean negotiations, the co-supported draft resolution ostensibly called for the "prompt resumption of the six-party talks or re-launch of multilateral consultations in any other similar format, with the goal of facilitating a peaceful and comprehensive solution through dialogue," signaling Russia and China's intensifying concern and interest in cooperating formally on the North Korean denuclearization process.[151]

While the Trump administration has long asserted that North Korea's complete denuclearization must precede sanctions relief, more recent indicators emphasize a shift in the White House in the direction of a progressively more accommodating negotiation position. At a UN Security Council meeting on December 11, 2019, the U.S. ambassador to the United Nations, Kelly Craft, remarked that the administration would now "remain ready to take actions in parallel, and to simultaneously take concrete steps toward this agreement," noting further that it was "prepared to be flexible," recognizing "the need for a balanced agreement that addresses the concerns of all parties."[152] At the same meeting, a Chinese representative said that it was "imperative" that economic sanctions on North Korea be eased. China's ambassador to the United Nations, Zhang Jun, called on the international community to ease the tensions over the Korean Peninsula through political solutions and peace talks. For Beijing, it was crucial "to maintain the international consensus and momentum for a political solution" and to "support and urge the United States and the Democratic People's Republic of Korea to move toward each other, and do everything we can to head off a dramatic reversal of the peninsula's situation."[153] This position was further supported by Nebenzya, who argued that progress was impossible as long as North Korea was "told to unequivocally agree to all conditions that are imposed for the promise of future benefits."[154] These comments closely echoed Foreign Minister Lavrov's at the Moscow Non-proliferation Conference on November 8, speaking on Moscow's and Beijing's preference for an "action-by-action, step-by-step" approach to North Korean denuclearization.[155] Despite the potential tensions that such "converging" actions by Russia and China could produce, in this instance, a multilateral approach providing a circuit breaker to the peninsula was very much required. Of course, how the Trump administration interprets such developments and responds next in its negotiations with North Korea will be the decisive factor on where the issue ends.

Taiwan

If the Trump doctrine can be described as transactional, at times erratic, and "policy-on-the-fly," followed by the penchant for jarring American "friends and allies," then the Taiwan-China issue can be considered an apt example of Trump's ebbing and flowing style in play. For the Chinese, first impressions upon Trump's election victory were troubling to say the least. Almost as a first action, Trump appeared to put the long-standing one-China policy on notice, famously questioning its efficacy and taking a congratulatory call from Taiwan's president, Tsai Ing-wen. Secretary of State-designate Rex Tillerson was quick to clear this up, reiterating on January 11 the U.S. commitment to Taiwan (based on the Taiwan Relations Act (TRA)) and the Six Assurances (from the United States-China Joint Communiqué) at his Senate confirmation hearing. He also suggested that he was not aware of "any plans to alter" the U.S. one-China policy.[156] This was followed by Trump himself, who took the opportunity to use a February 9 call with Xi Jinping to reaffirm the United States' commitment to the said policy.[157] In a further attempt to placate Chinese concerns, worried about a shift in U.S.-Taiwan policy, the

Trump administration's NSS stated that the United States would "maintain our strong ties with Taiwan in accordance with our 'One-China' policy, including our commitments under the Taiwan Relations Act to provide for Taiwan's legitimate defense needs and deter coercion."[158]

That said, the Trump administration's language on Taiwan has evolved since 2017 with a preparedness to regularly run precariously close to the diplomatic line on the issue. In 2018, for instance, in a major turn in U.S. diplomatic practice, the 115th Congress passed, with Trump's signature, the Taiwan Travel Act, calling on U.S. policy to permit U.S. officials at all levels, "including Cabinet level national security officials, general officers, and other executive branch officials," to visit Taiwan for meetings with equivalent posts. In reciprocating these exchanges, it further allowed high-level Taiwan representatives to enter the United States under civil terms to convene with U.S. officials, "including officials from the Department of State and the Department of Defense and other Cabinet agencies."[159] In May 2019, the United States hosted a meeting between the U.S. and Taiwanese national security advisers, the first such meeting publicly disclosed since the United States ended diplomatic relations with Taiwan in 1979.[160]

In further formal, albeit ambiguous, developments, the DoD's June 2019 IPSR discussed America's position on Taiwan without specifically referencing the U.S. one-China policy. This was followed by a second high-profile U.S. government report on the current era of unofficial relations with Taiwan, this time referring to the island ambiguously as a "country" rather than an autonomous territory of China, and a nation under peril. The strategy document introduced Taiwan, along with Singapore, New Zealand, and Mongolia, as Indo-Pacific democracies that were considered "reliable, capable, and natural partners of the United States," with all having "a vital interest in upholding the rules-based international order, which includes a strong, prosperous, and democratic Taiwan."[161] Whether these "adjustments" were intentional and/or represented a conceptual shift in Washington's evolving Taiwan policy, the White House did not elaborate.

In July 2019, the Trump administration appeared to escalate these changes on the Taiwan issue by permitting President Tsai

Ing-wen to make high-profile transit visits through New York City and Denver, on her way to and from visiting diplomatic partners in the Caribbean. While not out of the ordinary, in terms of previous practice, the White House this time agreed to allow Tsai to include a short private speech at Columbia University, a visit to Central Park, and a function at Taiwan's representative office for the UN representatives of Taiwan's diplomatic allies.[162] These allowances, including the subtle changes to diplomatic practices, pushed the boundaries of the U.S-China relationship over Taiwan to new levels. Indeed, the last time a (former) Taiwanese president spoke at a United States university a crisis was caused to erupt in the Taiwan Strait. As such, if Trump perceived them to be meaningless in terms of the one-China policy, Chinese perceptions indicated otherwise. In the context of the broader contours of U.S.-China relations pertaining to the SCS, the evolving trade war, and concerns about the BRI (to name but a few), Trump's preparedness to traverse the one-China policy clearly reflected a strategic and political intent.

In looking back, when it made the landmark decision to recognize the PRC and *de*-recognize the Republic of China (ROC) in 1979, the U.S. stated that the government of the PRC was "the sole legal Government of China." In this context, "sole" meant that the PRC *was* and *is* the only China, with no understanding of the ROC as a distinct sovereign entity. The United States, however, did not concede wholly to Chinese mandates that it recognize Chinese sovereignty over Taiwan. Instead, the U.S. "acknowledged" (but did not formally "recognize") the Chinese position that Taiwan was part of China, and for a range of geopolitical reasons, both states were prepared to proceed forward despite their divergences on this issue.[163] The logical conclusion to these actions on Taiwan by the Trump administration suggests principally one of two things: that Trump was prepared to use Taiwan as a means to needle China on the international stage and garner strategic traction wherever possible, or that Congress has been largely leading this course of policy from behind.

Trump's signing of the Hong Kong Human Rights and Democracy Act, authorizing the United States to sanction individuals responsible for human-rights abuses in Hong Kong, illustrates this Congressional involvement more specifically. Trump, for his part, has been generally dismissive of democracy promotion and human rights, threatening even to veto the Hong Kong Human Rights and Democracy Act, while noting also that Xi had acted "very responsibly" on Hong Kong.[164] Regardless of these diverging narratives, policy toward Taiwan has become increasingly bipartisan and dynamic, reflecting a more serious shift in the United States in terms of the 1979 TRA. Chinese officials, upon the signing of the Hong Kong Human Rights and Democracy Act, reciprocated by condemning the move, and imposing sanctions on several U.S.-based organizations and U.S. warship visits to Hong Kong.[165] But the more significant outcome has come from Taiwan, with observers noting that such actions by Washington have been watched very closely in Taipei by both citizens and policymakers. To add further trouble to Beijing's Taiwan dilemma, noted Taiwan foreign minister Joseph Wu, reflecting on the 2020 Taiwan presidential election, "young voters here in Taiwan" had been watching "the young demonstrators in Hong Kong fighting for their freedom and democracy [and realized] if they don't come out and try to save our country through the democratic process, Taiwan might become a second Hong Kong."[166]

In January 2020, the people of Taiwan provided a defining rebuke to China when they defeated the pro-Beijing Nationalists and re-elected President Tsai in a landslide victory. In the preceding year, Tsai appeared to be in political danger after her Democratic Progressive Party experienced significant losses to the Nationalists in local elections. Undeterred by significant Chinese attempts to boost her challenger, Han Kuo-yu, Tsai won a record 8.2 million votes, more than any Taiwanese leader since the start of direct presidential elections in 1996.[167] In a statement that angered Beijing, U.S. secretary of state Mike Pompeo observed that Taiwan's democratic system, free market economy, and civil society made it "a model for the Indo-Pacific region and a force for good in the world." Further, "the United States thanks President Tsai for her leadership in developing a strong partnership with the United States and applauds her commitment to maintaining cross-Strait stability in the face of unrelenting pressure." Although Pompeo did not mention Beijing specifically, his remarks clearly referred to the pressure Tsai had encountered from China during her first term in office.[168] These remarks, and others like them, we note, illustrate the shift undertaken by the Trump administration during its tenure thus far. On Trump's watch, U.S. warships have sailed through the Taiwan Strait on a regular basis, contrasted with their marginal deployment under President Obama. While both Obama and George W. Bush declined Taiwan's requests to buy U.S. F-16s for concern of provoking Beijing's indignation, Trump authorized a fighter-jet transaction for the first time since 1992. Additionally, a U.S.-Taiwan free trade agreement is imminent and will most certainly attain significant bipartisan support in Congress. Although the deal would contribute to the U.S. economy and increase U.S. exports, it also augments the administration's strategy as it seeks "to broaden and deepen the security relationship with Taiwan." These actions, undoubtedly, have been commensurate with assessments that brand China a revisionist power, seeking to diminish the U.S. influence in East Asia. The Pentagon's IPSR has conveyed in these terms the importance of Taiwan to the Trump administration: that a "strong, prosperous, and democratic Taiwan" is part of the rules-based order that America has a vital interest in upholding; and that the U.S. is pursuing a "strong partnership with Taiwan, particularly in light of Beijing's pressure campaign against Taiwan."[169]

Conclusion

In assessing the Trump administration's approach to security challenges with China, the three pillars—aside from the focus on trade—of military modernization, the SCS, and the BRI, illuminate notable changes and varied adjustments to strategy pursued across the Bush and Obama administrations. As this chapter illustrates, the periodical intensification of competition was the major theme, buttressed of course by a strong military and an expanded unilateral American position in U.S.-led multilateral organizations. The strengthening of barriers and obstacles to China's SCS maritime claims has been undertaken, as well as a general re-energizing of the military—despite debates pertaining to shortfalls in resources and budget limitations. Additionally, official concerns and disagreement over the strategic drive of China's BRI have been firmly articulated, causing, partly as a result, the implementation of counter-policies designed to meet the emerging strategic economic threat. A broader change identified in this analysis has been Trump's, at times, siloed approach in dealing with China, often in opposition to the "whole of government" approach emphasized in the DoD, the NSC, the State Department, and Congress. In this regard, in eschewing diplomacy amid greater military posturing and replacing economic integration with limited and seemingly self-defeating "America First" trade policies, Trump's strategy, such as it has been, has spoken to the domain of undisciplined campaign politics more than a sophisticated comprehension of geopolitical implications and considerations for grand strategy. For Trump's Asia-Pacific partners, this "unnuanced" approach to challenging the increasingly provocative China in the region has been met with some support, oftentimes confusion, and occasionally derision.

In reviewing Trump's White House management and leadership qualities, these views come as unsurprising. Disorder and inconsistency define the Trump administration's management style, no more evident than in its (mis)handling of the COVID-19 crisis and the very related race protests in May/June 2020. In looking back to 2016, while many were willing to wait and see before judging the efficacy of Trump's foreign policy team, they did not have to wait long to assess that the first year had been generally unsatisfactory.[170] Secretary of State Rex Tillerson, thought to be an experienced operator from his time as ExxonMobil CEO, was given little room to influence foreign affairs or even choose his own management team. At this time, too, the State Department underwent a restructuring in funds and personnel as important positions remained vacant. National Security Adviser H. R. McMaster, who replaced Michael Flynn in February 2017 following scandal, added more sophistication to foreign policy, as did Secretary of Defense James Mattis, but their advice was often countermanded and ignored by Trump, who disdained intellectuals and intelligence officials. By the middle of the second year, all but Mattis had departed from their positions or had been fired by Trump.

The broader contours of this outcome in policy and personnel can be seen in Trump's delayed and mismatched policy toward China and the Indo-Pacific. With the notable exception of INDOPACOM's augmented FoN strategy in the SCS, the gap between strategy, as delineated in the NSS and the NDS, and the policies adopted illustrates the discernible incongruences between promises and action. Budget allocations for reinforcing regional allies and bolstering U.S.-partner relationships in the Indo-Pacific have not sufficiently met the increase in significance that China's purported challenge has warranted. In some areas, budgets have actually been scaled back. Despite the explicit break in foreign policy doctrine from strategic engagement to strategic competition, the Trump administration continued to prioritize trade over a coordinated response encompassing soft ideational and diplomatic factors with hard military ones.

That said, changes to the Trump administration's China policies by late 2018 had begun to recognize, and reconcile with, some of these ostensible gaps in action and strategy. An increase in vocal opposition to China's SCS militarization and predatory BRI practices, including more diplomatic engagement with Indo-Pacific partners, was forthcoming from Vice President Mike Pence and Secretary of State Mike Pompeo. At this time too, the U.S.-China trade war added impetus to Congressional initiatives, including the BUILD Act and FIRRMA, both designed to compete more strategically with China's BRI and stymie the transference of critical technologies from America to China. In terms of Trump's leadership in this area, the record, however, is ambiguous. While he has allowed Pence and Pompeo to take charge of voicing Washington's Indo-Pacific strategies, it is yet unclear the extent to which this has been coordinated in the White House. Trump has maintained that he means no ill will toward China and that Washington and Beijing get along well. At the same time, increasing competition in strategic areas belies this attitude. Inside information has presented Trump as at times aloof, moronic, unhinged, and disinterested.[171]

Judging the current record, Trump's China policy has evolved year-on-year to resemble something more sophisticated and coordinated. This has been helped along by Congress and importantly China's president, Xi Jinping, whose expansionistic and increasingly zero-sum policies have spurred greater opposition in the United States and, in some ways, engendered a clearer focus from the administration. Of course, given the security developments emanating from the COVID-19 crisis, the administration's poor and inconsistent responses to the pandemic, its penchant to align blame solely on China—not to mention an unbridled preparedness to fan the flames of unresolved racial tensions and police violence—the Trump administration's actions only promise to accelerate and exacerbate frictions between the two countries.

Afterword

Looking ahead, the challenges for the next administration are manifold. Already, the beginning of the new decade has witnessed several clear, stability-eroding disruptions to international security, an evident reality which will require nuanced and novel solutions involving international cooperation. Unmistakable in this picture is the role of climate change, illustrated by the ruinous destruction of widespread bush fires in Australia, fueled by extreme heat and the country's driest spring on record. In the Middle East, tensions have risen further following President Trump's decision to openly condone the assassination in January 2020 of Iranian general Qasem Soleimani. Directly related to this incident was the accidental shooting down of a Ukrainian passenger airliner by Iran the following week. Additionally, the emergence of the COVID-19 viral pandemic in China and beyond, and the misguided delays in global responses have caused an international widening of the contagion. As COVID-19-related deaths have skyrocketed, and quarantines and lockdowns spurred the contraction of commerce, so too have the prospects of an elongated global financial crisis taken hold. Moreover, the refusal and/or incapacity of Trump to provide substantive leadership during race-related protests that have swept America, and the absence of even the most basic inclination to call for calm and unity, has no doubt further marred the administration's reputation both at home and abroad.

How the United States itself responds to these crises will of course impact upon the decisions and relationships of allies, partners, and periphery countries in the ongoing security challenges now evident between Washington and Beijing. While it might be routine to suggest that leadership will be required in great profusion moving forward, there is little evidence to suggest the Trump White House comprehends the current gap in this area. Under Trump, a nationally defined criterion for engagement, or at the least cooperation on areas of mutual interest, with China and partners has been notably absent. Meanwhile, definitional and implementation shortfalls in concepts such as the Free and Open Indo-Pacific, strategic competition, and the BUILD Act have tormented the administration's response to China. Here, the implications of Washington's shrinking diplomatic program, too, have converged to complicate the administration's message. Whereas secretaries of state Condoleezza Rice under George W. Bush and Hillary Clinton under Barack Obama both sought increases to the diplomatic budget to refocus on partners and emerging concerns in the Indo-Pacific, the Trump administration has cut deeply into these and other international programs for greater spending on the military.

The ability of the United States to respond to such events in a transitioning global system will in no small way require a reset of the post-Cold War operational scripture: reconciliation between the unilateralism of American presidential administrations and the reality of what now is a multipolar, crisis-prone, porous, and interdependent world. In this regard, one of the first lessons of the Trump administration is that while leading and "winning" are not mutually exclusive, they are methodologically complex, requiring above all nuance and government-wide cooperation. Given this consideration, a reassessment and rethinking of "America First" and the geopolitically confronting Indo-Pacific strategy is imperative. It requires, further, the assessment of the Bush and Obama years, accepting without prejudice the positive and negative aspects as lessons for policy development. On this point the "security trap" of the Bush years in the Middle East looms large. By attempting to solve the nation's problems through the primary execution of military force, the experience is likely to be resistance and backlash in the international community, isolation among friends, and the engendering of greater insecurity.[1]

Great-power conflict in the twenty-first century

Great-power conflict has emerged as a significant and dynamic new challenge to international security. The rapid rise of China and its search for stature and regional influence has been a long-recognized phenomenon, explaining much of the trepidation among Western analysts and policymakers advocating engagement with Beijing. While it is evident that such fears have been warranted, the engagement strategies of the Bush and Obama administrations in their attempt to militate against the rise of a revisionist peer-competitor have not aged well. At the same time, a return to zero-sum policies, unilateralism, and brash and arrogant rhetoric followed by divisive policy departures, have characterized an assertiveness in both the United States and China that have only aggravated competition. In assessing what course of action to take, the experiences of the twenty-first-century administrations will be instructive. Which engagement mechanisms have worked? Which ones have failed? Has diplomacy emboldened administration initiatives, and if not, why not? What regional initiatives have been successful? These are the questions that need to be examined moving forward in the next administration. Outright rejection of former presidential initiatives, and ignorance of their political and international struggles, are illustrative in all three presidential administrations discussed over the course of this book, the examples of which have led to policy short-termism, reassessment, and at times a redressing of former policy applications.

As China maintains its destabilizing militarization of contested islands in the SCS, continues to modernize the military without the transparent and diplomatic tools to prevent misperception, and seizes opportunities to dismantle liberal international democratic norms, the White House will have to decide how to respond. For the next administration, regardless of who wins the 2020 presidential election, the question of the extent to which the United States can live in a world where it shares power with another peer-competitor will require a response. Given the historical context of the Cold War and the divergent pathways in governance and foreign relations between the U.S. and China, the answer is likely to be negative. There are structural reasons for this, as realists and power-transition theorists argue: the powerful get to write the rules of the road, to decide upon financial and economic structures, and to profit from the fruits of the international system. More importantly, being the hegemon also denotes a level of security of the highest kind, drawing upon disproportionate resources in times of conflict to defeat unwanted challengers. That said, there are also constructed facets to this image, equally decisive to the question at hand.

For the United States, the strategic and historical trajectory from emancipated colony to global superpower has been infused with a deep-seated belief in the exceptional quality of American political and moral ability. In this context, as long as China continues to disabuse the global commons of its humanitarian program; deny basic rights, such as religious freedoms, to its 1.4 billion citizens; and seek to export its system abroad, it will be in America's national interest to compete with and if possible dismantle the Chinese Communist Party. That the CCP sees in its own image equally worthy and exceptional qualities will reinforce a positive feedback loop. Xi Jinping's "China Dream," emphasizing the rejuvenation of the nation, reflects a similar promise to return China to the Middle Kingdom of antiquity and emboldening patriotic themes of greatness. Together with organized nationalism—narrowed to inflate Party worth and the one hundred years of humiliation—the campaign for Made in China 2025, and tools such as the Belt and Road Initiative (BRI), illustrate the strategies for national development and offer a socio-cultural-economic rationale for strategic competition.

In this context, the new great-power contest will look and behave in ways unrecognizable to the conflict that defined the Cold War between the United States and the Soviet Union. There are notable and consequential reasons for this. The first is that the China of today is monumentally larger, more sophisticated, wealthier, better organized, and more globally integrated than the Soviet Union was even at its most powerful point. Further, despite the differences in political systems between democratic America and autocratic China, the ideological divide is much weaker. The PRC is now a global hub for liberal trade and financial exchange. As much as the United States may seek to decouple with or sanction elements of China's economy and commercial sector, its allies will not so easily be persuaded by such destabilizing departures in policy. The case of Huawei and 5G is illustrative. As this book goes to print, Britain, a member of the Five Eyes intelligence network along with Australia, the U.S., New Zealand, and Canada, is still considering Huawei's tender to build its 5G networks, despite great protestations from the U.S. and Australia. If Britain had continued to solicit the services of Huawei, the very foundation and composition of the grouping and the apparent independence of the group's intelligence gathering would have been called into question. As this example shows, the vertical and horizontal aspects of the new great-power competition will increasingly disrupt traditional alliance agreements as states seek to manage their economies and growth strategies in times of volatility.

Indicatively, the most noteworthy aspect of this twenty-first-century power dynamic is that ideational and economic strengths, not just military might, will be the defining characteristics of national power. In other words, the power to persuade, cajole, influence, and even coerce global partners, allies, and importantly periphery nations through global institutions, via international laws and norms, trade deals and development projects, and outreach programs, whether purely diplomatic or defense-related, will define the competitive strength of the United States. From this purview, the competition offered by China's BRI and America's alternative will become pivotal. While it is trite to say a fracturing of this power has taken place under the administration of President Donald Trump, the foundations of America's liberal traditions have not been completely eroded. That said, nor are they infinitely resilient. As the Huawei case demonstrates, the informal power of American leadership is waning. This speaks to a further condition of the new power dynamic: no longer will a single or bipolar structure dominate the international focus.

Ongoing challenges

As states seek to build upon national security foundations, whether through the independent search for military security or in direct response to the rise of new threats, the continual "advancements" in dual-use critical technologies, cyber security processes, artificial intelligence, and arms development will create further uncertainty. The management of these emerging, and possibly game-changing, challenges to existing differences will put a premium on the ability for policymakers to avoid their escalation in ongoing confrontations. The scholarship on this broader discourse has partially met this expanding emphasis on the new great-power conflict, although the continued struggle in assessing material and ideational dynamics and perceptions of shifting power across the world is evident. In this context, differentiating the former lessons of the Cold War struggles from the new conditions of the twenty-first century will require innovative, multi-disciplinary approaches, targeting, for instance, how 5G can be used to influence politics across BRI countries, and seeking to understand how to influence operations can drive perceptions and shape policy choices.

What is evident in these times and among such challenges is that there is a need for cautious policies and restrained rhetoric. The BRI is a case in point. China's global development program may suffer from notable shortcomings in financing structures, transparency, building and financial safeguards, and questions of viability. But indications also suggest the BRI is more alive and dynamic than monolithic, and singularly purposeful. In other words, its programs and processes are more subject to international concerns, opinions, and challenges than they are otherwise given credit for. In Beijing, the government has responded to international criticism of its predatory loans, and accusations of debt diplomacy, by implementing more safeguards, greater transparency, and more flexible financial options. As this example demonstrates, the risk of recognizing deception in all actions produces only self-fulfilling prophecies as counter-policies are adopted to address new areas of perceived competition. This is not to say also that accidents of benign intention—such as how China perceives its strategic footholds in the Indian Ocean to be—are without outcomes of malign utility.

As this line of thinking suggests, accountability is all-important. On this point, there are notable contradictions worthy of further analysis and attention at the national and international level. For one, it is imperative to point out that engagement on China's behalf has been predominantly selective, self-serving, and dissatisfying. Nowhere has this been the case more than on issues of nuclear weapons proliferation and North Korea. While Beijing has participated in UN sanctions against North Korean provocation, it has consistently sought to water down the imposition for these sanctions to take full effect. Moreover, it has refused to join the Proliferation Security Initiative due to claims that interdiction programs at sea are counter to international law. What have been the outcomes of these barriers? On North Korea, to the extent that outside influence can change behaviors, the Bush, Obama, and Trump administrations have collectively tried sundry hard-line, conciliatory, and ground-breaking approaches. For the fact that these approaches have failed, including the sanctions regimes encompassed, the Chinese authorities deserve credit. As to international law, China's pursuit of islands in the SCS, its militarization of those islands, and the harassment of regional neighbors and fellow claimants repudiate the claim that international legal documents are important or that they cannot be altered by such agreements as the PSI. On sanctions too, the object of China's periodical refusal to accept harsh sanctions against Pyongyang and Tehran out of principle has fallen flat in the face of its own sanctions against nations it perceives as upsetting to Chinese feelings. These inconsistencies mark a departure from the narrative Beijing seeks of the benign and cooperative global partner.

Finally, and as the divisive and divergent responses in the United States and China to the COVID-19 pandemic illustrate, the loss of U.S. international leadership has created a vacuum which autocracies such as China have been able to exploit to their own ends. Here, the implications for the further erosion of the liberal world order are perceived as acute. Discordant voices in the U.S. COVID-19 narrative and charged differences between states and the federal government in Washington to the correct response have revealed a nation divided, inarticulate, and fundamentally unprepared at a time of national and international crisis. Critical interventions by Trump, such as the hijacking of personal protective equipment (PPE) supplies from traditional partners such as France and Canada, and attempting to buy out potential vaccine patents for exclusive U.S. use in Germany, has for many laid bare the interests of the Trump administration and the United States more broadly.[2] When it comes to such crises, the United States, this message portrays, will act alone and in the face of reassuring rhetoric pronouncing its dedication to cooperation, alliance relationships, and democratic partnerships.

Meanwhile, in China the message from leaders has been equally eccentric: it has attempted to display leadership, for instance, by touting its successful national response as a template for export and shipping PPE supplies to countries in need while at the same time excoriating Western nations perceived as unduly critical of its part in the spread of the virus. This attempt has for the time being been repudiated in the international community as the brash and polemical statements of China's ambassadors—so-called "Wolf Warrior" diplomats, named after the popular Chinese movie (2017)—have caused some states to reassess their relationships with Beijing. But the point serves to reveal a more enduring image of Beijing's capabilities (despite the undiplomatic assertiveness of its ambassadors) and a truism of the current international environment, a point fundamentally missed in Trump's strategy for dealing with China thus far. In short, the norms of appropriateness in international affairs are being constantly reassessed by states in light of the perceived effectiveness of autocratic systems to deal with the perennial headaches so familiar to underdeveloped states—challenges such as resource insecurity, growing urban migration, social inequality, and international crisis, which have so obviously been ignored by the former great Western powers. In this equation, Trump's harmful response to addressing COVID-19 in the United States, blaming China as a strategy to deflect criticism at home, has worked to embellish sentiments that liberal democracy in the American image is an unworthy tradeoff for the easier and more prompt acquisition of development and finance from China.

The damage to America's credibility will be a source of the next administration's enduring troubles in trying to convince nations, particularly those in the Indo-Pacific, that Washington should have an influential voice in their affairs when it has so shamelessly ignored the experiences of states to deal even with its own COVID-19 response.

Closing thoughts

The notable disjuncture in the Trump administration between narrative, strategy, and perceptions of threat has weakened the authority and legitimacy of American leadership in international affairs. Where Trump has allowed his Defense Department, and to an extent his NSC, to drive security strategy, he has consistently undermined their narratives by creating a perceptively false, or at the very least an overly simplistic image of Xi Jinping and Beijing's foreign policy goals—counter to the claims made by his defense establishment. There are two alarming concerns associated with this contradiction here. The first is that it denies the "whole of government" approach necessary to compete with Beijing, which is, to be sure, competing at all levels of government. The second, perhaps more enduring and critical challenge, is that such contradictions, notwithstanding Trump's antipathy for the media and his delegitimizing rhetoric, has fueled and will fuel a trust deficit between the executive government, the legislative branch, and the American people on policy and action toward China. The implications are substantive, and here the lessons of history are illustrative: when the United States has united to compete against a perceived or even real foe, its capacity and resolve to succeed have been awesomely formidable. When unity and trust have eroded, and when confidence in the government is low, however, the ability to compete and win protracted contests has been demonstrably weak. The example of Vietnam here comes to mind, and although it is unlikely a ground war will erupt in the Indo-Pacific in the near future, the implications are the same. Will a divided and confused America, concerned about standards of living, socio-economic well-being, racial dichotomies, and jobs, stand behind a policy to disruptively compete against China in a twenty-first-century Cold War? The answer so far suggests not.

Should Trump lose the presidential election in November 2020, the next president will have to deal with this incongruous mix of images, perceptions, and policies. A new president from an opposing political party will likely seek to readdress the bureaucratic approach, working assumptions, and policies of government in association with their perceptions of foreign affairs. Whereas the practice for outgoing presidents has been to support new policy approaches, or at the very least remain silent on the differences in them, there is little guarantee this will remain the tradition with Trump. His attitude and personality belies a capability for self-control and censorship in this area. In this case, the potential for political disruption is even more acute. Should Trump remain in office, on the other hand, he will in one way or another be forced to reconcile with this narrative, to face the complications of policies poorly implemented, or indeed, policy failures. Further, as military strategies become increasingly competitive and uncertain, and the balance of military assets unfavorable in the Indo-Pacific, the immeasurable, non-contractual, and ideational characteristics of the twenty-first-century great-power challenge will come increasingly to the fore as requiring more attention. The implications of the current ideational deficit in the Trump administration have yet to be fully quantified. A preliminary assessment is, however, that by the beginning of the next administration, the president will be playing catch-up.

In looking ahead, there are significant lessons to draw upon for moral, conceptual, and strategic nuance in the experiences of the Bush, Obama, and Trump administrations. For one, it is impossible to overlook the fact that, at least under Bush and Obama, engagement has been strategized, trialed, and embraced at the highest levels of government and at the highest levels of national security. It is difficult, too, to discount the point that America has been instrumental in China's modernization and its substantial growth in economic, financial, and even military capabilities. In this case, it would be remiss of critics to deny that, while there have been challenges, the American-led liberal system has provided China with the means to reach its national potential. These are extraordinary talking points worth embracing in every rhetorical act concerning China. Denying them, as Trump has, delegitimizes the lessons that these experiences have produced and the policies that former administrations adopted. As nations in the Indo-Pacific search for stability, consistency, and trust in regional partnerships, these peculiarities in the Trump administration will have lasting implications, not the least being the impression that credibility, respect, and authenticity have become virtues of the past. That this is taking place at a time when nations are increasingly looking to China for economic partnership and development support, presents another critical challenge for the United States.

Notes

Introduction

1. Zbigniew Brzezinski, "Living with China," *National Interest*, Spring 2000, 5–21. On territorial claims, for instance, Fravel observes that China's leaders have been more cooperative and conciliatory in solving seventeen of its twenty-three disputes since 1949, "usually receiving less than 50 percent of the contested land." M. Taylor Fravel, "Regime Insecurity and International Cooperation: Explaining China's Compromises in Territorial Disputes," *International Security* 30, no. 2, 2005, 46–83.
2. Robert S. Ross, "China II: Beijing as a Conservative Power," *Foreign Affairs*, March/April 1997, 34; Elizabeth Economy and Michel Oksenberg, *China Joins the World: Progress and Prospects*, New York: Council on Foreign Relations Press, 1999.
3. Michael R. Pompeo, "The West Is Winning," speech at Munich Security Conference, February 15, 2020, <https://www.state.gov/the-west-is-winning> (accessed April 23, 2020).
4. Kurt M. Campbell and Ely Ratner, "The China Reckoning: How Beijing Defied American Expectations," *Foreign Affairs*, March/April 2018, 60–70, at 60.
5. Zhang Qingmin and Eric Hyer, "U.S. 'Dual Track' Policy: Arms Sales and Technology Transfer to China Mainland and Taiwan," *Journal of Contemporary China* 10, no. 26, 2001, 89–105, at 91.
6. Robert S. Ross, "Engagement in US China Policy," in Alastair Iain Johnston and Robert S. Ross (eds.), *Engaging China: The Management of an Emerging Power*, Abingdon, England: Routledge, 1999, 185.
7. Michael Walzer, "On Humanitarianism: Is Helping Others Charity, or Duty, or Both?" *Foreign Affairs*, July/August 2011, 69–80, at 77; Mel Gurtov, *Will This Be China's Century? A Skeptic's View*, Boulder: Lynne Rienner, 2013, 99.

8. For this school see Bill Gertz, *The China Threat: How the People's Republic Targets America*, Washington, DC: Regnery, 2000; Edward Timperlake and William C. Triplett II, *Red Dragon Rising: Communist China's Military Threat to America*, Washington, DC: Regnery, 1999.

9. This argument pertains more generally to the offensive-realist school of international relations; see for instance John J. Mearsheimer, *The Tragedy of Great Power Politics*, New York: W. W. Norton, 2001; Denny Roy, "The 'China Threat' Issue: Major Arguments," *Asian Survey* 36, no. 8, 1996, 758–71; Yong Deng, "Reputation and the Security Dilemma: China Reacts to the China Threat Theory," in Alastair Iain Johnston and Robert S. Ross (eds), *New Directions in the Study of China's Foreign Policy*, Stanford, CA: Stanford University Press, 2006.

10. Yi Edward Yang and Xinsheng Liu, "The 'China Threat' through the Lens of US Print Media 1992–2006," *Journal of Contemporary China* 21, no. 76, 2012, 695–711, at 704–5.

11. See for instance David M. Lampton, *Following the Leader: Ruling China, from Deng Xiaoping to Xi Jinping*, Berkeley: University of California Press, 2014, 225–6; David Shambaugh, "The Coming Chinese Crackup," *Wall Street Journal*, March 6, 2015; Jeffrey Reeves, "U.S. Perspectives on China: Trends and Attitudes in U.S. Public Opinion, Media, Scholarship and Leadership Statements," in Andrew T. H. Tan (ed.), *Handbook of U.S.-China Relations*, Cheltenham, England: Edward Elgar, 2016, 83–6.

12. Evan S. Medeiros, "The Changing Fundamentals of U.S.-China Relations," *Washington Quarterly* 42, no. 3, 2019, 93–119.

13. Robert O. Work and Greg Grant, "Beating the Americans at Their Own Game: An Offset Strategy with Chinese Characteristics," Center for a New American Security, June 6, 2019, <https://www.cnas.org/publications/reports/beating-the-americans-at-their-own-game> (accessed April 23, 2020).

14. Medeiros, "The Changing Fundamentals of US-China Relations."

15. Anne-Marie Brady, "Magic Weapons: China's Political Influence Activities under Xi Jinping," Wilson Center, September 18, 2017, <https://www.wilsoncenter.org/article/magic-weapons-chinas-political-influence-activities-under-xi-jinping> (accessed April 23, 2020).

16. Medeiros, "The Changing Fundamentals of US-China Relations."

17. Ibid.

18. Pendleton Herring, *Presidential Leadership: The Chief Relations of Congress and the Chief Executive*, New York: Farrar & Rinehart,

1940. See also Michael Patrick Cullinane and Clare Frances Elliot, *Perspectives on Presidential Leadership: An International View of the White House*, New York: Routledge, 2014, 3.

19. Charles W. Kegley, Jr., and Eugene R. Wittkopf, *American Foreign Policy: Pattern and Process*, New York: St. Martin's Press, 1979, 333–4; see also Herbert A. Simon, *Administrative Behavior: A Study of Decision-Making Processes in Administrative Organizations*, 3rd ed., New York: Free Press, 1969; Graham Allison, *Essence of Decision: Explaining the Cuban Missile Crisis*, Boston: Little, Brown, 1971.

20. Medeiros, "The Changing Fundamentals of US-China Relations."

21. "Remarks by President Trump in Press Conference: Osaka, Japan," White House, June 29, 2019, <https://www.whitehouse.gov/briefings-statements/remarks-president-trump-press-conference-osaka-japan> (accessed April 24, 2020).

22. Gerry Shih, "As U.S.-China Relations Fray, Beijing Directs Its Fury at One Target: Mike Pompeo," *Washington Post*, June 27, 2019, <https://www.washingtonpost.com/world/as-u-s-china-relations-tumble-beijing-unleashes-fury-at-one-target-mike-pompeo/2019/06/27/c952ec90-98c9-11e9-a027-c571fd3d394d_story.html> (accessed April 24, 2020).

23. Condoleezza Rice, "Campaign 2000: Promoting the National Interest," *Foreign Affairs*, January/February 2000, 45–62.

24. Medeiros, "The Changing Fundamentals of U.S.-China Relations."

25. Richard Haass, "The Pandemic Will Accelerate History Rather than Reshape It," *Foreign Affairs*, April 7, 2020, <https://www.foreignaffairs.com/articles/united-states/2020-04-07/pandemic-will-accelerate-history-rather-reshape-it> (accessed June 15, 2020).

Chapter 1

1. Charles Krauthammer, "The Bush Doctrine," *Weekly Standard,* June 4, 2001, <https://www.weeklystandard.com/charles-krauthammer/the-bush-doctrine-1776> (accessed April 24, 2020).

2. Stefan Halper and Jonathan Clarke, *America Alone: The Neoconservatives and the Global Order*, Cambridge, England: Cambridge University Press, 2004, 103.

3. Maria Ryan, *Neoconservatism and the New American Century*, New York: Palgrave Macmillan, 2010, 145.

4. Quote in Editorial, *Atlanta Journal and Constitution*, March 19, 2001. See also Andrew Scobell, "Crouching Korea, Hidden China: Bush Administration Policy toward Pyongyang and Beijing," *Asian Survey* 42, no. 2, 2002, 343–68, at 366–8.

5. Guy Roberts, *U.S. Foreign Policy and China: Bush's First Term*, Abingdon, England: Routledge, 2015, 23.

6. Scobell, "Crouching Korea, Hidden China," 356.

7. Ibid., 356.

8. Zalmay Khalilzad, "Congage China," RAND, Issue Paper 187, 1999, <https://rand.org/pubs/issue_papers/IP187/IP187.html>.

9. Halper and Clarke, *America Alone*, 173.

10. Some have gone as far as to say that a neoconservative foreign policy establishment not only existed but thrived in the Bush administration. Prominent among these were Scooter Libby, chief of staff to the vice president; Elliot Abrams, special assistant to the National Security Council; Richard Perle, chairman of the Defense Policy Board Advisory Committee; John Bolton, ambassador to the United Nations; Zalmay Khalilzad, head of the Bush transition team and later counsellor to Rumsfeld at Defense; Dov Zakheim at the Pentagon; Devon Cross on the Defense Policy Board; and Douglas Feith, undersecretary of defense for policy. Inderjeet Parmar, "A Neo-conservative-Dominated U.S. Foreign Policy Establishment?" in Kenneth Christie (ed.), *United States Foreign Policy and National Identity in the Twenty-First Century*, Abingdon, England: Routledge, 2008; Scobell, "Crouching Korea, Hidden China."

11. *Rebuilding America's Defenses: Strategy, Forces, and Resources for a New Century*, Project for the New American Century, September 2000, 2.

12. Kevin Pollpeter, *U.S.-China Security Management: Assessing the Military-to-Military Relationship*, Santa Monica, CA: RAND, 2004.

13. Melvyn P. Leffler, "9/11 and the Past and Future of American Foreign Policy," *International Affairs* 79, no. 5, 2003, 1045–63, at 1055.

14. John Higley, "The Bush Elite: Aberration or Harbinger?" in Brendan O'Connor and Martin Griffiths (eds), *The Rise of Anti-Americanism*, Abingdon, England: Routledge, 2006, 157; see also Parmar, "A Neo-conservative-Dominated U.S. Foreign Policy Establishment?" 42.

15. See for instance Khalilzad, "Congage China."

16. Jim George, "Leo Strauss, Neoconservatism and U.S. Foreign Policy: Esoteric Nihilism and the Bush Doctrine," *International Politics* 42, 2005, 174–202, at 176.

17. Quoted in "A Slower Boat to China," *Weekly Standard*, March 27, 2000, <https://www.weeklystandard.com/the-scrapbook/a-slower-boat-to-china> (accessed April 24, 2020).

18. *Quadrennial Defense Review Report*, U.S. Department of Defense, September 30, 2001, 25, <https://archive.defense.gov/pubs/qdr2001.pdf> (accessed April 24, 2020).

19. *Report of the Select Committee on U.S. National Security and Military/Commercial Concerns with the People's Republic of China*, House of Representatives, 105th Congress, 2nd Session, 105–851, May 25, 1999. See pp. 166–77 for recommendations.

20. Matthew Rees, "Congress's China Challenge," *Weekly Standard*, March 22, 1999, <https://www.weeklystandard.com/matthew-rees/congresss-china-challenge> (accessed April 24, 2020).

21. Khalilzad, "Congage China."

22. See for instance, "Excerpts from Pentagon's Plan: Prevent the Re-emergence of a New Rival," *New York Times*, March 8, 1992, 14; Stephen Yates, "No Concessions to China after Mistaken Embassy Bombing," Heritage Foundation, May 28, 1999, <https://www.heritage.org/asia/report/no-concessions-china-after-the-mistaken-embassy-bombing> (accessed April 24, 2020); Constantine C. Menges, *China: The Gathering Threat*, Nashville: Nelson Current, 2005.

23. John R. Bolton, "Time for a Two-China Policy," American Enterprise Institute, August 9, 1999, <https://www.aei.org/articles/time-for-a-two-china-policy> (accessed April 24, 2020).

24. See Roberts, *U.S. Foreign Policy and China*.

25. Ibid.

26. Jack L. Goldsmith, *The Terror Presidency: Law and Judgment inside the Bush Administration*, New York: W. W. Norton, 2007, 205; also James P. Pfiffner, "The Contemporary President: Decision Making in the Bush White House," *Presidential Studies Quarterly* 39, no. 2, 2009, 363–84, at 367.

27. Khalilzad, "Congage China."

28. David Shambaugh, "Sino-American Strategic Relations: From Partners to Competitors," *Survival* 42, no. 1, 2000, 97–115, at 107–10.

29. George W. Bush, "State of the Union Address to the 107th Congress," in *Selected Speeches of President George W. Bush, 2001–2008*, <http://georgewbush-whitehouse.archives.gov/infocus/bushrecord/

documents/Selected_Speeches_George_W_Bush.pdf> (accessed April 24, 2020).

30. John J. Mearsheimer, *The Tragedy of Great Power Politics*, New York: W. W. Norton, 2001.
31. Christopher Layne, "The Unipolar Illusion: Why New Great Powers Will Rise," *International Security* 17, no. 4, 1993, 5–51, at 38.
32. Samuel P. Huntington, *The Clash of Civilizations and the Remaking of World Order*, London: Simon & Schuster, 1997, 218–38, 238–9.
33. Arthur Waldron, "China after Communism," American Enterprise Institute, September 11, 2000, <https://www.aei.org/publication/china-after-communism> (accessed April 24, 2020).
34. Patrick E. Tyler, "Rebels' New Cause: A Book for Yankee Bashing," *New York Times*, September 4, 1996, <https://www.nytimes.com/1996/09/04/world/rebels-new-cause-a-book-for-yankee-bashing.html> (accessed April 24, 2020).
35. Song Qiang et al., *Zhongguo keyi shuobu* ("China Can Say No"), Beijing: Zhonghua gongshang lianhe chubanshe, 1996.
36. Richard Bernstein and Ross H. Munro, *The Coming Conflict with China*, New York: Alfred A. Knopf, 1997, 49.
37. Edward Timperlake and William C. Triplett II, *Red Dragon Rising: Communist China's Military Threat to America*, Washington, DC: Regnery, 1999, 42. See also Bill Gertz, *The China Threat: How the People's Republic Targets America*, Washington, DC: Regnery, 2000, xii–xiii. For more on the China threat analysis see Denny Roy, "Hegemon on the Horizon? China's Threat to East Asian Security," *International Security* 19, no. 1, 1994, 149–68; Nicholas Kristof, "The Rise of China," *Foreign Affairs*, November/December 1993, 59–74, at 72; Douglas H. Paal, "China II: Insecurity Complex; Why Chinese Spies Love Us," *National Review*, May 1999, 26–8; Emma V. Broomfield, "Perceptions of Danger: The China Threat Theory," *Journal of Contemporary China* 12, no. 35, 2003, 265–84.
38. Chengxin Pan, *Knowledge, Desire and Power in Global Politics: Western Representations of China's Rise*, Cheltenham, England: Edward Elgar, 2012, 44.
39. Paul Wolfowitz, "Transfer of Missile Technology to China," Congressional Testimony by Federal Document Clearing House, September 17, 1998, quoted in Pan, *Knowledge, Desire and Power in Global Politics*, 47. For more on the discussion of realism and the German analogy see particularly Aaron L. Friedberg, "Will Europe's Past Be Asia's Future?" *Survival* 42, no. 3, 2000, 147–59.
40. Pan, *Knowledge, Desire and Power in Global Politics*, 45.

41. "Security Issues and Strategic Perceptions," Hearing before the U.S.-China Security Review Commission, August 3, 2001, 389, transcript available at <https://www.uscc.gov/sites/default/files/transcripts/8.3.01HT.pdf> (accessed May 8, 2020).

42. *Report to Congress of the U.S.-China Security Review Commission: The National Security Implications of the Economic Relationship between the United States and China*, July 2002, available at <https://www.uscc.gov/sites/default/files/annual_reports/2002%20Annual%20Report%20to%20Congress.pdf> (accessed April 24, 2020). See executive summary, 4.

43. "Security Issues and Strategic Perceptions," 403.

44. Ibid., 441.

45. Murray Hiebert, "Red Scare," *Far Eastern Economic Review*, October 12, 2000, available at <https://gertzfile.com/gertzfile/FEERarticle.html> (accessed April 27, 2020).

46. Ibid.

47. Ibid.

48. "Security Issues and Strategic Perceptions," 433.

49. Bolton, "Time for a Two-China Policy."

50. Jiemian Yang, "Sino-U.S. and Cross-Strait Relations under the Post-'11 September' Strategic Settings," *Journal of Contemporary China* 11, no. 33, 2002, 657–72, at 662.

51. Harry Harding, "American China Policy under the Bush Administration: Change and Continuity," in Arthur Lewis Rosenbaum (ed.), *U.S.-China Relations and the Bush Administration: A New Paradigm or Continuing Modalities*, Claremont, CA: Keck Center for International and Strategic Studies, 2001, 57–79.

52. Robert S. Ross, "Navigating the Taiwan Strait: Deterrence, Escalation Dominance, and U.S.-China Relations," *International Security* 27, no. 2, 2002, 48–85, at 50.

53. Marc Lacey and David E. Sanger, "First Meeting: China Testing Firmer Way of Bush Team," *New York Times*, March 23, 2001, 5.

54. Colin Powell, CNN interview, May 14, 2001, cited in Marc Lacey, "Powell to Allow Taiwan's President to Stop Briefly," *New York Times*, May 15, 2001, 10. On those who claim justification for this language see Roberts, *U.S. Foreign Policy and China*; Lawrence E. Grinter, "Handling the Taiwan Issue: Bush Administration Policy toward Beijing and Taipei," *Asian Affairs: An American Review* 29, no. 1, 2002, 3–15, at 4.

55. The lesson that illustrates the finer points of perception, in particular the false certainty that one knows one's opponents, is Dean Acheson's comments in response to questions about the at-times provocative

actions of U.S. and UN forces toward the border between North Korea and the PRC. As American bombs accidentally crossed the Yalu, as the United States sought protector status over Taiwan, and as Republicans in Congress called for the eradication of communism in China, it was believed nonetheless that the Chinese understood American intentions as they themselves believed them, that "no possible shred of evidence could have existed in the minds of the Chinese Communist authorities about the peaceful intentions of the forces of the United Nations." See Adam S. R. Bartley, *Perceptions of China and White House Decision-Making, 1941–1963: Spears of Promise, Shields of Truth*, New York: Routledge, 2020. The Chinese were known to refer to Chen's stopovers in America as "transit diplomacy." By all indications, they didn't see them as innocent at all. Yang, "Sino-U.S. and Cross-Strait Relations."

56. For Rumsfeld's comments on "unknown unknowns," see "Press Conference by US Secretary of Defence, Donald Rumsfeld," NATO, June 6, 2002, <https://www.nato.int/docu/speech/2002/s020606g.htm> (accessed June 15, 2020); Ryan, *Neoconservatism and the New American Century*, 119–20.

57. *Report to Congress of the U.S.-China Economic and Security Review Commission*, 165. For Bush's May 1 speech see "Remarks by the President to Students and Faculty at National Defense University," White House, May 1, 2001, <https://georgewbush-whitehouse.archives.gov/news/releases/2001/05/20010501-10.html> (accessed April 27, 2020).

58. Jing-dong Yuan, "Chinese Responses to U.S. Missile Defenses: Implications for Arms Control and Regional Security," *Nonproliferation Review* 10, no. 1, 2003, 75–96, at 79.

59. In 2004, a report by the U.S.-China Economic and Security Review Commission announced that there had been a "dramatic change in the military balance between China and Taiwan. In the past years, China has increasingly developed a quantitative and qualitative advantage over Taiwan." "2004 Report to Congress of the U.S.-China Economic and Security Review Commission," 108th Congress, 2nd Session, June 2004, 193, available at <https://www.uscc.gov/sites/default/files/annual_reports/2004-Report-to-Congress.pdf> (accessed May 8, 2020).

60. Cited in Roberts, *U.S. Foreign Policy and China*, 90.

61. Craig S. Smith, "Students' Unease over Weakness Could Threaten Beijing's Leaders," *New York Times*, April 6, 2001.

62. James Mulvenon, "Civil-Military Relations and the EP-3 Crisis: A Content Analysis," *China Leadership Monitor*, Winter 2002, 5,

<www.hoover.org/publications/clm/issues/2906891.html> (accessed April 27, 2020).

63. Ibid.

64. Susan Shirk, *China: Fragile Superpower*, New York: Oxford University Press, 2008, 232; Suisheng Zhao, "Chinese Nationalism and Its Foreign Policy Ramifications," in Christopher Marsh and June Teufel Dreyer (eds), *U.S.-China Relations in the Twenty-First Century: Polices, Prospects, and Possibilities*, Lanham, MD: Lexington, 2003, 71.

65. John W. Garver, "Sino-American Relations in 2001: The Difficult Accommodation of Two Great Powers," *International Journal* 57, no. 2, 2002, 283–310; David Sanger and Steve Myers, "Collision with China: The Negotiations," *New York Times*, April 13, 2001, 1; "White House Says it Sees Some Hope to End Standoff," *New York Times*, April 6, 2001, 1, 10.

66. For more on the contents of the letter see "War of Words," *Newsweek*, April 23, 2001, 21–4.

67. Robert Kagan and William Kristol, "A National Humiliation," *Weekly Standard*, April 15, 2001.

68. The case for a consistent and nuanced China policy is made by Roberts, *U.S. Foreign Policy and China*, 88–94.

69. Garver, "Sino-American Relations in 2001," 293; this is also shared by Quansheng Zhao, "America's Response to the Rise of China and Sino-U.S. Relations," *Asian Journal of Political Science* 13, no. 2, 2005, 1–27, at 4.

70. A number of internal political attributes, thought to have influenced the decision-making process in Beijing, are justified in understanding China's confused response. A first was that the military had monopolized the response with their version of events, seen by leaders in Beijing as politically risky to oppose. No leader was thought able to challenge the military hierarchy with the 16th Party Congress down the road in 2002. Jiang Zemin was to step down from his political posts, but was thought to, and did, retain the chairmanship of the Central Military Commission. Similarly, Hu Jintao, tasked with responding to the crisis, was as yet unsure of his political capital among the military. A second point was that leaders were unlikely to move against the current of nationalism spoiling for a more assertive response to America's perceived provocation. As James Mulvenon notes, "once Wang Wei [the Chinese pilot] was effectively designated as a martyr, any possibility of backing away from the official story of the collision was eliminated." Mulvenon, "Civil-Military Relations and the EP-3 Crisis," 5.

71. David Shambaugh, "Sino-American Relations since September 11: Can the New Stability Last?" *Current History*, September 2002, 243–9, at 244.
72. The President's remarks were not completely denied or fixed in follow-up interviews to reflect current Taiwan policy. As Dennis Van Vranken Hickey notes, Bush's apparent "slip of the tongue" continued to be "cited by senior administration officials as official U.S. policy." Dennis Van Vranken Hickey, "Continuity and Change: The Administration of George W. Bush and U.S. Policy toward Taiwan," *Journal of Contemporary China* 13, no. 40, 2004, 461–78, at 470 n56.
73. Roberts, *U.S. Foreign Policy and China*.
74. Yang, "Sino-U.S. and Cross-Strait Relations," 670.
75. Robert Sutter, "Bush Administration Policy toward Beijing and Taipei," *Journal of Contemporary China* 12, no. 36, 2003, 477–92, at 478.
76. Ibid., 479.
77. Jia Qingguo, "Impact of 9.11 on Sino-U.S. Relations: A Preliminary Assessment," paper for the Brookings Institution, July 2002, available at <https://www.brookings.edu/wp-content/uploads/2016/06/2002_qingguo.pdf> (accessed April 27, 2020).
78. Aaron L. Friedberg, "11 September and the Future of Sino-American Relations," *Survival* 44, no. 1, 2002, 33–50, at 36; see also J. Mohan Malik, "Dragon on Terrorism: Assessing China's Tactical Gains and Strategic Losses after 11 September," *Contemporary Southeast Asia* 24, no. 2, 2002, 252–93.
79. Adam Ward, "China and America: Trouble Ahead?" *Survival* 45, no. 3, 2003, 35–56, at 36.
80. These points are illustrated in Bonnie S. Glaser, "Playing Up the Positive on the Eve of the Crawford Summit," *Comparative Connections* 4, no. 3, 2002, 6.
81. Robert Sutter, "The Taiwan Problem in the Second George W. Bush Administration—U.S. Officials' Views and Their Implications for U.S. Policy," *Journal of Contemporary China* 15, no. 48, 2006, 417–41, at 425.
82. Ibid., 429.
83. Michael R. Gordon, "U.S. Nuclear Plan Sees New Weapons and New Targets," *New York Times*, March 10, 2002.
84. Ted Garlen Carpenter, "U.S. Goes Too Far with Visit of Taiwan Official," Cato Institute, March 25, 2002, <https://www.cato.org/publications/commentary/us-goes-too-far-visit-taiwan-official> (accessed April 27, 2020); Nancy B. Tucker, "Strategic Ambiguity or Strategic Rivalry," in Nancy B. Tucker (ed.), *Dangerous Strait:*

The U.S.-Taiwan-China Crisis, New York: Columbia University Press, 2005, 177.

85. Wolfowitz here reiterated Bush's support to do whatever it took to help Taiwan. Harding, "American China Policy under the Bush Administration," 70.

86. "Survey of Programs on United States-China Relations and Security Issues," National Committee on United States-China Relations, China Policy Series no. XXIII, March 2007, 13, <https://www.ncuscr.org/sites/default/files/page_attachments/Survey-Programs-US-China-Relations-Security-Issues.pdf> (accessed April 27, 2020).

87. A good example here is the U.S. 2002 Supplemental Appropriations Act and Powell's inability to assuage Chinese concerns about American intentions. Notably, Beijing viewed this as a unilateral change to the status quo. See page 43 for more on this. In response to Bush's Taiwan policies, on March 15, 2005 Beijing enacted the Anti-Secession Law, prescribing the use of "non-peaceful means" for unification should Taiwan seek independence. The administration was to view this as a unilateral change of the status quo rather than a response to Bush's policies.

88. Condoleezza Rice, *No Higher Honor: A Memoir of My Years in Washington*. New York: Crown, 2011, 518.

Chapter 2

1. Robert B. Zoellick, "Whither China? From Membership to Responsibility," Remarks to National Committee on U.S.-China Relations, September 21, 2005, <https://2001-2009.state.gov/s/d/former/zoellick/rem/53682.htm> (accessed April 27, 2020).

2. "The President's Budget for Foreign Affairs and Business Meeting to Vote Out the Nomination of Robert B. Zoellick to be Deputy Secretary of State," Hearing before the Committee on Foreign Relations, United States Senate, 109th Congress, 1st Session, S. Hrg.109-98, February 16, 2005, 3, transcript available at <https://www.foreign.senate.gov/imo/media/doc/021605_Transcript_The%20President's%20Budget%20for%20Foreign%20Affairs%20and%20Business%20Meeting.pdf> (accessed April 27, 2020).

3. Kennon H. Nakamura and Susan B. Epstein, "Diplomacy for the 21st Century: Transformational Diplomacy," CRS Report for Congress, August 23, 2007; Condoleezza Rice, "Transformational Diplomacy," speech at Georgetown University, January 18, 2006,

<https://2001-2009.state.gov/secretary/rm/2006/59306.htm>
(accessed April 27, 2020); Yuan Peng, "Sino-American Relations:
New Changes and New Challenges," *Australian Journal of International Affairs* 61, no. 1, 2007, 98–113, at 102.

4. See Condoleezza Rice, "U.S. Policy toward Asia," Address at the Heritage Foundation, Washington, D.C., June 18, 2008, <http://2001-2009.state.gov/secretary/rm/2008/06/106034.htm> (accessed April 27, 2020); Michael J. Green, "The Iraq War and Asia: Assessing the Legacy," *Washington Quarterly* 31, no. 2, 2008, 181–200, at 181.

5. Mel Gurtov, "Northeast Asia Policy under George W. Bush: Doctrine in Search of Policy," *North Korean Review* 3, no. 1, 2007, 72–85; Barry Buzan, "A Leader without Followers? The United States in World Politics after Bush," *International Politics* 45, no. 5, 2008, 554–70; Satu P. Limaye, "Minding the Gaps: The Bush Administration and U.S.-Southeast Asia Relations," *Contemporary Southeast Asia* 26, no. 1, 2004, 73–93, at 75.

6. Ralph Cossa, "Condoleezza Rice's Unfortunate Decision," *Japan Times*, July 25, 2005; Michael Vatikiotis, "No Rice for ASEAN This Year," *New York Times*, July 9, 2005; Anne Davies, "Asia Hit as White House Focuses on Iraq," *The Age*, July 26, 2007.

7. "America's Image Slips, but Allies Share U.S. Concerns over Iran, Hamas," Pew Research Center, June 13, 2006, <http://pewglobal.org/reports/display.php?ReportID=252> (accessed April 27, 2020); "Global Economic Gloom—China and India Notable Exceptions," Pew Research Center, June 12, 2008, <https://www.pewresearch.org/global/2008/06/12/global-economic-gloom-china-and-india-notable-exceptions> (accessed May 12, 2020).

8. Gurtov, "Northeast Asia Policy under George W. Bush," 83; Alison D. Ba, "China-ASEAN Relations: Political Significance of an ASEAN Free Trade Area," in T. J. Cheng et al. (eds), *China under the Fourth Generation Leadership: Opportunities, Dangers, and Dilemmas*, Singapore: World Scientific, 2005.

9. The term "habits of cooperation" is taken from Carin Zissis, "Hills: U.S.-Chinese Relations Need Habits of Cooperation," Council on Foreign Relations, April 10, 2007, <https://www.cfr.org/interview/hills-us-chinese-relations-need-habits-cooperation> (accessed April 27, 2020).

10. Victor D. Cha, "Winning Asia: Washington's Untold Success Story," *Foreign Affairs*, November/December 2007, 98–113, at 98–9.

11. T. J. Pempel, "How Bush Bungled Asia: Militarism, Economic Indifference and Unilateralism Have Weakened the United States across Asia," *Pacific Review* 21, no. 5, 2008, 547–81, at 551.

12. "China's Role in the World: Is China a Responsible Stakeholder?" Hearing before the U.S.-China Economic and Security Review Commission, 109th Congress, 2nd Session, August 3–4, 2006, 40, transcript available at <https://www.uscc.gov/sites/default/files/transcripts/8.3-4.06HearingTrascript.pdf> (accessed April 27, 2020). Thomas Christensen, deputy assistant secretary of state for East Asian and Pacific affairs, makes the comment that the U.S. had made "real progress" on North Korea by urging China to take a leadership role (40).

13. *Renmin Ribao* (People's Daily), October, 20, 2001.

14. Francis X. Taylor, "U.S.-China Inter-agency Partnership to Fight Terrorism," remarks to the press, Beijing, December 6, 2001, <https://2001-2009.state.gov/s/ct/rls/rm/2001/6689.htm> (accessed April 28, 2020).

15. Denny Roy, "China and the War on Terrorism," *Orbis* 46, no. 3, 2002, 511–21; Joshua Kurlantzick, "China's Dubious Role in the War on Terror," *Current History*, December 2003, 432–5; Shirley A. Kan, "U.S.-China Counter-terrorism Cooperation: Issues for U.S. Policy," Congressional Research Service, December 7, 2004, available at <https://fas.org/irp/crs/RS21995.pdf> (accessed May 11, 2020).

16. Bonnie S. Glaser, "Fleshing Out the Candid, Cooperative and Constructive Relationship," *Comparative Connections* 4, no. 2, 2002.

17. Jonathan Manthorpe, "Terror War Throws a Curve Ball: China's Handling of Its 'Internal Affairs' Crops Up in a Game Already Charged with Suspicion and Mistrust," *Vancouver Sun*, September 10, 2002.

18. James Kelly, "U.S.-East Asia Policy: Three Aspects," Woodrow Wilson Center, Washington, D.C., December 11, 2002; Kan, "U.S.-China Counter-terrorism Cooperation," 5.

19. Taylor, "U.S.-China Inter-agency Partnership to Fight Terrorism."

20. Foreign Press Center Briefing, General Tommy Franks, Commander, U.S. Central Command, Washington, D.C., April 11, 2002; Press Roundtable with Adm. Dennis Blair, Commander, U.S. Pacific Command, Hong Kong, April 18, 2002. Quote in Kan, "U.S.-China Counter-terrorism Cooperation," 2.

21. "Identify, Disrupt and Dismantle: Coordinating the Government's Attack on Terrorist Financing," Joint Hearing before the Subcommittee on Technology, Information Policy, Intergovernmental Relations and Census and the Subcommittee on Government Efficiency and Financial Management of the Committee on Government Reform, House of Representatives, 108th Congress, 1st Session, December 15, 2003, 108–140, transcript available at <https://www.govinfo.gov/content/pkg/CHRG-108hhrg93428/html/CHRG-108hhrg93428.htm> (accessed April 28, 2020).

22. "Counterterror Initiatives in the Terror Finance Program," Hearings before the Committee on Banking, Housing, and Urban Affairs, United States Senate, 108th Congress, 1st and 2nd Sessions, September 25, 2003, October 22, 2003, April 29, 2004, and September 29, 2004, S. Hrg. 108–802, <https://www.govinfo.gov/content/pkg/CHRG-108shrg20396/html/CHRG-108shrg20396.htm> (accessed April 28, 2020). China did finally join the task force in 2005 but only as an observer.

23. "Testimony of Kenneth Lawson, Assistant Secretary of Office of Enforcement, U.S. Department of the Treasury, the Subcommittee on National Security, Veterans Affairs and International Relations, Rightsizing the U.S. Presence Abroad," press release, U.S. Department of the Treasury, May 1, 2002, <https://www.treasury.gov/press-center/press-releases/Pages/po3066.aspx> (accessed April 28, 2020).

24. These bodies have included anti-laundering institutions such as the Asia-Pacific Group on Money Laundering, The Eurasia Group on Money Laundering and Terrorist Financing, the Financial Action Task Force, and the UN International Convention for the Suppression of the Financing of Terrorism. *Country Reports on Terrorism 2006*, U.S. Department of State, April 2007, 33, <https://2009-2017.state.gov/documents/organization/83383.pdf> (accessed April 28, 2020).

25. *Country Reports on Terrorism 2005*, U.S. Department of State, April 2006, 66, <https://2009-2017.state.gov/documents/organization/65462.pdf>; Murray Scott Tanner and James Bellacqua, "China's Response to Terrorism," CNA Analysis & Solutions, June 2016, 106–7, <https://www.cna.org/cna_files/pdf/IRM-2016-U-013542-Final.pdf> (both accessed April 28, 2020).

26. *Country Reports on Terrorism 2004*, U.S. Department of State, April 2005, 33, <https://2001-2009.state.gov/documents/organization/45313.pdf> (accessed April 28, 2020); CRT 2005, pp. 66-67, Tanner and Bellacqua, "China's Response to Terrorism," 111–12.

27. *Patterns of Global Terrorism 2001*, U.S. Department of State, May 2002, 16, <https://2001-2009.state.gov/documents/organization/10319.pdf> (accessed April 28, 2020).

28. *Country Reports on Terrorism 2010*, U.S. Department of State, August 2011, 33, <https://2009-2017.state.gov/documents/organization/170479.pdf> (accessed April 28, 2020); Tanner and Bellacqua, "China's Response to Terrorism," 105.

29. Irvin F. J. Lim, "Not Yet All Aboard . . . but Already All at Sea over Container Security Initiative," Working Paper no. 35, Institute of Defence and Strategic Studies, Singapore, October 2002.

30. *Container Security Initiative: 2006–2011 Strategic Plan*, U.S. Customs and Border Protection, August 2006, 5, available at <https://www.hsdl.org/?abstract&did=468251>; "Supply Chain Security: Examinations of High-Risk Cargo at Foreign Seaports Have Increased, but Improved Data Collection and Performance Measures are Needed," U.S. Government Accountability Office, Report to Congressional Requesters, January 2008, 9, <https://www.gao.gov/new.items/d08187.pdf> (both accessed April 28, 2020).

31. Lim, "Not Yet All Aboard"; Andrew S. Erickson, Lyle J. Goldstein, and Nan Li (eds), *China, the United States, and 21st-Century Sea Power: Defining a Maritime Security Partnership*, Annapolis, MD: Naval Institute Press, 2010.

32. One example, on this charge for instance, is information exchange and outcome on proliferation activities. According to David Sedney, deputy assistant secretary of defense for East Asian affairs, U.S. officials had given information on Chinese entities in breach of proliferation laws to their counterparts with the aim of ceasing such activities. The response had been silence and secrecy on the Chinese side, what Sedney referred to as the "wall." The Chinese, he noted, "won't tell us what they've done" with the information. "China's Proliferation and the Impact on Trade Policy on Defense Industries in the United States and China," Hearing before the U.S.-China Economic and Security Review Commission, 110th Congress, 1st Session, July 12–13, 2007, 19, transcript available at <https://www.uscc.gov/sites/default/files/transcripts/7.12-13.07HearingTranscript.pdf> (accessed April 28, 2020).

33. "U.S. Official Praises HK, Mainland for Cooperation against Terrorism," Embassy of the People's Republic of China in the United States of America, August 1, 2003, <www.china-embassy.org/eng/zt/mgryzdzg/t36538.htm> (accessed April 28, 2020).

34. Feng Qing, "Shanghai and Shenzhen Join 'Antiterror Treaty' for Container Shipping," *21 Shiji Jingji Baodao*, August 4, 2003; "100% Scanning Does Not Equate to 100% Security According to Esteemed Port of Hamburg Executive: An Exclusive Interview with Dr. Jurgen Sorgenfrei, Chairman," *Maritime and Border Security News*, December 20, 2007; Erickson, Goldstein, and Li (eds), *China, the United States, and 21st-Century Sea Power.*

35. See Dave Eberhart, "Container Ships—The Next Terrorist Weapon?" *NewsMax*, April 14, 2002, <https://www.newsmax.com/pre-2008/container-ships-the-next/2002/04/14/id/666281> (accessed April 28, 2020); Lim, "Not Yet All Aboard," 15.

36. Damien McElroy, "Beijing Produces Videos Glorifying Terrorist Attacks on 'Arrogant' U.S.," *The Telegraph*, November 4, 2001, <http://www.telegraph.co.uk/news/worldnews/asia/china/1361461/ Beijing-produces-videos-glorifying-terrorist-attacks-on-arrogant-US. html> (accessed April 28, 2020).

37. Denny Roy, *Return of the Dragon: Rising China and Regional Security*, New York: Columbia University Press, 2013, 247–8.

38. Erickson, Goldstein, and Li (eds), *China, the United States, and 21st-Century Sea Power*, 79.

39. "China's Role in the World," 91.

40. Erickson, Goldstein, and Li (eds), *China, the United States, and 21st-Century Sea Power*, 80.

41. "Department of Homeland Security Appropriations for 2005," Hearings before a Subcommittee on Appropriations, House of Representatives, 108th Congress, 2nd Session, March 4, 2004, 294.

42. "China's Role in the World," 40, 42; "China's Proliferation to North Korea and Iran, and Its Role in Addressing the Nuclear and Missile Situations in Both Nations," Hearing before the U.S.-China Economic and Security Review Commission, 109th Congress, 2nd Session, September 14, 2006, 37, transcript available at <https:// www.uscc.gov/sites/default/files/transcripts/9.14.06HearingTransc ript.pdf> (accessed April 28, 2020).

43. Michael D. Swaine, *America's Challenge: Engaging a Rising China in the Twenty-First Century*, Washington, DC: Carnegie Endowment for International Peace, 2012.

44. Kan, "U.S.-China Counterterrorism Cooperation," 25.

45. "Current and Projected Threats to the National Security," Hearing before the Select Committee on Intelligence of the United States Senate,110thCongress,2ndSession,February5,2008,S.Hrg.110-824, testimony of J. Michael McConnell, <https://www.intelligence. senate.gov/hearings/current-and-projected-threats-national-security- february-5-2008#> (accessed April 28, 2020).

46. Gardner Bovingdon, *Autonomy in Xinjiang: Han Nationalist Imperatives and Uyghur Discontent*, Washington, DC: East-West Center, 2004, quote on p. 47; Abanti Bhattacharya, "Conceptualising Uyghur Separatism in Chinese Nationalism," *Strategic Analysis* 27, no. 3, 2003, 357–81, at 359; Herbert S. Yee, "Ethnic Relations in Xinjiang: A Survey of Uygur-Han Relations in Urumqi," *Journal of Contemporary China* 12, no. 36, 2003, 431–52, at 444; Paul J. Smith, "China's Power Ascendancy and the Global Terrorism Burden: Opportunities for U.S.-China Cooperation," in Erickson,

Goldstein, and Li (eds), *China, the United States, and 21st-Century Sea Power*, 113; "Looking West: China and Central Asia," Hearing before the U.S.-China Economic and Security Review Commission, 114th Congress, 1st Session, March 18, 2015, testimony of Raffaello Pantucci, transcript available at <https://www.uscc.gov/sites/default/files/transcripts/March%2018,%202015%20Hearing%20Transcript.pdf> (accessed April 28, 2020); "Why Is There Tension between China and the Uighurs?" BBC News, September 26, 2014, <http://www.bbc.com/news/world-asia-china-26414014> (accessed April 28, 2020).

47. Tanner and Bellacqua, "China's Response to Terrorism," 26.
48. Beina Xu, Holly Fletcher, and Jayshree Bajora, *The East Turkistan Islamic Movement (ETIM)*, Council on Foreign Relations, September 4, 2014, <https://www.cfr.org/backgrounder/east-turkestan-islamic-movement-etim> (accessed April 28, 2020). Paul J. Smith gives a good account of terrorist attacks in "China's Power Ascendency and the Global Terrorism Burden."
49. Tanner and Bellacqua, "China's Response to Terrorism," 29. On judgments of China's labeling these groups terrorists, see "Uighurs Fleeing Persecution as China Wages its 'War on Terror,'" Amnesty International, July 6, 2004, <https://www.amnesty.org/en/documents/ASA17/021/2004/en>; "Political Persecution of Uyghurs in the Era of the 'War on Terror'," Uyghur Human Rights Project, October 16, 2007, <http://docs.uyghuramerican.org/Persecution_of_Uyghurs_in_the_Era_of_the_War_on_Terror.pdf> (both accessed April 28, 2020).
50. "Terror List with Links to al Qaeda Unveiled," *China Daily*, December 16, 2003, <http://www.chinadaily.com.cn/en/doc/2003-12/16/content_290658.htm> (accessed April 28, 2020).
51. Kan, "U.S.-China Counter-terrorism Cooperation," 6.
52. Gaye Christoffersen, "Constituting the Uyghur in U.S.-China Relations: The Geopolitics of Identity Formation in the War on Terrorism," *Strategic Insights* 1, no. 7, 2002.
53. Kurlantzick, "China's Dubious Role in the War on Terror." Curiously, Bush seemed to invert this emphasis on rewarding good behavior when it came to North Korea and nuclear proliferation, more on which is below.
54. Richard Bernstein, "When China Convinced the U.S. that Uighurs Were Waging Jihad," *The Atlantic*, March 19, 2019.
55. Guy Dinmore and James Kynge, "China Torture Fears Curb Guantanamo Releases," *Financial Times*, June 23, 2004; David Cloud and Ian Johnson, "In Post-9/11 World, Chinese Dissidents Pose U.S. Dilemma," *Wall Street Journal*, August 3, 2004; Josh White

and Robin Wright, "Detainee Cleared for Release Is in Limbo at Guantanamo," *Washington Post*, December 15, 2005; Robin Wright, "Chinese Detainees Are Men without a Country," *Washington Post*, August 24, 2005; Kan, "U.S.-China Counter-terrorism Cooperation," 5–6.

56. Kiyemba v. Obama, 559 U.S. Court of Appeals, D.C. Circuit, February 18, 2009.
57. Kan, "U.S.-China Counter-terrorism Cooperation," 9.
58. "China's Role in the World," 91.
59. "China's Proliferation and the Impact on Trade Policy," 13. See also "Current and Projected Threats to the National Security," testimony of J. Michael McConnell, 55.
60. "China's Role in the World," 91–3.
61. "China's Proliferation to North Korea and Iran," 13.
62. Ibid., 6.
63. John J. Tkacik, Jr., "Revenge of the Panda Hugger," *Weekly Standard*, February 27, 2006, 18.
64. Jim Wolf, "U.S. Faults China on Shipments to Iran," Reuters, July 12, 2007, <https://www.reuters.com/article/idUSN12351086> (accessed April 28, 2020); Neil King, Jr., "China-Iran Trade Surge Vexes U.S.," *Wall Street Journal*, July 27, 2007; Shirley A. Kan, "China and Proliferation of Weapons of Mass Destruction and Missiles: Policy Issues," *Current Politics and Economics of Northern and Western Asia* 23, no. 1/2, 2014, 220.
65. Kan, "China and Proliferation of Weapons of Mass Destruction and Missiles," 211.
66. "China's Proliferation Practices and Role in the North Korean Crisis," Hearing before the U.S.-China Economic and Security Review Commission, 109th Congress, 1st Session, March 10, 2005, 16, transcript available at <https://www.uscc.gov/sites/default/files/transcripts/3.10.05ht.pdf> (accessed April 28, 2020).
67. "China's Proliferation Practices, and the Development of Its Cyber and Space Capabilities," Hearing before the U.S.-China Economic and Security Review Commission, 110th Congress, 2nd Session, May 20, 2008, 108, transcript available at <https://www.uscc.gov/sites/default/files/transcripts/5.20.08HearingTranscript.pdf> (accessed April 28, 2020).
68. Ibid.
69. Willem van Kemenade, "China vs. the Western Campaign for Iran Sanctions," *Washington Quarterly* 33, no. 3, 2010, 99–114, at 109–10.
70. Three times more citizens in China viewed the administration's war in Iraq as more threatening than weapons proliferation in

North Korea; see "America's Image Slips." See also Pempel, "How Bush Bungled Asia," 558.

71. "China's Proliferation and the Impact on Trade Policy," 11; "China's Endeavors for Arms Control, Disarmament and Non-proliferation," Information Office of the State Council of the People's Republic of China, September 2005, <http://en.people.cn/whitepaper/arms/arms.html> (accessed April 28, 2020).

72. Dingli Shen, "Can Sanctions Stop Proliferation?" *Washington Quarterly* 31, no. 3, 2008, 89–100, at 92.

73. John W. Garver, "Is China Playing a Dual Game in Iran?" *Washington Quarterly* 34, no. 1, 2011, 75–88, at 82–3.

74. United Nations Security Council, "Note by the President of the Security Council," January 31, 1992, UN Doc. S/23500.

75. United Nations Security Council, Resolution 1540 (2004), April 28, 2004, <https://www.un.org/ga/search/view_doc.asp?symbol=S/RES/1540%20(2004)> (accessed April 29, 2020). It should be noted here too that while Beijing sought to embolden its non-proliferation credentials by stating in the white paper "China's Endeavors for Arms Control, Disarmament, and Non-proliferation" that it joined and participated in all non-proliferation regimes, it completely ignored the PSI as belonging to the regimes.

76. Zhang Yan, news conference, September 1, 2005, cited in Jinyuan Su, "The Proliferation Security Initiative (PSI) and Interdiction at Sea: A Chinese Perspective," *Ocean Development and International Law* 43, no. 1, 2012, 96–118, at 98.

77. "The Lifting of the EU Arms Embargo on China," Hearing before the Committee on Foreign Relations, United States Senate, 109th Congress, 1st Session, March 16, 2005, S. Hrg. 109-94, 1, transcript available at <https://www.foreign.senate.gov/imo/media/doc/031605_Transcript_The%20Lifting%20of%20the%20EU%20Arms%20Embargo%20on%20China.pdf> (accessed April 29, 2020).

78. "China's Proliferation Practices and Role in the North Korean Crisis," 2.

79. Kan, "China and Proliferation of Weapons of Mass Destruction and Missiles," 236.

80. Charles L. Pritchard, *Failed Diplomacy: The Tragic Story of How North Korea Got the Bomb*, Washington, DC: Brookings Institution Press, 2007, 53.

81. "President Delivers State of the Union Address," White House, January 29, 2002, <https://georgewbush-whitehouse.archives.gov/news/releases/2002/01/20020129-11.html> (accessed April 29, 2020); Glenn Kessler, "Three Little Words Matter to N. Korea,"

Washington Post, February 22, 2005, p. 10; "Press Conference of the President," White House, April 28, 2005, <https://georgewbush-whitehouse.archives.gov/news/releases/2005/04/20050428-9. html> (accessed April 29, 2020).

82. Pritchard, *Failed Diplomacy*, 55–6.
83. See Gregory J. Moore, "America's Failed North Korea Nuclear Policy: A New Approach," *Asian Perspective* 32, no. 4, 2008, 9–27; C. Kenneth Quinones, "Dualism in the Bush Administration's North Korea Policy," *Asian Perspective* 27, no. 1, 2003, 197–224; Pritchard, *Failed Diplomacy*. This deep divide in views among advisers in the administration was personified at first by Pritchard and Bob Joseph, undersecretary of state for arms control, and by the second-term lead negotiator for talks with North Korea, Christopher Hill, and arms control specialist and ambassador to the UN John Bolton. Moore, "America's Failed North Korea Nuclear Policy."
84. For North Korean remarks on this point, see Korean Central News Agency, June 18, 2001; "Spokesman for DPRK Foreign Ministry Slams Bush's Remark," Korean Central News Agency, October 23, 2001; Commentary, *Minju Choson*, October 29, 2001; Pritchard, *Failed Diplomacy*.
85. "U.S. Tells Iran, Syria, N. Korea 'Learn from Iraq,'" Reuters, April 9, 2003; see also Andrew Newman, "Arms Control, Proliferation and Terrorism: The Bush Administration's Post-September 11 Security Strategy," *Journal of Strategic Studies* 27, no. 1, 2004, 59–88, at 76.
86. Kan, "China and Proliferation of Weapons of Mass Destruction and Missiles," 241.
87. Condoleezza Rice, *No Higher Honor: A Memoir of My Years in Washington*, New York: Crown, 2011, 525; Victor Cha, *The Impossible State: North Korea, Past and Future*, London: Bodley Head, 2012, 284.
88. Kan, "China and Proliferation of Weapons of Mass Destruction and Missiles," 241. Bonnie S. Glaser further observes that when Rice met with Chinese leaders on March 20 to convince them of the incompatibility between stability and nuclear North Korea, there were no signs she had convinced her hosts. Bonnie S. Glaser, "Rice Seeks to Caution, Cajole, and Cooperate with Beijing," *Comparative Connections* 7, no. 1, 2005, 2.
89. Cha, *The Impossible State*, 313.
90. Andrew Scobell, "China and North Korea: From Comrades-in-Arms to Allies at Arm's Length," Strategic Studies Institute, March 2004, 11–12, <https://publications.armywarcollege.edu/ pubs/1672.pdf> (accessed April 29, 2020).

91. "Rice Reassures Japan on Security Commitment," NBC News, October 18, 2006, <http://www.nbcnews.com/id/15313151/ns/world_news-asia_pacific/t/rice-reassures-japan-security-commitment> (accessed April 29, 2020). See comments also by Nicholas R. Burns, undersecretary of state for political affairs: "China, North Korea's largest trading partner and main conduit to the outside world, has committed to enforce 1718. As China follows through, the North Korean regime will feel the pain. It will be deprived of hard currency it earns from exporting WMD and missile technology and conventional arms. And the North Korean elite will lose access to prized luxury goods. We are hopeful this pressure will convince the North to do the right thing." "North Korea's Nuclear Test: Next Steps," Hearing before the Committee on International Relations, House of Representatives, 109th Congress, 2nd Session, 109-242, November 15, 2006, 24, transcript available at <https://www.govinfo.gov/content/pkg/CHRG-109hhrg30902/pdf/CHRG-109hhrg30902.pdf> (accessed April 29, 2020).
92. Gordon Fairclough, "Close-out Sale: North Korea's Elite Shop While They Can," *Wall Street Journal*, December 18, 2006; Nicholas Kralev, "Chinese Exports Blunt U.N. Sanctions," *Washington Times*, December 19, 2008; Kan, "China and Proliferation of Weapons of Mass Destruction and Missiles," 245.
93. "North Korea's Nuclear Test: Next Steps," 12, 15.
94. Cited in Jean Edward Smith, *Bush*, New York: Simon & Schuster, 2016, 649.
95. "China's Proliferation to North Korea and Iran," 96–7.
96. Dan Blumenthal and Aaron Friedberg, "Not Too Late to Curb Dear Leader," *Weekly Standard*, February 12, 2007, 14.
97. "China's Proliferation to North Korea and Iran," 9.
98. Rice, *No Higher Honor*, 526.

Chapter 3

1. Kerry Dumbaugh, "China-U.S. Relations: Current Issues and Implications for U.S. Policy," Congressional Research Service, October 8, 2009, 1, available at <https://fas.org/sgp/crs/row/R40457.pdf> (accessed April 29, 2020).
2. Hillary Clinton, "Remarks with Chinese Foreign Minister Yang Jiechi, Beijing, China," U.S. Department of State, February 21, 2009, <https://2009-2017.state.gov/secretary/20092013clinton/rm/2009a/02/119432.htm> (accessed April 29, 2020).

3. Dumbaugh, "China-U.S. Relations," 1–2.
4. "National Security Strategy," White House, May 2010, 43, <https://obamawhitehouse.archives.gov/sites/default/files/rss_viewer/national_security_strategy.pdf> (accessed April 29, 2020).
5. Ibid.
6. James Fallows, "China's Great Leap Backward," *The Atlantic*, December 2016, <https://www.theatlantic.com/magazine/archive/2016/12/chinas-great-leap-backward/505817> (accessed April 29, 2020); "Investigating the Chinese Threat, Part I: Military and Economic Aggression," Hearing before the Committee on Foreign Affairs, House of Representatives, 112th Congress, 2nd Session, 112–137, March 28, 2012, transcript available at <https://www.govinfo.gov/content/pkg/CHRG-112hhrg73536/pdf/CHRG-112hhrg73536.pdf> (accessed April 29, 2020).
7. This point is made in Chapter 2 in terms of China's counter-terror cooperation. It is worth noting also that this follows along the lines of John J. Mearsheimer's argument that "talk is cheap," intentions are unknown, and interests are power-oriented. Because China is not yet powerful enough to expel America from East Asia, it is logical to expect that it will participate nominally in international institutions to lessen the fear that its rise will correspond with revisionist ambitions. John J. Mearsheimer, "The Gathering Storm: China's Challenge to U.S. Power in Asia," *The Chinese Journal of International Politics* 3, no. 4, 2010, 381–96. Christopher Layne refers to this as part of Beijing's "reassurance strategy." Christopher Layne, "China's Challenge to US Hegemony," *Current History*, January 2008, 16.
8. John J. Tkacik, Jr., remarks on the point that "in the world today, virtually every one of America's adversaries are [*sic*] China's friend," and that this was not a coincidence. "Investigating the China Threat, Part I," 25.
9. Dumbaugh, "China-U.S. Relations," 3.
10. Ibid., 1–2.
11. John R. Bolton, "Obama's Reckless, Ridiculous China Policy," American Enterprise Institute, February 4, 2010, <https://www.aei.org/articles/obamas-reckless-ridiculous-china-policy> (accessed April 29, 2020).
12. Gregory Chin makes the point that as China rises and integrates further within the global economic system it will increasingly seek moderate, rather than drastic, changes to the international order which, given its great power, it was entitled to. The U.S. therefore would be better to engage and accommodate where

appropriate to manage this transition. Gregory Chin, "China's Rising International Influence," in Alan S. Alexandroff and Andrew F. Cooper (eds), *Rising States, Rising Institutions: Challenges for Global Governance*, Washington, DC: Brookings Institution Press, 2010, 100.

13. Dumbaugh, "China-U.S. Relations," 1–2.
14. See for instance, Hugh White, *The China Choice: Why We Should Share Power*, Oxford: Oxford University Press, 2012.
15. David Shambaugh, *China Goes Global: The Partial Power*, New York: Oxford University Press, 2013, 315.
16. Dumbaugh, "China-U.S. Relations," 1–2.
17. Kenneth Lieberthal and Wang Jisi, "Addressing U.S.-China Strategic Distrust," John L. Thornton Center Monograph Series no. 4, Brookings Institution, March 2012, <https://www.brookings.edu/wp-content/uploads/2016/06/0330_china_lieberthal.pdf> (accessed April 29, 2020).
18. Dumbaugh, "China-U.S. Relations," 6.
19. "Pentagon Says Chinese Vessels Harassed U.S. Ship," CNN, March 9, 2009, <https://edition.cnn.com/2009/POLITICS/03/09/us.navy.china/index.html>; "U.S. Accuses the Chinese of Harassing Naval Vessel," *New York Times*, March 9, 2009, <https://www.nytimes.com/2009/03/09/world/asia/09iht-ship.3.20710715.html> (both accessed April 29, 2020).
20. "U.S. Accuses the Chinese of Harassing Naval Vessel."
21. Shirley A. Kan, "U.S.-China Military Contacts: Issues for Congress," Congressional Research Service, October 27, 2014, 77, available at <https://fas.org/sgp/crs/natsec/RL32496.pdf> (accessed April 29, 2020).
22. Dumbaugh, "China-U.S. Relations," 7.
23. "Foreign Ministry Spokesperson Ma Zhaoxu's Regular Press Conference," Chinese Ministry of Foreign Affairs, March 10, 2009, <https://www.fmprc.gov.cn/zflt/eng/fyrth/t541713.htm> (accessed April 29, 2020)
24. Guoli Liu, *China Rising: Chinese Foreign Policy in a Changing World*, London: Palgrave, 2017, 56.
25. Ibid.
26. Office of the Secretary of Defense, "Annual Report to Congress: Military Power of the People's Republic of China 2007," U.S. Department of Defense, 1, available at <https://fas.org/nuke/guide/china/dod-2007.pdf> (accessed April 29, 2020).

27. ChinaPower Team, "What Does China Really Spend on Its Military?" ChinaPower, December 28, 2015, updated August 6, 2019, <https://chinapower.csis.org/military-spending> (accessed April 29, 2020).

28. Dumbaugh, "China-U.S. Relations," 8.

29. Ibid.

30. John Pomfret, "America vs. China: A Competitive Face-off between Two Pacific Powers," *Washington Post*, November 18, 2016, <https://www.washingtonpost.com/graphics/national/obama-legacy/relations-with-china.html> (accessed April 30, 2020).

31. Bree Feng, "Obama's 'Free Rider' Comment Draws Chinese Criticism," *New York Times*, August 13, 2014, <https://sinosphere.blogs.nytimes.com/2014/08/13/obamas-free-rider-comment-draws-chinese-criticism> (accessed April 30, 2020).

32. Thomas J. Christensen, "Obama and Asia: Confronting the China Challenge," *Foreign Affairs*, September/October 2015, <https://www.foreignaffairs.com/articles/asia/obama-and-asia> (accessed April 30, 2020).

33. "U.S.-China Joint Announcement on Climate Change," press release, White House, November 11, 2014, <https://obamawhitehouse.archives.gov/the-press-office/2014/11/11/us-china-joint-announcement-climate-change> (accessed April 30, 2020).

34. Pomfret, "America vs. China."

35. "U.S.-China Joint Statement ," White House, November 17, 2009, <https://obamawhitehouse.archives.gov/realitycheck/the-press-office/us-china-joint-statement> (accessed May 1, 2020)."

36. Christensen, "Obama and Asia."

37. Ibid.

38. Michael McDevitt, "Deterring North Korean Provocations," Brookings Institution, February 7, 2011, <https://www.brookings.edu/research/deterring-north-korean-provocations> (accessed April 30, 2020).

39. Hillary R. Clinton, "Remarks at Press Availability," National Convention Center, Hanoi, Vietnam, U.S. Department of State, July 23, 2010, <https://2009-2017.state.gov/secretary/20092013clinton/rm/2010/07/145095.htm> (accessed April 30, 2020).

40. Christensen, "Obama and Asia."

41. Ibid.

42. Jonathan G. Odom, "What Does a 'Pivot' or 'Rebalance' Look Like? Elements of the U.S. Strategic Turn towards Security in the Asia-Pacific

Region and Its Waters," *Asian-Pacific Law and Policy Journal* 14, no. 1, 2012, 2–33.

43. Richard Weitz, "Pivot Out, Rebalance In," *The Diplomat*, May 3, 2012, <https://thediplomat.com/2012/05/pivot-out-rebalance-in> (accessed April 30, 2020).

44. Hillary Clinton, "America's Pacific Century," *Foreign Policy*, October 11, 2011, <https://foreignpolicy.com/2011/10/11/americas-pacific-century> (accessed April 30, 2020).

45. Ibid.

46. Ibid.

47. Clark Sorensen and Task Force 2016, "The Obama Administration's Pivot to Asia," Henry M. Jackson School of International Studies, University of Washington, 2016, <https://jsis.washington.edu/news/obama-administrations-pivot-asia> (accessed April 30, 2020).

48. Clinton, "America's Pacific Century."

49. Laura Southgate, "The Asia Pivot as a Strategy of Foreign Policy: A Source of Peace or a Harbinger of Conflict?" International Studies Association conference, Hong Kong, June 15–17, 2017, transcript available at <http://dspace.lib.cranfield.ac.uk/handle/1826/12071> (accessed April 30, 2020).

50. "Remarks by President Obama to the Australian Parliament," White House, November 17, 2011, <https://obamawhitehouse.archives.gov/the-press-office/2011/11/17/remarks-president-obama-australian-parliament> (accessed April 30, 2020).

51. Ibid.

52. Tom Donilon, "America Is Back in the Pacific and Will Uphold the Rules," *Financial Times*, November 27, 2011, <https://www.ft.com/content/4f3febac-1761-11e1-b00e-00144feabdc0> (accessed April 30, 2020).

53. Mark E. Manyin, Stephen Daggett, Ben Dolven, Susan V. Lawrence, Michael F. Martin, Ronald O'Rourke, and Bruce Vaughn, "Pivot to the Pacific? The Obama Administration's 'Rebalancing' toward Asia," Congressional Research Service, March 28, 2012, available at <https://fas.org/sgp/crs/natsec/R42448.pdf> (accessed April 30, 2020).

54. Ibid.

55. "Sustaining U.S. Global Leadership: Priorities for 21st Century Defense," U.S. Department of Defense, January 2012, <https://archive.defense.gov/news/Defense_Strategic_Guidance.pdf> (accessed April 30, 2020).

56. Ibid.

57. Evan A. Feigenbaum and Bernard Gwertzman, "Strengthening the U.S. Role in Asia," Council on Foreign Relations" November 16, 2011, <https://www.cfr.org/interview/strengthening-us-role-asia> (accessed April 30, 2020).
58. Ibid.
59. Robert Sutter, "The Obama Administration and U.S. Policy in Asia," *Contemporary Southeast Asia* 31, no. 2, 2009, 189–216, at 206. See also Jörn Dosch, "The U.S. and Southeast Asia," in Mark Beeson (ed.), *Contemporary Southeast Asia*, 2nd ed., Basingstoke, England: Palgrave Macmillan, 2009, 223.
60. Manyin et al., "Pivot to the Pacific?"
61. Hillary R. Clinton and Surin Pitsuwan, "Beginning a New Era of Diplomacy in Asia," U.S. Department of State, February 18, 2009, <https://2009-2017.state.gov/secretary/20092013clinton/rm/2009a/02/119422.htm> (accessed April 30, 2020).
62. Manyin et al., "Pivot to the Pacific?"
63. David S. McDonough, "Obama's Pacific Pivot in US Grand Strategy: A Canadian Perspective," *Asian Security* 9, no. 3, 2013, 165–84.
64. Manyin et al., "Pivot to the Pacific?"
65. Craig Whitlock, "Australia May Host U.S. Drones at Cocos," *Sydney Morning Herald*, March 28, 2012, <https://www.smh.com.au/politics/federal/australia-may-host-us-drones-at-cocos-20120327-1vwmm.html> (accessed April 30, 2020).
66. Ibid.
67. Ibid.
68. "Defence White Paper 2013," Australian Government, Department of Defence, 2013, 11, <https://www.defence.gov.au/Whitepaper/2013/docs/WP_2013_web.pdf> (accessed April 30, 2020).
69. Littoral combat ships are shallow-draft vessels that operate in coastal waters and can counter coastal mines, quiet diesel submarines, and small, fast, armed boats.
70. Manyin at al., "Pivot to the Pacific?"
71. Andrea Shalal-Esa, "Update 2—US Navy Eyes Stationing Ships in Singapore," Reuters, December 16, 2011, <https://www.reuters.com/article/usa-navy-asia/update-2-us-navy-eyes-stationing-ships-in-singapore-idUSL3E7NG06I20111216> (accessed April 30, 2020).
72. Manyin et al., "Pivot to the Pacific?" 8. It is worth noting here, that as of 2020, China has continued to stall on a commitment to agree on a code of conduct in the SCS, marking eighteen years since the code was announced.
73. Ibid.

74. Ibid.
75. Robert S. Ross, "The Problem with the Pivot: Obama's New Asia Policy Is Unnecessary and Counterproductive," *Foreign Affairs*, November/December 2012, <https://www.foreignaffairs.com/articles/asia/2012-11-01/problem-pivot> (accessed April 30, 2020).
76. Ibid.
77. Susan V. Lawrence, "U.S.-China Relations: An Overview of Policy Issues," Congressional Research Service, August 1, 2013, 7, available at <https://fas.org/sgp/crs/row/R41108.pdf> (accessed April 30, 2020).
78. Dean Cheng and Bruce Klingner, "U.S. Asian Policy: America's Security Commitment to Asia Needs More Forces," Heritage Foundation, August 7, 2012, <https://www.heritage.org/asia/report/us-asian-policy-americas-security-commitment-asia-needs-more-forces>.
79. Ibid.
80. John O'Callaghan and Manuel Mogato, "The U.S. Military Pivot to Asia: When Bases Are Not Bases," Reuters, November 14, 2012, <https://www.reuters.com/article/us-usa-asia-military/the-u-s-military-pivot-to-asia-when-bases-are-not-bases-idUSBRE8AD05Y20121114> (accessed April 30, 2020). According to Michael Pillsbury, these "hawks" have been more influential in their advice and planning for PLA and PLAN objectives than many believe. Michael Pillsbury, *The Hundred-Year Marathon: China's Secret Strategy to Replace America as the Global Superpower*, New York: Henry Holt, 2015, 3.
81. Lanxin Xiang, "China and the 'Pivot,'" *Survival* 54, no. 5, 2012, 113–28, at 114.
82. "Remarks by Chinese Vice President Xi Jinping at a Luncheon Co-hosted by the U.S. China Business Council and the National Committee on U.S.-China Relations," Federal News Service, February 15, 2012.
83. Cui Tiankai and Pang Hanzhao, "China-US Relations in China's Overall Diplomacy in the New Era: On China and US Working Together to Build a New-Type Relationship between Major Countries," *China International Strategy Review 2012*, <http://en.iiss.pku.edu.cn/research/discuss/2012/2370.html> (accessed May 11, 2020).
84. Ibid.
85. "Remarks by Secretary Hagel at the IISS Asia Security Summit, Shangri-La Hotel, Singapore," U.S. Department of Defense, June 1, 2013, <https://archive.defense.gov/transcripts/transcript.aspx?transcriptid=5251> (accessed April 30, 2020).
86. "Press Briefing by National Security Advisor Tom Donilon," White House, June 8, 2013, <https://obamawhitehouse.archives.

gov/the-press-office/2013/06/09/press-briefing-national-security-advisor-tom-donilon>.

87. Lawrence, "U.S.-China Relations."
88. Jeffrey A. Bader and David Dollar, "Why the TPP Is the Linchpin of the Asia Rebalance," Brookings Institution, July 28, 2015, <https://www.brookings.edu/blog/order-from-chaos/2015/07/28/why-the-tpp-is-the-linchpin-of-the-asia-rebalance> (accessed April 30, 2020).
89. Ian F. Fergusson and Brock R. Williams, "The Trans-Pacific Partnership (TPP): Key Provisions and Issues for Congress," Congressional Research Service, June 14, 2016, 5, available at <https://fas.org/sgp/crs/row/R44489.pdf> (accessed April 30, 2020).
90. Daniel Slane and Michael Wessel (guest bloggers for Edward Alden), "The TPP: Why It Won't Address Security Concerns with China," Council on Foreign Relations, May 15, 2015, <https://www.cfr.org/blog/tpp-why-it-wont-address-security-concerns-china>.
91. Ibid.
92. Fergusson and Williams, "The Trans-Pacific Partnership (TPP)," 5.
93. Simon Lester, "Chinese Free Trade Is No Threat to American Free Trade", Cato Institute, April 22, 2015, <https://www.cato.org/publications/free-trade-bulletin/chinese-free-trade-no-threat-american-free-trade> (accessed April 30, 2020).
94. Christensen, "Obama and Asia."
95. Ibid.
96. Ibid.

Chapter 4

1. Susan V. Lawrence, "U.S.-China Relations: An Overview of Policy Issues," Congressional Research Service, August 1, 2013, 1, available at <https://fas.org/sgp/crs/row/R41108.pdf> (accessed April 30, 2020).
2. Ibid.
3. Jean-Pierre Cabestan, "Is Xi Jinping the Reformist Leader China Needs?" *China Perspectives*, no. 3 (91), 2012, 69–76; Keith B. Richburg, "Xi Jinping, Likely China's Next Leader, Seen as Pragmatic, Low Key," *Washington Post*, August 15, 2011; Louisa Lim, "A Pragmatic Princeling Next in Line to Lead China," NPR, February 14, 2012, <https://www.npr.org/2012/02/14/146815991/a-pragmatic-princeling-next-in-line-to-lead-china?t=1588322037659> (accessed May 1, 2020).

4. Susan V. Lawrence, "China's Vice President Xi Jinping Visits the United States: What Is at Stake?" Congressional Research Service, February 6, 2012, available at <https://fas.org/sgp/crs/row/R42342.pdf> (accessed May 1, 2020).

5. Susan V. Lawrence, Caitlin Campbell, Rachel F. Fefer, Jane A. Leggett, Thomas Lum, Michael F. Martin, and Andres B. Schwarzenberg, "U.S.-China Relations," Congressional Research Service, September 3, 2019, <https://crsreports.congress.gov/product/pdf/R/R45898> (accessed May 1, 2020).

6. Ibid.

7. Jean Garrison and Marc Wall, "The Rise of Hedging and Regionalism: An Explanation and Evaluation of President Obama's China Policy," *Asian Affairs: An American Review* 43, no. 2, 2016, 47–63.

8. "Remarks by Vice President Biden and Chinese Vice President Xi at the State Department Luncheon," White House, February 14, 2012, <https://obamawhitehouse.archives.gov/the-press-office/2012/02/14/remarks-vice-president-biden-and-chinese-vice-president-xi-state-departm> (accessed May 1, 2020).

9. "U.S.-China Joint Statement," White House, November 17, 2009, <https://obamawhitehouse.archives.gov/realitycheck/the-press-office/us-china-joint-statement> (accessed May 1, 2020).

10. Lawrence, "U.S.-China Relations," 1–3.

11. Ibid.

12. "United States and China Agree to Work Together on Phase Down of HFCs," White House, June 8, 2013, <https://obamawhitehouse.archives.gov/the-press-office/2013/06/08/united-states-and-china-agree-work-together-phase-down-hfcs> (accessed May 1, 2020).

13. "Joint U.S.-China Statement on Climate Change," U.S. Department of State, April 13, 2013, <https://2009-2017.state.gov/r/pa/prs/ps/2013/04/207465.htm> (accessed May 1, 2020).

14. Lawrence, "U.S.-China Relations," 2.

15. "What Does Xi Jinping's China Dream mean?" BBC News, June 6, 2013, <https://www.bbc.com/news/world-asia-china-22726375>; Faine Greenwood, "Xi Jinping Describes 'Chinese Dream' at Closing of National People's Congress," PRI, March 17, 2013, <https://www.pri.org/stories/2013-03-17/xi-jinping-describes-chinese-dream-closing-national-peoples-congress> (both accessed May 1, 2020).

16. Richard McGregor, "Party Man: Xi Jinping's Quest to Dominate China," *Foreign Affairs*, September/October 2019, <https://www.foreignaffairs.com/articles/china/2019-08-14/party-man> (accessed May 1, 2020).

17. Joshua Kucera, "The New Silk Road?" *The Diplomat*, November 11, 2011, <https://thediplomat.com/2011/11/the-new-silk-road> (accessed May 1, 2020).
18. McGregor, "Party Man."
19. Bates Gill, "Xi Jinping's Grip on Power Is Absolute, but There Are New Threats to His 'Chinese Dream,'" *The Conversation*, June 28, 2019, <https://theconversation.com/xi-jinpings-grip-on-power-is-absolute-but-there-are-new-threats-to-his-chinese-dream-118921> (accessed May 1, 2020).
20. Ibid.
21. Chen Fei, "On Strengthening the Role of the Communist Party of China in the Armed Forces in the New Situation: A Study of Xi Jinping's Important Expositions on Strengthening the Role of the Communist Party of China in the Armed Forces," *China Military Science*, no. 4, 2014, 86–92.
22. "Xi Jinping Calls for PLA 'Real Combat' Awareness," China Central Television, December 12, 2012.
23. Kevin McCauley, "President Xi Clears the Way for Military Reform: PLA Corruption, Clique Breaking and Making, and Personnel Shuffle," *China Brief* 15, no. 3, 2015, 9–13; Zhao Shengnan, "Reshuffle Brings In Younger Officers," *China Daily*, August 4, 2015, <https://www.chinadaily.com.cn/china/2015-08/04/content_21493316.htm> (accessed May 1, 2020).
24. Ian E. Rinehart, "The Chinese Military: Overview and Issues for Congress," Congressional Research Service, March 24, 2016, 8–9, available at <https://fas.org/sgp/crs/row/R44196.pdf> (accessed May 1, 2020).
25. "Sustaining U.S. Global Leadership: Priorities for 21st Century Defense," U.S. Department of Defense, January 2012, 2, <https://archive.defense.gov/news/Defense_Strategic_Guidance.pdf> (accessed April 30, 2020).
26. Ibid.
27. "Remarks by President Obama and President Xi Jinping of the People's Republic of China after Bilateral Meeting," White House, June 8, 2013, <https://obamawhitehouse.archives.gov/the-press-office/2013/06/08/remarks-president-obama-and-president-xi-jinping-peoples-republic-china-> (accessed May 1, 2020).
28. Lawrence, "U.S.-China Relations," 17.
29. Office of the Secretary of Defense, "Annual Report to Congress: Military and Security Developments Involving the People's Republic of China 2013," U.S. Department of Defense, May 7, 2013, 17,

<https://archive.defense.gov/pubs/2013_China_Report_FINAL. pdf> (accessed May 1, 2020).

30. Lawrence, "U.S.-China Relations," 17.
31. Ibid.
32. "China's Military Strategy," State Council, People's Republic of China, May 2015, <http://english.www.gov.cn/archive/white_paper/2015/ 05/27/content_281475115610833.htm> (accessed May 1, 2020).
33. Xu Jian, "Rethinking China's Period of Strategic Opportunity," *China International Studies*, March/April 2014, 51–70, <http:// www.ciis.org.cn/english/2014-05/28/content_6942258.htm>; Rinehart, "The Chinese Military," 8.
34. "China's Military Strategy."
35. Ibid.
36. Ibid.
37. Zhang Xiaolin and Cao Yang, "Promote the Transformation of Naval Strategy, Safeguard Maritime Security," *Navy Today*, June 2015, 20–3. Translation by China Maritime Studies Institute, U.S. Naval War College; Rinehart, "The Chinese Military," 8–9.
38. "China's Military Strategy."
39. Susan Turner Haynes, *Chinese Nuclear Proliferation: How Global Politics Is Transforming China's Weapons Buildup and Modernization*, Lincoln, NE: Potomac, 2016.
40. Stockholm International Peace Research Institute, *SIPRI Yearbook 2018*, Oxford: Oxford University Press, 2018, 260.
41. Bill Gertz, "China Flight Tests New Submarine-Launched Missile," *Washington Free Beacon*, December 18, 2018, <https://freebeacon. com/national-security/china-flight-tests-new-submarine-launched-missile> (accessed May 1, 2020).
42. Hans M. Kristensen and Robert S. Norris, "Chinese Nuclear Forces, 2016," *Bulletin of the Atomic Scientists* 72, no. 4, 2016, 205–11.
43. "China: Nuclear," Nuclear Threat Initiative, April 2015, <https:// www.nti.org/learn/countries/china/nuclear> (accessed May 1, 2020).
44. "The United States Strengthens Its Nuclear Superiority, and China Cannot Afford to Ignore It," *Global Times*, January 9, 2018, <http://opinion.huanqiu.com/editorial/2018-01/11506799.html> (accessed May 1, 2020); Haynes, *Chinese Nuclear Proliferation*, 77–8.
45. Susan Turner Haynes, "Chinese Nuclear Strategy," in Aiden Warren and Philip M. Baxter (eds), *Nuclear Modernization in the 21st Century*, Abingdon, England: Routledge, 2020, 78.
46. "China's Military Strategy."

47. Timothy R. Heath, "Trump's National Security Strategy Ratchets Up U.S. Competition with China", *World Politics Review*, December 26, 2017, <https://www.worldpoliticsreview.com/articles/23889/trump-s-national-security-strategy-ratchets-up-u-s-competition-with-china> (accessed May 1, 2020).
48. Lawrence, "U.S.-China Relations," 20–21.
49. Hillary Rodham Clinton, "Remarks with Japanese Foreign Minister Fumio Kishida after Their Meeting," U.S. Department of State, January 18, 2013, <https://2009-2017.state.gov/secretary/20092013clinton/rm/2013/01/203050.htm>; "Press Conference with Secretary Hagel and Defense Minister Onodera from the Pentagon," U.S. Department of Defense, April 29, 2013, <https://content.govdelivery.com/accounts/USDOD/bulletins/78e2bb> (both accessed May 1, 2020).
50. Clinton, "Remarks with Japanese Foreign Minister Fumio Kishida after Their Meeting."
51. "Press Briefing by National Security Advisor Tom Donilon," White House, June 8, 2013, <https://obamawhitehouse.archives.gov/the-press-office/2013/06/08/press-briefing-national-security-advisor-tom-donilon> (accessed May 1, 2020).
52. "China Opposes U.S. Comments about Diaoyu Islands: Spokesman," Xinhua News Agency, January 20, 2013.
53. "Press Briefing by National Security Advisor Tom Donilon"; Lawrence, "U.S.-China Relations," 21.
54. The seven Spratly Islands reefs that China controls are Cuarteron Reef (known in China as Huayang Jiao), Fiery Cross Reef (Yongshu Jiao), Gaven Reef (Nanxun Jiao), Hugh Reef (Dongmen Jiao), Johnson Reef (Chigua Jiao), Mischief Reef (Meiji Jiao), and Subi Reef (Zhubi Jiao).
55. It should be noted that in February 2020, Philippine president Rodrigo Duterte formally delivered a notice to terminate the Visiting Forces Agreement to the United States, thereby deepening the uncertainty about the implications for the U.S.-Philippine alliance. See Prashanth Parameswaran, "The Significance of Ending the US-Philippines Visiting Forces Agreement," *The Diplomat*, February 12, 2020, <https://thediplomat.com/2020/02/the-significance-of-ending-the-us-philippines-visiting-forces-agreement> (accessed June 15, 2020).
56. "China, ASEAN to Hold Meetings on South China Sea in September," Xinhua News Service, June 30, 2013; Lawrence, "U.S.-China Relations," 21.
57. Michael D. Swaine, "Beyond American Predominance in the Western Pacific: The Need for a Stable U.S.-China Balance of Power,"

Carnegie Endowment for International Peace, April 20, 2015, <http://carnegieendowment.org/2015/04/20/beyond-american-pre-dominance-in-western-pacific-need-for-stable-u.s.-china-balance-of-power> (accessed May 1, 2020).

58. Jeremy Page and Julian E. Barnes, "China Expands Island Construction in Disputed South China Sea," *Wall Street Journal*, February 18, 2015; Jun Kaminishikawara, "U.S. Could Change Military Posture if China Expands Air Defense Zone," Kyodo News Agency, January 31, 2014.

59. Kyle Rempfer, "U.S. Military Posture in Asia Could Change if China Declares Another Air Defense Identification Zone," *Air Force Times*, September 28, 2018, <https://www.airforcetimes.com/news/2018/09/28/us-military-posture-in-asia-could-change-if-china-declares-another-air-defense-identification-zone> (accessed May 1, 2020).

60. "Safeguarding American Interests in the East and South China Seas," Hearing before the Committee on Foreign Relations, United States Senate, 114th Congress, 1st Session, May 13, 2015, S. Hrg. 114-75, testimony of David Shear, <https://www.foreign.senate.gov/hearings/safeguarding-american-interests-in-the-east-and-south-china-seas>; Ben Dolven, Jennifer K. Elsea, Susan V. Lawrence, Ronald O'Rourke, and Ian E. Rinehart, "Chinese Land Reclamation in the South China Sea: Implications and Policy Options," Congressional Research Service, June 18, 2015, 22, available at <https://fas.org/sgp/crs/row/R44072.pdf> (both accessed May 1, 2020).

61. Andrew Jacobs, "Kerry Expected to Bring Up China's Sea Claims during Visit," *New York Times*, May 15, 2015, <https://www.nytimes.com/2015/05/16/world/asia/kerry-china-south-sea-dispute.html> (accessed May 1, 2020).

62. David Brunnstrom, "Carter Says U.S. Will Sail, Fly and Operate Wherever International Law Allows," Reuters, October 14, 2015, <https://www.reuters.com/article/us-usa-australia-southchinasea-carter-idUSKCN0S72MG20151013> (accessed May 1, 2020).

63. Mira Rapp-Hooper, "In Defense of Facts in the South China Sea," Asia Maritime Transparency Initiative, June 2, 2015, <http://amti.csis.org/in-defense-of-facts-in-the-south-china-sea> (accessed May 1, 2020).

64. Ash Carter, "IISS Shangri-La Dialogue: 'A Regional Security Architecture Where Everyone Rises,'" U.S. Department of Defense, May 30, 2015, <https://www.defense.gov/Newsroom/Speeches/Speech/Article/606676> (accessed May 5, 2020).

65. Rapp-Hooper, "In Defense of Facts in the South China Sea."

66. Prashanth Parameswaran, "U.S. Launches New Maritime Security Initiative at Shangri La Dialogue 2015," *The Diplomat*, June 2, 2015, <https://thediplomat.com/2015/06/us-launches-new-maritime-security-initiative-at-shangri-la-dialogue-2015> (accessed May 1, 2020).

67. Dolven et al., "Chinese Land Reclamation in the South China Sea," 22.

68. "China's Menacing Sandcastles in the South China Sea," *War on the Rocks*, March 2, 2015, <https://warontherocks.com/2015/03/chinas-menacing-sandcastles-in-the-south-china-sea> (accessed May 1, 2020; a collection of short writings by several authors; see in particular those by Ely Ratner, Shawn Brimley, Robert Haddick, Mira Rapp-Hooper, and Zack Cooper); Richard Fontaine, "Chinese Land Reclamation Pushes Boundaries," *Wall Street Journal*, March 3, 2015; Michael Mazza, "Obama's China Tool Kit: In Need of Serious Repair," American Enterprise Institute, March 5, 2015, <https://www.aei.org/articles/obamas-china-toolkit-need-serious-repair> (accessed May 1, 2020); Harry Kazianis, "Superpower Showdown: America Can Stop Chinese Aggression in Asia," *National Interest*, March 6, 2015, <https://nationalinterest.org/feature/superpower-showdown-america-can-stop-chinese-aggression-asia-12368> (accessed May 1, 2020); Michael J. Green and Mira Rapp-Hooper, "China's New Maritime Provocation," *Washington Post*, March 13, 2015; John Schaus, "Concrete Steps for the U.S. in the South China Sea," *War on the Rocks*, March 16, 2015, <http://warontherocks.com/2015/03/concrete-steps-for-the-u-s-in-the-south-china-sea> (accessed May 1, 2020).

69. Mazza, "Obama's China Tool Kit."

70. Ibid.

71. Quoted in Dolven et al., "Chinese Land Reclamation in the South China Sea," 23.

72. Parameswaran, "U.S. Launches New Maritime Security Initiative"; Dolven et al., "Chinese Land Reclamation in the South China Sea," 23.

73. Carter, "IISS Shangri-La Dialogue."

74. Brahma Chellaney, "Who Lost the South China Sea?" *Maritime Executive*, June 15, 2018, <https://www.maritime-executive.com/editorials/who-lost-the-south-china-sea> (accessed May 1, 2020).

75. Wayne M. Morrison, "China's Economic Rise: History, Trends, Challenges, and Implications for the United States," Congressional Research Service, June 25, 2019, 1, available at <https://fas.org/sgp/crs/row/RL33534.pdf> (accessed May 4, 2020).

76. "Assessment on U.S. Defense Implications of China's Expanding Global Access," U.S. Department of Defense, December 2018, <https://

media.defense.gov/2019/Jan/14/2002079292/-1/-1/1/EXPANDING-GLOBALACCESS-REPORT-FINAL.PDF> (accessed May 4, 2020).

77. Dolven et al., "Chinese Land Reclamation in the South China Sea," 26.
78. "Assessment on U.S. Defense Implications of China's Expanding Global Access."
79. "Full Text of Chinese President Xi's Address at APEC CEO Summit," XinhuaNet, November 11, 2017, <http://www.xinhuanet.com/english/2017-11/11/c_136743492.htm> (accessed May 4, 2020).
80. Jacob Stokes, "China's Road Rules: Beijing Looks West toward Eurasian Integration," *Foreign Affairs*, April 19, 2015, <https://www.foreignaffairs.com/articles/asia/2015-04-19/chinas-road-rules> (accessed May 4, 2020).
81. Ibid.
82. Andrea Kendall-Taylor and David Shullman, "A Russian-Chinese Partnership Is a Threat to U.S. Interests: Can Washington Act before It's Too Late?" *Foreign Affairs*, May 14, 2019, <https://www.foreignaffairs.com/articles/china/2019-05-14/russian-chinese-partnership-threat-us-interests> (accessed May 4, 2020).
83. Elizabeth C. Economy, "China's New Revolution: The Reign of Xi Jinping," *Foreign Affairs*, May/June 2018, <https://www.foreignaffairs.com/articles/china/2018-04-17/chinas-new-revolution> (accessed May 4, 2020).
84. Ibid.
85. Peter Cai, "Understanding China's Belt and Road Initiative," Lowy Institute, March 2017, <https://www.lowyinstitute.org/sites/default/files/documents/Understanding%20China%E2%80%99s%20Belt%20and%20Road%20Initiative_WEB_1.pdf> (accessed May 4, 2020).
86. Gal Luft, "China's Infrastructure Play: Why Washington Should Accept the New Silk Road," *Foreign Affairs*, September/October 2016, <https://www.foreignaffairs.com/articles/asia/chinas-infra-structure-play>.
87. David E. Sanger and Edward Wong, "As Obama Plays China Card on Trade, Chinese Pursue Their Own Deals," *New York Times*, May 12, 2015. <https://www.nytimes.com/2015/05/13/us/politics/as-obama-plays-china-card-on-trade-chinese-pursue-their-own-deals.html>.
88. Kevin Rudd, "The Price of Mistrust," *Foreign Policy*, May 7, 2015, <https://foreignpolicy.com/2015/05/07/china-us-relations-washington-beijing> (accessed May 4, 2020).
89. Kelsey Davenport, "Chronology of U.S.-North Korean Nuclear and Missile Diplomacy," Arms Control Association, April 2020,

<https://www.armscontrol.org/factsheets/dprkchron> (accessed May 4, 2020).

90. Anna Fifield, "North Korea Conducts Fifth Nuclear Test, Claims It Has Made Warheads with 'Higher Strike Power,'" *Washington Post,* September 9, 2016, <https://www.washingtonpost.com/world/north-korea-conducts-fifth-nuclear-test-as-regime-celebrates-national-holiday/2016/09/08/9332c01d-6921-4fe3-8f68-c611dc59f5a9_story.html>; Joby Warrick, "A North Korean H-bomb? Not Likely, Experts Say," *Washington Post,* January 6, 2016, <https://www.washingtonpost.com/world/national-security/a-north-korean-h-bomb-not-likely-experts-say/2016/01/06/93ec6b14-b49b-11e5-9388-466021d971de_story.html> (both accessed May 4, 2020).

91. "Kim Jong Un Visits Reconstructed Pyongchon Revolutionary Site," *Rodong Sinmun,* December 10, 2015, available at <http://www.nkleadershipwatch.org/2015/12/09/kim-jong-un-visits-pyongchon-revolutionary-site> (accessed May 4, 2020).

92. Declan Butler and Elizabeth Gibney, "What Kind of Bomb Did North Korea Detonate?" *Nature,* January 8, 2016, <https://www.nature.com/news/what-kind-of-bomb-did-north-korea-deto-nate-1.19132> (accessed May 4, 2020).

93. "North Korea," Nuclear Threat Initiative, August 2019, <http://www.nti.org/learn/countries/north-korea> (accessed May 4, 2020).

94. Davenport, "Chronology of US-North Korean Nuclear and Missile Diplomacy."

95. Steven Lee Myers and Choe Sang-Hun, "North Korea Agrees to Curb Nuclear Work; US Offers Aid," *New York Times,* February 29, 2012, <http://www.nytimes.com/2012/03/01/world/asia/us-says-north-korea-agrees-to-curb-nuclear-work.html> (accessed May 4, 2020).

96. See Aiden Warren, *The Obama Administration's Nuclear Weapon Strategy: The Promises of Prague,* Abingdon, England: Routledge, 2014, 144–57.

97. "Remarks by Tom Donilon, National Security Advisor to the President: 'The United States and the Asia-Pacific in 2013,'" White House, March 11, 2013, <https://obamawhitehouse.archives.gov/the-press-office/2013/03/11/remarks-tom-donilon-national-security-advisor-president-united-states-an> (accessed May 4, 2020).

98. Jane Perlez, "North Korea Tests the Patience of Its Closest Ally," *New York Times,* June 24, 2012, <https://www.nytimes.com/2012/06/25/world/asia/north-korea-tests-the-patience-of-its-ally-china.html> (accessed May 4, 2020); "Security Council Tightens Sanctions on DPR Korea in Wake of Latest Nuclear Blast," *UN News,* March 7, 2013, <https://news.un.org/en/story/2013/

03/433722-security-council-tightens-sanctions-dpr-korea-wake-latest-nuclear-blast> (accessed May 4, 2020); "Remarks by Tom Donilon, National Security Advisor to the President."

99. Celia Hatton, "Is China Ready to Abandon North Korea?" BBC News, April 12, 2013, <https://www.bbc.com/news/world-asia-china-22062589> (accessed May 4, 2020)

100. Heng Xie and Megha Rajagopalan, "Bank of China Closes Account of Key North Korean Bank," Reuters, May 7, 2013, <https://www.reuters.com/article/us-korea-north-china-bank-idUSBRE9460CX20130507> (accessed May 4, 2020).

101. Qian Zhou, "In Talks with ROK President Park Geun-hye, Xi Jinping Emphasizes Comprehensively Promoting Mutually Beneficial Cooperation, Spurring Still Greater Development of Sino-ROK Relations," Xinhua News Agency, June 27, 2013.

102. "U.S.-China Strategic and Economic Dialogue Outcomes of the Strategic Track," U.S. Department of State, July 12, 2013, <https://2009-2017.state.gov/r/pa/prs/ps/2013/07/211861.htm> (accessed May 4, 2020).

103. "H. Res. 65—Condemning the Government of North Korea for its flagrant and repeated violations of multiple United Nations Security Council resolutions, for its repeated provocations that threaten international peace and stability, and for its February 12, 2013, test of a nuclear device," House of Representatives, 113rd Congress, February 13, 2013, <https://www.congress.gov/bill/113th-congress/house-resolution/65/text> (accessed May 4, 2020).

104. Fifield, "North Korea Conducts Fifth Nuclear Test."

105. Julian Borger, "Kim Jong-un's Growing Nuclear Arsenal Could Force U.S. Back to Negotiating Table," *The Guardian*, September 9, 2016, <https://www.theguardian.com/world/2016/sep/09/north-koreas-growing-ambition-nuclear-arsenal-force-us-negotiating-table> (accessed May 4, 2020).

106. Ibid.

107. Lesley Wroughton and Yeganeh Torbati, "Exclusive: U.S. Warns China It Will Target Firms for Illicit North Korea Business," Reuters, December 2, 2016, <https://www.reuters.com/article/us-northkorea-usa-sanctions-idUSKBN13R28E> (accessed May 4, 2020).

108. Emma Chanlett-Avery, Mark E. Manyin, Mary Beth D. Nikitin, Caitlin Elizabeth Campbell, and Wil Mackey, "North Korea: U.S. Relations, Nuclear Diplomacy, and Internal Situation," Congressional Research Service, July 27, 2018, available at <https://fas.org/sgp/crs/nuke/R41259.pdf> (accessed May 4, 2020).

109. Victor Cha, "The Unfinished Legacy of Obama's Pivot to Asia," *Foreign Policy*, September 6, 2016, <https://foreignpolicy.com/2016/09/06/the-unfinished-legacy-of-obamas-pivot-to-asia> (accessed May 4, 2020).

110. Garrison and Wall, "The Rise of Hedging and Regionalism."

Chapter 5

1. "Hearing on U.S.-China Relations in 2019: A Year in Review," Hearing before the U.S.-China Economic and Security Review Commission, 116th Congress, 1st Session, September 4, 2019, 6, transcript available at <https://www.uscc.gov/sites/default/files/2019-10/September%204,%202019%20Hearing%20Transcript.pdf> (accessed May 4, 2020).

2. Michal Kolmaš and Šárka Kolmašová, "A 'Pivot' That Never Existed: America's Asian Strategy under Obama and Trump," *Cambridge Review of International Affairs* 32, no. 1, 2019, 61–79, at 71.

3. Scott W. Howard, remarks in "The Future of U.S.-China Military Relations," *Chinafile*, March 1, 2019, <http://www.chinafile.com/conversation/future-of-china-us-military-relations> (accessed May 4, 2020).

4. David R. Stilwell, "The U.S., China, and Pluralism in International Affairs," speech at Brookings Institution, December 2, 2019, transcript available at <https://fj.usembassy.gov/the-u-s-china-and-pluralism-in-international-affairs> (accessed May 4, 2020).

5. Jason A. Edwards, "Make America Great Again: Donald Trump and Redefining the U.S. Role in the World," *Communication Quarterly* 66, no. 2, 2018, 176–95, at 181.

6. Max Fisher, "Stephen K. Bannon's CPAC Comments, Annotated and Explained," *New York Times*, February 24, 2017.

7. Hal Brands, "The Unexceptional Superpower: American Grand Strategy in the Age of Trump," *Survival* 59, no. 6, 2017, 7–40, at 12–13; Robert Sutter, "Congress and Trump Administration China Policy: Overlapping Priorities, Uneasy Adjustments and Hardening toward Beijing," *Journal of Contemporary China* 28, no. 118, 2019, 519–37, at 526.

8. Martha Joynt Kumar, "The Contemporary Presidency: Energy or Chaos? Turnover at the Top of President Trump's White House," *Presidential Studies Quarterly* 49, no. 1, 2019, 219–36, at 220. By

the beginning of 2020, Trump had gone through five national security advisers, one secretary of state, and four secretaries of defense,
including acting positions.

9. David E. Lewis, Patrick Bernhard, and Emily You, "President
Trump as Manager: Reflections on the First Year," *Presiden-
tial Studies Quarterly* 48, no. 3, 2018, 480–501, at 488; David
E. Sanger and Maggie Haberman, "50 G.O.P. Officials Warn
Donald Trump Would Put Nation's Security 'at Risk,'" *New York
Times*, August 8, 2016.

10. Robbie Gramer and Maya Gandhi, "Tillerson to Kushner: We've
Got to Stop Meeting like This," *Foreign Policy*, June 27, 2019,
<https://foreignpolicy.com/2019/06/27/tillerson-secretary-of-
state-testimony-transcript-house-foreign-affairs-committee-jared-
kushner-role-trump-administration> (accessed May 4, 2020); Ben
Kesling and Dustin Volz, "Rex Tillerson Says Jared Kushner Often
Kept Him out of the Loop," *Wall Street Journal*, June 27, 2019;
Sharon LaFraniere, Maggie Haberman, and Peter Baker, "Jared
Kushner's Vast Duties, and Visibility in the White House, Shrink,"
New York Times, November 25, 2017.

11. Mark Bowden, "Top Military Officers Unload on Trump," *The
Atlantic*, November 2019, <https://www.theatlantic.com/maga-
zine/archive/2019/11/military-officers-trump/598360> (accessed
May 4, 2020).

12. John Walcott, "'Willful Ignorance': Inside President Trump's Troubled Intelligence Briefings," *Time*, February 5, 2019, <https://time.
com/5518947/donald-trump-intelligence-briefings-national-security>
(accessed May 4, 2020); Eliot A. Cohen, "America's Long Goodbye:
The Real Crisis of the Trump Era," *Foreign Affairs*, January/February
2019, 138.

13. "Memorandum: National Security and Foreign Policy Authorities on
President Obama's Trade Agenda," Office of the United States Trade
Representative, <https://ustr.gov/memorandum-national-security-and-
foreign-policy-authorities-president-obama%E2%80%99s-trade-
agenda> (accessed May 4, 2020); Aaron L. Friedberg, "Competing
with China," *Survival* 60, no. 3, 2018, 7–64, at 41.

14. Erica Werner, Seung Min Kim, and Damian Paletta, "Trump Weighs
Rejoining Trans-Pacific Partnership He Once Called a 'Disaster,'"
Washington Post, April 12, 2018. Larry Kudlow, who replaced Gary
Cohn as director of the National Economic Council, was reported
to be looking to create a trade "coalition of the willing" not unlike
the TPP to confront China. Paul Blustein, *Schism: China, America*

and the *Fracturing of the Global Trading System*, Waterloo, ON: Centre for International Governance Innovation, 2019.

15. David M. Lampton, "A Tipping Point in U.S.-China Relations Is upon U.S.," *US-China Perception Monitor*, May 11, 2015.

16. Elizabeth C. Economy, "The Debate on U.S.-China Relations: Make Room, Make Way, or Make Hay," *RealClear World*, May 22, 2015, <https://www.realclearworld.com/articles/2015/05/22/the_debate_on_us-china_relations_make_room_make_way_or_make_haycidotr-partner_site-rcw_111210.html> (accessed May 4, 2020); Robert D. Blackwill and Ashley J. Tellis, "Revising U.S. Grand Strategy toward China," Council on Foreign Relations, Special Report no. 72, April 2015, <https://www.cfr.org/report/revising-us-grand-strategy-toward-china> (accessed May 4, 2020); Suisheng Zhao, "American Reflections on the Engagement with China and Responses to President Xi's New Model of Major Power Relations," *Journal of Contemporary China* 26, no. 106, 2017, 489–503.

17. Michael Pillsbury, *The Hundred-Year Marathon: China's Secret Strategy to Replace America as the Global Superpower*, New York: Henry Holt, 2015; Ben Schreckinger and Daniel Lippman, "The China Hawk Who Captured Trump's 'Very, Very Large Brain,'" *Politico*, November 30, 2018, <https://www.politico.com/story/2018/11/30/trump-china-xi-jinping-g20-michael-pillsbury-1034610> (accessed May 4, 2020). For Navarro's anti-China books, see Peter Navarro, *The Coming China Wars: Where They Will Be Fought and How They Will Be Won*, Upper Saddle River, NJ: Financial Times Press, 2008; Peter Navarro and Greg Autry, *Death by China: Confronting the Dragon—A Global Call to Action*, Upper Saddle River, NJ: Prentice Hall, 2011; Peter Navarro, *Crouching Tiger: What China's Militarism Means for the World*, Amherst, NY: Prometheus, 2015.

18. See for instance, Sam Parker and Gabrielle Chefitz, "Debt Book Diplomacy: China's Strategic Leveraging of its Newfound Economic Influence and Consequences for U.S. Foreign Policy," Belfer Center, Harvard Kennedy School, May 2018, <https://www.belfercenter.org/sites/default/files/files/publication/Debtbook%20Diplomacy%20PDF.pdf> (accessed May 4, 2020).

19. Quoted in Megan Cassella and Doug Palmer, "Lawmakers, U.S. Allies Sound Alarm over Trump's Latest Tariff Moves," *Politico*, July 11, 2018, <https://www.politico.com/story/2018/07/11/new-trump-tariffs-trade-war-china-678252>; David Lauter and Jonathan Kaiman,

"Trump's China Tariffs Get Bipartisan Support, Reflecting Widespread U.S. Disillusionment with Beijing," *Los Angeles Times*, March 22, 2018, <https://www.latimes.com/politics/la-na-pol-trump-china-tariffs-20180322-story.html> (both accessed May 4, 2020).

20. Michael Brown and Pavneet Singh, "China's Technology Transfer Strategy: How Chinese Investments in Emerging Technology Enable a Strategic Competitor to Access the Crown Jewels of U.S. Innovation," Defense Innovation Unit Experimental (DIUx), January 2018, 2, <https://admin.govexec.com/media/diux_chinatechnologytransferstudy_jan_2018_(1).pdf> (accessed May 4, 2020). This report was made available to Defense Department personnel and security establishment insiders in mid-2017.

21. Rosemary Foot and Amy King, "Assessing the Deterioration in China-U.S. Relations: U.S. Governmental Perspectives on the Economic-Security Nexus," *China International Strategy Review* 1, no. 1, 2019, 39–50, at 44.

22. Comments made by senior members of the PLA at the 16th Annual East Asia Security Symposium, hosted by the Center for Strategic and Peace Studies, China Foreign Affairs University, Beijing, June 24–28, 2019. Due to Chatham House rules, the names of the speakers and interviewees have been omitted.

23. "National Security Strategy of the United States of America," White House, December 2017, 2, <https://www.whitehouse.gov/wp-content/uploads/2017/12/NSS-Final-12-18-2017-0905.pdf> (accessed May 5, 2020).

24. Christina Lin, "A Tipping Point for Sino-US Relations?" *Asia Times*, May 13, 2019, <https://www.asiatimes.com/2019/05/article/a-tipping-point-for-sino-us-relations> (accessed May 5, 2020).

25. Hearing to Receive Testimony on China and Russia, Committee on Armed Services, United States Senate, January 29, 2019, 10, transcript available at <https://www.armed-services.senate.gov/imo/media/doc/19-02_1-29-19.pdf> (accessed May 5, 2020). See also "Summary of the 2018 National Defense Strategy of the United States of America: Sharpening the American Military's Competitive Edge," U.S. Department of Defense, 1–2, <https://dod.defense.gov/Portals/1/Documents/pubs/2018-National-Defense-Strategy-Summary.pdf> (accessed May 5, 2020).

26. "Hearing on U.S.-China Relations in 2019," 51.

27. "Remarks by President Trump on the Administration's National Security Strategy," White House, December 18, 2017, <https://www.whitehouse.gov/briefings-statements/remarks-president-trump-administrations-national-security-strategy> (accessed May 5, 2020).

28. "Summary of the 2018 National Defense Strategy," 1–2.

29. "Remarks by Vice President Pence on the Administration's Policy toward China," White House, October 4, 2018, <https://www.whitehouse.gov/briefings-statements/remarks-vice-president-pence-administrations-policy-toward-china> (accessed May 5, 2020).

30. "Full Transcript: Trump's 2020 State of the Union Address," *New York Times*, February 5, 2020, <https://www.nytimes.com/2020/02/05/us/politics/state-of-union-transcript.html> (accessed May 5, 2020).

31. "Political warfare" refers to attempts to shape perceptions in regional governments and publics of the opportunity for wealth and power presented by China, rather than the threat of hegemonic control, while painting United States leadership and policies as unstable, unreliable, or threatening.

32. Hearing to Receive Testimony on China and Russia, 14.

33. Hearing to Receive Testimony on Policy and Strategy in the Asia-Pacific, Committee on Armed Services, United States Senate, April 25, 2017, 13, transcript available at <https://www.armed-services.senate.gov/imo/media/doc/17-35_04-25-17.pdf> (accessed May 5, 2020).

34. Gordon Lubold, "U.S. Wants to Spend Added Billions on Military in Asia," *Wall Street Journal*, May 7, 2017.

35. "Remarks by President Trump at APEC CEO Summit: Da Nang, Vietnam," White House, November 10, 2017, <https://www.whitehouse.gov/briefings-statements/remarks-president-trump-apec-ceo-summit-da-nang-vietnam> (accessed May 5, 2020)

36. DoD News, "Pacific Command Change Highlights Growing Importance of Indian Ocean Area," U.S. Indo-Pacific Command, May 31, 2018, <https://www.pacom.mil/Media/News/News-Article-View/Article/1537107/pacific-command-change-highlights-growing-importance-of-indian-ocean-area> (accessed May 5, 2020).

37. "Sec. Pompeo Remarks on 'America's Indo-Pacific Economic Vision,'" U.S. Mission to ASEAN, July 30, 2018, <https://asean.usmission.gov/sec-pompeo-remarks-on-americas-indo-pacific-economic-vision>; Jean-Loup Samaan, "Confronting the Flaws in America's Indo-Pacific Strategy," *War on the Rocks*, February 11, 2019, <https://warontherocks.com/2019/02/confronting-the-flaws-in-americas-indo-pacific-strategy> (both accessed May 5, 2020).

38. Susan B. Epstein, Marian L. Lawson, and Cory R. Gill, "Department of State, Foreign Operations, and Related Programs: FY2018 Budget and Appropriations," Congressional Research Service, April 13, 2018, 14, <https://crsreports.congress.gov/product/pdf/R/R44890> (accessed May 5, 2020).

39. "Indo-Pacific Strategy Report: Preparedness, Partnerships, and Promoting a Networked Region," U.S. Department of Defense, June 1, 2019, <https://media.defense.gov/2019/Jul/01/2002152311/-1/-1/1/DEPARTMENT-OF-DEFENSE-INDO-PACIFIC-STRATEGY-REPORT-2019.PDF> (accessed May 5, 2020).

40. Epstein, Lawson, and Gill, "Department of State, Foreign Operations, and Related Programs," 16.

41. James M. Roberts, "Will the BUILD Act Improve Lending in Poor Countries and Counter China? The Jury's Still Out," Heritage Foundation, May 24, 2019, <https://www.heritage.org/budget-and-spending/commentary/will-the-build-act-improve-lending-poor-countries-and-counter-china> (accessed May 5, 2020).

42. "U.S. International Development Finance Corporation Begins Operations," DFC, January 2, 2020, <https://www.dfc.gov/media/press-releases/us-international-development-finance-corporation-begins-operations> (accessed May 5, 2020). For more on the IPSR, see Mark Montgomery and Eric Sayers, "Addressing America's Operational Shortfall in the Pacific," *War on the Rocks*, June 18, 2019, <https://warontherocks.com/2019/06/addressing-americas-operational-shortfall-in-the-pacific> (accessed May 5, 2020).

43. Ashley Townshend, Brendan Thomas-Noone, and Matilda Steward, "Averting Crisis: American Strategy, Military Spending and Collective Defence in the Indo-Pacific," United States Studies Centre, University of Sydney, August 19, 2019, <https://www.ussc.edu.au/analysis/averting-crisis-american-strategy-military-spending-and-collective-defence-in-the-indo-pacific#america%E2%80%99s-troubled-defence-budget> (accessed May 5, 2020).

44. Ibid.

45. Hearing to Receive Testimony on the Department of Defense Budget Posture in Review of the Defense Authorization Request for Fiscal Year 2019 and the Future Years Defense Program, Committee on Armed Services, United States Senate, April 26, 2018, 29, transcript available at <https://www.armed-services.senate.gov/imo/media/doc/18-44_04-26-18.pdf> (accessed May 5, 2020).

46. Cortez A. Cooper, III, *PLA Military Modernization: Drivers, Force Restructuring, and Implications*, Santa Monica, CA: Rand, 2018, 12.

47. Hearing to Receive Testimony on China and Russia, 14.

48. "2017 Report to Congress of the U.S.-China Economic and Security Review Commission," 115th Congress, 1st Session, November 2017, 507, <https://www.uscc.gov/sites/default/files/2019-09/2017_Annual_Report_to_Congress.pdf> (accessed May 5, 2020).

49. Ibid., 555.
50. Ronald O'Rourke, "China Naval Modernization: Implications for U.S. Navy Capabilities—Background and Issues for Congress," Congressional Research Service, April 24, 2020, 6, <https://crsreports.congress.gov/product/pdf/RL/RL33153> (accessed May 5, 2020).
51. Hannah Beech, "China's Sea Control Is a Done Deal, 'Short of War with the U.S.,'" *New York Times*, September 20, 2018, <https://www.nytimes.com/2018/09/20/world/asia/south-china-sea-navy.html> (accessed May 5, 2020).
52. O'Rourke, "China Naval Modernization," 26; John Power, "Has the US Already Lost the Battle for the South China Sea?" *South China Morning Post*, January 18, 2020; Kerry K. Gershaneck and James E. Fanell, "This Is How China's Will Fight and Win a War in the South China Sea [*sic*]," *National Interest*, January 18, 2020, <https://nationalinterest.org/blog/buzz/how-chinas-will-fight-and-win-war-south-china-sea-115061> (accessed May 5, 2020).
53. "2019 Report to Congress of the U.S.-China Economic and Security Review Commission," 116th Congress, 1st Session, November 2019, 470, <https://www.uscc.gov/sites/default/files/2019-11/2019%20Annual%20Report%20to%20Congress.pdf> (accessed May 5, 2020).
54. Oriana Skylar Mastro, "China's Military Modernization Program: Trends and Implications," American Enterprise Institute, September 4, 2019, 86, available at <https://www.uscc.gov/sites/default/files/Panel%20II%20Mastro_Written%20Testimony.pdf> (accessed May 5, 2020).
55. "Hearing on China's Military Reforms and Modernization: Implications for the United States," Hearing before the U.S.-China Economic and Security Review Commission, 115th Congress, 2nd Session, February 15, 2018, 47, transcript available at <https://www.uscc.gov/sites/default/files/transcripts/Hearing%20Transcript%20-%20February%2015,%202018.pdf> (accessed May 5, 2020).
56. Jane Perlez and Steven Lee Myers, "U.S. and China Are Playing 'Game of Chicken' in South China Sea," *New York Times*, November 8, 2018, <https://www.nytimes.com/2018/11/08/world/asia/south-china-sea-risks.html> (accessed May 5, 2020).
57. Ronald O'Rourke, "U.S.-China Strategic Competition in South and East China Seas: Background and Issues for Congress," Congressional Research Service, April 24, 2020, 1, available at <https://fas.org/sgp/crs/row/R42784.pdf> (accessed May 5, 2020).
58. "National Security Strategy of the United States of America," 45–6.

59. "Prime Minister's Keynote Address at Shangri La Dialogue (June 01, 2018)," Ministry of External Affairs, Government of India, June 1, 2018, <https://mea.gov.in/Speeches-Statements.htm?dtl/29943/Prime+Ministers+Keynote+Address+at+Shangri+La+Dialogue+June+01+2018> (accessed May 5, 2020). See also Aparne Pande and Satoru Nagao, "Whose Indo-Pacific?" *American Interest*, August 3, 2018, <https://www.the-american-interest.com/2018/08/03/whose-indo-pacific> (accessed May 5, 2020).

60. "'Confluence of the Two Seas': Speech by H.E. Mr. Shinzo Abe, Prime Minister of Japan at the Parliament of the Republic of India," Japanese Ministry of Foreign Affairs, August 22, 2007, <http://www.mofa.go.jp/region/asia-paci/pmv0708/speech-2.html> (accessed May 5, 2020).

61. "National Security Strategy of the United States of America," 46.

62. Josh Rogin, "Trump's National Security Strategy Marks a Hawkish Turn on China," *Washington Post*, December 18, 2017, <https://www.washingtonpost.com/news/josh-rogin/wp/2017/12/18/trumps-national-security-strategy-marks-a-hawkish-turn-on-china> (accessed May 5, 2020).

63. "National Security Strategy of the United States of America," 47.

64. Alex N. Wong, "Briefing on the Indo-Pacific Strategy," U.S. Department of State, April 2, 2018, <https://www.state.gov/briefing-on-the-indo-pacific-strategy> (accessed May 5, 2020).

65. See Dzirhan Mahadzir, "Air Force Keeping Up Presence Operations over South China Sea," *USNI News*, December 11, 2019, <https://news.usni.org/2019/12/11/air-force-keeping-up-presence-operations-over-south-china-sea>; Liu Zhen, "U.S, Warplanes on Beijing's Radar in South China Sea, American Air Force Chiefs Say," *South China Morning Post*, December 9, 2019.

66. RIMPAC is a U.S.-led, multilateral naval exercise in the Pacific involving naval forces from more than two dozen countries that is held every two years. At DoD's invitation, China participated in the 2014 and 2016 RIMPAC exercises. DoD had invited China to participate in the 2018 RIMPAC exercise, and China had accepted that invitation. DoD's statement regarding the withdrawal of the invitation was reprinted in Megan Eckstein, "China Disinvited from Participating in 2018 RIMPAC Exercise," *USNI News*, May 23, 2018, <https://news.usni.org/2018/05/23/china-disinvited-participating-2018-rimpac-exercise> (accessed May 5, 2020).

67. Robert Burns, "Mattis Pushes Closer Ties to Vietnam amid Tension with China," Associated Press, October 14, 2018, <https://apnews.com/fe078dfe838e48dc9ffdbf84529bba04> (accessed May 5, 2020).

68. O'Rourke, "U.S.-China Strategic Competition in South and East China Seas," 18.

69. Ash Carter, "IISS Shangri-La Dialogue: 'A Regional Security Architecture Where Everyone Rises,'" U.S. Department of Defense, May 30, 2015, <https://www.defense.gov/Newsroom/Speeches/Speech/Article/606676> (accessed May 5, 2020). See Aaron Mehta, "Carter Announces $425M in Pacific Partnership Funding," *Defense News*, May 30, 2015, <https://www.defensenews.com/home/2015/05/30/carter-announces-425m-in-pacific-partnership-funding> (accessed May 5, 2020); Prashanth Parameswaran, "America's New Maritime Security Initiative for Southeast Asia," *The Diplomat*, April 2, 2016, <https://thediplomat.com/2016/04/americas-new-maritime-security-initiative-for-southeast-asia> (accessed May 5, 2020); Prashanth Parameswaran, "U.S, Launches New Maritime Security Initiative at Shangri-La Dialogue 2015," *The Diplomat*, June 2, 2015, <https://thediplomat.com/2015/06/us-launches-new-maritime-security-initiative-at-shangri-la-dialogue-2015> (accessed May 1, 2020).

70. William Gallo, "Mattis in Southeast Asia, amid Fresh U.S. Focus on China," VOA News, January 22, 2018, <https://www.voanews.com/east-asia-pacific/mattis-southeast-asia-amid-fresh-us-focus-china>; Richard Javad Heydarian, "Mattis Signals Harder Line in South China Sea," *Asia Times*, January 25, 2018, <https://asiatimes.com/2018/01/mattis-signals-harder-line-south-china-sea>; Patrick M. Cronin and Marvin C. Ott, "Deepening the U.S.,-Indonesian Strategic Partnership," *The Diplomat*, February 17, 2018, <https://thediplomat.com/2018/02/deepening-the-us-indonesian-strategic-partnership>; Nike Ching, "U.S., Vietnam to Cooperate on Freedom of Navigation in Disputed South China Sea," VOA News, July 9, 2018, <https://www.voanews.com/east-asia-pacific/us-vietnam-cooperate-freedom-navigation-disputed-south-china-sea>; Bill Gertz, "Trump Courts Vietnam to Ward Off Beijing in South China Sea," *Asia Times*, November 14, 2017, <https://asiatimes.com/2017/11/trump-courts-vietnam-ward-off-beijing-south-china-sea> (all accessed May 5, 2020); Burns, "Mattis Pushes Closer Ties to Vietnam amid Tension with China".

71. Jake Maxwell Watts, "Bolton Warns China against Limiting Free Passage in South China Sea," *Wall Street Journal*, November 13, 2018, <https://www.wsj.com/articles/bolton-warns-china-against-limiting-free-passage-in-south-china-sea-1542110191> (accessed May 5, 2020).

72. Michael R. Pompeo, "Remarks with Philippine Foreign Secretary Teodoro Locsin, Jr. at a Press Availability," U.S. Department of

State, March 1, 2019, <https://www.state.gov/remarks-with-philip-pine-foreign-secretary-teodoro-locsin-jr> (accessed May 5, 2020).

73. Simon Tisdall, "Little Blue Men: The Maritime Militias Pushing China's Claims," *The Guardian*, May 16, 2016, <https://www.theguardian.com/world/2016/may/16/little-blue-men-the-maritime-militias-pushing-chinas-claims-in-south-china-sea>; Ryan Pickrell, "China's South China Sea Strategy Takes a Hit as the U.S. Navy Threatens to Get Tough on Beijing's Sea Forces," *Business Insider*, April 30, 2019, <https://www.businessinsider.com.au/us-navy-tough-on-china-paramilitary-fishing-fleet-gray-zone-tactics-2019-4> (both accessed May 5, 2020).

74. Ankit Panda, "The U.S. Navy's Shifting View of China's Coast Guard and 'Maritime Militia,'" *The Diplomat*, April 30, 2019, <https://thediplomat.com/2019/04/the-us-navys-shifting-view-of-chinas-coast-guard-and-maritime-militia> (accessed May 5, 2020); Shirley Tay, "U.S. Reportedly Warns China over Hostile Non-naval Vessels in South China Sea," CNBC, April 29, 2019, <https://www.cnbc.com/2019/04/29/south-china-sea-us-warns-china-over-non-naval-vessels-ft.html> (accessed May 5, 2020); Pickrell, "China's South China Sea Strategy Takes a Hit"; Ryan Pickrell, "It Looks Like the U.S. Has Been Quietly Lowering the Threshold for Conflict in the South China Sea," *Business Insider*, June 17, 2019, <https://www.businessinsider.com/us-quietly-lowers-threshold-for-conflict-in-south-china-sea-2019-6> (accessed May 5, 2020); Demetri Sevastopulo and Kathrin Hille, "U.S. Warns China on Aggressive Acts by Fishing Boats and Coast Guard," *Financial Times*, April 28, 2019.

75. Perlez and Myers, "U.S. and China Are Playing 'Game of Chicken' in South China Sea."

76. "Department of Defense Report to Congress: Annual Freedom of Navigation Report—Fiscal Year 2018," U.S. Department of Defense, December 31, 2018, 2–3, <https://policy.defense.gov/Portals/11/Documents/FY18%20DoD%20Annual%20FON%20Report%20(final).pdf?ver=2019-03-19-103517-010> (accessed May 5, 2020).

77. Andreo Calonzo and Glen Carey, "U.S. Increased Sea Patrols to Send Message to China, Defense Secretary Says," Bloomberg, November 19, 2019, <https://www.bloomberg.com/news/articles/2019-11-19/u-s-says-increased-sea-patrols-aimed-at-china> (accessed May 5, 2020). See Deutsche Presse-Agentur and Associated Press, "U.S. to Boost Military Alliance with Philippines as South China Sea

Tensions Grow," *South China Morning Post*, November 19, 2019; O'Rourke, "U.S.-China Strategic Competition in South and East China Seas," 13.

78. Mark J. Valencia, "U.S. FONOPS in the South China Sea: Intent, Effectiveness, and Necessity," *The Diplomat*, July 11, 2017, <https://thediplomat.com/2017/07/us-fonops-in-the-south-china-sea-intent-effectiveness-and-necessity> (accessed May 5, 2020).

79. John Power and Catherine Wong, "Exclusive Details and Footage Emerge of Near Collision between Warships in South China Sea," *South China Morning Post*, November 4, 2018, <https://www.scmp.com/week-asia/geopolitics/article/2171596/exclusive-details-and-footage-emerge-near-collision-between> (accessed May 5, 2020). See Perlez and Myers, "U.S. and China Are Playing 'Game of Chicken' in South China Sea"; James Holmes, "South China Sea Showdown: What Happens if a U.S. Navy and Chinese Vessel Collide?" *National Interest*, October 6, 2018, <https://nationalinterest.org/blog/buzz/south-china-sea-showdown-what-happens-if-us-navy-and-chinese-vessel-collide-32612> (accessed May 5, 2020); Kristin Huang and Keegan Elmer, "Beijing's Challenge to U.S. Warship in South China Sea 'Deliberate and Calculated,' Observers Say," *South China Morning Post*, October 5, 2018; Stacie E. Goddard, "The U.S. and China Are Playing a Dangerous Game. What Comes Next?" *Washington Post*, October 3, 2018; O'Rourke, "U.S.-China Strategic Competition in South and East China Seas," 40.

80. Ryan Browne, "U.S. Navy Has Had 18 Unsafe or Unprofessional Encounters with China since 2016," CNN, November 3, 2018, <https://edition.cnn.com/2018/11/03/politics/navy-unsafe-encounters-china/index.html> (accessed May 5, 2020). See Kristin Huang, "China Has a History of Playing Chicken with the U.S. Military—Sometimes These Dangerous Games End in Disaster," *Business Insider*, October 2, 2018.

81. Alex Lockie, "China Has Jamming Equipment in the South China Sea—and the U.S. May 'Not Look Kindly on It,'" *Business Insider*, April 18, 2018, <https://www.businessinsider.com/china-jamming-us-navy-jets-off-aircraft-carriers-pacific-2018-4>; Asia Times Staff, "China 'Crosses Threshold' with Missiles at South China Sea Outposts," *Asia Times*, May 4, 2018, <https://asiatimes.com/2018/05/china-crosses-threshold-with-missiles-at-south-china-sea-outposts>; Mike Yeo, "How Far Can China's Long-Range Missiles Reach in the South China Sea?" *Defense News*, May 4, 2018,

<https://www.defensenews.com/naval/2018/05/04/how-far-can-chinas-long-range-missiles-reach-in-the-south-china-sea>; Amanda Macias, "China Quietly Installed Defensive Missile Systems on Strategic Spratly Islands in Hotly Contested South China Sea," CNBC, May 2, 2018, <https://www.cnbc.com/2018/05/02/china-added-missile-systems-on-spratly-islands-in-south-china-sea.html>; "China Installs Cruise Missiles on South China Sea Outposts—CNBC Report," Reuters, May 2, 2018, <https://uk.reuters.com/article/southchinasea-china-missiles/china-installs-cruise-missiles-on-south-china-sea-outposts-cnbc-report-idUKL8N1S9934> (all accessed May 5, 2020).

82. Amanda Macias, "China Is Quietly Conducting Electronic Warfare Tests in the South China Sea," CNBC, July 5, 2018, <https://www.cnbc.com/2018/07/05/us-intel-report-china-quietly-testing-electronic-warfare-assets-on-sp.html> (accessed May 6, 2020). For more on China's "active defense" strategy see M. Taylor Fravel, *Active Defense: China's Military Strategy since 1949*, Princeton, NJ: Princeton University Press, 2019.

83. O'Rourke, "U.S.-China Strategic Competition in South and East China Seas," 63; Jesse Johnson, "In First, China Permanently Stations Search-and-Rescue Vessel in South China Sea's Spratly Chain," *Japan Times*, July 29, 2018, <https://www.japantimes.co.jp/news/2018/07/29/asia-pacific/first-china-permanently-stations-search-rescue-vessel-south-china-seas-spratly-chain> (accessed May 6, 2020).

84. "Advance Policy Questions for Admiral Philip Davidson, USN Expected Nominee for Commander, U.S. Pacific Command," 18, <https://www.armed-services.senate.gov/imo/media/doc/Davidson_APQs_04-17-18.pdf> (accessed May 6, 2020). See also ibid., 8, 16, 17, 19, 43; Beech, "China's Sea Control Is a Done Deal."

85. O'Rourke, "U.S.-China Strategic Competition in South and East China Seas," 41; Office of the Secretary of Defense: "Annual Report to Congress: Military and Security Developments Involving the People's Republic of China 2018," U.S. Department of Defense, May 16, 2018, 67–8, <https://media.defense.gov/2018/Aug/16/2001955282/-1/-1/1/2018-CHINA-MILITARY-POWER-REPORT.PDF> (accessed May 6, 2020). See Christopher Woody, "This New Defense Department Map Shows How China Says One Thing and Does Another with Its Military Operations at Sea," *Business Insider*, August 17, 2018, <https://www.businessinsider.com/defense-department-map-shows-chinas-naval-operations-in-maritime-eezs-2018-8> (accessed May 6, 2020).

86. Quoted in Perlez and Myers, "U.S. and China Are Playing 'Game of Chicken' in South China Sea."

87. Leng Shumei and Liu Xuanzun, "China Warns U.S. Ships to Leave Sea," *Global Times*, May 6, 2019, <http://www.globaltimes.cn/content/1148768.shtml> (accessed May 6, 2020).

88. "Department of Defense Report to Congress: Annual Freedom of Navigation Report—Fiscal Year 2017," U.S. Department of Defense, December 31, 2017, 2, <https://policy.defense.gov/Portals/11/FY17%20DOD%20FON%20Report.pdf?ver=2018-01-19-163418-053> (accessed May 6, 2020).

89. Tuan N. Pham, "Chinese Double Standards in the Maritime Domain," *The Diplomat*, August 16, 2017, <https://thediplomat.com/2017/08/chinese-double-standards-in-the-maritime-domain>; Mark J. Valencia, "The U.S.-China Maritime Surveillance Debate," *The Diplomat*, August 4, 2017, <https://thediplomat.com/2017/08/the-us-china-maritime-surveillance-debate> (both accessed May 6, 2020).

90. Perlez and Myers, "U.S. and China Are Playing 'Game of Chicken' in South China Sea."

91. O'Rourke, "U.S.-China Strategic Competition in South and East China Seas," 22–3.

92. Eric Sayers, "Assessing America's Indo-Pacific Budget Shortfall," *War on the Rocks*, November 15, 2018, <https://warontherocks.com/2018/11/assessing-americas-indo-pacific-budget-shortfall> (accessed May 6, 2020).

93. Ibid.

94. Townshend, Thomas-Noone, and Steward, "Averting Crisis."

95. Jesse Johnson, "U.S. Looks to Deploy New Missiles to Asia, Defense Chief Says amid Tensions with China," August 4, 2019, <https://www.japantimes.co.jp/news/2019/08/04/asia-pacific/u-s-looks-deploy-new-missiles-asia-defense-chief-says-amid-tensions-china> (accessed May 6, 2020).

96. Toshi Yoshihara and Jacob Cohn, "The Case for Deploying U.S. Land-Based Missiles in Asia," *National Interest*, May 13, 2019, <https://nationalinterest.org/blog/buzz/case-deploying-us-land-based-missiles-asia-57322> (accessed May 6, 2020).

97. Jacob Cohn, Timothy A. Walton, Adam Lemon, and Toshi Yoshihara, "Leveling the Playing Field: Reintroducing U.S. Theater-Range Missiles in a Post-INF World," Center for Strategic and Budgetary Assessments, May 21, 2019 <https://csbaonline.org/research/publications/leveling-the-playing-field-reintroducing-us-theater-range-missiles-in-a-post-INF-world/publication/1> (accessed May 6, 2020).

https://csbaonline.org/research/publications/leveling-the-play-
ing-field-reintroducing-us-theater-range-missiles-in-a-post-INF-
world/publication/1

98. Nathan Levine, "Why America Leaving the INF Treaty is China's
New Nightmare," *National Interest*, October 22, 2018, <https://
nationalinterest.org/blog/buzz/why-america-leaving-inf-treaty-
chinas-new-nightmare-34087> (accessed May 6, 2020).

99. Montgomery and Sayers, "Addressing America's Operational
Shortfall in the Pacific."

100. Sugio Takahashi and Eric Sayers, "America and Japan in a Post-INF
World," *War on the Rocks*, March 8, 2019, <https://warontherocks.
com/2019/03/america-and-japan-in-a-post-inf-world>   (accessed
May 6, 2020).

101. Clive Williams, "Pacific Collateral from the INF Treaty Collapse,"
The Interpreter, January 31, 2019, <https://www.lowyinstitute.org/
the-interpreter/pacific-collateral-inf-treaty-collapse> (accessed May
6, 2020).

102. Tom Countryman and Kingston Reif, "Intermediate-Range Missiles
Are the Wrong Weapon for Today's Security Challenges," *War on
the Rocks*, August 13, 2019, <https://warontherocks.com/2019/08/
intermediate-range-missiles-are-the-wrong-weapon-for-todays-
security-challenges> (accessed May 6, 2020).

103. Ibid.; Zack Brown, "China Is No Reason to Abandon the INF,"
Defense One, November 6, 2018, <https://www.defenseone.com/
ideas/2018/11/china-no-reason-abandon-inf/152607/?oref=defense_
one_breaking_nl> (accessed May 6, 2020).

104. James Cameron, "Withdrawing from the INF Treaty Is a Mistake," Foreign Policy Research Institute, October 22, 2018,
<https://www.fpri.org/article/2018/10/withdrawing-from-the-inf-
treaty-is-a-mistake> (accessed May 6, 2020).

105. Pranay Vaddi, "Leaving the INF Treaty Won't Help Trump
Counter China," Carnegie Endowment for International Peace,
January 31, 2019, <https://carnegieendowment.org/2019/01/31/
leaving-inf-treaty-won-t-help-trump-counter-china-pub-78262>
(accessed May 6, 2020).

106. Quoted in Ankit Panda, "China Won't Join the INF Treaty—But
Can It Forever Dodge Arms Control?" *The Diplomat*, February
25, 2019, <https://thediplomat.com/2019/02/china-wont-join-the-
inf-treaty-but-can-it-forever-dodge-arms-control> (accessed May 6,
2020).

107. Peter Ferdinand, "Westward Ho—the China Dream and 'One Belt, One Road': Chinese Foreign Policy under Xi Jinping," *International Affairs* 92, no. 4, 2016, 941–57.
108. Enda Curran, "China's Marshall Plan," Bloomberg, August 7, 2016, <https://www.bloomberg.com/news/articles/2016-08-07/china-s-marshall-plan>; Joseph S. Nye, Jr., "Xi Jinping's Marco Polo Strategy," *Project Syndicate*, June 12, 2017, <https://www.project-syndicate.org/commentary/china-belt-and-road-grand-strategy-by-joseph-s--nye-2017-06> (both accessed May 6, 2020).
109. Nadège Rolland, "China's 'Belt and Road Initiative': Underwhelming or Game-Changer?" *Washington Quarterly* 40, no. 1, 2017, 127–42, at 136.
110. Bonnie S. Glaser and Alexandra Viers, "U.S.-China Relations: Trump and Xi Break the Ice at Mar-a-Lago," *Comparative Connections* 19, no. 1, 2017, 21–32.
111. "National Security Strategy of the United States of America," 25.
112. Ibid., 39.
113. Heather Nauert, "Australia-India-Japan-U.S. Consultations on the Indo-Pacific," U.S. State Department, November 12, 2017, <https://www.state.gov/australia-india-japan-u-s-consultations-on-the-indo-pacific>; Joel Wuthnow, "Securing China's Belt and Road Initiative: Dimensions and Implications," <https://www.uscc.gov/sites/default/files/Wuthnow_USCC%20Testimony_20180123.pdf> (both accessed May 6, 2020).
114. Aaron L. Connelly, "Autopilot: East Asia Policy under Trump," Lowy Institute, October 31, 2017, <https://www.lowyinstitute.org/publications/autopilot-east-asia-policy-under-trump> (accessed May 6, 2020).
115. "Press Conference by Prime Minister Shinzo Abe Following His Attendance at the APEC Economic Leaders' Meeting, ASEAN-Related Summit Meetings, and Other Related Meetings," Prime Minister of Japan and His Cabinet, November 14, 2017, <https://japan.kantei.go.jp/98_abe/statement/201711/_00007.html> (accessed May 6, 2020).
116. Suresh Nanwani, "Belt and Road Initiative: Responses from Japan and India—Bilateralism, Multilateralism and Collaborations," *Global Policy* 10, no. 2, 2019, 284–9, at 285.
117. "Partnership for Quality Infrastructure," Japanese Ministry of Foreign Affairs, May 21, 2015, 1–2, <https://www.mofa.go.jp/files/000117998.pdf> (accessed May 6, 2020).

118. "Asia-Africa Growth Corridor: Partnership for Sustainable and Innovative Development," presentation at African Development Bank meeting, May 2017.

119. "Remarks by Vice President Pence on the Administration's Policy Toward China."

120. PTI Washington, "BRI has a National Security Element: Pompeo," *BusinessLine*, March 29, 2019, <https://www.thehindubusinessline.com/news/world/bri-has-a-national-security-element-pompeo/article26673918.ece> (accessed May 6, 2020).

121. Daniel R. Russel and Blake Berger, "Navigating the Belt and Road Initiative," Asia Society Policy Institute, June 2019, 11, <https://asiasociety.org/sites/default/files/2019-06/Navigating%20the%20Belt%20and%20Road%20Initiative_2.pdf> (accessed May 6, 2020).

122. Ibid.

123. Shayerah Ilias Akhtar and Marian L. Lawson, "BUILD Act: Frequently Asked Questions about the New U.S. International Development Finance Corporation," Congressional Research Service, January 15, 2019, available at <https://fas.org/sgp/crs/misc/R45461.pdf> (accessed May 6, 2020).

124. Michael R. Pompeo, "Landmark Development Finance Legislation Improves America's Competitiveness Overseas," U.S. Department of State, October 3, 2018, <https://www.state.gov/landmark-development-finance-legislation-improves-americas-competitiveness-overseas> (accessed May 6, 2020).

125. Daniel F. Runde and Romina Bandura, "The BUILD Act Has Passed: What's Next?" Center for Strategic and International Studies, October 12, 2018, <https://www.csis.org/analysis/build-act-has-passed-whats-next> (accessed May 6, 2020).

126. Ibid.

127. Ibid.

128. U.S. Department of Commerce, Bureau of Industry and Security, "Addition of Entities to the Entity List," 84 Federal Register 22961, May 21, 2019.

129. Arjun Kharpal, "Huawei's 4 Big Issues in 2020—From the Blacklist to the Decision over Its Operating System's Future," CNBC, December 30, 2019, <https://www.cnbc.com/2019/12/31/huawei-2020-outlook-us-blacklist-harmonyos-cfo-trial.html> (accessed May 6, 2020).

130. Brad Glosserman, "Huawei and the Realities of the 5G World," *Japan Times*, February 3, 2020, <https://www.japantimes.co.jp/

opinion/2020/02/03/commentary/world-commentary/huawei-realities-5g-world> (accessed May 6, 2020).

131. Björn Alexander Düben, "Try as It Might, Germany Isn't Warming to Huawei," *The Diplomat*, January 9, 2020, <https://thediplomat.com/2020/01/try-as-it-might-germany-isnt-warming-to-huawei> (accessed May 6, 2020).

132. Susan V. Lawrence, Caitlin Campbell, Rachel F. Fefer, Jane A. Leggett, Thomas Lum, Michael F. Martin, and Andres B. Schwarzenberg, "U.S.-China Relations," Congressional Research Service, September 3, 2019, 2, <https://crsreports.congress.gov/product/pdf/R/R45898 (accessed May 1, 2020); Donald J. Trump (@realDonaldTrump), Twitter, August 23, 2019, <https://twitter.com/realdonaldtrump/status/1164914960046133249> and August 24, 2019, <https://twitter.com/realdonaldtrump/status/1165111122510237696> (accessed May 6, 2020); "Remarks by President Trump and Prime Minister Johnson of the United Kingdom in Working Breakfast, Biarritz, France," White House, August 25, 2019, <https://www.whitehouse.gov/briefings-statements/remarks-president-trump-prime-minister-johnson-united-kingdom-working-breakfast-biarritz-france> (accessed May 6, 2020).

133. Priyanka Boghani, "The U.S. and North Korea on the Brink: A Timeline," *Frontline*, February 28, 2019, <https://www.pbs.org/wgbh/frontline/article/the-u-s-and-north-korea-on-the-brink-a-timeline> (accessed May 6, 2020).

134. Kelsey Davenport, "Chronology of U.S.-North Korean Nuclear and Missile Diplomacy," Arms Control Association, April 2020, <https://www.armscontrol.org/factsheets/dprkchron> (accessed May 4, 2020).

135. "Report to Congress on Strategy to Address the Threats Posed by, and the Capabilities of, the Democratic Republic of Korea," U.S. Department of State, April 2019.

136. "Trump Blames Stagnant North Korea Talks on U.S.-China Trade War," Al Jazeera, August 30, 2018, <https://www.aljazeera.com/news/2018/08/trump-blames-stagnant-north-korea-talks-china-trade-war-180830085022067.html> (accessed May 6, 2020).

137. "Specially Designated Nationals and Blocked Persons List (SDN) Human Readable Lists," U.S. Department of the Treasury, January 5, 2020, <https://www.treasury.gov/resource-center/sanctions/SDN-List/Pages/default.aspx> (accessed May 7, 2020).

138. Edith M. Lederer, "Russia, China Block UN from Saying NKorea Violated Sanctions," Associated Press, June 19, 2019, <https://

www.apnews.com/cb6be1337d2a48ecbde14dac590be083>
(accessed May 7, 2020).

139. "Remarks to Press by Secretary Pompeo and Ambassador Haley at the UN," U.S. Mission to the United Nations, July 20, 2018, <https://usun.usmission.gov/remarks-to-press-by-secretary-pompeo-and-ambassador-haley-at-the-un> (accessed May 7, 2020).

140. Lederer, "Russia, China Block UN from Saying NKorea Violated Sanctions."

141. "Adhering to the 'Dual-Track Approach': The Realization of Denuclearization of the Korean Peninsula and the Establishment of Peaceful Mechanism on the Korean Peninsula," Ministry of Foreign Affairs of the PRC, April 5, 2018, <https://www.fmprc.gov.cn/mfa_eng/zxxx_662805/t1548991.shtml> (accessed May 7, 2020); "Wang Yi Talks about Promoting the Political Settlement Process of the Korean Peninsula Issue," Ministry of Foreign Affairs of the PRC, August 2, 2019, <https://www.fmprc.gov.cn/mfa_eng/zxxx_662805/t1686491.shtml> (accessed May 7, 2020); Lawrence et al., "U.S.-China Relations," 28.

142. Lederer, "Russia, China Block UN from Saying NKorea Violated Sanctions."

143. Kelsey Davenport and Julia Masterson, "North Korea Reiterates End to Test Moratorium: North Korea Denuclearization Digest," Arms Control Association, January 30, 2020, <https://www.armscontrol.org/blog/2020-01-30/north-korea-denuclearization-digest> (accessed May 7, 2020).

144. Jacob Fromer, "Echoing Kim Jong Un, North Korean Diplomat Warns Nuclear Test Moratorium May End," *NK News*, January 21, 2020, <https://www.nknews.org/2020/01/echoing-kim-jong-un-north-korean-diplomat-warns-nuclear-test-moratorium-may-end> (accessed May 7, 2020).

145. Jeff Mason and David Brunnstrom, "Trump Expects Second Kim Meeting in 'Not-Too-Distant Future,'" Reuters, January 2, 2019, <https://www.reuters.com/article/us-northkorea-usa/trump-expects-second-kim-meeting-in-not-too-distant-future-idUSKCN1OW1D5>; Robert Carlin, "Hints for 2019: Kim Jong Un's New Year's Address," *38 North*, January 3, 2019, <https://www.38north.org/2019/01/rcarlin010319> (both accessed May 7, 2020).

146. Agence France-Presse, "North Korea Says May Seek 'New Path' of Weapons Build-up," *DefenceTalk*, January 22, 2020, <https://www.defencetalk.com/north-korea-says-may-seek-new-path-of-weapons-build-up-73270> (accessed May 7, 2020).

147. Davenport and Masterson, "North Korea Reiterates End to Test Moratorium"; Jesse Johnson, "North Korea's Kim Warns of 'New Strategic Weapon' as Nuclear Freeze Falters," *Japan Times*, January 1, 2020, <https://www.japantimes.co.jp/news/2020/01/01/asia-pacific/politics-diplomacy-asia-pacific/kim-warns-new-strategic-weapon-north-korea-snubs-arms-test-moratorium-face-gangster-like-u-s> (accessed May 7, 2020).

148. Julia Masterson, "North Korea, China, Russia Converge Positions," *Arms Control Today*, January/February 2020, <https://www.armscontrol.org/act/2020-01/news/north-korea-china-russia-converge-positions> (accessed May 7, 2020).

149. "Russia, China Prepare UN SC Resolution for N. Korea Sanctions Relief, Dialogue," TASS, December 16, 2019, <https://tass.com/world/1099993> (accessed May 7, 2020).

150. Masterson, "North Korea, China, Russia Converge Positions."

151. Edith M. Lederer, "China, Russia Urge NKorea Sanction Lift," *The Standard*, December 17, 2019, <https://www.standard.net.au/story/6547011/china-russia-urge-nkorea-sanction-lift> (accessed May 7, 2020).

152. Hong Xiao, "Chinese Envoy Calls for Peace Talks to Ease Tensions on Korean Peninsula," *China Daily*, December 13, 2019, <https://global.chinadaily.com.cn/a/201912/13/WS5df2e-f24a310cf3e3557de88.html> (accessed May 7, 2020).

153. Ibid.

154. "North Korea's Denuclearization Possible Only through Trust-Building Measures—Diplomat," TASS, December 11, 2020, <https://tass.com/world/1098547> (accessed May 7, 2020).

155. "Foreign Minister Sergey Lavrov's Remarks at the Moscow Non-proliferation Conference on 'Foreign Policy Priorities of the Russian Federation in Arms Control and Non-proliferation in the Context of Changes in the Global Security Architecture' Moscow, November 8, 2019," Ministry of Foreign Affairs of the Russian Federation, November 8, 2019, <https://www.mid.ru/en/vistupleniya_ministra/-/asset_publisher/MCZ7HQuMdqBY/content/id/3891674> (accessed May 7, 2020).

156. Bonnie S. Glaser and Michael J. Green, "What Is the U.S. 'One China' Policy, and Why Does It Matter?" Center for Strategic and International Studies, January 13, 2017, <https://www.csis.org/analysis/what-us-one-china-policy-and-why-does-it-matter> (accessed May 7, 2020).

157. "Readout of the President's Call with President Xi Jinping of China," White House, February 9, 2017, <https://www.whitehouse.gov/

briefings-statements/readout-presidents-call-president-xi-jinping-china> (accessed May 7, 2020).

158. "National Security Strategy of the United States of America," 47.

159. Taiwan Travel Act, 2018, HR 535, 115th Congress, 1st Session, March 16, 2018, <https://www.congress.gov/bill/115th-congress/house-bill/535> (accessed May 7, 2020).

160. Yimou Lee and Ben Blanchard, "China Bridles at Rare Meeting between Taiwan and U.S. Security Officials," Reuters, May 27, 2019, <https://www.reuters.com/article/us-usa-taiwan/china-bridles-at-rare-meeting-between-taiwanand-u-s-security-officials-idUSKCN1SX077> (accessed May 7, 2020).

161. "Indo-Pacific Strategy Report."

162. Wen Kuei-hsiang and Elizabeth Hsu, "Taiwan President Meets with Envoys to U.N. during New York Stopover," *Focus Taiwan*, July 12, 2019, <https://focustaiwan.tw/politics/201907120002>; Stacy Hsu and Ozzy Yin, "Tsai Calls for Global Support for 'Free Taiwan' at Columbia Speech," *Focus Taiwan*, July 13, 2019, <http://focustaiwan.tw/politics/201907130005> (both accessed May 7, 2020).

163. Glaser and Green, "What Is the U.S. 'One China' Policy, and Why Does it Matter?"

164. "Trump Says China's Xi Has Acted Responsibly on Hong Kong Protests," Reuters, July 23, 2019, <https://www.reuters.com/article/us-usa-trade-china/trump-says-chinas-xi-has-acted-responsibly-on-hong-kong-protests-idUSKCN1UH20Q> (accessed May 7, 2020).

165. "Timeline: U.S. Relations with China 1949–2020," Council for Foreign Relations, <https://www.cfr.org/timeline/us-relations-china> (accessed May 7, 2020).

166. Marc A. Thiessen, "Donald Trump Is the Most Pro-Taiwan President in U.S. History," *Washington Post*, January 14, 2020, <https://www.washingtonpost.com/opinions/2020/01/14/donald-trump-is-most-pro-taiwan-president-us-history> (accessed May 7, 2020).

167. Ibid.

168. Jonathan Landay and David Brunnstrom, "U.S. Applauds Tsai's Re-election as Taiwan President: Pompeo," Reuters, January 11, 2020, <https://www.reuters.com/article/us-taiwan-election-usa/u-s-applauds-tsais-re-election-as-taiwan-president-pompeo-idUSK-BN1ZA0M3> (accessed May 7, 2020).

169. Quoted in Richard C. Bush, "The Trump Administration's Policies toward Taiwan," Brookings Institution, June 5, 2019, <https://www.brookings.edu/on-the-record/the-trump-administrations-policies-toward-taiwan> (accessed May 7, 2020); Thiessen, "Donald Trump Is the Most Pro-Taiwan President in U.S. History."

170. See for instance Mathew Kroenig, "The Case for Trump's Foreign Policy: The Right People, The Right Positions," *Foreign Affairs*, May/June 2017, 30–4.
171. Rebecca Morin, "'Idiot,' 'Dope,' 'Moron': How Trump's Aides Have Insulted the Boss," *Politico*, September 4, 2018, <https://www.politico.com/story/2018/09/04/trumps-insults-idiot-woodward-806455> (accessed May 7, 2020).

Afterword

1. G. John Ikenberry, "The Security Trap," *Democracy: A Journal of Ideas*, no. 2, 2006.
2. Kim Willsher, Oliver Holmes, Bethan McKernan, and Lorenzo Tondo, "US Hijacking Mask Shipments in Rush for Coronavirus Protection," *The Guardian*, April 3, 2020, <https://www.theguardian.com/world/2020/apr/02/global-battle-coronavirus-equipment-masks-tests>; "Coronavirus: US Accused of 'Piracy' over Mask 'Confiscation,'" BBC News, April 4, 2020, <https://www.bbc.com/news/world-52161995>; Aitor Hernández-Morales, "Germany Confirms that Trump Tried to Buy Firm Working on Coronavirus Vaccine," *Politico*, March 15, 2020, <https://www.politico.eu/article/germany-confirms-that-donald-trump-tried-to-buy-firm-working-on-coronavirus-vaccine> (all accessed June 15, 2020).

Bibliography

"100% Scanning Does Not Equate to 100% Security According to Esteemed Port of Hamburg Executive: An Exclusive Interview with Dr. Jurgen Sorgenfrei, Chairman," *Maritime & Border Security News*, December 20, 2007.

"2004 Report to Congress of the U.S.-China Economic and Security Review Commission," 108th Congress, 2nd Session, June 2004, <https://www.uscc.gov/sites/default/files/annual_reports/2004-Report-to-Congress.pdf>.

"2017 Report to Congress of the U.S.-China Economic and Security Review Commission," 115th Congress, 1st Session, November 2017, <https://www.uscc.gov/sites/default/files/2019-09/2017_Annual_Report_to_Congress.pdf>.

"2019 Report to Congress of the U.S.-China Economic and Security Review Commission," 116th Congress, 1st Session, November 2019, <https://www.uscc.gov/sites/default/files/2019-11/2019%20Annual%20Report%20to%20Congress.pdf>.

"Adhering to the 'Dual-Track Approach': The Realization of Denuclearization of the Korean Peninsula and the Establishment of Peaceful Mechanism on the Korean Peninsula," Ministry of Foreign Affairs of the PRC, April 5, 2018, <https://www.fmprc.gov.cn/mfa_eng/zxxx_662805/t1548991.shtml>.

"Advance Policy Questions for Admiral Philip Davidson, USN Expected Nominee for Commander, U.S. Pacific Command," <https://www.armed-services.senate.gov/imo/media/doc/Davidson_APQs_04-17-18.pdf>.

"America's Image Slips, but Allies Share U.S. Concerns over Iran, Hamas," Pew Research Center, June 13, 2006, <http://pewglobal.org/reports/display.php?ReportID=252>.

"Asia Africa Growth Corridor: Partnership for Sustainable and Innovative Development," presentation at African Development Bank meeting, May 2017.

274

"Assessment on U.S. Defense Implications of China's Expanding Global Access," U.S. Department of Defense, December 2018, <https://media.defense.gov/2019/Jan/14/2002079292/-1/-1/1/EXPANDING-GLOBALACCESS-REPORT-FINAL.PDF>.

"China, ASEAN to Hold Meetings on South China Sea in September," Xinhua News Service, June 30, 2013.

"China Installs Cruise Missiles on South China Sea Outposts—CNBC Report," Reuters, May 2, 2018, <https://uk.reuters.com/article/southchinasea-china-missiles/china-installs-cruise-missiles-on-south-china-sea-outposts-cnbc-report-idUKL8N1S9934>.

"China: Nuclear," Nuclear Threat Initiative, April 2015, <https://www.nti.org/learn/countries/china/nuclear>.

"China Opposes U.S. Comments about Diaoyu Islands: Spokesman," Xinhua News Agency, January 20, 2013.

"China's Endeavors for Arms Control, Disarmament and Non-proliferation," Information Office of the State Council of the People's Republic of China, September 2005, <http://en.people.cn/whitepaper/arms/arms.html>.

"China's Menacing Sandcastles in the South China Sea," *War on the Rocks*, March 2, 2015, <https://warontherocks.com/2015/03/chinas-menacing-sandcastles-in-the-south-china-sea>.

"China's Military Strategy," State Council, People's Republic of China, May 2015, <http://english.www.gov.cn/archive/white_paper/2015/05/27/content_281475115610833.htm>.

"China's Proliferation and the Impact on Trade Policy on Defense Industries in the United States and China," Hearing before the U.S.-China Economic and Security Review Commission, 110th Congress, 1st Session, July 12–13, 2007, transcript available at <https://www.uscc.gov/sites/default/files/transcripts/7.12-13.07HearingTranscript.pdf>.

"China's Proliferation Practices and Role in the North Korean Crisis," Hearing before the U.S.-China Economic and Security Review Commission, 109th Congress, 1st Session, March 10, 2005, transcript available at <https://www.uscc.gov/sites/default/files/transcripts/3.10.05ht.pdf>.

"China's Proliferation Practices, and the Development of Its Cyber and Space Capabilities," Hearing before the U.S.-China Economic and Security Review Commission, 110th Congress, 2nd Session, May 20, 2008, transcript available at <https://www.uscc.gov/sites/default/files/transcripts/5.20.08HearingTranscript.pdf>

"China's Proliferation to North Korea and Iran, and Its Role in Addressing the Nuclear and Missile Situations in Both Nations," Hearing before the U.S.-China Economic and Security Review Commission,

109th Congress, 2nd Session, September 14, 2006, transcript available at <https://www.uscc.gov/sites/default/files/transcripts/9.14.06H earingTranscript.pdf>.

"China's Role in the World: Is China a Responsible Stakeholder?" Hearing before the U.S.-China Economic and Security Review Commission, 109th Congress, 2nd Session, August 3–4, 2006, transcript available at <https://www.uscc.gov/sites/default/files/transcripts/8.3-4.06HearingTrascript.pdf>.

"'Confluence of the Two Seas': Speech by H.E. Mr. Shinzo Abe, Prime Minister of Japan at the Parliament of the Republic of India," Japanese Ministry of Foreign Affairs, August 22, 2007, <http://www.mofa.go.jp/region/asia-paci/pmv0708/speech-2.html>.

Container Security Initiative: 2006–2011 Strategic Plan, U.S. Customs and Border Protection, August 2006, available at <https://www.hsdl.org/?abstract&did=468251>.

"Coronavirus: US Accused of 'Piracy' over Mask 'Confiscation,'" BBC News, April 4, 2020, <https://www.bbc.com/news/world-52161995>.

"Counterterror Initiatives in the Terror Finance Program," Hearings before the Committee on Banking, Housing, and Urban Affairs, United States Senate, 108th Congress, 1st and 2nd Sessions, September 25, 2003, October 22, 2003, April 29, 2004, and September 29, 2004, S. Hrg. 108-802, <https://www.govinfo.gov/content/pkg/CHRG-108shrg20396/html/CHRG-108shrg20396.htm>.

Country Reports on Terrorism 2004, U.S. Department of State, April 2005, <https://2001-2009.state.gov/documents/organization/45313.pdf>.

Country Reports on Terrorism 2005, U.S. Department of State, April 2006, <https://2009-2017.state.gov/documents/organization/65462.pdf>.

Country Reports on Terrorism 2006, U.S. Department of State, April 2007, <https://2009-2017.state.gov/documents/organization/83383.pdf>.

Country Reports on Terrorism 2010, U.S. Department of State, August 2011, <https://2009-2017.state.gov/documents/organization/170479.pdf>.

"Current and Projected Threats to the National Security," Hearing before the Select Committee on Intelligence of the United States Senate, 110th Congress, 2nd Session, February 5, 2008, S. Hrg. 110-824, <https://www.intelligence.senate.gov/hearings/current-and-projected-threats-national-security-february-5-2008#>.

"Defence White Paper 2013," Australian Government, Department of Defence, 2013, <https://www.defence.gov.au/Whitepaper/2013/docs/WP_2013_web.pdf>.

"Department of Defense Report to Congress: Annual Freedom of Navigation Report—Fiscal Year 2017," U.S. Department of Defense,

December 31, 2017, <https://policy.defense.gov/Portals/11/FY17%20 DOD%20FON%20Report.pdf?ver=2018-01-19-163418-053>.

"Department of Defense Report to Congress: Annual Freedom of Navigation Report—Fiscal Year 2018," U.S. Department of Defense, December 31, 2018, <https://policy.defense.gov/Portals/11/ Documents/FY18%20DoD%20Annual%20FON%20Report%20 (final).pdf?ver=2019-03-19-103517-010>.

"Department of Homeland Security Appropriations for 2005," Hearings before a Subcommittee on Appropriations, House of Representatives, 108th Congress, 2nd Session, March 4, 2004.

Editorial, *Atlanta Journal and Constitution*, March 19, 2001.

"Excerpts from Pentagon's Plan: Prevent the Re-emergence of a New Rival," *New York Times*, March 8, 1992, p 14.

"Foreign Minister Sergey Lavrov's Remarks at the Moscow Non-proliferation Conference on 'Foreign Policy Priorities of the Russian Federation in Arms Control and Non-proliferation in the Context of Changes in the Global Security Architecture' Moscow, November 8, 2019," Ministry of Foreign Affairs of the Russian Federation, November 8, 2019, <https://www.mid.ru/en/vistupleniya_ministra/-/asset_publisher/ MCZ7HQuMdqBY/content/id/3891674>

"Foreign Ministry Spokesperson Ma Zhaoxu's Regular Press Conference," Chinese Ministry of Foreign Affairs, March 10, 2009, <https:// www.fmprc.gov.cn/zflt/eng/fyrth/t541713.htm>.

Foreign Press Center Briefing, General Tommy Franks, Commander, U.S. Central Command, Washington, D.C., April 11, 2002.

"Full Text of Chinese President Xi's Address at APEC CEO Summit," XinhuaNet, November 11, 2017, <http://www.xinhuanet.com/ english/2017-11/11/c_136743492.htm>.

"Full Transcript: Trump's 2020 State of the Union Address," *New York Times*, February 5, 2020, <https://www.nytimes.com/2020/02/05/us/ politics/state-of-union-transcript.html>.

"The Future of U.S.-China Military Relations," *Chinafile*, March 1, 2019, <http://www.chinafile.com/conversation/future-of-china-us-military- relations>.

"Global Economic Gloom—China and India Notable Exceptions," Pew Research Center, June 12, 2008, <https://www.pewresearch. org/global/2008/06/12/global-economic-gloom-china-and-india- notable-exceptions>.

"H. Res. 65—Condemning the Government of North Korea for its flagrant and repeated violations of multiple United Nations Security Council resolutions, for its repeated provocations that threaten international peace and stability, and for its February 12, 2013, test of a nuclear device," U.S. House of Representatives, 113rd Congress, February 13, 2013, <https://www.congress.gov/bill/113th-congress/house-resolution/65/text>.

"Hearing on China's Military Reforms and Modernization: Implications for the United States," Hearing before the U.S.-China Economic and Security Review Commission, 115th Congress, 2nd Sess., February 15, 2018, transcript available at <https://www.uscc.gov/sites/default/files/transcripts/Hearing%20Transcript%20-%20February%20 15,%202018.pdf>.

"Hearing on U.S.-China Relations in 2019: A Year in Review," Hearing Before the U.S.-China Economic and Security Review Commission, 116th Congress, 1st Session, September 4, 2019, transcript available at <https://www.uscc.gov/sites/default/files/2019-10/September%20 4,%202019%20Hearing%20Transcript.pdf>.

Hearing to Receive Testimony on China and Russia, Committee on Armed Services, United States Senate, January 29, 2019, transcript available at <https://www.armed-services.senate.gov/imo/media/doc/19-02_1-29-19.pdf>.

Hearing to Receive Testimony on Policy and Strategy in the Asia-Pacific, Committee on Armed Services, United States Senate, April 25, 2017, transcript available at <https://www.armed-services.senate.gov/imo/media/doc/17-35_04-25-17.pdf>

Hearing to Receive Testimony on the Department of Defense Budget Posture in Review of the Defense Authorization Request for Fiscal Year 2019 and the Future Years Defense Program, Committee on Armed Services, United States Senate, April 26, 2018, transcript available at <https://www.armed-services.senate.gov/imo/media/doc/18-44_04-26-18.pdf>.

"Identify, Disrupt and Dismantle: Coordinating the Government's Attack on Terrorist Financing," Joint Hearing before the Subcommittee on Technology, Information Policy, Intergovernmental Relations and Census and the Subcommittee on Government Efficiency and Financial Management of the Committee on Government Reform, House of Representatives, 108th Congress, 1st Session, December 15, 2003, 108-140, transcript available at <https://www.govinfo.gov/content/pkg/CHRG-108hhrg93428/html/CHRG-108hhrg93428.htm>.

"Indo-Pacific Strategy Report: Preparedness, Partnerships, and Promoting a Networked Region," U.S. Department of Defense, June 1, 2019, <https://media.defense.gov/2019/Jul/01/2002152311/-1/-1/1/DEPARTMENT-OF-DEFENSE-INDO-PACIFIC-STRATEGY-REPORT-2019.PDF>.

"Investigating the Chinese Threat, Part I: Military and Economic Aggression," Hearing before the Committee on Foreign Affairs, House of Representatives, 112th Congress, 2nd Session, 112-137, March 28, 2012, transcript available at <https://www.govinfo.gov/content/pkg/CHRG-112hhrg73536/pdf/CHRG-112hhrg73536.pdf>.

"Joint U.S.-China Statement on Climate Change," U.S. Department of State, April 13, 2013, <https://2009-2017.state.gov/r/pa/prs/ps/2013/04/207465.htm>.

"Kim Jong Un Visits Reconstructed Pyongchon Revolutionary Site," *Rodong Sinmun*, December 10, 2015, available at <http://www.nkleadershipwatch.org/2015/12/09/kim-jong-un-visits-pyongchon-revolutionary-site>.

Kiyemba v. Obama, 559 U.S. Court of Appeals, D.C. Circuit, February 18, 2009, <https://www.iris-france.org/wp-content/uploads/2017/12/Asia-focus-56.pdf>.

"The Lifting of the EU Arms Embargo on China," Hearing before the Committee on Foreign Relations, United States Senate, 109th Congress, 1st Session, March 16, 2005, S. Hrg. 109-94, transcript available at <https://www.foreign.senate.gov/imo/media/doc/031605_Transcript_The%20Lifting%20of%20the%20EU%20Arms%20Embargo%20on%20China.pdf>.

"Looking West: China and Central Asia," Hearing before the U.S.-China Economic and Security Review Commission, 114th Congress, 1st Session, March 18, 2015, transcript available at <https://www.uscc.gov/sites/default/files/transcripts/March%2018,%202015%20Hearing%20Transcript.pdf>.

"Memorandum: National Security and Foreign Policy Authorities on President Obama's Trade Agenda," Office of the United States Trade Representative, <https://ustr.gov/memorandum-national-security-and-foreign-policy-authorities-president-obama%E2%80%99s-trade-agenda>.

"National Security Strategy," White House, May 2010, <https://obamawhitehouse.archives.gov/sites/default/files/rss_viewer/national_security_strategy.pdf>.

"National Security Strategy of the United States of America," White House, December 2017, <https://www.whitehouse.gov/wp-content/uploads/2017/12/NSS-Final-12-18-2017-0905.pdf>.

"North Korea," Nuclear Threat Initiative, August 2019, <http://www.nti.org/learn/countries/north-korea>.

"North Korea's Denuclearization Possible Only through Trust-Building Measures—Diplomat," TASS, December 11, 2020, <https://tass.com/world/1098547>.

"North Korea's Nuclear Test: Next Steps," Hearing before the Committee on International Relations, House of Representatives, 109th Congress, 2nd Session, 109–242, November 15, 2006, transcript available at <https://www.govinfo.gov/content/pkg/CHRG-109hhrg30902/pdf/CHRG-109hhrg30902.pdf>.

"Partnership for Quality Infrastructure," Japanese Ministry of Foreign Affairs, May 21, 2015, <https://www.mofa.go.jp/files/000117998.pdf>.

Patterns of Global Terrorism 2001, U.S. Department of State, May 2002, <https://2001-2009.state.gov/documents/organization/10319.pdf>.

"Pentagon Says Chinese Vessels Harassed U.S. Ship," CNN, March 9, 2009, <https://edition.cnn.com/2009/POLITICS/03/09/us.navy.china/index.html>.

"Political Persecution of Uyghurs in the Era of the 'War on Terror,'" Uyghur Human Rights Project, October 16, 2007, <http://docs.uyghuramerican.org/Persecution_of_Uyghurs_in_the_Era_of_the_War_on_Terror.pdf>.

"President Delivers State of the Union Address," White House, January 29, 2002, <https://georgewbush-whitehouse.archives.gov/news/releases/2002/01/20020129-11.html>

"The President's Budget for Foreign Affairs and Business Meeting to Vote Out the Nomination of Robert B. Zoellick to be Deputy Secretary of State," Hearing before the Committee on Foreign Relations, United States Senate, 109th Congress, 1st Session, S. Hrg.109-98, February 16, 2005, transcript available at <https://www.foreign.senate.gov/imo/media/doc/021605_Transcript_The%20President's%20Budget%20for%20Foreign%20Affairs%20and%20Business%20Meeting.pdf>.

"Press Briefing by National Security Advisor Tom Donilon," White House, June 8, 2013, <https://obamawhitehouse.archives.gov/the-press-office/2013/06/09/press-briefing-national-securityadvisor-tom-donilon>.

"Press Conference by Prime Minister Shinzo Abe Following His Attendance at the APEC Economic Leaders' Meeting, ASEAN-Related Summit Meetings, and Other Related Meetings," Prime Minister of Japan and His Cabinet, November 14, 2017, <https://japan.kantei.go.jp/98_abe/statement/201711/_00007.html>.

"Press Conference by US Secretary of Defence, Donald Rumsfeld," NATO, June 6, 2002, <https://www.nato.int/docu/speech/2002/s020606g.htm>.

"Press Conference of the President," White House, April 28, 2005, <https://georgewbush-whitehouse.archives.gov/news/releases/2005/04/20050428-9.html>

"Press Conference with Secretary Hagel and Defense Minister Onodera from the Pentagon," U.S. Department of Defense, April 29, 2013, <https://content.govdelivery.com/accounts/USDOD/bulletins/78e2bb>.

Press Roundtable with Adm. Dennis Blair, Commander, U.S. Pacific Command, Hong Kong, April 18, 2002.

"Prime Minister's Keynote Address at Shangri La Dialogue (June 01, 2018)," Ministry of External Affairs, Government of India, June 1, 2018, <https://mea.gov.in/Speeches-Statements.htm?dtl/29943/Prime+Ministers+Keynote+Address+at+Shangri+La+Dialogue+June+01+2018>.

Quadrennial Defense Review Report, U.S. Department of Defense, September 30, 2001, <https://archive.defense.gov/pubs/qdr2001.pdf>.

"Readout of the President's Call with President Xi Jinping of China," White House, February 9, 2017, <https://www.whitehouse.gov/briefings-statements/readout-presidents-call-president-xi-jinping-china>.

Rebuilding America's Defenses: Strategy, Forces and Resources for a New Century, Project for the New American Century, September 2000.

"Remarks by Chinese Vice President Xi Jinping at a Luncheon Co-hosted by the U.S. China Business Council and the National Committee on U.S.-China Relations," Federal News Service, February 15, 2012.

"Remarks by President Obama and President Xi Jinping of the People's Republic of China after Bilateral Meeting," White House, June 8, 2013, <https://obamawhitehouse.archives.gov/the-press-office/2013/06/08/remarks-president-obama-and-president-xi-jinping-peoples-republic-china->.

"Remarks by President Obama to the Australian Parliament," White House, November 17, 2011, <https://obamawhitehouse.archives.gov/the-press-office/2011/11/17/remarks-president-obama-australian-parliament>.

"Remarks by President Trump and Prime Minister Johnson of the United Kingdom in Working Breakfast, Biarritz, France," White House, August 25, 2019, <https://www.whitehouse.gov/briefings-statements/remarks-president-trump-prime-minister-johnson-united-kingdom-working-breakfast-biarritz-france>.

"Remarks by President Trump at APEC CEO Summit: Da Nang, Vietnam," White House, November 10, 2017, <https://www.whitehouse.gov/briefings-statements/remarks-president-trump-apec-ceo-summit-da-nang-vietnam>.

"Remarks by President Trump in Press Conference: Osaka, Japan," White House, June 29, 2019, <https://www.whitehouse.gov/briefings-statements/remarks-president-trump-press-conference-osaka-japan>.

"Remarks by President Trump on the Administration's National Security Strategy," White House, December 18, 2017, <https://www.whitehouse.gov/briefings-statements/remarks-president-trump-administrations-national-security-strategy>.

"Remarks by Secretary Hagel at the IISS Asia Security Summit, Shangri-La Hotel, Singapore," U.S. Department of Defense, June 1, 2013, <https://archive.defense.gov/transcripts/transcript.aspx?transcriptid=5251>.

"Remarks by the President to Students and Faculty at National Defense University," White House, May 1, 2001, <https://georgewbush-whitehouse.archives.gov/news/releases/2001/05/20010501-10.html>

"Remarks by Tom Donilon, National Security Advisor to the President: 'The United States and the Asia-Pacific in 2013,'" White House, March 11, 2013, <https://obamawhitehouse.archives.gov/the-press-office/2013/03/11/remarks-tom-donilon-national-security-advisor-president-united-states-an>.

"Remarks by Vice President Biden and Chinese Vice President Xi at the State Department Luncheon," White House, February 14, 2012, <https://obamawhitehouse.archives.gov/the-press-office/2012/02/14/remarks-vice-president-biden-and-chinese-vice-president-xi-state-departm>.

"Remarks by Vice President Pence on the Administration's Policy toward China," White House, October 4, 2018, <https://www.whitehouse.gov/briefings-statements/remarks-vice-president-pence-administrations-policy-toward-china>.

"Remarks to Press by Secretary Pompeo and Ambassador Haley at the UN," U.S. Mission to the United Nations, July 20, 2018, <https://usun.usmission.gov/remarks-to-press-by-secretary-pompeo-and-ambassador-haley-at-the-un>.

Report of the Select Committee on U.S. National Security and Military/Commercial Concerns with the People's Republic of China, House of Representatives, 105th Congress, 2nd Session, 105–851, May 25, 1999.

Report to Congress of the U.S.-China Economic and Security Review Commission: The National Security Implications of the Economic Relationship between the United States and China, July 2002, available at <https://www.uscc.gov/sites/default/files/annual_reports/2002%20Annual%20Report%20to%20Congress.pdf>.

"Report to Congress on Strategy to Address the Threats Posed by, and the Capabilities of, the Democratic Republic of Korea," U.S. Department of State, April 2019.

"Rice Reassures Japan on Security Commitment," NBC News, October 18, 2006, <http://www.nbcnews.com/id/15313151/ns/world_news-asia_pacific/t/rice-reassures-japan-security-commitment>.

"Russia, China Prepare UN SC Resolution for N. Korea Sanctions Relief, Dialogue," TASS, December 16, 2019, <https://tass.com/world/1099993>.

"Safeguarding American Interests in the East and South China Seas," Hearing before the Committee on Foreign Relations, United States Senate, 114th Congress, 1st Session, May 13, 2015, S. Hrg. 114–75, <https://www.foreign.senate.gov/hearings/safeguarding-american-interests-in-the-east-and-south-china-seas>.

"Sec. Pompeo Remarks on 'America's Indo-Pacific Economic Vision,'" U.S. Mission to ASEAN, July 30, 2018, <https://asean.usmission.gov/sec-pompeo-remarks-on-americas-indo-pacific-economic-vision>.

"Security Council Tightens Sanctions on DPR Korea in Wake of Latest Nuclear Blast," UN News, March 7, 2013, <https://news.un.org/en/story/2013/03/433722-security-council-tightens-sanctions-dpr-korea-wake-latest-nuclear-blast>.

"Security Issues and Strategic Perceptions," Hearing before the U.S.-China Economic and Security Review Commission, August 3, 2001, transcript available at <https://www.uscc.gov/sites/default/files/transcripts/8.3.01HT.pdf>.

"Specially Designated Nationals and Blocked Persons List (SDN) Human Readable Lists," U.S. Department of the Treasury, January 5, 2020, <https://www.treasury.gov/resource-center/sanctions/SDN-List/Pages/default.aspx>.

"Spokesman for DPRK Foreign Ministry Slams Bush's Remark," Korean Central News Agency, October 23, 2001.

"Summary of the 2018 National Defense Strategy of the United States of America: Sharpening the American Military's Competitive Edge," U.S. Department of Defense, <https://dod.defense.gov/Portals/1/Documents/pubs/2018-National-Defense-Strategy-Summary.pdf>.

"Supply Chain Security: Examinations of High-Risk Cargo at Foreign Seaports Have Increased, but Improved Data Collection and Performance Measures Are Needed," U.S. Government Accountability Office, Report to Congressional Requesters, January 2008, <https://www.gao.gov/new.items/d08187.pdf>.

"Survey of Programs on United States-China Relations and Security Issues," National Committee on United States-China Relations, China Policy Series no. XXIII, March 2007, <https://www.ncuscr.org/sites/default/files/page_attachments/Survey-Programs-U.S.-China-Relations-Security-Issues.pdf>.

"Sustaining U.S. Global Leadership: Priorities for 21st Century Defense," U.S. Department of Defense, January 2012, <https://archive.defense.gov/news/Defense_Strategic_Guidance.pdf>.

Taiwan Travel Act, 2018, HR 535, 115th Congress, 1st Session, March 16, 2018, <https://www.congress.gov/bill/115th-congress/house-bill/535>.

"Terror List with Links to al Qaeda Unveiled," *China Daily*, December 16, 2003, <http://www.chinadaily.com.cn/en/doc/2003-12/16/content_290658.htm>.

"Testimony of Kenneth Lawson, Assistant Secretary of Office of Enforcement, U.S. Department of the Treasury, the Subcommittee on National Security, Veterans Affairs and International Relations, Rightsizing the U.S. Presence Abroad," press release, U.S. Department of the Treasury, May 1, 2002, <https://www.treasury.gov/press-center/press-releases/Pages/po3066.aspx>.

"Timeline: U.S. Relations with China 1949–2020," Council for Foreign Relations, <https://www.cfr.org/timeline/us-relations-china>.

"Trump Blames Stagnant North Korea Talks on U.S.-China Trade War," Al Jazeera, August 30, 2018, <https://www.aljazeera.com/news/2018/08/trump-blames-stagnant-north-korea-talks-china-trade-war-180830085022067.html>.

"Trump Says China's Xi Has Acted Responsibly on Hong Kong Protests," Reuters, July 23, 2019, <https://www.reuters.com/article/us-usa-trade-china/trump-says-chinas-xi-has-acted-responsibly-on-hong-kong-protests-idUSKCN1UH20Q>.

"Uighurs Fleeing Persecution as China Wages its 'War on Terror,'" Amnesty International, July 6, 2004, <https://www.amnesty.org/en/documents/ASA17/021/2004/en>.

"United States and China Agree to Work Together on Phase Down of HFCs," White House, June 8, 2013, <https://obamawhitehouse.archives.gov/the-press-office/2013/06/08/united-states-and-china-agree-work-together-phase-down-hfcs>.

"The United States Strengthens Its Nuclear Superiority, and China Cannot Afford to Ignore It," *Global Times*, January 9, 2018, <http://opinion.huanqiu.com/ editorial/2018-01/11506799.html>.

"U.S. Accuses the Chinese of Harassing Naval Vessel," *New York Times*, March 9, 2009, <https://www.nytimes.com/2009/03/09/world/asia/09iht-ship.3.20710715.html>.

"U.S.-China Joint Announcement on Climate Change," press release, White House, November 11, 2014, <https://obamawhitehouse.archives.gov/the-press-office/2014/11/11/us-china-joint-announcement-climate-change>.

"U.S.-China Joint Statement," White House, November 17, 2009, <https://obamawhitehouse.archives.gov/realitycheck/the-press-office/us-china-joint-statement>.

"U.S.-China Strategic and Economic Dialogue Outcomes of the Strategic Track," U.S. Department of State, July 12, 2013, <https://2009-2017.state.gov/r/pa/prs/ps/2013/07/211861.htm>.

"U.S. International Development Finance Corporation Begins Operations," DFC, January 2, 2020, <https://www.dfc.gov/media/press-releases/us-international-development-finance-corporation-begins-operations>.

"U.S. Official Praises HK, Mainland for Cooperation against Terrorism," Embassy of the People's Republic of China in the United States of America, August 1, 2003, <www.china-embassy.org/eng/zt/mgryzdzg/t36538.htm>.

"U.S. Tells Iran, Syria, N. Korea 'Learn from Iraq,'" Reuters, April 9, 2003.

"Wang Yi Talks about Promoting the Political Settlement Process of the Korean Peninsula Issue," Ministry of Foreign Affairs of the PRC, August 2, 2019, <https://www.fmprc.gov.cn/mfa_eng/zxxx_662805/t1686491.shtml>.

"War of Words," *Newsweek*, April 23, 2001.

"What Does Xi Jinping's China Dream Mean?" BBC News, June 6, 2013, <https://www.bbc.com/news/world-asia-china-22726375>.

"White House Says It Sees Some Hope in to End Standoff," *New York Times*, April 6, 2001.

"Why Is There Tension between China and the Uighurs?" BBC News, September 26, 2014, <http://www.bbc.com/news/world-asia-china-26414014>.

"Xi Jinping Calls for PLA 'Real Combat' Awareness," China Central Television, December 12, 2012.

Agence France-Presse, "North Korea Says May Seek 'New Path' of Weapons Build-Up," *DefenceTalk*, January 22, 2020, <https://www.defencetalk.com/north-korea-says-may-seek-new-path-of-weapons-build-up-73270>.

Akhtar, Shayerah Ilias and Lawson, Marian L., "BUILD Act: Frequently Asked Questions about the New U.S. International Development Finance Corporation," Congressional Research Service, January 15, 2019, available at <https://fas.org/sgp/crs/misc/R45461.pdf>.

Allison, Graham, *Essence of Decision: Explaining the Cuban Missile Crisis*, Boston: Little, Brown, 1971.

Asia Times Staff, "China 'Crosses Threshold' with Missiles at South China Sea Outposts," *Asia Times*, May 4, 2018, <https://asiatimes.

com/2018/05/china-crosses-threshold-with-missiles-at-south-china-sea-outposts>.

Ba, Alison D., "China-ASEAN Relations: Political Significance of an ASEAN Free Trade Area," in T. J. Cheng et al. (eds), *China under the Fourth Generation Leadership: Opportunities, Dangers, and Dilemmas*, Singapore: World Scientific, 2005.

Bader, Jeffrey A. and Dollar, David, "Why the TPP Is the Linchpin of the Asia Rebalance," Brookings Institution, July 28, 2015, <https://www.brookings.edu/blog/order-from-chaos/2015/07/28/why-the-tpp-is-the-linchpin-of-the-asia-rebalance>.

Bartley, Adam S. R., *Perceptions of China and White House Decision-Making, 1941–1963: Spears of Promise, Shields of Truth*, New York: Routledge, 2020.

Beech, Hannah, "China's Sea Control Is a Done Deal, 'Short of War with the U.S.,'" *New York Times*, September 20, 2018, <https://www.nytimes.com/2018/09/20/world/asia/south-china-sea-navy.html>.

Bernstein, Richard, "When China Convinced the U.S. that Uighurs Were Waging Jihad," *The Atlantic*, March 19, 2019.

Bernstein, Richard and Munro, Ross H., *The Coming Conflict with China*. New York: Alfred A. Knopf, 1997.

Bhattacharya, Abanti, "Conceptualising Uyghur Separatism in Chinese Nationalism," *Strategic Analysis* 27, no. 3, 2003.

Blackwill, Robert D. and Tellis, Ashley J., "Revising U.S. Grand Strategy toward China," Council on Foreign Relations, Special Report no. 72, April 2015, <https://www.cfr.org/report/revising-us-grand-strategy-toward-china>.

Blumenthal, Dan and Friedberg, Aaron, "Not Too Late to Curb Dear Leader," *Weekly Standard*, February 12, 2007.

Blustein, Paul, *Schism: China, America and the Fracturing of the Global Trading System*, Waterloo, ON: Centre for International Governance Innovation, 2019.

Boghani, Priyanka, "The U.S. and North Korea on the Brink: A Timeline," *Frontline*, February 28, 2019, <https://www.pbs.org/wgbh/frontline/article/the-u-s-and-north-korea-on-the-brink-a-timeline>.

Bolton, John R., "Obama's Reckless, Ridiculous China Policy," American Enterprise Institute, February 4, 2010, <https://www.aei.org/articles/obamas-reckless-ridiculous-china-policy>.

Bolton, John R., "Time for a Two-China Policy," American Enterprise Institute, August 9, 1999, <https://www.aei.org/publication/time-for-a-two-china-policy>.

Borger, Julian, "Kim Jong-un's Growing Nuclear Arsenal Could Force U.S. Back to Negotiating Table," *The Guardian*, September 9, 2016,

<https://www.theguardian.com/world/2016/sep/09/north-koreas-growing-ambition-nuclear-arsenal-force-us-negotiating-table>.

Bovingdon, Gardner, *Autonomy in Xinjiang: Han Nationalist Imperatives and Uyghur Discontent*, Washington, D C: East-West Center, 2004.

Bowden, Mark, "Top Military Officers Unload on Trump," *The Atlantic*, November 2019, <https://www.theatlantic.com/magazine/archive/2019/11/military-officers-trump/598360>.

Brady, Anne-Marie, "Magic Weapons: China's Political Influence Activities under Xi Jinping," Wilson Center, September 18, 2017, <https://www.wilsoncenter.org/article/magic-weapons-chinas-political-influence-activities-under-xi-jinping>.

Brands, Hal, "The Unexceptional Superpower: American Grand Strategy in the Age of Trump," *Survival* 59, no. 6, 2017.

Broomfield, Emma V., "Perceptions of Danger: The China Threat Theory," *Journal of Contemporary China* 12, no. 35, 2003.

Brown, Michael and Singh, Pavneet, "China's Technology Transfer Strategy: How Chinese Investments in Emerging Technology Enable a Strategic Competitor to Access the Crown Jewels of U.S. Innovation," Defense Innovation Unit Experimental (DIUx), January 2018, <https://admin.govexec.com/media/diux_chinatechnologytransfer-study_jan_2018_(1).pdf>.

Brown, Zack, "China Is No Reason to Abandon the INF," *Defense One*, November 6, 2018, <https://www.defenseone.com/ideas/2018/11/china-no-reason-abandon-inf/152607/?oref=defense_one_breaking_nl>.

Browne, Ryan, "U.S. Navy Has Had 18 Unsafe or Unprofessional Encounters with China since 2016," CNN, November 3, 2018, <https://edition.cnn.com/2018/11/03/politics/navy-unsafe-encounters-china/index.html>.

Brunnstrom, David, "Carter Says U.S. Will Sail, Fly and Operate Wherever International Law Allows," Reuters, October 14, 2015, <https://www.reuters.com/article/us-usa-australia-southchinasea-carter-idUSKCN0S72MG20151013>.

Brzezinski, Zbigniew, "Living with China," *National Interest*, Spring 2000.

Burns, Robert, "Mattis Pushes Closer Ties to Vietnam amid Tension with China," Associated Press, October 14, 2018, <https://apnews.com/fe078dfe838e48dc9ffdbf84529bba04>.

Bush, George W., "State of the Union Address to the 107th Congress," in *Selected Speeches of President George W. Bush, 2001–2008*, <http://georgewbush-whitehouse.archives.gov/infocus/bushrecord/documents/Selected_Speeches_George_W_Bush.pdf>.

Bush, Richard C., "The Trump Administration's Policies toward Taiwan," Brookings Institution, June 5, 2019, <https://www.brookings.edu/on-the-record/the-trump-administrations-policies-toward-taiwan>.

Butler, Declan and Gibney, Elizabeth, "What Kind of Bomb Did North Korea Detonate?" *Nature*, January 8, 2016, <https://www.nature.com/news/what-kind-of-bomb-did-north-korea-detonate-1.19132>.

Buzan, Barry, "A Leader without Followers? The United States in World Politics after Bush," *International Politics* 45, no. 5, 2008.

Cabestan, Jean-Pierre, "Is Xi Jinping the Reformist Leader China Needs?" *China Perspectives*, no. 3 (91), 2012.

Cai, Peter, "Understanding China's Belt and Road Initiative," Lowy Institute, March 2017, <https://www.lowyinstitute.org/sites/default/files/documents/Understanding%20China%E2%80%99s%20Belt%20and%20Road%20Initiative_WEB_1.pdf>.

Calonzo, Andreo and Carey, Glen, "U.S. Increased Sea Patrols to Send Message to China, Defense Secretary Says," Bloomberg, November 19, 2019, <https://www.bloomberg.com/news/articles/2019-11-19/u-s-says-increased-sea-patrols-aimed-at-china>.

Cameron, James, "Withdrawing from the INF Treaty Is a Mistake," Foreign Policy Research Institute, October 22, 2018, <https://www.fpri.org/article/2018/10/withdrawing-from-the-inf-treaty-is-a-mistake>.

Campbell, Kurt M. and Ratner, Ely, "The China Reckoning: How Beijing Defied American Expectations," *Foreign Affairs*, March/April 2018.

Carlin, Robert, "Hints for 2019: Kim Jong Un's New Year's Address," *38 North*, January 3, 2019, <https://www.38north.org/2019/01/rcarlin010319>.

Carpenter, Ted Garlen, "U.S. Goes Too Far with Visit of Taiwan Official," Cato Institute, March 25, 2002, <https://www.cato.org/publications/commentary/us-goes-too-far-visit-taiwan-official>.

Carter, Ash, "IISS Shangri-la Dialogue: 'A Regional Security Architecture Where Everyone Rises,'" U.S. Department of Defense, May 30, 2015, <https://www.defense.gov/Newsroom/Speeches/Speech/Article/606676>.

Cassella, Megan and Palmer, Doug, "Lawmakers, U.S. Allies Sound Alarm over Trump's Latest Tariff Moves," *Politico*, July 11, 2018, <https://www.politico.com/story/2018/07/11/new-trump-tariffs-trade-war-china-678252.

Cha, Victor, *The Impossible State: North Korea, Past and Future*, London: Bodley Head, 2012.

Cha, Victor, "The Unfinished Legacy of Obama's Pivot to Asia," *Foreign Policy*, September 6, 2016, <https://foreignpolicy.com/2016/09/06/the-unfinished-legacy-of-obamas-pivot-to-asia>.

Cha, Victor D., "Winning Asia: Washington's Untold Success Story," *Foreign Affairs*, November/December 2007.

Chanlett-Avery, Emma, Manyin, Mark E., Nikitin, Mary Beth D., Campbell, Caitlin Elizabeth, and Mackey, Wil, "North Korea: U.S. Relations, Nuclear Diplomacy, and Internal Situation," Congressional Research Service, July 27, 2018, available at <https://fas.org/sgp/crs/nuke/R41259.pdf>.

Chellaney, Brahma, "Who Lost the South China Sea?" *Maritime Executive*, June 15, 2018, <https://www.maritime-executive.com/editorials/who-lost-the-south-china-sea>.

Chen Fei, "On Strengthening the Role of the Communist Party of China in the Armed Forces in the New Situation: A Study of Xi Jinping's Important Expositions on Strengthening the Role of the Communist Party of China in the Armed Forces," *China Military Science*, no. 4, 2014.

Cheng, Dean and Klingner, Bruce, "U.S. Asian Policy: America's Security Commitment to Asia Needs More Forces," Heritage Foundation, August 7, 2012, <https://www.heritage.org/asia/report/us-asian-policy-americas-security-commitment-asia-needs-more-forces>.

Chin, Gregory, "China's Rising International Influence," in Alan S. Alexandroff and Andrew F. Cooper (eds), *Rising States, Rising Institutions: Challenges for Global Governance*, Washington, DC: Brookings Institute Press, 2010.

ChinaPower Team, "What Does China Really Spend on Its Military?" ChinaPower, December 28, 2015, updated August 6, 2019, <https://chinapower.csis.org/military-spending>.

Ching, Nike, "U.S., Vietnam to Cooperate on Freedom of Navigation in Disputed South China Sea," VOA News, July 9, 2018, <https://www.voanews.com/east-asia-pacific/us-vietnam-cooperate-freedom-navigation-disputed-south-china-sea>.

Christensen, Thomas J., "Obama and Asia: Confronting the China Challenge," *Foreign Affairs*, September/October 2015, <https://www.foreignaffairs.com/articles/asia/obama-and-asia>.

Christoffersen, Gaye, "Constituting the Uyghur in U.S.-China Relations: The Geopolitics of Identity Formation in the War on Terrorism," *Strategic Insights* 1, no. 7, 2002.

Clinton, Hillary, "America's Pacific Century," *Foreign Policy*, October 11, 2011, <https://foreignpolicy.com/2011/10/11/americas-pacific-century>.

Clinton, Hillary R., "Remarks at Press Availability," National Convention Center, Hanoi, Vietnam, U.S. Department of State, July 23, 2010, <https://2009-2017.state.gov/secretary/20092013clinton/rm/2010/07/145095.htm>.

Clinton, Hillary, "Remarks with Chinese Foreign Minister Yang Jie-chi, Beijing, China," U.S. Department of State, February 21, 2009, <https://2009-2017.state.gov/secretary/20092013clinton/rm/2009a/02/119432.htm>.

Clinton, Hillary Rodham, "Remarks with Japanese Foreign Minister Fumio Kishida after Their Meeting," U.S. Department of State, January 18, 2013, <https://2009-2017.state.gov/secretary/20092013clinton/rm/2013/01/203050.htm>.

Clinton, Hillary R. and Pitsuwan, Surin, "Beginning a New Era of Diplomacy in Asia," U.S. Department of State, February 18, 2009, <https://2009-2017.state.gov/secretary/20092013clinton/rm/2009a/02/119422.htm>.

Cloud, David and Johnson, Ian, "In Post-9/11 World, Chinese Dissidents Pose U.S. Dilemma," *Wall Street Journal*, August 3, 2004.

Cohen, Eliot A., "America's Long Goodbye: The Real Crisis of the Trump Era," *Foreign Affairs*, January/February 2019.

Cohn, Jacob, Walton, Timothy A., Lemon, Adam, and Yoshihara, Toshi, "Leveling the Playing Field: Reintroducing U.S. Theater-Range Missiles in a Post-INF World," Center for Strategic and Budgetary Assessments, May 21, 2019, <https://csbaonline.org/research/publications/leveling-the-playing-field-reintroducing-us-theater-range-missiles-in-a-post-INF-world/publication/1>.

Connelly, Aaron L., "Autopilot: East Asia Policy under Trump," Lowy Institute, October 31, 2017, <https://www.lowyinstitute.org/publications/autopilot-east-asia-policy-under-trump>.

Cooper, Cortez A., *PLA Military Modernization: Drivers, Force Restructuring, and Implications*, Santa Monica, CA: Rand, 2018.

Cossa, Ralph, "Condoleezza Rice's Unfortunate Decision," *Japan Times*, July 25, 2005.

Countryman, Tom and Reif, Kingston, "Intermediate-Range Missiles Are the Wrong Weapon for Today's Security Challenges," *War on the Rocks*, August 13, 2019, <https://warontherocks.com/2019/08/intermediate-range-missiles-are-the-wrong-weapon-for-todays-security-challenges>.

Cronin, Patrick M. and Ott, Marvin C., "Deepening the U.S.-Indonesian Strategic Partnership," *The Diplomat*, February 17, 2018, <https://thediplomat.com/2018/02/deepening-the-us-indonesian-strategic-partnership>.

Cui Tiankai and Pang Hanzhao, "China-US Relations in China's Overall Diplomacy in the New Era: On China and US Working Together to Build a New-Type Relationship between Major Countries," *China International Strategy Review 2012*, <http://en.iiss.pku.edu.cn/research/discuss/2012/2370.html>

Cullinane, Michael Patrick and Elliot, Clare Frances, *Perspectives on Presidential Leadership: An International View of the White House*, New York: Routledge, 2014.

Curran, Enda, "China's Marshall Plan," Bloomberg, August 7, 2016, <https://www.bloomberg.com/news/articles/2016-08-07/china-s-marshall-plan>.

Davenport, Kelsey, "Chronology of U.S.-North Korean Nuclear and Missile Diplomacy," Arms Control Association, April 2020, <https://www.armscontrol.org/factsheets/dprkchron>.

Davenport, Kelsey and Masterson, Julia, "North Korea Reiterates End to Test Moratorium: North Korea Denuclearization Digest," Arms Control Association, January 30, 2020, <https://www.armscontrol.org/blog/2020-01-30/north-korea-denuclearization-digest>.

Davies, Anne, "Asia Hit as White House Focuses on Iraq," *The Age*, July 26, 2007.

Deng, Yong, "Reputation and the Security Dilemma: China Reacts to the China Threat Theory," in Alastair Iain Johnston and Robert S. Ross (eds), *New Directions in the Study of China's Foreign Policy*. Stanford, CA: Stanford University Press, 2006.

Deutsche Presse-Agentur and Associated Press, "U.S. to Boost Military Alliance with Philippines as South China Sea Tensions Grow," *South China Morning Post*, November 19, 2019.

Dinmore, Guy and Kynge, James, "China Torture Fears Curb Guantanamo Releases," *Financial Times*, June 23, 2004.

DoD News, "Pacific Command Change Highlights Growing Importance of Indian Ocean Area," U.S. Indo-Pacific Command, May 31, 2018, <https://www.pacom.mil/Media/News/News-Article-View/Article/1537107/pacific-command-change-highlights-growing-importance-of-indian-ocean-area>.

Dolven, Ben, Elsea, Jennifer K., Lawrence, Susan V., O'Rourke, Ronald, and Rinehart, Ian E., "Chinese Land Reclamation in the South China Sea: Implications and Policy Options," Congressional Research Service, June 18, 2015, available at <https://fas.org/sgp/crs/row/R44072.pdf>.

Donilon, Tom, "America Is Back in the Pacific and Will Uphold the Rules," *Financial Times*, November 27, 2011, <https://www.ft.com/content/4f3febac-1761-11e1-b00e-00144feabdc0>.

Dosch, Jörn, "The U.S. and Southeast Asia," in Mark Beeson (ed.), *Contemporary Southeast Asia*, 2nd ed., Basingstoke, England: Palgrave Macmillan, 2009.

Düben, Björn Alexander, "Try as It Might, Germany Isn't Warming to Huawei," *The Diplomat*, January 9, 2020, <https://thediplomat.com/2020/01/try-as-it-might-germany-isnt-warming-to-huawei>.

Dumbaugh, Kerry, "China-U.S. Relations: Current Issues and Implications for U.S. Policy," Congressional Research Service, October 8, 2009, available at <https://fas.org/sgp/crs/row/R40457.pdf>.

Eberhart, Dave, "Container Ships—The Next Terrorist Weapon?" NewsMax, April 14, 2002, <https://www.newsmax.com/pre-2008/container-ships-the-next/2002/04/14/id/666281>.

Eckstein, Megan, "China Disinvited from Participating in 2018 RIMPAC Exercise," USNI News, May 23, 2018, <https://news.usni.org/2018/05/23/china-disinvited-participating-2018-rimpac-exercise>.

Economy, Elizabeth C., "China's New Revolution: The Reign of Xi Jinping," Foreign Affairs, May/June 2018, <https://www.foreignaffairs.com/articles/china/2018-04-17/chinas-new-revolution>.

Economy, Elizabeth C., "The Debate on U.S.-China Relations: Make Room, Make Way, or Make Hay," Rea Clear World, May 22, 2015, <https://www.realclearworld.com/articles/2015/05/22/the_debate_on_us-china_relations_make_room_make_way_or_make_haycidotr-partner_site-rcw_111210.html>.

Economy, Elizabeth and Oksenberg, Michel, China Joins the World: Progress and Prospects, New York: Council on Foreign Relations Press, 1999.

Edwards, Jason A., "Make America Great Again: Donald Trump and Redefining the U.S. Role in the World," Communication Quarterly 66, no. 2, 2018.

Epstein, Susan B., Lawson, Marian L., and Gill, Cory R., "Department of State, Foreign Operations, and Related Programs: FY2018 Budget and Appropriations," Congressional Research Service, April 13, 2018, <https://crsreports.congress.gov/product/pdf/R/R44890>.

Erickson, Andrew S., Goldstein, Lyle J., and Li, Nan (eds.), China, the United States, and 21st-Century Sea Power: Defining a Maritime Security Partnership, Annapolis, MD: Naval Institute Press, 2010.

Fairclough, Gordon, "Close-out Sale: North Korea's Elite Shop While They Can," Wall Street Journal, December 18, 2006.

Fallows, James, "China's Great Leap Backward," The Atlantic, December 2016, <https://www.theatlantic.com/magazine/archive/2016/12/chinas-great-leap-backward/505817>.

Feigenbaum, Evan A. and Gwertzman, Bernard, "Strengthening the U.S. Role in Asia," Council on Foreign Relations, November 16, 2011, <https://www.cfr.org/interview/strengthening-us-role-asia>.

Feng, Bree, "Obama's 'Free Rider' Comment Draws Chinese Criticism," New York Times, August 13, 2014, <https://sinosphere.blogs.nytimes.com/2014/08/13/obamas-free-rider-comment-draws-chinese-criticism>.

Feng Qing, "Shanghai and Shenzhen Join 'Antiterror Treaty' for Container Shipping," *21 Shiji Jingji Baodao*, August 4, 2003.

Ferdinand, Peter, "Westward Ho—the China Dream and 'One Belt, One Road': Chinese Foreign Policy under Xi Jinping," *International Affairs* 92, no. 4, 2016.

Fergusson, Ian F. and Williams, Brock R., "The Trans-Pacific Partnership (TPP): Key Provisions and Issues for Congress," Congressional Research Service, June 14, 2016, available at <https://fas.org/sgp/crs/row/R44489.pdf>.

Fifield, Anna, "North Korea Conducts Fifth Nuclear Test, Claims It Has Made Warheads with 'Higher Strike Power,'" *Washington Post*, September 9, 2016, <https://www.washingtonpost.com/world/north-korea-conducts-fifth-nuclear-test-as-regime-celebrates-national-holiday/2016/09/08/9332c01d-6921-4fe3-8f68-c611dc59f5a9_story.html>.

Fisher, Max, "Stephen K. Bannon's CPAC Comments, Annotated and Explained," *New York Times*, February 24, 2017.

Fontaine, Richard, "Chinese Land Reclamation Pushes Boundaries," *Wall Street Journal*, March 3, 2015.

Foot, Rosemary and King, Amy, "Assessing the Deterioration in China-U.S. Relations: U.S. Governmental Perspectives on the Economic-Security Nexus," *China International Strategy Review* 1, no. 1, 2019.

Fravel, M. Taylor, *Active Defense: China's Military Strategy since 1949*, Princeton, NJ: Princeton University Press, 2019.

Fravel, M. Taylor, "Regime Insecurity and International Cooperation: Explaining China's Compromises in Territorial Disputes," *International Security* 30, no. 2, 2005.

Friedberg, Aaron L., "11 September and the Future of Sino-American Relations," *Survival* 44, no. 1, 2002.

Friedberg, Aaron L., "Competing with China," *Survival* 60, no. 3, 2018.

Friedberg, Aaron L., "Will Europe's Past Be Asia's Future?" *Survival* 42, no. 3, 2000.

Fromer, Jacob, "Echoing Kim Jong Un, North Korean Diplomat Warns Nuclear Test Moratorium May End," *NK News*, January 21, 2020, <https://www.nknews.org/2020/01/echoing-kim-jong-un-north-korean-diplomat-warns-nuclear-test-moratorium-may-end>.

Gallo, William, "Mattis in Southeast Asia, amid Fresh U.S. Focus on China," VOA News, January 22, 2018, <https://www.voanews.com/east-asia-pacific/mattis-southeast-asia-amid-fresh-us-focus-china>.

Garrison, Jean and Wall, Marc, "The Rise of Hedging and Regionalism: An Explanation and Evaluation of President Obama's China Policy," *Asian Affairs: An American Review* 43, no. 2, 2016.

Garver, John W., "Is China Playing a Dual Game in Iran?" *Washington Quarterly* 34, no. 1, 2011.

Garver, John W., "Sino-American Relations in 2001: The Difficult Accommodation of Two Great Powers," *International Journal* 57, no. 2, 2002.

George, Jim, "Leo Strauss, Neoconservatism and U.S. Foreign Policy: Esoteric Nihilism and the Bush Doctrine," *International Politics* 42, 2005.

Gershaneck, Kerry K. and Fanell, James E., "This Is How China's Will Fight and Win a War in the South China Sea [*sic*]," *National Interest*, January 18, 2020, <https://nationalinterest.org/blog/buzz/how-chinas-will-fight-and-win-war-south-china-sea-115061>.

Gertz, Bill, "China Flight Tests New Submarine-Launched Missile," *Washington Free Beacon*, December 18, 2018, <https://freebeacon.com/national-security/china-flight-tests-new-submarine-launched-missile>.

Gertz, Bill, *The China Threat: How the People's Republic Targets America*, Washington DC: Regnery, 2000.

Gertz, Bill, "Trump Courts Vietnam to Ward Off Beijing in South China Sea," *Asia Times*, November 14, 2017, <https://asiatimes.com/2017/11/trump-courts-vietnam-ward-off-beijing-south-china-sea>.

Gill, Bates, "Xi Jinping's Grip on Power Is Absolute, but There Are New Threats to His 'Chinese Dream,'" *The Conversation*, June 28, 2019, <https://theconversation.com/xi-jinpings-grip-on-power-is-absolute-but-there-are-new-threats-to-his-chinese-dream-118921>.

Glaser, Bonnie S., "Fleshing Out the Candid, Cooperative and Constructive Relationship," *Comparative Connections* 4, no. 2, 2002.

Glaser, Bonnie S., "Playing Up the Positive on the Eve of the Crawford Summit," *Comparative Connections* 4, no. 3, 2002.

Glaser, Bonnie S., "Rice Seeks to Caution, Cajole, and Cooperate with Beijing," *Comparative Connections* 7, no. 1, 2005.

Glaser, Bonnie S. and Green, Michael J., "What Is the U.S. 'One China' Policy, and Why Does It Matter?" Center for Strategic and International Studies, January 13, 2017, <https://www.csis.org/analysis/what-us-one-china-policy-and-why-does-it-matter>.

Glaser, Bonnie S. and Viers, Alexandra, "U.S.-China Relations: Trump and Xi Break the Ice at Mar-a-Lago," *Comparative Connections* 19, no. 1, 2017.

Glosserman, Brad, "Huawei and the Realities of the 5G World," *Japan Times*, February 3, 2020, <https://www.japantimes.co.jp/opinion/2020/02/03/commentary/world-commentary/huawei-realities-5g-world>.

Goddard, Stacie E., "The U.S. and China Are Playing a Dangerous Game. What Comes Next?" *Washington Post*, October 3, 2018.

Goldsmith, Jack L., *The Terror Presidency: Law and Judgment inside the Bush Administration*, New York: W. W. Norton, 2007.

Gordon, Michael R., "U.S. Nuclear Plan Sees New Weapons and New Targets," *New York Times*, March 10, 2002.

Gramer, Robbie and Gandhi, Maya, "Tillerson to Kushner: We've Got to Stop Meeting like This," *Foreign Policy*, June 27, 2019, <https://foreignpolicy.com/2019/06/27/tillerson-secretary-of-state-testimony-transcript-house-foreign-affairs-committee-jared-kushner-role-trump-administration>.

Green, Michael J., "The Iraq War and Asia: Assessing the Legacy," *Washington Quarterly* 31, no. 2, 2008.

Green, Michael J. and Rapp-Hooper, Mira, "China's New Maritime Provocation," *Washington Post*, March 13, 2015.

Greenwood, Faine, "Xi Jinping Describes 'Chinese Dream' at Closing of National People's Congress," PRI, March 17, 2013, <https://www.pri.org/stories/2013-03-17/xi-jinping-describes-chinese-dream-closing-national-peoples-congress>.

Grinter, Lawrence E., "Handling the Taiwan Issue: Bush Administration Policy toward Beijing and Taipei," *Asian Affairs: An American Review* 29, no. 1, 2002.

Gurtov, Mel, "Northeast Asia Policy under George W. Bush: Doctrine in Search of Policy," *North Korean Review* 3, no. 1, 2007.

Gurtov, Mel, *Will This Be China's Century? A Skeptic's View*, Boulder: Lynne Rienner, 2013.

Haass, Richard, "The Pandemic Will Accelerate History Rather than Reshape It," *Foreign Affairs*, April 7, 2020, <https://www.foreignaffairs.com/articles/united-states/2020-04-07/pandemic-will-accelerate-history-rather-reshape-it>

Halper, Stefan and Clarke, Jonathan, *America Alone: The Neo-conservatives and the Global Order*, Cambridge, England: Cambridge University Press, 2004.

Harding, Harry, "American China Policy under the Bush Administration: Change and Continuity," in Arthur Lewis Rosenbaum (ed.), *U.S.-China Relations and the Bush Administration: A New Paradigm or Continuing Modalities*, Claremont, CA: Keck Center for International and Strategic Studies, 2001.

Hatton, Celia, "Is China Ready to Abandon North Korea?" BBC News, April 12, 2013, <https://www.bbc.com/news/world-asia-china-22062589>.

Haynes, Susan Turner, *Chinese Nuclear Proliferation: How Global Politics Is Transforming China's Weapons Buildup and Modernization*, Lincoln, NE: Potomac, 2016.

Haynes, Susan Turner, "Chinese Nuclear Strategy," in Aiden Warren and Phil Baxter (eds), *Nuclear Modernization in the 21st Century*, Abingdon, England: Routledge, 2020.

Heath, Timothy R., "Trump's National Security Strategy Ratchets Up U.S. Competition with China," *World Politics Review*, December 26, 2017, <https://www.worldpoliticsreview.com/articles/23889/trump-s-national-security-strategy-ratchets-up-u-s-competition-with-china>.

Hernández-Morales, Aitor, "Germany Confirms that Trump Tried to Buy Firm Working on Coronavirus Vaccine," *Politico*, March 15, 2020, <https://www.politico.eu/article/germany-confirms-that-donald-trump-tried-to-buy-firm-working-on-coronavirus-vaccine>.

Herring, Pendleton, *Presidential Leadership: The Chief Relations of Congress and the Chief Executive*, New York: Farrar & Rinehart, 1940.

Heydarian, Richard Javad, "Mattis Signals Harder Line in South China Sea," *Asia Times*, January 25, 2018, <https://asiatimes.com/2018/01/mattis-signals-harder-line-south-china-sea>.

Hickey, Dennis Van Vranken, "Continuity and Change: The Administration of George W. Bush and U.S. Policy toward Taiwan," *Journal of Contemporary China* 13, no. 40, 2004.

Hiebert, Murray, "Red Scare," *Far Eastern Economic Review*, October 12, 2000, available at <https://gertzfile.com/gertzfile/FEERarticle.html>.

Higley, John, "The Bush Elite: Aberration or Harbinger?" in Brendan O'Connor and Martin Griffiths (eds), *The Rise of Anti-Americanism*, Abingdon, England: Routledge, 2006.

Holmes, James, "South China Sea Showdown: What Happens if a U.S. Navy and Chinese Vessel Collide?" *National Interest*, October 6, 2018, <https://nationalinterest.org/blog/buzz/south-china-sea-showdown-what-happens-if-us-navy-and-chinese-vessel-collide-32612>.

Hong Xiao, "Chinese Envoy Calls for Peace Talks to Ease Tensions on Korean Peninsula," *China Daily*, December 13, 2019, <https://global.chinadaily.com.cn/a/201912/13/WS5df2ef24a310cf3e3557de88.html>.

Hsu, Stacy and Yin, Ozzy, "Tsai Calls for Global Support for 'Free Taiwan' at Columbia Speech," *Focus Taiwan*, July 13, 2019, <http://focustaiwan.tw/politics/201907130005>.

Huang, Kristin, "China Has a History of Playing Chicken with the U.S. Military—Sometimes These Dangerous Games End in Disaster," *Business Insider*, October 2, 2018.

Huang, Kristin and Elmer, Keegan, "Beijing's Challenge to U.S. Warship in South China Sea 'Deliberate and Calculated,' Observers Say," *South China Morning Post*, October 5, 2018.

Huntington, Samuel P., *The Clash of Civilizations and the Remaking of World Order*, London: Simon & Schuster, 1997.

Ikenberry, G. John, "The Security Trap," *Democracy: A Journal of Ideas*, no. 2, 2006.

Jacobs, Andrew, "Kerry Expected to Bring Up China's Sea Claims During Visit," *The New York Times*, May 15, 2015, <https://www.nytimes.com/2015/05/16/world/asia/kerry-china-south-sea-dispute.html>.

Jia Qingguo, "Impact of 9.11 on Sino-U.S. Relations: A Preliminary Assessment," paper for the Brookings Institution, July 2002, available at <https://www.brookings.edu/wp-content/uploads/2016/06/2002_qingguo.pdf>.

Johnson, Jesse, "In First, China Permanently Stations Search-and-Rescue Vessel in South China Sea's Spratly Chain," *Japan Times*, July 29, 2018, <https://www.japantimes.co.jp/news/2018/07/29/asia-pacific/first-china-permanently-stations-search-rescue-vessel-south-china-seas-spratly-chain>.

Johnson, Jesse, "North Korea's Kim Warns of 'New Strategic Weapon' as Nuclear Freeze Falters," *Japan Times*, January 1, 2020, <https://www.japantimes.co.jp/news/2020/01/01/asia-pacific/politics-diplomacy-asia-pacific/kim-warns-new-strategic-weapon-north-korea-snubs-arms-test-moratorium-face-gangster-like-u-s>.

Johnson, Jesse, "U.S. Looks to Deploy New Missiles to Asia, Defense Chief Says amid Tensions with China," *Japan Times*, August 4, 2016, <https://www.japantimes.co.jp/news/2019/08/04/asia-pacific/u-s-looks-deploy-new-missiles-asia-defense-chief-says-amid-tensions-china>.

Kagan, Robert and Kristol, William, "A National Humiliation," *Weekly Standard*, April 15, 2001.

Kaminishikawara, Jun, "U.S. Could Change Military Posture if China Expands Air Defense Zone," Kyodo News Agency, January 31, 2014.

Kan, Shirley A., "China and Proliferation of Weapons of Mass Destruction and Missiles: Policy Issues," *Current Politics and Economics of Northern and Western Asia* 23, no. 1/2, 2014.

Kan, Shirley, "U.S.-China Counter-terrorism Cooperation: Issues for U.S. Policy," Congressional Research Service, December 7, 2004, available at <https://fas.org/irp/crs/RS21995.pdf>.

Kan, Shirley A., "U.S.-China Counterterrorism Cooperation: Issues for U.S. Policy," Congressional Research Service, May 7, 2009.

Kan, Shirley A., "U.S.-China Military Contacts: Issues for Congress," Congressional Research Service, October 27, 2014, available at <https://fas.org/sgp/crs/natsec/RL32496.pdf>.

Kazianis, Harry, "Superpower Showdown: America Can Stop Chinese Aggression in Asia," *National Interest*, March 6, 2015, <https://nationalinterest.org/feature/superpower-showdown-america-can-stop-chinese-aggression-asia-12368>.

Kegley, Charles W., Jr. and Wittkopf, Eugene R., *American Foreign Policy: Pattern and Process*, New York: St. Martin's Press, 1979.

Kelly, James, "U.S.-East Asia Policy: Three Aspects," Woodrow Wilson Center, Washington, D.C., December 11, 2002.

Kemenade, Willem van, "China vs. the Western Campaign for Iran Sanctions," *Washington Quarterly* 33, no. 3, 2010.

Kendall-Taylor, Andrea and Shullman, David, "A Russian-Chinese Partnership Is a Threat to U.S. Interests: Can Washington Act before It's Too Late?" *Foreign Affairs*, May 14, 2019, <https://www.foreignaffairs.com/articles/china/2019-05-14/russian-chinese-partnership-threat-us-interests>.

Kesling, Ben and Volz, Dustin, "Rex Tillerson Says Jared Kushner Often Kept Him out of the Loop," *Wall Street Journal*, June 27, 2019.

Kessler, Glenn, "Three Little Words Matter to N. Korea," *Washington Post*, February 22, 2005.

Khalilzad, Zalmay, "Congage China," Rand, Issue Paper 187, 1999, <https://rand.org/pubs/issue_papers/IP187/IP187.html>.

Kharpal, Arjun, "Huawei's 4 Big Issues in 2020—From the Blacklist to the Decision over Its Operating System's Future," CNBC, December 30, 2019, <https://www.cnbc.com/2019/12/31/huawei-2020-outlook-us-blacklist-harmonyos-cfo-trial.html>.

King, Neil, Jr., "China-Iran Trade Surge Vexes U.S.," *Wall Street Journal*, July 27, 2007.

Kolmaš, Michal and Kolmašová, Šárka, "A 'Pivot' That Never Existed: America's Asian Strategy under Obama and Trump," *Cambridge Review of International Affairs* 32, no. 1, 2019.

Kralev, Nicholas, "Chinese Exports Blunt U.N. Sanctions," *Washington Times*, December 19, 2008.

Krauthammer, Charles, "The Bush Doctrine," *Weekly Standard,* June 4, 2001, <https://www.weeklystandard.com/charles-krauthammer/the-bush-doctrine-1776>.

Kristensen, Hans M. and Norris, Robert S., "Chinese Nuclear Forces," *Bulletin of the Atomic Scientists*, 72, no. 4, 2016.

Kristof, Nicholas, "The Rise of China," *Foreign Affairs*, November/December 1993.

Kroenig, Mathew, "The Case for Trump's Foreign Policy: The Right People, The Right Positions," *Foreign Affairs*, May/June 2017.

Kucera, Joshua, "The New Silk Road?" *The Diplomat*, November 11, 2011, <https://thediplomat.com/2011/11/the-new-silk-road>.

Kumar, Martha Joynt, "The Contemporary Presidency: Energy or Chaos? Turnover at the Top of President Trump's White House," *Presidential Studies Quarterly* 49, no. 1, 2019.

Kurlantzick, Joshua, "China's Dubious Role in the War on Terror," *Current History*, December 2003.

Lacey, Marc, "Powell to Allow Taiwan's President to Stop Briefly," *New York Times*, May 15, 2001.

Lacey, Marc and Sanger, David E., "First Meeting: China Testing Firmer Way of Bush Team," *New York Times*, March 23, 2001.

LaFraniere, Sharon, Haberman, Maggie, and Baker, Peter, "Jared Kushner's Vast Duties, and Visibility in the White House, Shrink," *New York Times*, November 25, 2017.

Lampton, David M., *Following the Leader: Ruling China, from Deng Xiaoping to Xi Jinping*, Berkeley: University of California Press, 2014.

Lampton, David M., "A Tipping Point in U.S.-China Relations Is upon U.S.," *US-China Perception Monitor*, May 11, 2015.

Landay, Jonathan and Brunnstrom, David, "U.S. Applauds Tsai's Re-election as Taiwan President: Pompeo," Reuters, January 11, 2020, <https://www.reuters.com/article/us-taiwan-election-usa/u-s-applauds-tsais-re-election-as-taiwan-president-pompeo-idUSKBN1ZA0M3>.

Lauter, David and Kaiman, Jonathan, "Trump's China Tariffs Get Bipartisan Support, Reflecting Widespread U.S. Disillusionment with Beijing," *Los Angeles Times*, March 22, 2018, <https://www.latimes.com/politics/la-na-pol-trump-china-tariffs-20180322-story.html>.

Lawrence, Susan V., "China's Vice President Xi Jinping Visits the United States: What Is at Stake?" Congressional Research Service, February 6, 2012, available at <https://fas.org/sgp/crs/row/R42342.pdf>.

Lawrence, Susan V., "U.S.-China Relations: An Overview of Policy Issues," Congressional Research Service, August 1, 2013, available at <https://fas.org/sgp/crs/row/R41108.pdf>.

Lawrence, Susan V., Campbell, Caitlin, Fefer, Rachel F., Leggett, Jane A., Lum, Thomas, Martin, Michael F., and Schwarzenberg, Andres B., "U.S.-China Relations," Congressional Research Service, September 3, 2019, <https://crsreports.congress.gov/product/pdf/R/R45898>.

Layne, Christopher, "The Unipolar Illusion: Why New Great Powers Will Rise," *International Security* 17, no. 4, 1993.

Layne, Christopher, "China's Challenge to U.S. Hegemony," *Current History*, January 2008.

Lederer, Edith M., "Russia, China Block UN from Saying NKorea Violated Sanctions," Associated Press, June 19, 2019, <https://www.apnews.com/cb6be1337d2a48ecbde14dac590be083>.

Lederer, Edith M., "China, Russia Urge NKorea Sanction Lift," *The Standard*, December 17, 2019, <https://www.standard.net.au/story/6547011/china-russia-urge-nkorea-sanction-lift>.

Lee, Yimou and Blanchard, Ben, "China Bridles at Rare Meeting between Taiwan and U.S. Security Officials," Reuters, May 27, 2019, <https://www.reuters.com/article/us-usa-taiwan/china-bridles-at-rare-meeting-between-taiwanand-u-s-security-officials-idUSKCN1SX077>.

Leffler, Melvyn P., "9/11 and the Past and Future of American Foreign Policy," *International Affairs* 79, no. 5, 2003.

Leng Shumei and Liu Xuanzun, "China Warns U.S. Ships to Leave Sea," *Global Times*, May 6, 2019, <http://www.globaltimes.cn/content/1148768.shtml>.

Lester, Simon, "Chinese Free Trade Is No Threat to American Free Trade", Cato Institute, April 22, 2015, <https://www.cato.org/publications/free-trade-bulletin/chinese-free-trade-no-threat-american-free-trade>.

Levine, Nathan, "Why America Leaving the INF Treaty is China's New Nightmare," *National Interest*, October 22, 2018, <https://nationalinterest.org/blog/buzz/why-america-leaving-inf-treaty-chinas-new-nightmare-34087>.

Lewis, David E., Bernhard, Patrick, and You, Emily, "President Trump as Manager: Reflections on the First Year," *Presidential Studies Quarterly* 48, no. 3, 2018.

Lieberthal, Kenneth and Wang Jisi, "Addressing U.S.-China Strategic Distrust," John L. Thornton Center Monograph Series no. 4, Brookings Institution, March 2012, <https://www.brookings.edu/wp-content/uploads/2016/06/0330_china_lieberthal.pdf>.

Lim, Irvin F. J., "Not Yet All Aboard . . . but Already All at Sea over Container Security Initiative," Working Paper no. 35, Institute of Defence and Strategic Studies, Singapore, October 2002.

Lim, Louisa, "A Pragmatic Princeling Next in Line to Lead China," NPR, February 14, 2012, <https://www.npr.org/2012/02/14/146815991/a-pragmatic-princeling-next-in-line-to-lead-china?t=1588322037659>.

Limaye, Satu P., "Minding the Gaps: The Bush Administration and U.S.-Southeast Asia Relations," *Contemporary Southeast Asia* 26, no. 1, 2004.

Lin, Christina, "A Tipping Point for Sino-US Relations?" *Asia Times*, May 13, 2019, <https://www.asiatimes.com/2019/05/article/a-tipping-point-for-sino-us-relations>.

Liu, Guoli, *China Rising: Chinese Foreign Policy in a Changing World*, London: Palgrave, 2017.

Liu Zhen, "U.S. Warplanes on Beijing's Radar in South China Sea, American Air Force Chiefs Say," *South China Morning Post*, December 9, 2019.

Lockie, Alex, "China Has Jamming Equipment in the South China Sea—and the U.S. May 'Not Look Kindly on It,'" *Business Insider*, April 18, 2018, <https://www.businessinsider.com/china-jamming-us-navy-jets-off-aircraft-carriers-pacific-2018-4>.

Lubold, Gordon, "U.S. Wants to Spend Added Billions on Military in Asia," *Wall Street Journal*, May 7, 2017.

Luft, Gal, "China's Infrastructure Play: Why Washington Should Accept the New Silk Road," *Foreign Affairs*, September/October 2016, <https://www.foreignaffairs.com/articles/asia/china-s-infrastructure-play>.

Macias, Amanda, "China Quietly Installed Defensive Missile Systems on Strategic Spratly Islands in Hotly Contested South China Sea," CNBC, May 2, 2018, <https://www.cnbc.com/2018/05/02/china-added-missile-systems-on-spratly-islands-in-south-china-sea.html>

Macias, Amanda, "China Is Quietly Conducting Electronic Warfare Tests in the South China Sea," CNBC, July 5, 2018, <https://www.cnbc.com/2018/07/05/us-intel-report-china-quietly-testing-electronic-warfare-assets-on-sp.html>.

Mahadzir, Dzirhan, "Air Force Keeping Up Presence Operations over South China Sea," *USNI News*, December 11, 2019, <https://news.usni.org/2019/12/11/air-force-keeping-up-presence-operations-over-south-china-sea>.

Malik, J. Mohan, "Dragon on Terrorism: Assessing China's Tactical Gains and Strategic Losses after 11 September," *Contemporary Southeast Asia* 24, no. 2, 2002.

Manthorpe, Jonathan, "Terror War Throws a Curve Ball: China's Handling of Its 'Internal Affairs' Crops Up in a Game Already Charged with Suspicion and Mistrust," *Vancouver Sun*, September 10, 2002.

Manyin, Mark E., Daggett, Stephen, Dolven, Ben, Lawrence, Susan V., Martin, Michael F., O'Rourke, Ronald, and Vaughn, Bruce, "Pivot to the Pacific? The Obama Administration's 'Rebalancing' toward Asia," Congressional Research Service, March 28, 2012, available at <https://fas.org/sgp/crs/natsec/R42448.pdf>.

Mason, Jeff and Brunnstrom, David, "Trump Expects Second Kim Meeting in 'Not-Too-Distant Future,'" Reuters, January 2, 2019, <https://www.reuters.com/article/us-northkorea-usa/trump-expects-second-kim-meeting-in-not-too-distant-future-idUSKCN1OW1D5>.

Masterson, Julia, "North Korea, China, Russia Converge Positions," *Arms Control Today*, January/February 2020, <https://www.armscontrol.org/act/2020-01/news/north-korea-china-russia-converge-positions>.

Mastro, Oriana Skylar, "China's Military Modernization Program: Trends and Implications," American Enterprise Institute, September 4, 2019, available at <https://www.uscc.gov/sites/default/files/Panel%20II%20Mastro_Written%20Testimony.pdf>.

Mazza, Michael, "Obama's China Tool Kit: In Need of Serious Repair," American Enterprise Institute, March 5, 2015, <https://www.aei.org/articles/obamas-china-toolkit-need-serious-repair>.

McCauley, Kevin, "President Xi Clears the Way for Military Reform: PLA Corruption, Clique Breaking and Making, and Personnel Shuffle," *China Brief* 15, no. 3, 2015.

McDevitt, Michael, "Deterring North Korean Provocations," Brookings Institution, February 7, 2011, <https://www.brookings.edu/research/deterring-north-korean-provocations>.

McDonough, David S., "Obama's Pacific Pivot in U.S. Grand Strategy: A Canadian Perspective," *Asian Security* 9, no. 3, 2013.

McElroy, Damien, "Beijing Produces Videos Glorifying Terrorist Attacks on 'Arrogant' U.S.," *The Telegraph*, November 4, 2001, <http://www.telegraph.co.uk/news/worldnews/asia/china/1361461/Beijing-produces-videos-glorifying-terrorist-attacks-on-arrogant-US.html>.

McGregor, Richard, "Party Man: Xi Jinping's Quest to Dominate China," *Foreign Affairs*, September/October 2019, <https://www.foreignaffairs.com/articles/china/2019-08-14/party-man>.

Mearsheimer, John J., *The Tragedy of Great Power Politics*, New York: W. W. Norton, 2001.

Mearsheimer, John J., "The Gathering Storm: China's Challenge to U.S. Power in Asia," *Chinese Journal of International Politics* 3, no.4, 2010.

Medeiros, Evan S., "The Changing Fundamentals of U.S.-China Relations," *Washington Quarterly* 42, no. 3, 2019.

Mehta, Aaron, "Carter Announces $425M in Pacific Partnership Funding," *Defense News*, May 30, 2015, <https://www.defensenews.com/home/2015/05/30/carter-announces-425m-in-pacific-partnership-funding>.

Mulvenon, James, "Civil-Military Relations and the EP-3 Crisis: A Content Analysis," *China Leadership Monitor*, Winter 2002, 5, <www.hoover.org/publications/clm/issues/2906891.html>.

Menges, Constantine C., *China: The Gathering Threat*, Nashville: Nelson Current, 2005.

Montgomery, Mark and Sayers, Eric, "Addressing America's Operational Shortfall in the Pacific," *War on the Rocks*, June 18, 2019, <https://warontherocks.com/2019/06/addressing-americas-operational-shortfall-in-the-pacific>.

Moore, Gregory J., "America's Failed North Korea Nuclear Policy: A New Approach," *Asian Perspective* 32, no. 4, 2008.

Morin, Rebecca, "'Idiot,' 'Dope,' 'Moron': How Trump's Aides Have Insulted the Boss," *Politico*, September 4, 2018, <https://www.politico.com/story/2018/09/04/trumps-insults-idiot-woodward-806455>.

Morrison, Wayne M., "China's Economic Rise: History, Trends, Challenges, and Implications for the United States," Congressional Research Service, June 25, 2019, available at <https://fas.org/sgp/crs/row/RL33534.pdf>.

Myers, Steven Lee and Choe Sang-Hun, "North Korea Agrees to Curb Nuclear Work; US Offers Aid," *New York Times*, February 29, 2012, <http://www.nytimes.com/2012/03/01/world/asia/us-says-north-korea-agrees-to-curb-nuclear-work.html>.

Nakamura, Kennon H. and Epstein, Susan B., "Diplomacy for the 21st Century: Transformational Diplomacy," CRS Report for Congress, August 23, 2007.

Nanwani, Suresh, "Belt and Road Initiative: Responses from Japan and India—Bilateralism, Multilateralism and Collaborations," *Global Policy* 10, no. 2, 2019.

Nauert, Heather, "Australia-India-Japan-U.S. Consultations on the Indo-Pacific," U.S. State Department, November 12, 2017, <https://www.state.gov/australia-india-japan-u-s-consultations-on-the-indo-pacific>.

Navarro, Peter, *The Coming China Wars: Where They Will Be Fought and How They Will Be Won*, Upper Saddle River, NJ: Financial Times Press, 2008.

Navarro, Peter, *Crouching Tiger: What China's Militarism Means for the World*, Amherst, NY: Prometheus, 2015.

Navarro, Peter and Autry, Greg, *Death by China: Confronting the Dragon—A Global Call to Action*, Upper Saddle River, NJ: Prentice Hall, 2011.

Newman, Andrew, "Arms Control, Proliferation and Terrorism: The Bush Administration's Post-September 11 Security Strategy," *Journal of Strategic Studies* 27, no. 1, 2004.

Nye, Joseph S., Jr., "Xi Jinping's Marco Polo Strategy," *Project Syndicate*, June 12, 2017, <https://www.project-syndicate.org/commentary/china-belt-and-road-grand-strategy-by-joseph-s--nye-2017-06>.

O'Callaghan, John and Mogato, Manuel, "The U.S. Military Pivot to Asia: When Bases Are Not Bases," Reuters, November 14, 2012, <https://www.reuters.com/article/us-usa-asia-military/the-u-s-military-pivot-to-asia-when-bases-are-not-bases-idUSBRE8AD05Y20121114>.

Odom, Jonathan G., "What Does a 'Pivot' or 'Rebalance' Look Like? Elements of the U.S. Strategic Turn towards Security in the Asia-Pacific Region and Its Waters," *Asian-Pacific Law & Policy Journal* 14, no. 1, 2012.

Office of the Secretary of Defense, "Annual Report to Congress: Military and Security Developments Involving the People's Republic of China 2013," U.S. Department of Defense, May 7, 2013, <https://archive.defense.gov/pubs/2013_China_Report_FINAL.pdf>.

Office of the Secretary of Defense, "Annual Report to Congress: Military and Security Developments Involving the People's Republic of China 2018," U.S. Department of Defense, May 16, 2018, <https://media.defense.gov/2018/Aug/16/2001955282/-1/-1/1/2018-CHINA-MILITARY-POWER-REPORT.PDF>.

Office of the Secretary of Defense, "Annual Report to Congress: Military Power of the People's Republic of China 2007," U.S. Department of Defense, available at <https://fas.org/nuke/guide/china/dod-2007.pdf>.

O'Rourke, Ronald, "China Naval Modernization: Implications for U.S. Navy Capabilities—Background and Issues for Congress," Congressional Research Service, April 24, 2020, <https://crsreports.congress.gov/product/pdf/RL/RL33153>.

O'Rourke, Ronald, "U.S.-China Strategic Competition in South and East China Seas: Background and Issues for Congress," Congressional Research Service, April 24, 2020, available at <https://fas.org/sgp/crs/row/R42784.pdf>.

Paal, Douglas H., "China II: Insecurity Complex; Why Chinese Spies Love Us," *National Review*, May 1999.

Page, Jeremy and Barnes, Julian E., "China Expands Island Construction in Disputed South China Sea," *Wall Street Journal*, February 18, 2015.

Pan, Chengxin, *Knowledge, Desire and Power in Global Politics: Western Representations of China's Rise*. Cheltenham, England: Edward Elgar, 2012.

Panda, Ankit, "China Won't Join the INF Treaty—But Can It Forever Dodge Arms Control?" *The Diplomat*, February 25, 2019, <https://thediplomat.com/2019/02/china-wont-join-the-inf-treaty-but-can-it-forever-dodge-arms-control>.

Panda, Ankit, "The U.S. Navy's Shifting View of China's Coast Guard and 'Maritime Militia,'" *The Diplomat*, April 30, 2019, <https://thediplomat.com/2019/04/the-us-navys-shifting-view-of-chinas-coast-guard-and-maritime-militia>.

Pande, Aparne and Nagao, Satoru, "Whose Indo-Pacific?" *American Interest*, August 3, 2018, <https://www.the-american-interest.com/2018/08/03/whose-indo-pacific>.

Parameswaran, Prashanth, "U.S. Launches New Maritime Security Initiative at Shangri La Dialogue 2015," *The Diplomat*, June 2, 2015, <https://thediplomat.com/2015/06/us-launches-new-maritime-security-initiative-at-shangri-la-dialogue-2015>.

Parameswaran, Prashanth, "America's New Maritime Security Initiative for Southeast Asia," *The Diplomat*, April 2, 2016, <https://thediplomat.com/2016/04/americas-new-maritime-security-initiative-for-southeast-asia>.

Parameswaran, Prashanth, "The Significance of Ending the US-Philippines Visiting Forces Agreement," *The Diplomat*, February 12, 2020, <https://thediplomat.com/2020/02/the-significance-of-ending-the-us-philippines-visiting-forces-agreement>.

Parker, Sam and Chefitz, Gabrielle, "Debt Book Diplomacy: China's Strategic Leveraging of its Newfound Economic Influence and Consequences for U.S. Foreign Policy," Belfer Center, Harvard Kennedy School, May 2018, <https://www.belfercenter.org/sites/default/files/files/publication/Debtbook%20Diplomacy%20PDF.pdf>.

Parmar, Inderjeet, "A Neo-conservative-Dominated U.S. Foreign Policy Establishment?" in Kenneth Christie (ed.), *United States Foreign Policy and National Identity in the Twenty-First Century*, Abingdon, England: Routledge, 2008.

Pempel, T. J., "How Bush Bungled Asia: Militarism, Economic Indifference and Unilateralism Have Weakened the United States across Asia," *Pacific Review* 21, no. 5, 2008.

Perlez, Jane, "North Korea Tests the Patience of Its Closest Ally," *New York Times*, June 24, 2012, <https://www.nytimes.com/2012/06/25/world/asia/north-korea-tests-the-patience-of-its-ally-china.html>.

Perlez, Jane and Myers, Steven Lee, "U.S. and China Are Playing 'Game of Chicken' in South China Sea," *New York Times*, November 8, 2018, <https://www.nytimes.com/2018/11/08/world/asia/south-china-sea-risks.html>.

Pfiffner, James P., "The Contemporary President: Decision Making in the Bush White House," *Presidential Studies Quarterly* 39, no. 2, 2009.

Pham, Tuan N., "Chinese Double Standards in the Maritime Domain," *The Diplomat*, August 16, 2017, <https://thediplomat.com/2017/08/chinese-double-standards-in-the-maritime-domain>.

Pickrell, Ryan, "China's South China Sea Strategy Takes a Hit as the U.S. Navy Threatens to Get Tough on Beijing's Sea Forces," *Business Insider*, April 30, 2019, <https://www.businessinsider.com.au/us-navy-tough-on-china-paramilitary-fishing-fleet-gray-zone-tactics-2019-4>.

Pickrell, Ryan, "It Looks Like the U.S, Has Been Quietly Lowering the Threshold for Conflict in the South China Sea," *Business Insider*, June 17, 2019, <https://www.businessinsider.com/us-quietly-lowers-threshold-for-conflict-in-south-china-sea-2019-6>.

Pillsbury, Michael, *The Hundred-Year Marathon: China's Secret Strategy to Replace America as the Global Superpower*, New York: Henry Holt, 2015.

Pollpeter, Kevin, *U.S.-China Security Management: Assessing the Military-to-Military Relationship*, Santa Monica, CA: Rand, 2004.

Pomfret, John, "America vs. China: A Competitive Face-off between Two Pacific Powers," *Washington Post*, November 18, 2016, <https://www.washingtonpost.com/graphics/national/obama-legacy/relations-with-china.html>.

Pompeo, Michael R., "Landmark Development Finance Legislation Improves America's Competitiveness Overseas," U.S. Department of State, October 3, 2018, <https://www.state.gov/landmark-development-finance-legislation-improves-americas-competitiveness-overseas>.

Pompeo, Michael R., "Remarks with Philippine Foreign Secretary Teodoro Locsin, Jr. at a Press Availability," U.S. Department of State, March 1, 2019, <https://www.state.gov/remarks-with-philippine-foreign-secretary-teodoro-locsin-jr>.

Pompeo, Michael R., "The West is Winning," speech at Munich Security Conference, February 15, 2020, <https://www.state.gov/the-west-is-winning>.

Power, John, "Has the US Already Lost the Battle for the South China Sea?" *South China Morning Post*, January 18, 2020.

Power, John and Wong, Catherine, "Exclusive Details and Footage Emerge of Near Collision between Warships in South China Sea," *South China Morning Post*, November 4, 2018, <https://www.scmp.com/week-asia/geopolitics/article/2171596/exclusive-details-and-footage-emerge-near-collision-between>.

Pritchard, Charles L., *Failed Diplomacy: The Tragic Story of How North Korea Got the Bomb*, Washington, DC: Brookings Institution Press, 2007.

PTI Washington, "BRI has a National Security Element: Pompeo," *BusinessLine*, March 29, 2019, <https://www.thehindubusinessline.com/news/world/bri-has-a-national-security-element-pompeo/article 26673918.ece>.

Qian Zhou, "In Talks with ROK President Park Geun-hye, Xi Jinping Emphasizes Comprehensively Promoting Mutually Beneficial Cooperation, Spurring Still Greater Development of Sino-ROK Relations," Xinhua News Agency, June 27, 2013.

Quinones, C. Kenneth, "Dualism in the Bush Administration's North Korea Policy," *Asian Perspective* 27, no. 1, 2003.

Rapp-Hooper, Mira, "In Defense of Facts in the South China Sea," Asia Maritime Transparency Initiative, June 2, 2015, <http://amti.csis.org/in-defense-of-facts-in-the-south-china-sea>.

Rees, Matthew, "Congress's China Challenge," *Weekly Standard*, March 22, 1999, <https://www.weeklystandard.com/matthew-rees/congresss-china-challenge>.

Reeves, Jeffrey, "U.S. Perspectives on China: Trends and Attitudes in U.S. Public Opinion, Media, Scholarship and Leadership Statements," in Andrew T. H. Tan (ed.), *Handbook of U.S.-China Relations*, Cheltenham, England: Edward Elgar, 2016.

Rempfer, Kyle, "U.S. Military Posture in Asia Could Change if China Declares Another Air Defense Identification Zone," *Air Force Times*, September 28, 2018, <https://www.airforcetimes.com/news/2018/09/28/us-military-posture-in-asia-could-change-if-china-declares-another-air-defense-identification-zone>.

Rice, Condoleezza, "Campaign 2000: Promoting the National Interest," *Foreign Affairs*, January/February 2000.

Rice, Condoleezza, "Transformational Diplomacy," speech at Georgetown University, January 18, 2006, <https://2001-2009.state.gov/secretary/rm/2006/59306.htm>.

Rice, Condoleezza, "U.S. Policy toward Asia," Address at the Heritage Foundation, Washington, D.C., June 18, 2008, <http://2001-2009.state.gov/secretary/rm/2008/06/106034.htm>.

Rice, Condoleezza, *No Higher Honor: A Memoir of My Years in Washington*, New York: Crown, 2011.

Richburg, Keith B., "Xi Jinping, Likely China's Next Leaders, Seen as Pragmatic, Low Key," *Washington Post*, August 15, 2011.

Rinehart, Ian E., "The Chinese Military: Overview and Issues for Congress," Congressional Research Service, March 24, 2016, available at <https://fas.org/sgp/crs/row/R44196.pdf>.

Roberts, Guy, *U.S. Foreign Policy and China: Bush's First Term*, Abingdon, England: Routledge, 2015.

Roberts, James M., "Will the BUILD Act Improve Lending in Poor Countries and Counter China? The Jury's Still Out," Heritage Foundation, May 24, 2019, <https://www.heritage.org/budget-and-spending/commentary/will-the-build-act-improve-lending-poor-countries-and-counter-china>.

Rogin, Josh, "Trump's National Security Strategy Marks a Hawkish Turn on China," *Washington Post*, December 18, 2017, <https://www.washingtonpost.com/news/josh-rogin/wp/2017/12/18/trumps-national-security-strategy-marks-a-hawkish-turn-on-china>.

Rolland, Nadège, "China's 'Belt and Road Initiative': Underwhelming or Game-Changer?" *Washington Quarterly* 40, no. 1, 2017.

Ross, Robert S., "China II: Beijing as a Conservative Power," *Foreign Affairs*, March/April 1997.

Ross, Robert S., "Engagement in US China Policy," in Alastair Iain Johnston and Robert S. Ross (eds.), *Engaging China: The Management of an Emerging Power*, Abingdon, England: Routledge, 1999.

Ross, Robert S., "Navigating the Taiwan Strait: Deterrence, Escalation Dominance, and U.S.-China Relations," *International Security* 27, no. 2, 2002.

Ross, Robert S., "The Problem with the Pivot: Obama's New Asia Policy Is Unnecessary and Counterproductive," *Foreign Affairs*, November/December 2012, <https://www.foreignaffairs.com/articles/asia/2012-11-01/problem-pivot>.

Roy, Denny, "China and the War on Terrorism," *Orbis* 46, no. 3, 2002.

Roy, Denny, "The 'China Threat' Issue: Major Arguments," *Asian Survey* 36, no. 8, 1996.

Roy, Denny, "Hegemon on the Horizon?: China's Threat to East Asian Security," *International Security* 19, no. 1, 1994.

Roy, Denny, *Return of the Dragon: Rising China and Regional Security*, New York: Columbia University Press, 2013.

Rudd, Kevin, "The Price of Mistrust," *Foreign Policy*, May 7, 2015, <https://foreignpolicy.com/2015/05/07/china-us-relations-washington-beijing>.

Runde, Daniel F. and Bandura, Romina, "The BUILD Act Has Passed: What's Next?" Center for Strategic and International Studies, October 12, 2018, <https://www.csis.org/analysis/build-act-has-passed-whats-next>.

Russel, Daniel R. and Berger, Blake, "Navigating the Belt and Road Initiative," Asia Society Policy Institute, June 2019, <https://asiasociety.org/sites/default/files/2019-06/Navigating%20the%20Belt%20and%20Road%20Initiative_2.pdf>.

Ryan, Maria, *Neoconservatism and the New American Century*, New York: Palgrave Macmillan, 2010.

Samaan, Jean-Loup, "Confronting the Flaws in America's Indo-Pacific Strategy," *War on the Rocks*, February 11, 2019, <https://warontherocks.com/2019/02/confronting-the-flaws-in-americas-indo-pacific-strategy>.

Sanger, David E. and Haberman, Maggie, "50 G.O.P. Officials Warn Donald Trump Would Put Nation's Security 'at Risk,'" *New York Times*, August 8, 2016.

Sanger, David and Myers, Steve, "Collision with China: The Negotiations," *New York Times*, April 13, 2001.

Sanger, David E. and Wong, Edward, "As Obama Plays China Card on Trade, Chinese Pursue Their Own Deals," *The New York Times*, May 12, 2015.

Sayers, Eric, "Assessing America's Indo-Pacific Budget Shortfall," *War on the Rocks*, November 15, 2018, <https://warontherocks.com/2018/11/assessing-americas-indo-pacific-budget-shortfall>.

Schaus, John, "Concrete Steps for the U.S. in the South China Sea," *War on the Rocks*, March 16, 2015, <http://warontherocks.com/2015/03/concrete-steps-for-the-u-s-in-the-south-china-sea>.

Schreckinger, Ben and Lippman, Daniel, "The China Hawk Who Captured Trump's 'Very, Very Large Brain,'" *Politico*, November 30, 2018, <https://www.politico.com/story/2018/11/30/trump-china-xi-jinping-g20-michael-pillsbury-1034610>.

Scobell, Andrew, "China and North Korea: From Comrades-in-Arms to Allies at Arm's Length," Strategic Studies Institute, March 2004, <https://publications.armywarcollege.edu/pubs/1672.pdf>.

Scobell, Andrew, "Crouching Korea, Hidden China: Bush Administration Policy toward Pyongyang and Beijing," *Asian Survey* 42, no. 2, 2002.

Sevastopulo, Demetri and Hille, Kathrin, "U.S. Warns China on Aggressive Acts by Fishing Boats and Coast Guard," *Financial Times*, April 28, 2019.

Shalal-Esa, Andrea, "Update 2—US Navy Eyes Stationing Ships in Singapore," Reuters, December 16, 2011, <https://www.reuters.com/article/usa-navy-asia/update-2-us-navy-eyes-stationing-ships-in-singapore-idUSL3E7NG06I20111216>.

Shambaugh, David, *China Goes Global: The Partial Power*, New York: Oxford University Press, 2013.

Shambaugh, David, "The Coming Chinese Crackup," *Wall Street Journal*, March 6, 2015.

Shambaugh, David, "Sino-American Relations since September 11: Can the New Stability Last?" *Current History*, September 2002.

Shambaugh, David, "Sino-American Strategic Relations: From Partners to Competitors," *Survival* 42, no. 1, 2000.

Shen, Dingli, "Can Sanctions Stop Proliferation?" *Washington Quarterly* 31, no. 3, 2008.

Shih, Gerry, "As U.S.-China Relations Fray, Beijing Directs Its Fury at One Target: Mike Pompeo," *Washington Post*, June 27, 2019, <https://www.washingtonpost.com/world/as-u-s-china-relations-tumble-beijing-unleashes-fury-at-one-target-mike-pompeo/2019/06/27/c952ec90-98c9-11e9-a027-c571fd3d394d_story.html>.

Shirk, Susan, *China: Fragile Superpower*, New York: Oxford University Press, 2008.

Simon, Herbert A., *Administrative Behavior: A Study of Decision-Making Processes in Administrative Organizations*, 3rd ed., New York: Free Press, 1969.

Slane, Daniel and Wessel, Michael (guest bloggers for Edward Alden), "The TPP: Why It Won't Address Security Concerns with China," Council on Foreign Relations, May 15, 2015, <https://www.cfr.org/blog/tpp-why-it-wont-address-security-concerns-china>.

Smith, Craig S., "Students' Unease over Weakness Could Threaten Beijing's Leaders," *New York Times*, April 6, 2001.

Smith, Jean Edward, *Bush*, New York: Simon & Schuster, 2016.

Smith, Paul J., "China's Power Ascendancy and the Global Terrorism Burden: Opportunities for U.S.-China Cooperation," in Andrew S. Erickson, Lyle J. Goldstein, and Nan Li (eds), *China, the United States, and 21st-Century Sea Power: Defining a Maritime Security Partnership*, Annapolis, MD: Naval Institute Press, 2010.

Song Qiang et al., *Zhongguo keyi shuobu* ("China Can Say No"), Beijing: Zhonghua gongshang lianhe chubanshe, 1996.

Sorensen, Clark and Task Force 2016, "The Obama Administration's Pivot to Asia," Henry M. Jackson School of International Studies, University of Washington, 2016, <https://jsis.washington.edu/news/obama-administrations-pivot-asia>.

Southgate, Laura, "The Asia Pivot as a Strategy of Foreign Policy: A Source of Peace or a Harbinger of Conflict?" International Studies Association conference, Hong Kong, June 15–17, 2017, transcript available at <http://dspace.lib.cranfield.ac.uk/handle/1826/12071>.

Stilwell, David R., "The U.S., China, and Pluralism in International Affairs," speech at Brookings Institution, December 2, 2019, transcript available at <https://fj.usembassy.gov/the-u-s-china-and-pluralism-in-international-affairs>.

Stockholm International Peace Research Institute, *SIPRI Yearbook 2018*, Oxford: Oxford University Press, 2018.

Stokes, Jacob, "China's Road Rules: Beijing Looks West toward Eurasian Integration," *Foreign Affairs*, April 19, 2015, <https://www.foreignaffairs.com/articles/asia/2015-04-19/chinas-road-rules>.

Su, Jinyuan, "The Proliferation Security Initiative (PSI) and Interdiction at Sea: A Chinese Perspective," *Ocean Development & International Law* 43, no. 1, 2012.

Sutter, Robert, "Bush Administration Policy toward Beijing and Taipei," *Journal of Contemporary China* 12, no. 36, 2003.

Sutter, Robert, "Congress and Trump Administration China Policy: Overlapping Priorities, Uneasy Adjustments and Hardening toward Beijing," *Journal of Contemporary China* 28, no. 118, 2019.

Sutter, Robert, "The Obama Administration and U.S. Policy in Asia," *Contemporary Southeast Asia* 31, no. 2, 2009.

Sutter, Robert, "The Taiwan Problem in the Second George W. Bush Administration—U.S. Officials' Views and Their Implications for U.S. Policy," *Journal of Contemporary China* 15, no. 48, 2006.

Swaine, Michael D., *America's Challenge: Engaging a Rising China in the Twenty-First Century*, Washington, DC: Carnegie Endowment for International Peace, 2012.

Swaine, Michael D., "Beyond American Predominance in the Western Pacific: The Need for a Stable U.S.-China Balance of Power," Carnegie Endowment for International Peace, April 20, 2015, <http://carnegieendowment.org/2015/04/20/beyond-american-predominance-in-western-pacific-need-for-stable-u.s.-china-balance-of-power>.

Takahashi, Sugio and Sayers, Eric, "America and Japan in a Post-INF World," *War on the Rocks*, March 8, 2019, <https://warontherocks.com/2019/03/america-and-japan-in-a-post-inf-world>.

Tanner, Murray Scott and Bellacqua, James, "China's Response to Terrorism," CNA Analysis & Solutions, June 2016, <https://www.cna.org/cna_files/pdf/IRM-2016-U-013542-Final.pdf>.

Tay, Shirley, "U.S. Reportedly Warns China over Hostile Non-naval Vessels in South China Sea," CNBC, April 29, 2019, <https://www.cnbc.com/2019/04/29/south-china-sea-us-warns-china-over-non-naval-vessels-ft.html>.

Taylor, Francis X., "U.S.-China Inter-agency Partnership to Fight Terrorism," remarks to the press, Beijing, December 6, 2001, <https://2001-2009.state.gov/s/ct/rls/rm/2001/6689.htm>.

Thiessen, Marc A., "Donald Trump Is the Most Pro-Taiwan President in U.S. History," *Washington Post*, January 14, 2020, <https://www.washingtonpost.com/opinions/2020/01/14/donald-trump-is-most-pro-taiwan-president-us-history>.

Timperlake, Edward and Triplett, William C., II, *Red Dragon Rising: Communist China's Military Threat to America*, Washington, DC: Regnery, 1999.

Tisdall, Simon, "Little Blue Men: The Maritime Militias Pushing China's Claims," *The Guardian*, May 16, 2016, <https://www.theguardian.com/world/2016/may/16/little-blue-men-the-maritime-militias-pushing-chinas-claims-in-south-china-sea>.

Tkacik, John J., Jr., "Revenge of the Panda Hugger," *Weekly Standard*, February 27, 2006.

Townshend, Ashley, Thomas-Noone, Brendan, and Steward, Matilda, "Averting Crisis: American Strategy, Military Spending and Collective Defence in the Indo-Pacific," United States Study Centre, University of Sydney, August 19, 2019, <https://www.ussc.edu.au/analysis/averting-crisis-american-strategy-military-spending-and-collective-defence-in-the-indo-pacific#america%E2%80%99s-troubled-defence-budget>.

Trump, Donald J. (@realDonaldTrump), Twitter, August 23, 2019, <https://twitter.com/realdonaldtrump/status/1164914960046133249>.

Trump, Donald J. (@realDonaldTrump), Twitter, August 24, 2019, <https://twitter.com/realdonaldtrump/status/1165111122510237696>

Tucker, Nancy B., "Strategic Ambiguity or Strategic Rivalry," in Nancy B. Tucker (ed.), *Dangerous Strait: The U.S.-Taiwan-China Crisis*, New York: Columbia University Press, 2005.

Tyler, Patrick E., "Rebels' New Cause: A Book for Yankee Bashing," *New York Times*, September 4, 1996, <https://www.nytimes.com/1996/09/04/world/rebels-new-cause-a-book-for-yankee-bashing.html>.

United Nations Security Council, "Note by the President of the Security Council," January 31, 1992, UN Doc. S/23500.

United Nations Security Council, Resolution 1540 (2004), April 28, 2004, <https://www.un.org/ga/search/view_doc.asp?symbol=S/RES/1540%20(2004)>.

U.S. Department of Commerce, Bureau of Industry and Security, "Addition of Entities to the Entity List," 84 Federal Register 22961, May 21, 2019.

U.S. Department of Defense, News Transcript, Presenter: Secretary of Defense Donald H. Rumsfeld, June 6, 2002, <http://www.defense-link.mil/transcripts/transcript.aspx?transcriptid=3491>.

Vaddi, Pranay, "Leaving the INF Treaty Won't Help Trump Counter China," Carnegie Endowment for International Peace, January 31, 2019, <https://carnegieendowment.org/2019/01/31/leaving-inf-treaty-won-t-help-trump-counter-china-pub-78262>.

Valencia, Mark J., "The U.S.-China Maritime Surveillance Debate," *The Diplomat*, August 4, 2017, <https://thediplomat.com/2017/08/the-us-china-maritime-surveillance-debate>.

Valencia, Mark J., "U.S. FONOPS in the South China Sea: Intent, Effectiveness, and Necessity," *The Diplomat*, July 11, 2017, <https://thediplomat.com/2017/07/us-fonops-in-the-south-china-sea-intent-effectiveness-and-necessity>.

Vatikiotis, Michael, "No Rice for ASEAN This Year," *New York Times*, July 9, 2005.

Walcott, John, "'Willful Ignorance': Inside President Trump's Troubled Intelligence Briefings," *Time*, February 5, 2019, <https://time.com/5518947/donald-trump-intelligence-briefings-national-security>.

Waldron, Arthur, "China after Communism," American Enterprise Institute, September 11, 2000, <https://www.aei.org/publication/china-after-communism>.

Walzer, Michael, "On Humanitarianism: Is Helping others Charity, or Duty, or Both?" *Foreign Affairs*, July/August 2011.

Ward, Adam, "China and America: Trouble Ahead?" *Survival* 45, no. 3, 2003.

Warren, Aiden, *The Obama Administration's Nuclear Weapon Strategy: The Promises of Prague*, Abingdon, England: Routledge, 2014.

Warrick, Joby, "A North Korean H-bomb? Not Likely, Experts Say," *The Washington Post*, January 6, 2016, <https://www.washingtonpost.com/world/national-security/a-north-korean-h-bomb-not-likely-experts-say/2016/01/06/93ec6b14-b49b-11e5-9388-466021d971de_story.html>.

Watts, Jake Maxwell, "Bolton Warns China against Limiting Free Passage in South China Sea," *Wall Street Journal*, November 13, 2018, <https://www.wsj.com/articles/bolton-warns-china-against-limiting-free-passage-in-south-china-sea-1542110191>.

Weitz, Richard, "Pivot Out, Rebalance In," *The Diplomat*, May 3, 2012, <https://thediplomat.com/2012/05/pivot-out-rebalance-in>.

Wen Kuei-hsiang and Hsu, Elizabeth, "Taiwan President Meets with Envoys to U.N. during New York Stopover," *Focus Taiwan*, July 12, 2019, <http://focustaiwan.tw/politics/201907120002.aspx>.

Werner, Erica, Kim, Seung Min, and Paletta, Damian, "Trump Weighs Rejoining Trans-Pacific Partnership He Once Called a 'Disaster,'" *The Washington Post*, April 12, 2018.

White, Hugh, *The China Choice: Why We Should Share Power*, Oxford: Oxford University Press, 2012.

White, Josh and Wright, Robin, "Detainee Cleared for Release Is in Limbo at Guantanamo," *Washington Post*, December 15, 2005.

Whitlock, Craig, "Australia May Host U.S. Drones at Cocos," *Sydney Morning Herald*, March 28, 2012, <https://www.smh.com.au/politics/federal/australia-may-host-us-drones-at-cocos-20120327-1vwmm.html>.

Williams, Clive, "Pacific Collateral from the INF Treaty Collapse," *The Interpreter*, January 31, 2019, <https://www.lowyinstitute.org/the-interpreter/pacific-collateral-inf-treaty-collapse>.

Willsher, Kim, Holmes, Oliver, McKernan, Bethan, and Tondo, Lorenzo, "US Hijacking Mask Shipments in Rush for Coronavirus Protection," *The Guardian*, April 3, 2020, <https://www.theguardian.com/world/2020/apr/02/global-battle-coronavirus-equipment-masks-tests>.

Wolf, Jim, "U.S. Faults China on Shipments to Iran," *Reuters*, July 12, 2007, <https://www.reuters.com/article/idUSN12351086>.

Wolfowitz, Paul, "Transfer of Missile Technology to China," Congressional Testimony by Federal Document Clearing House, September 17, 1998.

Wong, Alex N., "Briefing on the Indo-Pacific Strategy," U.S. Department of State, April 2, 2018, <https://www.state.gov/briefing-on-the-indo-pacific-strategy>.

Woody, Christopher, "This New Defense Department Map Shows How China Says One Thing and Does Another with Its Military Operations at Sea," *Business Insider*, August 17, 2018, <https://www.businessinsider.com/defense-department-map-shows-chinas-naval-operations-in-maritime-eezs-2018-8>.

Work, Robert O. and Grant, Greg, "Beating the Americans at Their Own Game: An Offset Strategy with Chinese Characteristics," Center for a New American Security, June 6, 2019, <https://www.cnas.org/publications/reports/beating-the-americans-at-their-own-game>.

Wright, Robin, "Chinese Detainees Are Men without a Country," *Washington Post*, August 24, 2005.

Wroughton, Lesley and Torbati, Yeganeh, "Exclusive: U.S. Warns China It Will Target Firms for Illicit North Korea Business," Reuters, December 2, 2016, <https://www.reuters.com/article/us-northkorea-usa-sanctions-idUSKBN13R28E>.

Wuthnow, Joel, "Securing China's Belt and Road Initiative: Dimensions and Implications," <https://www.uscc.gov/sites/default/files/Wuthnow_USCC%20Testimony_20180123.pdf>.

Xiang, Lanxin, "China and the 'Pivot,'" *Survival* 54, no. 5, 2012.

Xie, Heng and Rajagopalan, Megha, "Bank of China Closes Account of Key North Korean Bank," Reuters, May 7, 2013, <https://www.reuters.com/article/us-korea-north-china-bank-idUSBRE9460CX20130507>.

Xu, Beina, Fletcher, Holly, and Bajora, Jayshree, *The East Turkistan Islamic Movement (ETIM)*, Council on Foreign Relations, 2014, <https://www.cfr.org/backgrounder/east-turkestan-islamic-movement-etim>.

Xu Jian, "Rethinking China's Period of Strategic Opportunity," *China International Studies*, March/April 2014, <http://www.ciis.org.cn/english/2014-05/28/content_6942258.htm>.

Yang, Jiemian, "Sino-U.S. and Cross-Strait Relations under the Post-'11 September' Strategic Settings," *Journal of Contemporary China* 11, no. 33, 2002.

Yang, Yi Edward and Liu, Xinsheng, "The 'China Threat' through the Lens of US Print Media 1992–2006," *Journal of Contemporary China* 21, no. 76, 2012.

Yates, Stephen, "No Concessions to China after Mistaken Embassy Bombing," Heritage Foundation, May 28, 1999, <https://www.heritage.org/asia/report/no-concessions-china-after-the-mistaken-embassy-bombing>.

Yee, Herbert S., "Ethnic Relations in Xinjiang: A Survey of Uygur-Han Relations in Urumqi," *Journal of Contemporary China* 12, no. 36, 2003.

Yeo, Mike, "How Far Can China's Long-Range Missiles Reach in the South China Sea?" *Defense News*, May 4, 2018, <https://www.defensenews.com/naval/2018/05/04/how-far-can-chinas-long-range-missiles-reach-in-the-south-china-sea>.

Yoshihara, Toshi and Cohn, Jacob, "The Case for Deploying U.S. Land-Based Missiles in Asia," *National Interest*, May 13, 2019, <https://nationalinterest.org/blog/buzz/case-deploying-us-land-based-missiles-asia-57322>.

Yuan, Jing-dong, "Chinese Responses to U.S. Missile Defenses: Implications for Arms Control and Regional Security," *Nonproliferation Review* 10, no. 1, 2003.

Yuan Peng, "Sino-American Relations: New Changes and New Challenges," *Australian Journal of International Affairs* 61, no. 1, 2007.

Zhang Qingmin and Hyer, Eric, "U.S. 'Dual Track' Policy: Arms Sales and Technology Transfer to China Mainland and Taiwan," *Journal of Contemporary China*, 10, no. 26, 2001.

Zhang Xiaolin and Cao Yang, "Promote the Transformation of Naval Strategy, Safeguard Maritime Security," *Navy Today*, June 2015. Translation by China Maritime Studies Institute, U.S. Naval War College.

Zhao, Quansheng, "America's Response to the Rise of China and Sino-U.S. Relations," *Asian Journal of Political Science* 13, no. 2, 2005.

Zhao Shengnan, "Reshuffle Brings In Younger Officers," *China Daily*, August 4, 2015, <https://www.chinadaily.com.cn/china/2015-08/04/content_21493316.htm>.

Zhao, Suisheng, "American Reflections on the Engagement with China and Responses to President Xi's New Model of Major Power Relations," *Journal of Contemporary China* 26, no. 106, 2017.

Zhao, Suisheng, "Chinese Nationalism and Its Foreign Policy Ramifications," in Christopher Marsh and Teufel Dreyer (eds.), *U.S.-China Relations in the Twenty-First Century: Polices, Prospects, and Possibilities*, Lanham, MD: Lexington, 2003.

Zissis, Carin, "Hills: U.S.-Chinese Relations Need Habits of Cooperation," Council on Foreign Relations, April 10, 2007, <https://www.cfr.org/interview/hills-us-chinese-relations-need-habits-cooperation>.

Zoellick, Robert B., "Whither China? From Membership to Responsibility," remarks to National Committee on U.S.-China relations, September 21, 2005, <https://2001-2009.state.gov/s/d/former/zoellick/rem/53682.htm>.

Index

Belt and Road Initiative (BRI), 6, 9,
115, 120, 135–7, 158, 168, 199,
201–3, 208, 210
charge of debt diplomacy, 186–7
Obama administration's response,
119, 138–40
Trump administration's response,
153, 160–4, 183–91
Biden, Joe, 115, 117
Blair, Dennis, 56
Blinken, Antony, 146
Boao Forum, 143
Bolton, John, 32, 85
as national security adviser, 172
as senior policy analyst for the
American Enterprise Institute,
24
as undersecretary of state for arms
control and international security
affairs, 74
Bonner, Robert, 58
Brown, Charles Q., 171
Brunei, 43, 97–8, 129
BUILD ACT (Better Utilization
of Investments Leading to
Development Act), 153, 163–4,
180, 188, 203, 206
Bush, George H. W., 4
administration, 20–1
Bush, George W., 1, 4–5, 27, 36–8, 47,
116, 156, 159, 201, 206
doctrine, 23, 25
as governor, 26
meeting with Jiang Zemin, 41
pragmatism, 45
years of, 2, 6
views toward China, 24
Bush administration, 6, 10, 18, 18–80,
81, 84, 101, 122, 154, 165, 201,
207, 211, 214
aggressiveness toward Iran, 69
aggressiveness toward North
Korea, 50
arms sales to Taiwan, 38–9, 40,
42, 45

on China's policies in the XUAR,
63, 65
China policy, 24, 34, 42, 48
conservative hawks, 21, 25
conservative pragmatists, 21
counter-terrorism cooperation
with China, 46–7, 53, 56, 79
on engagement with China, 48,
50, 52–3, 69, 78
Guantanamo Bay and Uighur
detainees, 64–5
handling of EP-3 incident; see also
EP-3 incident, 36–9, 46
on Iranian arms proliferation, 70
on non-proliferation cooperation
with China, 67
North Korea policy, 52, 71–6
relations with South Korea, 51
relationship with Asian Allies, 51
sanctions on Chinese SOEs, 68
terrorism cooperation with China,
43, 51, 54, 57–61, 66
Taiwan policy, 40, 42–5, 47

Campbell, Kurt M., 3
Canada, 98, 209, 212
Caribbean, 199
Carter, Ashton, 111, 130–1, 134
Carter, Jimmy, 2, 4, 20, 142
Central Command (USCENTCOM),
56
Central Intelligence Agency (CIA), 35
Central Military Commission, 121,
176
Cha, Victor, 52, 74, 75
Cheney, Richard (Dick), 19, 21, 36,
69, 73, 75
Chen Shui-bian, 33, 44–5, 48
Chile, 98
China (PRC)
"active defense," 176
allegations of arms proliferation,
62
assertiveness in SCS, 82, 87–9,
111–12, 132, 175, 177, 211

China Dream, 6, 115, 118–21,
208
"closed internet," 138
Coast Guard, 8, 95, 166, 173, 176
and Container Security Initiative;
see also CSI, 58–61
counter terrorism cooperation
with U.S., 43, 51, 54, 5–61
counter-terrorism strategy,
55, 63
Covid-19, 205
diplomatic pressure, 8
economy, 135
as a great power, 41, 83
INF treaty, 182–3
investment in critical technologies,
159
"Made in China 2025," 6, 115,
208
maritime militia, 8, 166, 173, 176
mercantilist trade practices, 158
military modernization, 6, 8, 36,
83, 87, 89, 95, 114, 118–26,
162, 165, 167, 203
militarization of islands, 8, 174,
176, 207, 211
nationalism, 37
"near-peer competitor" status with
U.S., 165–8
nine-dash line, 171
and North Korea, 52, 66, 74–6,
78, 142–4, 147–8, 191–3, 196,
210
nuclear modernization, 9, 125–6
participation in U.N., 52
peaceful rise debate, 84
perception of containment, 7
policies toward Iran, 68, 71
policies in the XUAR, 62, 80
position on Proliferation Security
Initiative (PSI), 71
rise of, 4, 20, 35, 50, 84, 96,
113
"salami-slicing" strategy in SCS,
129–30, 135

State Owned Enterprises (SOEs),
62, 68, 119, 138
Strike Hard campaign, 41, 55, 62
as strategic competitor, 11, 20
suppression of Uighurs, 57, 80
territorial disputes, 8, 91, 96, 111,
128, 178
theft of IP, 154
vessel *Yinhe*, 72
victim of terrorism, 57, 63
views on Iranian proliferation, 70
views on "rebalance," 106, 108,
139
views on U.S. Taiwan relations,
34–5, 36, 43–4, 45, 47, 199
violation of U.N. sanctions, 62,
76, 84, 146
weapons proliferation, 54,
69, 79
Wolf Warrior diplomats, 212
China Bureau of Fisheries, 127
China Can Say No publication, 28,
29
China Development Bank, 189
China Maritime Surveillance, 127
China Precision Machinery Import
and Export Corporation, 62
China threat narrative, 4, 5, 20,
21, 23, 24, 26, 27–32, 46,
53, 157
China's Endeavors for Arms
Control, Disarmament, and
Non-proliferation, white paper
(2005), 67, 70, 124
China's National Defense, white
paper (2004), 67
climate change, 82–3, 90, 113
Paris Agreement 148
Clinton, Bill, 4
China policy, 19, 47
Administration, 20, 23, 27–8, 52,
Clinton, Hillary, 81, 93, 95–7, 101,
119, 128, 206
Cohn, Gary, 155
Colby, Elbridge, 166

319

EU representative:
Easy Access System Europe
Mustamäe tee 50, 10621 Tallinn, Estonia
Gpsr.requests@easproject.com

www.ingramcontent.com/pod-product-compliance
Lightning Source LLC
Chambersburg PA
CBHW070842300326
41935CB00039B/1350